MORNINGS with JESUS
2015

DAILY ENCOURAGEMENT *for your* SOUL

365 DEVOTIONS

SUSANNA FOTH AUGHTMON

GWEN FORD FAULKENBERRY

GRACE FOX

TRICIA GOYER

SHARON HINCK

REBECCA BARLOW JORDAN

ERIN KEELEY MARSHALL

DIANNE NEAL MATTHEWS

CYNTHIA RUCHTI

SUZANNE DAVENPORT TIETJEN

ALICE J. WISLER

Guideposts

New York

Mornings with Jesus 2015

Published by Guideposts Books & Inspirational Media
110 William Street
New York, New York 10038
Guideposts.org

Acknowledgments

Every attempt has been made to credit the sources of copyrighted material used in this book. If any such acknowledgment has been inadvertently omitted or miscredited, receipt of such information would be appreciated.

"Joyfully" by Ed Cash, Mia Fieldes, and Kari Jobe Copyright © 2009 SHOUT! Music Publishing (APRA) Gateway Create Publishing (BMI) (Adm. at EMICMGPublishing.com)/ Wondrously Made Songs (BMI) All Rights Reserved. Used by permission. International Copyright Secured. All Rights Reserved. Used by Permission.

Scripture quotations marked (AMP) are taken from *The Amplified Bible*, © 1954, 1958, 1962, 1964, 1965, 1987 by The Lockman Foundation. Used by permission. www.Lockman.org

Scripture quotations marked (CEB) are taken from *Common English Bible*. Copyright © 2011 Common English Bible.

Scripture quotations marked (ESV) are taken from the Holy Bible, English Standard Version, copyright © 2001 by Crossway Bibles, a division of Good News Publishers. Used by permission. All rights reserved.

Scripture quotations marked (GNT) are taken from *Good News Translation*. Copyright © 1992 by American Bible Society.

Scripture quotations marked (GW) are taken from *God's Word Translation*. Copyright © 1995 by God's Word to the Nations. Used by permission of Baker Publishing Group.

Scripture quotations marked (HCS) are taken from the Holman Christian Standard Bible. Copyright © 1999, 2000, 2002, 2003 by Holman Bible Publishers, Nashville, Tennessee. All rights reserved.

Scripture quotations marked (KJV) are taken from *The King James Version of the Bible*.

Scripture quotations marked (MSG) are taken from *The Message*. Copyright © 1993, 1994, 1995, 1996, 2000, 2001, 2002 by Eugene H. Peterson.

Scripture quotations marked (NAS) are taken from the *New American Standard Bible*, copyright © 1960, 1962, 1963, 1968, 1971, 1972, 1973, 1975, 1977, 1995 by the Lockman Foundation. Used by permission. www.Lockman.org

Scripture quotations marked (NCV) are taken from the *New Century Version*. Copyright © 2005 by Thomas Nelson, Inc. Used by permission. All rights reserved.

Scripture quotations marked (NIV) are taken from two editions: *The Holy Bible, New International Version, NIV*. Copyright © 1973, 1978, 1984, 2011 by Biblica. All rights reserved worldwide. *The Holy Bible, New International Version*. Copyright © 1973, 1978, 1984 International Bible Society. Used by permission of Zondervan Bible Publishers.

Scripture quotations marked (NKJV) are taken from *The Holy Bible, New King James Version*. Copyright © 1997, 1990, 1985, 1983 by Thomas Nelson, Inc.

Scripture quotations marked (NLT) are taken from the *Holy Bible*, New Living Translation. Copyright © 1996. Used by permission of Tyndale House Publishers, Inc., Wheaton, Illinois 60189. All rights reserved.

Scripture quotations marked (NRSV) are taken from the *New Revised Standard Version Bible*. Copyright © 1989 by the Division of Christian Education of the National Council of the Churches of Christ in the U.S.A. Used by permission. All rights reserved.

Scripture quotations marked (RSV) are taken from the *Revised Standard Version of the Bible*, copyright © 1946, 1952, and 1971 the Division of Christian Education of the National Council of the Churches of Christ in the United States of America. Used by permission. All rights reserved.

Scripture quotations marked (VOICE) are taken from *The Voice Bible*. Copyright © 2012 Thomas Nelson, Inc. The Voice™ translation © 2012 Ecclesia Bible Society. All rights reserved.

Cover and interior design by Müllerhaus
Cover photo by Shutterstock
Indexed by Indexing Research
Typeset by Aptara

Printed and bound in the United States of America
10 9 8 7 6 5 4 3 2 1

INTRODUCTION

When Jesus was about to return to His Father in heaven, He, out of His great love for His disciples, made a point of sitting with them and comforting them: "Peace I leave with you; my peace I give you. I do not give to you as the world gives. Do not let your hearts be troubled and do not be afraid" (John 14:27, NIV). Jesus was about to leave, yet He told His disciples not to be afraid because He knew He would never be far from them and wanted them to rest in that truth.

Just as Jesus made a point of instructing His disciples to trust in Him despite any physical distance they felt from their Friend, He invites us, here and now, to learn from Him, to pray with Him, to be like Him, to love as He loves. He wants us to rely fully on Him because He is the only One Who can give us a strong foundation. It's why we don't have to be troubled or afraid.

As I delve into these brand-new devotions, I feel how real and powerful Jesus's presence is. We can live in that truth every moment of every day, in thoughtful prayer and devotion, drinking from His never-failing compassion and feasting on His endless mercies (Lamentations 3:22).

Mornings with Jesus 2015 is an easy-to-use devotional. There is a one-page reading for every day of the year. A Bible verse opens each devotion, written by one of our eleven contributors (all women), including best-selling authors Tricia Goyer and Cynthia Ruchti, who connect the Scripture to a moment in their lives, sharing their wisdom and insights with the deep desire to encourage and uplift you. A "Faith Step" grounds each reflection and is a practical way to apply what you've read to your life and to continue to think about the day's lesson by implementing its truth. These daily "Faith Steps" will challenge you to look at a Scripture passage in a new way, ask a question that will help you make a change in your life, or simply encourage you to praise and thank Jesus.

It is my hope that you'll find abundant inspiration and encouragement to lay aside your fears, doubts, and, inevitably, failures and, instead, seek the kingdom of God, revel in the simplicity of Jesus's love, and hold tight to Him as He works all things together—for your good.

Faithfully yours,
Keren Baltzer
Mornings with Jesus Editor

Mornings with Jesus in Your In-box

Now you can enjoy the daily encouragement of *Mornings with Jesus 2015* wherever you are! Receive each day's devotion on your computer, tablet, or smartphone. Visit MorningswithJesus.org/MWJ2015 and enter this code: MWJ2015.

Sign up for the online newsletter *Mornings with Jesus* through Guideposts.org. Each week you'll receive an inspiring devotion or personal thoughts from one of the authors about her own devotional time, prayer life, how focusing on Jesus shapes her relationship with Him, and much more.

THURSDAY, JANUARY 1

For I'm going to do a brand-new thing. See, I have already begun!
Don't you see it? Isaiah 43:19 (TLB)

ONE OF MY FAVORITE THINGS about New Year's Day is slipping a new calendar into the wooden frame on my kitchen wall. I buy the calendars from a company that makes beautiful ones illustrated by different artists representing every style, from country folk art to contemporary. The choices include every topic I could imagine, and then some. Cats, roses, the Civil War, England, snowmen, butterflies, poetry, roosters—you name it. Last year I chose the theme of primitive barns; this year it's country churches.

I love seeing all those blank spaces just waiting to be filled. First, I'll write in the names of loved ones on their birth dates. Later, I'll add meetings, appointments, and special events as they come up. To me, that new calendar represents a whole year's worth of opportunities and life experiences to come, some sweet and doubtless some bitter. Three hundred sixty-five days of possibilities.

During His last Passover meal with His disciples, Jesus announced the beginning of the new covenant, represented by His blood that would pay for the world's sins. Once we accept the gift of forgiveness made possible by His sacrifice, we become a new creation. But Jesus doesn't stop there. He lives inside us, helping us become more like Him and enjoy a life of meaning and fulfillment.

As we grow closer to Jesus, we come to understand Him on a new level. He offers new opportunities for us to serve Him. He may plant a new dream in our heart or show us a fresh way to use our gifts. Every year, every day represents a chance to embrace Jesus's love, mercy, and grace in a new way. —DIANNE NEAL MATTHEWS

FAITH STEP: *Ask Jesus to show you one new thing He would like to do in your life this year. Write it down on a slip of paper to keep in your Bible so you can talk to Him about it on a regular basis.*

FRIDAY, JANUARY 2

Therefore, if anyone is in Christ, the new creation has come: The old has gone, the new is here! 2 Corinthians 5:17 (NIV)

THIS PAST WEEK I WENT on a field trip with Addison to see the monarch butterflies wintering at Natural Bridges State Park. After showing a video illustrating the life cycle of the monarch, three parents were called upon to demonstrate the life stages. I was the butterfly.

I knew that Addison was likely to die of embarrassment. I myself was a little nervous faced with the polka-dot hoody, feelers, and goggles. But I thought to myself…this may be the only time I ever get to play a butterfly. So I embraced it. When they called my name I did a lovely butterfly ballet. There was some swooping. And prancing. And a finishing curtsy.

Addison was laughing….and completely mortified. I asked him later if that was his favorite part of the field trip. He said it was the worst part. This made me laugh. My dance may not have been inspirational, but the butterfly is. How much does one insect have to go through to become what it is truly meant to be? How much do we?

Because of Jesus, we are also on a transformational journey. Some of us are more caterpillar than butterfly. Some of us are holed up in a long spiritual winter, a cocooning of sorts. And some of us are just beginning to spread our wings. The beauty is that when we are journeying with Jesus, He keeps changing us. Out with the old and in with the new. Out with the sins and the hatred and the bitterness. In with the love and the grace and the mercy that comes from being around Him. And that is truly beautiful. —SUSANNA FOTH AUGHTMON

FAITH STEP: *Draw a picture of a butterfly. Fill its wings with words that describe how Jesus has transformed you.*

SATURDAY, JANUARY 3

Watch the way you talk. Let nothing foul or dirty come out of your mouth. Say only what helps, each word a gift. Ephesians 4:29 (MSG)

I COULD FEEL MY SARCASM twitching to pounce. The perfect retort was on the tip of my tongue, ready to launch at the arrogant person who deserved to be put in his place. I certainly wasn't at fault here, and he needed to know how wrong he was.

Can you feel the grace? Sort of makes you want to break out in a chorus of "Kumbaya."

Fortunately Jesus's Spirit caught me before I ruined a perfectly good opportunity to act wisely and zip my lip.

I love wit; wit is fun. But there's a fine line between wit and sarcasm, and is there anything positive that comes from sarcasm? I'm pretty sure not. Wit is the innocent form of sarcasm, but too often the two meld together and true biting sarcasm develops and begins to cut.

Even the word itself sounds on edge: "sar-chasm," like a foxhole it digs between people. Sarcasm is a divider of hearts, and what every person on God's green earth needs instead are words that unify, words that gather up frayed ends.

Jesus used plenty of wit as He taught and loved and drew others to truth, but He did not dilute His impact by resorting to sarcasm.

I looked up Ephesians 4:29 in several translations. *The Message* version clarifies the difference between jolly-good wit and more subversive sarcasm. If each word is a gift, what are we offering someone (or ourselves) with the things we say?

Who knows what wrath or arrogance or other destructive trait can be redeemed by the gift of a life-giving word? —ERIN KEELEY MARSHALL

FAITH STEP: *Pray over 1 Peter 3:8–9 (MSG). "Be loving, be compassionate, be humble. That goes for all of you, no exceptions. No retaliation. No sharp-tongued sarcasm. Instead, bless—that's your job—to bless. You'll be a blessing and also get a blessing."*

SUNDAY, JANUARY 4

---

*God, make a fresh start in me, shape a Genesis week from the chaos of my life.
Don't throw me out with the trash, or fail to breathe holiness in me. Bring me back
from gray exile, put a fresh wind in my sails! Psalm 51:10–11 (MSG)*

EVER HAVE A BAD DAY? You know, the kind where the car won't start; the electricity goes off; you break your toe trying to find the light switch; and your child throws up all over your brand-new carpet? We could all exchange stories where life challenged us to the max. Some of us would even admit to having a bad year.

The Psalmist David certainly had those kinds of days—and even years. Different circumstances, of course. He battled a giant, ran for his life from a jealous king, lost his rebellious son, and endured multiple family difficulties. He also committed adultery and even added "murderer" to his résumé. And that's just for starters. Is it any wonder when the prophet Nathan confronted David with his errant behavior, David wanted and needed a fresh start? The chaos of his life had grown out of control, and he begged for a new beginning—a "Genesis week."

Our bad days last year may never top David's—let's hope not. But we could easily enumerate experiences like unexpected surgery, death of loved ones, financial losses, or even some foolish, personal decisions that left us in "gray exile."

Whatever the past has brought you, Jesus wants to put a fresh wind in your sails this year. He's the only One Who can bring good out of otherwise chaotic circumstances. He's "huge in mercy," and "generous in love," (Psalm 51: 1–2, MSG). What great promises!

I especially like what David asked for in verse 15. It's a great New Year's prayer: "Unbutton my lips, dear God; I'll let loose with your praise." —REBECCA BARLOW JORDAN

FAITH STEP: *What will you ask Jesus to do this year? Be creative. Write out your own New Year's prayer, and place it where you'll see it often.*

MONDAY, JANUARY 5

"'I will shake all nations, and the Desire of All Nations shall come to this Temple, and I will fill this place with my glory,' says the Lord Almighty." Haggai 2:7 (TLB)

I'D NEVER HEARD OF A "word for the year" until fairly recently. First, I saw posts online by authors talking about prayerfully choosing a word to focus on during the coming year. Then I read an article in a major magazine by someone who has practiced this for quite a while. Although she often didn't understand why she felt compelled to claim a specific word, at the end of the year she was always amazed to see how that word related to her life circumstances and the spiritual lessons she'd learned.

A couple of years ago, I decided to choose a word; by the end of January I'd completely forgotten it. But last December a word jumped out at me as I heard two of my favorite Christmas carols on the radio. "Come, Thou Long Expected Jesus" refers to Jesus as "dear desire of every nation, joy of every longing heart." "Hark the Herald Angels Sing" invites Him to "Come, Desire of Nations, Come." After that, Bible verses with the word "desire" seemed to be constantly popping up. So I chose to focus on that word for a year.

I have to admit that sometimes unworthy desires cause me to take my eyes off of Jesus. Deep down I know that I will only be truly satisfied when I seek Him first, above all else. But longing for material possessions, pleasure, or worldly success can throw my priorities off balance. I want my heart's desire to be to know Jesus more intimately and follow Him more closely. At the end of the year, I want to want the right things so I can say, "He fulfills the desire of those who fear him" (Psalm 145:19, ESV). —DIANNE NEAL MATTHEWS

FAITH STEP: *Examine your heart's desires. List the ones that aren't pleasing to Jesus; ask Him to change those. And then consider praying about your own word for the year.*

TUESDAY, JANUARY 6

And this is eternal life, that they may know You, the only true God, and Jesus Christ whom You have sent. John 17:3 (NKJV)

WHEN I STARTED DATING MY husband he told me this was his favorite verse, so I did a little word study on it. I found out that in the original language, the word "know" here means "to know intimately." I thought that was cool—the idea that eternal life means we get to know God intimately through Jesus, here and now and then forever in heaven.

I thought about that again the other day when I went to see my friend Cheryl. I really can't express in words how close I am to her except to say that she's pretty much like family, and for me family is everything. She is battling stage four breast cancer. Last week I spent a day with her. She showed me the port in her chest that she uses for chemo and let me touch her bald head. We looked at old pictures and laughed, and ate some yummy lunch together. We also had a serious time of talking about her disease.

"I'm not ready to die. I haven't done all of the stuff I want to do."

"You can't. I don't even want to imagine a world without you in it."

I have no natural curiosity about the experience of dealing with cancer. But because it is a part of her life I want to know everything. I want to enter into it as much as another person can because I love her. We know each other intimately. Just as much as I want all of the fun times we've had, now I want to feel her pain.

Perhaps this is what is meant by coming to know Jesus intimately through the fellowship of His sufferings. When we have to die, or experience pain or loss, it's a little taste of the Cross. And thank God that as we go to the Cross with Him we also know His Resurrection. We will rise again. —GWEN FORD FAULKENBERRY

FAITH STEP: *Whatever you're going through, Jesus understands. Use it as a time to get to know Him more intimately. And hear Him whisper, "I have overcome. And so will you."*

WEDNESDAY, JANUARY 7

"I needed clothes, and you gave me something to wear."
Matthew 25:36 (GW)

I COULDN'T REMEMBER THE LAST time I'd felt that miserable. Six below zero, not counting the wind chill factor, and I had to stop for gas. Stepping out into the bitter cold from the heated leather seat of the car raked against my comfort zone. My gloves weren't thick enough to keep my hands from feeling the biting temperatures as I swiped my credit card, picked up the nozzle, punched the button, and slid the nozzle into the gas tank.

I hunched into my coat's collar, slapped my hands together, and danced from foot to foot while the tank filled. At the ten-dollar mark, I considered saying, "That's enough for now," and getting back into my warm car.

But, brave woman that I am, I toughed it out until the nozzle popped off. More foot stomping to ward off frostbite in my toes while I waited for the receipt to print out.

Finally. Done. I got behind the wheel and thought, *Well, that was miserable.*

I hadn't even pulled out of the gas station before a new thought rushed in: "miserable" for two or three minutes. At the end of that short stretch was a warm car and a warm home to return to. The coatless, homeless, carless, gloveless, jobless would say, "Lady, that's my whole life!"

My misery shouldn't have even registered, compared to theirs.

Jesus not only taught but also lived a life that demonstrated how we must forget our small annoyances and be aware of, sympathetic to, and responsive in a practical way to those truly in need, those who have a right to use the word "miserable."

Lord Jesus, my constant prayer: make me more like You. —CYNTHIA RUCHTI

FAITH STEP: *Choose to be uncomfortable today in a way that will comfort somebody else. Instead of eating out, buy a gift card so someone else can—a single parent, someone on a fixed income, someone with no income. Find a way to let your small discomforts remind you of those with uncomfortable lifetimes.*

THURSDAY, JANUARY 8

You are the light of the world. A town built on a hill cannot be hidden. Neither do people light a lamp and put it under a bowl. Instead they put it on its stand, and it gives light to everyone in the house. In the same way, let your light shine before others, that they may see your good deeds and glorify your Father in heaven. Matthew 5: 14–16 (NIV)

I LIKE TO STARGAZE, ESPECIALLY on cold crisp nights when the stars seem brightest. Standing under a magnificent sky, I marvel at how small I am in comparison to what is overhead. There might be days when I want it to be all about me, but the reality is, I am just one person in this huge world. Being observant of the night sky is a great way to be humbled and to put life into perspective. As the light of the stars twinkles like jewels on velvet, I think of the familiar song: *This little light of mine, I'm gonna let it shine.*

Innocently and enthusiastically, children sing this song in churches. But when you stop to ponder the words from where the verses came—*We are the light of the world*—it's hard to keep standing because as our ears process the meaning behind the statement, our knees want to buckle. When I hear that I am the light of the world, I know that those words come as both a daunting task that brings me to my knees and a great privilege, which makes me want to sing along with every Vacation Bible School class! Can I be that? Can I shine?

Like stars in the universe, we were made to give praise and glory to God. Wow! —ALICE J. WISLER

FAITH STEP: *What does being a light mean to you? What steps can you take to grow more into the likeness of Jesus, developing His characteristics?*

FRIDAY, JANUARY 9

Like a shepherd, he will care for his flock, gathering the lambs in
his arms, hugging them as he carries them, leading the nursing ewes
to good pasture. Isaiah 40:11 (MSG)

As a former shepherd, I know this verse well so I was surprised to see something new in it this time around.

Lambing season is my favorite time of the year. First, we ready the barn, filling pens with fresh straw. We watch the ewes for lambing signs. Every year a few fool us, lambing in the snow banks.

Once a ewe chooses a spot (especially if her water broke there), she won't move. Warm barns and shepherds aren't in her birthing plan. She knows where she wants to do this.

You could force her into the barn but it's hard without help—she'll "have her brakes on" all the way. Rather than fight, stopping her labor and guaranteeing a sleepless night, I'd get out of the wind and wait for the first lamb to be born. Then I'd use the lamb to move the ewe.

You see, the only thing she wants more than that piece of ground is her baby. Carrying the lamb slowly to the barn entices the ewe to follow. Most mamas will dart back a time or two before walking into the pen. In the end, they follow their lambs.

The shepherd described by Isaiah knew the power of attraction. He, too, drew the sheep to follow. How? By carrying their lambs. Moving newly delivered sheep was just as hard then. As hard as convincing someone like me to leave the familiar for the new and scary. But sometimes Jesus needs to do this. He'll guide us and safely hold what we consider most precious. He is the Good Shepherd who draws all people to Himself.

It's safe (and best) to follow Him. —Suzanne Davenport Tietjen

Faith Step: *Ask Jesus to keep you open to His will, to take the next step in your faith walk. Be open to however He chooses to work.*

SATURDAY, JANUARY 10

The thief comes only to steal and kill and destroy; I have come that they may have life, and have it to the full. John 10:10 (NIV)

THIS PAST YEAR WAS A hard year. It yanked the joy out of me. But I really like joy. I like laughter. I like hope. From listening to me you would think that I like crankiness. And depression. And that I enjoy a hearty portion of irritability. It's as if I have taken on an Eeyore worldview.

I have been thinking about what it would take for me to wake up and feel a sense of expectation at what the day holds instead of dread at the thought of *What is required of me?* What would it take to turn my heart inside out, empty it of the sadness and fill it with hope?

I know that some of my sadness comes from losing a dear friend recently. But I also know that some of it comes from choosing to focus on the hard things in my life instead of choosing to see the beauty that each day holds. Jesus said that He came so that we could have life and have it to the full. He came to offer joy and hope in the midst of our sadness. In spite of our circumstances. I want to seek Him out and embrace the joy He has for me.

I am on a mission to be joy-full this year. I am making a decision to ask Jesus to reshape how I think—to transform me by the renewing of my mind. I am setting out on a path that is headed toward seeing life differently and embracing the loveliness that is already surrounding me. Why don't you join me? —SUSANNA FOTH AUGHTMON

FAITH STEP: *Put on your favorite upbeat worship music and dance your heart out for ten minutes. Remind yourself that Jesus has come so that you can live life to the fullest and that He has joy for you today.*

SUNDAY, JANUARY 11

Therefore, my beloved brothers, be steadfast, immovable, always abounding in the work of the Lord, knowing that in the Lord your labor is not in vain.
1 Corinthians 15:58 (ESV)

EACH YEAR, I PICK A word or theme for the coming months. Hope, faith, courage, joy, or other qualities on which I want to focus my attention have had their turn. This year, my word is *diligence*. It's not a fun sort of word—not the kind of theme that evokes confetti and streamers and upbeat music. But it's a theme that's become important to me.

When I work on writing a novel, I face the daunting task of composing and refining several hundred pages. To help make consistent progress, I break the job into smaller goals. Last summer I labored to finish one good page each day to ultimately complete a manuscript. There were many days when I was tempted to believe the labor was in vain. Although it often seemed impossible, one day in early autumn, the final page was done. I was so glad I'd persisted.

Being steadfast is vital as we follow Jesus long term. We keep praying for the family member who doesn't accept Christ, even when years pass without glimmers of change. We keep volunteering at our local congregation, even though our efforts often seem to bring insignificant results. We give voice to our songs of praise, even when our throats are thick with tears.

In *Mere Christianity*, C. S. Lewis wrote, "That is why the little decisions you and I make every day are of such infinite importance. The smallest good act today is the capture of a strategic point from which, a few months later, you may be able to go on to victories you never dreamed of."

Being "steadfast" or diligent may not sound exciting, but Jesus can grow extravagant fruit from quiet faithfulness. —SHARON HINCK

FAITH STEP: *Think about a long-term project in your life. Ask Jesus to reassure you that your work is not in vain, and ask His help in making you steadfast and diligent.*

MONDAY, JANUARY 12

Thomas said, "Master, we have no idea where you're going. How do you expect us to know the road?" Jesus said, "I am the Road, also the Truth, also the Life. No one gets to the Father apart from me." John 14:5–6 (MSG)

I LIVE IN THE UPPER Peninsula of Michigan, an hour from work. My commute through the Hiawatha Forest or along Lake Superior can be hazardous. I drive in blizzards with a survival backpack. If I call in because of weather, the hospital will send someone out to get me, doubling the risk. So I check the DOT Web site and call the NICU with my route so they'll know if I go missing. Rumble strips on the center and edge of the road keep me on course. And, oh yeah, I pray. You bet.

I thought I knew winter driving before, but there's always more to learn—like how to deal with giant snowplows. If the snow's coming down hard, I trail them at a distance. When I see blinking lights in what looks like an oncoming horizontal white tornado, I pray harder. That's a snowplow big enough to create its own weather, stirring up the snow for half a mile or more. With only a few seconds to get it right, I lift my foot off the gas and, rather than stare at the plow, I look at the road, memorizing its shape in the distance. I imagine driving it blind because soon I will be—when the snowplow arrives. I coast down the visualized road and eventually emerge from the swirl of snow, get my bearings, and resume a safe speed.

Life can be scary like that. Some threat looms, blotting out everything else. But there is always a way through. Jesus is that Way. We can look to Him in every moment, no matter how lost we feel.
—SUZANNE DAVENPORT TIETJEN

FAITH STEP: *Is there an area of your life where you feel lost, the path obscured? Look to Jesus and ask Him to make Himself vivid and real to you.*

TUESDAY, JANUARY 13

Rejoice in the Lord always; again I will say, rejoice.
Philippians 4:4 (ESV)

IN MY LATTER YEARS (SINCE I've become fifty), I have a tendency to run late. I could blame it on my DNA; after all, my dad has run late for as long as I've known him. But the other day I was reminded of how slowing down and taking time can bring a new focus on living.

Before Sunday school, I dropped off my child at her place of work and then drove to church. Since she had to be at work at 9:00 AM and the class didn't start till nearly 10:00 AM, I had extra time. I had time to note the sky, the crisp January weather, the color of the pine trees. I had time to pray in the silence of my car, away from the usual distractions of home. I had time to write prayers for others.

Inside church I went to the library, a place, sad to say, that I don't usually go, even though they are sweet to stock my novels. Conversations with the librarians were lengthy and relaxed; I was in no hurry. As I walked up to the classroom, instead of the usual rush and quick hellos, I was able to take time to engage in the lives of a few others and hear their needs for prayer.

I rejoiced in the way Jesus opened my eyes to others, grateful for a unique morning that would not have occurred had I been operating in my usual Sunday rush. —ALICE J. WISLER

FAITH STEP: *What hinders you from slowing down? From rejoicing? Ask Jesus to make you "awake" to the blessings He has for you today.*

WEDNESDAY, JANUARY 14

Whenever the Cloud lifted from The Dwelling, the People of Israel set out on their travels, but if the Cloud did not lift, they wouldn't set out until it did lift. The Cloud of God was over The Dwelling during the day and the fire was in it at night, visible to all the Israelites in all their travels. Exodus 40:36–38 (MSG)

I OPENED THE BLINDS. GRAY, puffy clouds hovered—the perfect cozy morning for reading, writing, or enjoying coffee.

But the ominous heavens didn't always create such a cheerful mood for me. In years past, those clouds often represented dark times: postpartum depression, PMS (which I called "premonster syndrome"), illness, or loss of loved ones. Sometimes those days stretched out forever, and I longed for the fiery sun to warm my spirits again.

When Moses and the Israelites fled their captivity from Egypt, God led them through a cloud by day and fire by night. He also covered the completed Tabernacle during the day with a cloud. Even at night, a fiery cloud shone over the dwelling of His presence. The people used the cloud as a guide. When it lifted, they moved. When it hovered, they stayed. The entire tabernacle, especially the Ark of the Covenant, foreshadowed the indwelling presence of Jesus one day in our lives.

When I lacked wisdom and direction, when the future was uncertain, or when clouds of anxiety hovered overhead, those clouds were for a reason. In the meantime, I could bask in the glory of His presence. He is in the clouds.

And even during the "night," in the fires of my trials and travels, I've learned that Jesus is there, leading me as well. I no longer fear the clouds. I welcome them. I can rest in the knowledge that Jesus's presence will never leave me, day or night. —REBECCA BARLOW JORDAN

FAITH STEP: *Think about the clouds that have hovered over your life. Thank Jesus today for His presence with you, day and night.*

THURSDAY, JANUARY 15

Do not let your hearts be troubled. You believe in God; believe also in me.
My Father's house has many rooms; if that were not so, would I have told you
that I am going there to prepare a place for you? John 14:1–2 (NIV)

I SAT IN THE AUDIENCE of a small theater watching a talented college cast that included my youngest daughter. In abstract vignettes and powerful scenes they were presenting a new play that looked at the housing crisis. Actors depicted people buying dream homes, losing their homes, and longing for a sense of home.

The play made me think of the various places I've lived. In the first few years of marriage, my husband and I occupied married-student housing, the upstairs of his parents' home, a modest rental in a rough neighborhood, an apartment on the edge of a cow field in a small town, and, eventually, our first little fixer-upper house. Moving was always hard work, but once we cleaned, painted, and settled in, we felt the wonderful secure sensation of being home.

Jesus knows our longing for a sense of home. I love His promise that His Father's house has room for us, and that He is preparing a place for each of us that will truly feel like home. Whether we rest in a tent, a mansion, a rundown motel room, or a luxurious condo, whether we are on the road, in a foreign country, or in the same town where we were born, as long as we are on this planet, the places we live are only shadows of the beautiful home to come.

I'm grateful for the experiences I've had of feeling "at home," and even more grateful that one day Jesus will welcome me into my true perfect home. —SHARON HINCK

FAITH STEP: *Look around the place you call home today. Thank Jesus for His provision of shelter, but also thank Him for the home He is preparing for you.*

FRIDAY, JANUARY 16

And God raised us up with Christ and seated us with him in the heavenly realms in Christ Jesus, in order that in the coming ages he might show the incomparable riches of his grace, expressed in his kindness to us in Christ Jesus. Ephesians 2:6–7 (NIV)

WHEN MY HUSBAND AND I returned to the area we'd lived in for many years, our friends Kathryn and Fred invited us to stay at their home. They treated us like special guests at a bed-and-breakfast. The first morning Kathryn served oven-baked French toast with fresh fruit and whipped cream; the second morning, eggs and bacon. We began each day enjoying a nice visit over a delicious meal; during the day, Richard and I visited family members.

Since we planned to attend Sunday services together on the last day of our visit, Kathryn prepared cinnamon rolls to rise in the refrigerator overnight. The next morning she set the rolls out, jumped in the shower, and suddenly panicked. She replayed the prep of the rolls in her mind over and over, but could not remember adding yeast. Hating the idea of serving flat rolls, Kathryn began to pray: *Lord Jesus, You rose from the dead. You can make these rolls rise whether or not I added the yeast. Please?*

We'll never know for sure whether the cinnamon rolls (which were perfect) rose through supernatural power or as a result of yeast action. Either way, they were a sweet reminder of friendship with each other and with Christ. When Jesus rose from the dead, we were raised up with Him and figuratively seated with Him in heaven. Now we are showered with kindness from a Lord who cares about every detail of our life. We can share every concern with Jesus, even when it involves cinnamon rolls that may or may not have yeast in them. —DIANNE NEAL MATTHEWS

FAITH STEP: *As you go about your day, don't hesitate to share your concerns with Jesus, no matter how trivial they seem. Look for evidences of His kindness to you all day long.*

SATURDAY, JANUARY 17

*He will once again fill your mouth with laughter and
your lips with shouts of joy. Job 8:21 (NLT)*

THIS WEEKEND I TOOK MY cousin Beth with me to a women's conference
I was speaking at. There is one thing that Beth and I love to do when
we are together: laugh. We also love coffee, but mostly we love to laugh.
When life is real and hard and stressful, there is almost nothing better
than a good belly laugh. And I think that Jesus knew that I needed a good
long laugh to start off the New Year. To shake off the stress and sit back
with one of my favorite people and laugh until my stomach hurt.

Everyone could use a good dose of joy, a moment of gasping for air at
the thought of the craziness of life and how it can take us right out at the
knees, and how, if we can find it, even in the saddest of situations, laughter
can open us up to be real and honest with each other and ourselves. I
always think that if we are laughing at ourselves it is a whole lot easier to
hear the truth about who we really are.

When Jesus walked the earth, joy followed in His wake. I can't help
but think that when He brought Jairus's daughter back to life, there
were shouts of laughter filling the house. Or that when He healed blind
Bartimaeus, there were giggles of glee spilling from smiling lips and tears
of joy spilling from perfect eyes. I think laughter will be one of the sounds
we hear most when we get to meet Jesus in heaven. And I can't wait to
hear it! —SUSANNA FOTH AUGHTMON

FAITH STEP: *Make a coffee date with a good friend who always makes you laugh.
Know that when you are together, Jesus is with you in the midst of your joy.*

SUNDAY, JANUARY 18

---

*So, chosen by God for this new life of love, dress in the wardrobe God picked
out for you: compassion, kindness, humility, quiet strength, discipline.
Be even-tempered, content with second place, quick to forgive an
offense. . . . And regardless of what else you put on, wear love. It's your
basic all-purpose garment. Never be without it. Colossians 3:12–14 (MSG)*

WINTER IS MY FAVORITE SEASON, and I say that coming off a week of record
cold temperatures. Like most people in the Upper Peninsula of Michigan,
our family doesn't huddle around the fire waiting for spring. We get out
in the weather—snowshoeing, sledding, skiing, and riding snowmobiles.

I even enjoy getting dressed for it. I slide into shearling slippers, look
outside. and check the thermometer. In January, after basic undergar-
ments, I slide into the first layer, thin silk long underwear. It warms up as
soon as it touches my skin. Then, I put on wool socks, their cuffs pinning
the ankles of the long johns so they'll stay down. Next I'll don a turtleneck, then fleece-lined water-repellant pants (jeans are killers in this kind
of cold). I tuck in the turtleneck—no gaps! Maybe I'll add a sweater, then
choose from a basket of mittens, gloves, and hats, and stuff my selections
in the pockets of my down coat before I lace up my boots. And winter is
only fun (and safe) if you dress for it.

The Bible repeats the metaphor of dressing from Genesis to Revelation.
Job said he was clothed in righteousness. And what about the armor of
God? Sackcloth for repentance, priestly garments, a seamless robe—
clothing communicates.

We may be confused about how to live out our faith. Will others
see Jesus in us? Maybe we're making it harder than it has to be. By
faith we're God's children, hidden in Christ, clothed in Jesus's love.
—SUZANNE DAVENPORT TIETJEN

FAITH STEP: *Put on Christ! Put on love, which holds everything together. God's Word
says this is the way to live our faith and avoid sin. Claim this when you dress for the day.*

MONDAY, JANUARY 19

"Be still, and know that I am God! I will be honored by every nation. I will be honored throughout the world." Psalm 46:10 (NLT)

I'M A MOM OF SIX children, three of them six years old and younger, and there is rarely a quiet moment in our home. But there are a few…and those happen when the kids are still sleeping. I often wake up before the alarm clock, grab my Bible, journal, and coffee, and slip into the living room for time with Jesus. It's a tradition that's not exclusive to moms who live in noisy households.

"For Quakers, wisdom begins in silence," I read in *A Quaker Book of Wisdom.* "Quakers believe that only when we have silence in our voices and our souls can we hear the 'still small voice' that dwells within each of us—the voice of God that speaks to us and that we express to others through our deeds."

When I make room for silence in my life, I make room for Jesus to speak. It's easy to let the noise overwhelm me. In addition to the kids, there is the television, the radio, my cell phone, and numerous other intrusive things. Only in the quiet can I focus and not be distracted by other voices. I can center on Jesus's voice—and I do. I can tell the difference deep in my soul, and my family can tell too. My "deeds" reflect my heart, and a mom with a quiet heart is greatly appreciated, especially on noisy days!

Finally, I also teach my children about being still before Jesus. Sometimes this includes a Bible study or a prayer, but other times we just sit and "think about Jesus." It's training now that will develop a good habit that can last a lifetime. —TRICIA GOYER

FAITH STEP: *Set a timer and sit still before Jesus for ten minutes. Sit and consider all of His wonderful attributes. Praise Jesus for Who He is. Let your soul breathe deeply and know Jesus in a new way you've never experienced before.*

TUESDAY, JANUARY 20

With Jesus' help, let us continually offer our sacrifice of praise to God by proclaiming the glory of his name. Hebrews 13:15 (NLT)

MY HUSBAND BOUGHT ME A GPS a couple of years ago. He'd seen me—his directionally challenged wife—stress about driving in unfamiliar territory, and he knew my tendency for getting lost, especially after dark. Investing in a technological gizmo that could supply both visual and verbal directions seemed not only kind but smart as well.

That GPS has become my good friend. She travels everywhere with me, tells me where to go, and always shows me how to get home. Only heaven knows where I'd be without her help.

Spiritually speaking, I'm somewhat directionally challenged too. Scripture tells me how to live, but sometimes I don't "get" it. Thankfully, God—knowing my tendency to wander—made a way for me to navigate life successfully. He sent Jesus to guide me and to help me do what He commands. The same is true for you.

"...May the God of peace, who brought again from the dead our Lord Jesus, equip you with all you need for doing his will. May he produce in you, through the power of Jesus Christ, all that is pleasing to him" (Hebrews 13:20–21, NLT).

Navigate the highway of forgiveness? Jesus will help us.

Travel the road of suffering? Jesus will help us.

Drive the boulevard of uncertainty? Jesus will help us.

Jesus travels with us everywhere we go. He knows what lies ahead, and He directs our way. He's our good friend. Only heaven knows where we'd be without His help. —GRACE FOX

FAITH STEP: *Think about your life as a map. Recall an instance or two when you faced a crossroads in your journey. How did Jesus keep you moving in the right direction?*

WEDNESDAY, JANUARY 21

Don't burn out; keep yourselves fueled and aflame. Be alert
servants of the Master. Romans 12:11 (MSG)

I AWOKE WITH A SCRATCHY throat and deep voice. My nose felt like an overfilled balloon about to explode; my eyes burned and watered; my body ached like I'd played football the day before; and the tissue box was emptying fast.

I was sick, and it wasn't pretty.

I'd had a hunch I'd been overdoing it as I kept up with an overextended schedule. I had reminded myself late at night that I'd pay for my lack of moderation. I'd even had the haunting sense that germs were pouncing, but I hadn't positioned myself to fight back.

Sometimes I need to wise up sooner and pay attention to Jesus's example of prioritizing rest. The needs around Him were never-ending and dire. He had only twenty-four hours a day to do His work, and, surely, someone was always ready to let Him know if He wasn't measuring up to their standards.

Yet He didn't shove the need for rest to a corner to attend to last. He kept Himself refilled by downtime spent with His Father before He reached total burnout. Even if the demands didn't slow their assault, He did His work and then acted assertively to ensure the pauses He needed.

I paused all right, but the rest came from the barrel of sickness that knocked me over in its downhill tumble.

Jesus gives us common sense and His Spirit's help to live day to day at our best. Part of being people who can accomplish much for Him means giving ourselves the adequate tools to succeed. Life is a marathon, and He invites us to proactively pace ourselves so we don't burn out.

Achoo! Excuse me; I'm taking a break now. —ERIN KEELEY MARSHALL

FAITH STEP: *Sit down for fifteen minutes today, before it's late at night, before you're exhausted. Thank Jesus for rest, and don't feel guilty!*

THURSDAY, JANUARY 22

"Come and see . . . and see . . . [and] see." John 1:39, 46, 50 (CEB)

IT CAN GET ME OUT of my chair faster than the smoke alarm or a washing machine thumping across the laundry room floor—a grandchild who tugs at my hand and says, "Come and see, Grammie! You just have to see this!"

The destination of our "come and see" excursion could be the world's tiniest toad, the world's stickiest pinecones, a pail of acorns, an overflowing bathtub, or a peanut butter sandwich the little one made all by himself.

When His followers finally started to get a clue about Who He really was, some asked Jesus, "Where are You staying?" He answered, "Come and see" (John 1:39). Such a simple scene, but significant enough to have been recorded in Scripture. A short time later, Philip, a new follower, found Nathanael and invited him to follow Jesus too. Nathanael couldn't believe anything good could come from a town like Nazareth. Philip answered, "Come and see" (John 1:46), the very words Jesus had used.

Within minutes, Jesus convinced Nathanael He was more than a carpenter with a story to tell. He wowed Nathanael with knowledge about the very moment Philip had invited him to come and see Jesus. Jesus said, "Do you believe because I told you that I saw you under the fig tree? You will see greater things than these!" (John 1:50).

The invitation Jesus gave His followers—including us—isn't merely to "Come and see." It's to "Come and see . . . and see . . . [and] see!" See the magnificence of heaven in the everyday. See the love of Jesus in a child's eyes. See the sacrifice Jesus made for us, the affection He has for us, the limitlessness of grace He bought with His life. See the wonder waiting just beyond where you are now. —CYNTHIA RUCHTI

FAITH STEP: *Rise from your chair quickly today when Jesus whispers, "Come and see!" You don't want to miss what He has to show you.*

FRIDAY, JANUARY 23

For the grace of God has appeared that offers salvation to all people. It teaches us to say "No" to ungodliness and worldly passions, and to live self-controlled, upright and godly lives in this present age, while we wait for the blessed hope— the appearing of the glory of our great God and Savior, Jesus Christ, who gave himself for us to redeem us from all wickedness and to purify for himself a people that are his very own, eager to do what is good. Titus 2:11–14 (NIV)

THE THEATER HOUSE LIGHTS DIMMED. The orchestra began to play. The booming timpani quickened my heartbeat and the flute's trill built the anticipation. I'd looked forward to seeing this show for weeks, and I leaned forward as the curtains rose. Lights spilled onto the stage and illuminated a vibrant set. Performers lifted their voices in a swirl of movement and music. I was swept into the story.

There is nothing quite like the breathless excitement of the moment before the curtain rises. We may know a hint of what we'll discover, but much is a mystery until we experience it. We turn off our cell phones, stop rustling a piece of wrapped candy, even suppress a cough. Our attention is focused, eager.

In these verses in Titus, I glimpse that same sort of expectation. We are living every moment with the blessed hope of Jesus appearing. We exist in the moment before a great curtain rises on the fulfillment of His plan. Even better, He invites us to join Him. This isn't the overture of a story that we will passively watch. When Christ returns, we will join the celebration with Him. And while we wait, He invites us to join Him, "eager to do what is good." We can share His love with those around us. We can hum the distant melody of worship that will soon burst into full volume when He returns. —SHARON HINCK

FAITH STEP: *What creates anticipation in you? Ask Jesus to stir up the same eagerness for His return, and for serving Him in the meantime.*

SATURDAY, JANUARY 24

Who shall separate us from the love of Christ? Shall trouble or hardship or persecution or famine or nakedness or danger or sword? . . . No, in all these things we are more than conquerors through him who loved us. Romans 8:35–37 (NIV)

WHAT DOES IT MEAN TO you to be "more than a conqueror?" I've been thinking about these verses and feeling convicted about the way I respond to difficulty. I tend toward the melancholy side of my personality, and when bad things happen, the default mode for me is to go over the edge. This was made painfully obvious to me the other day when I visited my friend Cheryl who has cancer.

We were laughing and talking and then things got serious. "I need to tell you about my visit to the doctor," she said. "I got some bad news."

Cheryl went on to tell me about a change in her prognosis that was devastating. The doctor's words, as she repeated them to me, felt like a punch in the gut. It was all I could do not to fall apart right before her eyes. *Be strong. Be strong.* After I left, I let the tears flow all the way home.

The next day I received a text that she was at the ER. She'd developed a fever during the night, and severe stomach cramping. When the bloodwork was done at the local hospital, her oncologist sent a helicopter to fly her to the big hospital hours away for treatment. It was terrifying. I was basically incapacitated on the couch staring at my phone and willing it not to be true when her daughter sent me a picture. My friend was strapped into the helicopter with a black hat and surgical mask. The caption read, "Luke, I am your father." I pushed *call* immediately and she cackled with laughter.

Sometimes being more than a conqueror doesn't mean we ride out on a white horse, sword held high. Sometimes it's the choice to go on when we feel like quitting. Laughter in the face of fear. Trust in His love no matter what. —GWEN FORD FAULKENBERRY

FAITH STEP: *What is the worst thing you are facing right now? Thank God that even that cannot separate you from Jesus's love.*

SUNDAY, JANUARY 25

Because of the miraculous signs Jesus did in Jerusalem at the Passover celebration, many began to trust in him. But Jesus didn't trust them, because he knew human nature. No one needed to tell him what mankind is really like.

John 2:23–25 (NLT)

WHEN I SIT DOWN TO write, there is an excitement that stirs within, but when it comes to speaking to groups, I'm more nervous than anything else. I want to hold my breath until I can see if they laugh at my jokes or tear up at the right moments. Nothing feels as good as connecting with a crowd and seeing that my words are making an impact.

It seems to me that after so much time spent speaking to crowds Jesus would be excited that they finally believed…or did they? Jesus had crowds following Him, but mostly because they were seeking signs, rather than seeking a Savior. Jesus knew the men who followed Him weren't concerned about God's kingdom, but rather what they could get out of it for themselves. Jesus knew that gossip would spread faster than praise, and that their doubts would be easier to grasp than the Truth. Jesus didn't need the testimony of man…He had the testimony of God. He also knew in time that His identity would be revealed, and then all men would know Him and bow in worship.

As Romans 14:11 (NIV) says, "It is written: 'As surely as I live,' says the Lord, 'every knee will bow before me; every tongue will acknowledge God.'"

How about those you know? Do you know anyone who's missing the Truth of Who Jesus is, and instead is hanging around for His benefits? Pray that the trust they find in Christ will be real and true. Jesus may not trust human nature, but when we allow Him to fill us, we'll be able to know, believe and grasp all Who He truly is. —TRICIA GOYER

FAITH STEP: *Next time you're listening to a speaker, make eye contact, listen intently and smile. Also lift up a prayer for that person. It'll make a huge difference!*

MONDAY, JANUARY 26

"Come to me, all you who are struggling hard and carrying heavy loads, and I will give you rest." Matthew 11:28 (CEB)

A FRIEND OF MINE GOES to jail every Tuesday and Thursday. And those of us who love him couldn't be happier. He serves young men and women in the juvenile justice system. By serve, I mean that he listens to them, cares about them, encourages them—in most cases it's the only encouragement the young person receives—and coaches them through better life choices. In the name of Jesus.

He's seen the power of God's love at work when young men respond, "You care about what happens to me? Why?" It's not unusual for tears to fall. Most feel they're beyond the reach of anyone's concern for them. For far too many, it's a self-fulfilling prophesy. But some respond as if primed to receive a word of hope.

Most of the juvenile detention detainees are short-termers, but repeaters. They're in jail for an offense but out within a few days. Then they're back in for some new infraction.

My friend pours himself into the lives of these young men, in particular. "You're getting released tomorrow? Let's meet at the coffee shop at ten. My treat. We'll talk."

The young person always promises to show up. Two in twelve do.

After being stood up that many times, you'd think my friend would call it quits. But he doesn't. "I want them to know I care. I showed up."

Someone-who-cares-no-matter-what sits and waits—and waits. So few times, the invited one responds. Isn't that painfully like us with the invitation from Jesus to come, sit with Him, listen to Him, talk it out, or just sit? —CYNTHIA RUCHTI

FAITH STEP: *Is your appointment with Jesus written on your calendar in indelible ink? Or do you hope to fit in the time when you can? Either way, He's there. He shows up. Let that truth soak deep into your core.*

TUESDAY, JANUARY 27

Though the righteous fall seven times, they rise again.
Proverbs 24:16 (*NIV*)

SEVERAL YEARS AGO I READ about a man named Darren LaCroix, who won a world champion public-speaking contest. In only a seven-minute speech he linked his subject of failure to success. He had experienced multiple blunders in his own life, including a business venture and an attempted stand-up comedy act. And just to make his point clear, he literally fell down—to the floor. On purpose. He emphasized not to stay down too long or to give up. And did I mention his fear of public speaking?

I had a similar experience in my public-speaking class in college years ago. In explaining how to give a "chalk talk," one of my points was how to handle unexpected speaking failures. About that time, my carefully drawn, chalk-talk papers tumbled to the floor in a heap. Yes, that illustrated my point and brought a laugh to my classmates, but the "fall" was not on purpose. And did I mention my own fear of public speaking then?

All of us fall at one time or another. In fact, we have a "fallen" nature (Romans 3:23). We don't have to fall on purpose to prove it.

Most of us link that falling to failure. But I've told others many times that falling is not failing. Jesus, the Grace Giver, recognizes that we are dust, that we will make mistakes. But if we belong to Him as followers of Christ, we can and will learn from those falls. And we will get up again. And again. And again. Jesus's own disciples failed Him, but they learned—and were changed.

When we do fall, it's important that we not stay down long and give up in failure. Instead, we give *in* to Jesus. That kind of surrender is linked to success, not failure. —REBECCA BARLOW JORDAN

FAITH STEP: *What fallings (or failings) have you experienced? On a sheet of paper, list the lessons Jesus has taught you through those times, and thank Him for helping you to get up again.*

WEDNESDAY, JANUARY 28

*As Jesus approached Jericho, a blind man was sitting by the roadside begging.
When he heard the crowd going by, he asked what was happening. They told him,
"Jesus of Nazareth is passing by." He called out, "Jesus, Son of David,
have mercy on me!" Luke 18:35–38 (NIV)*

THIS PAST WEEK THE CLUTTER of life has been overwhelming me. Dishes, laundry, homework, book reports, writing deadlines, church schedules, car repairs. It is nothing out of the ordinary but sometimes the ordinary feels like it is too much. My children know when I have had enough because after dinner, they find me lying immobile on the couch, surrounded by unfolded laundry.

My youngest son, Addison, once mentioned, "Hey, Mom! I think you really like being on the couch." Yes. It would seem that I do. Or maybe it is more that life has flattened me with its fullness. It is in those moments that I need to be looking for Jesus. Reaching for Him. Calling out to Him. I keep thinking it is up to me to get me through life. This approach is not really working for me or anyone else who likes a seat on the couch.

I love the story of the blind man who hears that Jesus is passing by. He knows he can't get to Jesus in the crowd. But he also knows that Jesus is Who he needs. So he does what he can. He yells. He shouts. He screams. "Jesus! Help me! Have mercy on me!" And Jesus hears him. He floods his life with mercy. He brings healing to his life and sight to his eyes. He revolutionizes his world because…this man called to Him. He needed Him. He saw Him for Who He was: The Son of God. This week I am taking a different approach. The couch is out. Calling out to Jesus, the healer of my soul, is in. —SUSANNA FOTH AUGHTMON

FAITH STEP: *Pray out loud and let Jesus know that you need Him. That you want His mercy, His grace, His forgiveness, and His hope to flood your life.*

THURSDAY, JANUARY 29

Take delight in the Lord, and he will give you the desires of your heart.
Psalm 37:4 (NIV)

Do you ever wonder what Jesus wants you to do with your life? As a kid I shared a popular fear that He would send me to a remote wilderness to live on grubs and sleep in a hut. And while that way of living isn't out of the question for someone who is committed to following His lead, I needn't have worried so much.

I believe that knowing Jesus's will lies in discerning what makes our unique heart tick. This verse in Psalms has long been understood—perhaps mistakenly—to mean that if we love the Lord He'll give us what we want. However, we err in understanding its true meaning if our primary focus is on what we want. Its attention is on delighting in the Lord. Not just giving Him part of our heart, but handing it all over with joy and then letting Him define our desires.

If I've surrendered to Christ, then I'm allowing my natural desires to be altered, solidified, or reformed by Him. If He wants me to go to Africa and eat grubs, He'll plant and nurture a desire in me for the people over there. If I'm truly His, not just in word but in heart, then His desires for me will grow larger than my own selfish ones.

This morning I rediscovered a quote from Frederick Buechner: "The place where God calls you is where your deep gladness and the world's deep hunger meet."

The Bible's promise that our heart's desires will be met when we delight in Jesus lifts us as well as builds His kingdom. As we enjoy the Lord, He fills others through us, and He fills us too. —Erin Keeley Marshall

Faith Step: *Is there a dream you've nurtured or pushed away as impossible? Commit it to Jesus, and ask Him to do something with it. Let Him mold your desires into the more He has in store.*

FRIDAY, JANUARY 30

The unfailing love of the Lord never ends! By his mercies we have been kept from complete destruction. Great is his faithfulness; his mercies begin afresh each day. Lamentations 3:22–23 (NLT)

MY HUSBAND GIFTED ME WITH a coffee maker last year. It's a Tassimo machine—one that makes individual servings of both regular and specialty coffees, tea, and hot chocolate. Each morning I rise early, fetch a hot drink and then enjoy my quiet time with Jesus. Later in the day, I make another drink or two. At this rate, it doesn't take long for the water tank to empty. A red light flashes to let me know it's time for a refill.

How grateful I am that Jesus's love tank doesn't have a limited capacity. Imagine it draining a bit each time we yell at our kids, complain about the weather, and gripe about the price of gas and groceries. Imagine the "love level" visibly decreasing each time we worry, gossip, envy someone else's house, or neglect to do something the Lord prompts us to do. If Jesus's love tank were to run dry, we'd be in big trouble.

Thankfully, Scripture assures us that Jesus's love for us never ends and His mercies begin afresh every day. We wake in the morning, go through our day, and fall into bed at night surrounded by His presence and kept by His faithfulness. Nothing we do or say exhausts His mercy. Limitless, it is. More than ample toward all who acknowledge Him as Savior.

Go ahead—enjoy Jesus's love. Trust your well-being into His care. Cast your fears aside. Shed your doubt and shame. Embrace the abundant life He offers, knowing His love tank is always filled to the brim. —GRACE FOX

FAITH STEP: *Pour yourself a cup of your favorite drink. Now take a sip and note how the liquid level decreased. Thank Jesus that His love capacity for you never decreases but remains constant, filled to the brim.*

SATURDAY, JANUARY 31

If you carefully obey me and are faithful to the terms of my promise,
then out of all the nations you will be my own special possession,
even though the whole world is mine. Exodus 19:5 (GW)

LAST YEAR WE ADOPTED TWO children. We showed them love, and we told them that they'd found their forever-home. I could see in their eyes that they sometimes found that hard to believe, but, amazingly, it was something unexpected that helped our kids to trust our words. We taught them authority. We taught them obedience.

It is important for children to respect parental authority. We want our children to obey us so that they learn to grow and obey Jesus.

We wanted our children to know our love, yes, but through understanding the rules and standards of our family...they finally began to understand that they belonged. Outward molding led to inward believing. We guided them on how to eat around our table. How to treat our family members. "Our" meant all of us, them included. Our children learned to obey us because they belong to us. They are no longer orphans, they are ours. In the same way, we obey Jesus because we belong to Him. We are His special possession. He loves us more than we can imagine. And our obedience shows proof of our love too. You are my friends if you obey me, says John 15:14 (NLT). And John 14:15 says, "If you love me, obey my commandments."

Jesus doesn't ask us to obey just to give Himself an ego boost. Instead He knows we'll only truly understand what "belong" means if we fall in step behind the One Who's leading the way. Our outward compliance will lead to our inward faith as we see how following Jesus's commands will always lead us the right way. —TRICIA GOYER

FAITH STEP: *Make a list of as many of Jesus's rules as you can think of in three minutes. Then look at the list. How has obeying those rules helped you to better see yourself as Jesus's child?*

SUNDAY, FEBRUARY 1

"Come to me, all you who are weary and burdened, and I will give you rest. Take my yoke upon you and learn from me, for I am gentle and humble in heart, and you will find rest for your souls." Matthew 11:28–29 (NIV)

I HAVE BEEN TIRED LATELY. Somehow the weariness of life has crept down into my bones. Busy weekdays have bled into even busier weekends. This morning I found myself crawling out of bed only to want to crawl back in. Coffee is just not cutting it. I know that sooner or later something is going to give. Most likely it will be my cheery nature. It will be replaced by the cranky, whiny person that I become when I have too little time and too much to do in it.

I have been thinking about rest. True rest. It is something that Jesus offers us but we often bypass in the craziness of life. He calls to the weary and the worn in this world who are struggling to bear up under what life has handed them. That is us.

When He offers His yoke, He is offering to share the load. He wants to shift our burdens to His shoulders. He wants to offer His strength in place of our weakness. He wants to partner with us in life and teach us how to live. And I, for one, am ready for this shift. I can feel the dragging of my spirit and the weight of worry and anxiety pressing down on me. Jesus offers a different way of living. A way to rely on Him and follow His lead. In exchange, I get to rest. This is an offer I can't refuse.
—SUSANNA FOTH AUGHTMON

FAITH STEP: *Make a list of your worries, your responsibilities, and the things that are weighing on you. Ask Jesus for His guidance, His direction, and His wisdom as you plan out your day and commit these things to His care.*

MONDAY, FEBRUARY 2

Do not store up for yourselves treasures on earth, where moths and vermin destroy, and where thieves break in and steal. But store up for yourselves treasures in heaven, where moths and vermin do not destroy, and where thieves do not break in and steal. For where your treasure is, there your heart will be also.
Matthew 6:19–21 (NIV)

I LOVE MY CROCKPOT. IN the morning, I throw ingredients into it and go about my day. By suppertime when I'm too tired to think about preparing a meal, the food is ready. Even lesser quality meats turn tender after simmering all day. Yesterday I tossed in some stew meat and herbs, chopped carrots, onions, potato, and celery, and covered everything with beef broth. Humble ingredients, but they combined to create a satisfying stew for a cold winter evening.

When Jesus talks about storing up treasures in heaven, I think of my crockpot. The preparation comes long before the enjoyment. We are serving Him today, looking forward to the eventual feast.

What are the ingredients we're adding to the pot? Perhaps the quiet words of understanding and encouragement that we offered a friend yesterday. Or the financial gift we made to another's ministry. Maybe the song of praise we lifted to Jesus alone in the car as we drove across town. Or the effort it took to hold back an unkind word. A patient correction given to a child. A gentle hug. All the demonstrations of love to Jesus and others become part of the treasures stored up in heaven.

As the ingredients blend and simmer, Jesus stirs, adjusts, and adds His own components. I'm so excited for that time at the final banquet, where we'll discover what treasure was created from the humble bits and pieces of our lives. —SHARON HINCK

FAITH STEP: *Cook something today, and as you add in each ingredient, ask Jesus to show you various ways to add treasure to your heavenly storehouse.*

TUESDAY, FEBRUARY 3

I pray that from his glorious, unlimited resources he will empower you with inner strength through his Spirit. Then Christ will make his home in your hearts as you trust in him. Your roots will grow down into God's love and keep you strong.
Ephesians 3:16–17 (NLT)

My FAVORITE PLACE TO BE is home. In fact, if you could see me right now you'd know why I love it so much. I'm in my flannel pajamas, wearing no makeup, and I'm sitting in front of a rock fireplace in a leather recliner with my laptop. A fire crackles. Hot coffee steams beside me in my favorite mug. A fat Boston terrier snores by my feet. Sunshine spills through the window, enveloping me in natural light, and if I look outside I see woods and the Arkansas River. It's a sanctuary for a hermit like me.

What does it mean for Jesus to make His home in our hearts? I hope it means He is comfortable there, happy. It's not a place He's passing through, but His permanent residence. He takes care of it. It's a place He invests in, constantly making improvements. He decorates with all of His favorite things—beauty, joy, peace. We have good conversations here; we know one another intimately; we share everything.

What a lovely idea to imagine that wherever we go, we take Him with us in our hearts. He is there to stay, steady and secure, no matter what. We are never alone. I know that when I selected the place to build my house it was very special. I chose it because of the location, the view—it was where I wanted to be.

If you are a Christian, never doubt that Jesus lives in your heart. You are very special to Him. He chose you; your heart is where He wants to be. It is His sanctuary. —GWEN FORD FAULKENBERRY

FAITH STEP: *Meditate on the phrase "Christ will make His home in your hearts as you trust in Him." Write down what you think that means. How might this perspective change the way you go about your day?*

WEDNESDAY, FEBRUARY 4

"Come now, let us argue this out," says the Lord. "No matter how deep the stain of your sins, I can remove it. I can make you as clean as the freshly fallen snow. Even if you are stained as red as crimson, I can make you as white as wool."
Isaiah 1:18 (NLT)

SNOW FELL IN OUR AREA throughout last night and most of today. It covers the bare-branched trees, tops the fence posts, and blankets our lawn and driveway. It even conceals the flower baskets I've ignored since fall—the ones teeming with blooms long dead. Yes, beautiful is the freshly fallen snow outside, especially because no one's footprints mar it yet.

I gaze at the wintery scene as I sip my hot apple cider. Immediately a familiar Scripture comes to mind, and with it comes a new realization: Jesus gave His life on the Cross not to simply *cover* our sin stains as snow hides my dead flowers and leaf-strewn lawn. No, He shed His blood to *remove* our sin stains and to make us as spotless as the freshly fallen snow I see today.

Many of us wrestle with regrettable choices we've made. We beat ourselves up emotionally while trying to cover our past and our pain with plastic smiles and do-good behavior. On the inside, however, we doubt that God can use us. We feel tattered and dirty.

Take heart! Christ's shed blood washes away our stains. He makes us new, cleanses us completely, and leaves us pure and spotless as the snow cloaking my backyard shrubs.

Our finite minds grapple to understand this truth especially if our choices resulted in ongoing challenges, but it stands regardless. "Thank You, Jesus." —GRACE FOX

FAITH STEP: *Find an online photo or magazine picture depicting fresh snow. Print it or cut it out and then put it on your fridge. Each time you see it, thank Jesus for removing your sin stain and making you as clean as freshly fallen snow.*

THURSDAY, FEBRUARY 5

Praise be to the God and Father of our Lord Jesus Christ, who has blessed us in the heavenly realms with every spiritual blessing in Christ. Ephesians 1:3 (NIV)

IN 2013 MY HUSBAND AND I lived apart for three months after he started a new job sixteen hundred miles away. A couple of years earlier, we'd relocated across the country from our families, so I didn't have much of a support base. We'd made a handful of friends who were great, but they had their own families nearby and didn't live that close. Since we'd built a house in a developing subdivision, most of the neighbors on our little cul-de-sac were brand-new. I felt totally on my own, and prayed that I wouldn't have to deal with any emergencies during this period.

Then one morning, I woke up around 3:00 AM in pain. I tried to wait for Urgent Care to open at 7:00 but when the pain increased, I decided I had to do something sooner. While driving to the closest hospital in the predawn darkness, I remembered Emergency Room stories I'd heard. Sick people waiting for hours to be seen, sometimes sitting in hallways. I limped into the ER and within minutes saw a doctor, and got a diagnosis and prescriptions.

Back home, I thought about how things had worked out. The hospital was only twelve minutes from my home. I was able to drive myself there despite the pain. I was the only patient at 3:45 AM. Instead of questioning why God had allowed the crisis, as I usually do, I found reasons to praise Him. That ordeal served as a reminder that I can always find reasons to praise, whether in specific details or for spiritual blessings I have in Christ: my sins have been forgiven, my future is secure, and His presence guides me day by day—even during a kidney stone attack.
—DIANNE NEAL MATTHEWS

FAITH STEP: *Are you struggling with a hardship right now? Why not lay your questions aside for a few moments and thank God for the blessings you have in Jesus.*

FRIDAY, FEBRUARY 6

I will tell of the kindnesses of the Lord, the deeds for which he is to be praised, according to all the Lord has done for us—yes, the many good things he has done for Israel, according to his compassion and many kindnesses. Isaiah 63:7 (NIV)

SOMETIMES WHEN I PRAY, I am praying but I am not really believing that my prayers hold any weight. Even as I have been praying I have been doubting that my prayers would be answered in the way I wanted them to be. This is probably not the most effective way to pray.

Yesterday, when I was in the parking lot at the grocery store, I was shooting up a prayer to the Lord. I talk to Him a lot in the car. And this thought pierced my prayer midsentence. *You don't believe that I have good things for you.* I couldn't even deny it. I simply burst into tears.

This past year was a year of prayer and fasting for us. We prayed for a house. We prayed for our friend Shelly to live. We prayed for our church to grow exponentially. We prayed for a lot of things. We prayed and then we prayed some more. And when God did not move as I begged Him to, I lost my prayer mojo.

You would think I wouldn't be so fickle. Clearly, you don't know me. But I know that Jesus isn't done with me. When He zinged me in the parking lot with His truth, all I could say was, "You are right. Forgive me. Make me new." I think hands down it is the best prayer I have prayed yet.

The truth is, Jesus doesn't just have good things for me. *He has good upon good upon good things for me.* So gripping this truth with both hands, I am turning my heart toward Him once again. Rejoicing. Praying. Full of thanks. And that's good. —SUSANNA FOTH AUGHTMON

FAITH STEP: *Make a list of three things today: Something you can rejoice about, something you need prayer for, and something you are thankful for. Carry it in your pocket and read it often. Lift it up to Jesus and know that He has good things for you today.*

SATURDAY, FEBRUARY 7

In him all things hold together. Colossians 1:17 (NIV)

EVERY NOW AND THEN A fantastic word lodges itself in my psyche. (*Psyche* is one of them, by the way.) *Garfoofully* was birthed one tough afternoon when my brain was so frazzled, it was all I could utter when my husband asked me how my day went. And in recent months, *unflappable* has been memorable to me.

As life stays busy, my heart is increasingly sensitized to my need for Jesus's stabilizing effect. Keeping up with a family, paying attention to their hearts, feeding us, managing schoolwork and an activity or two, meeting writing deadlines, and volunteering here and there is a lot to handle, even more to handle well.

Each day as I consider how I'm doing with it all, the word *unflappable* rings in my thoughts—not because I am unflappable but because I aspire to be that way.

I want to be solid. More than that, I want those I care about to reap the benefits of living with stability. I want my husband to feel my support, my kids to thrive and be well-adjusted because they know Mom is consistent and what they'll get from me is filling for their hearts.

But the truth is, I can come undone by chaos. My voice rises (surely of its own accord, right?); my tone takes on an edge; my movements become harsher. I don't enjoy being me when I'm like that, and I can feel my family withdraw to calmer waters until I get hold of my senses once again.

I want more from life. I want to be more. So I seek the Source of stability: Jesus, the ever-unflappable one. He is never thrown. In fact, He's the holder-togetherer of all. (*Holder-togetherer* just lodged in your psyche, didn't it?)

The key to being held together by Him is to be *in* Him. In Jesus, I will discover unflappability. In Him I need not unravel, even if the day turns garfoofully. —ERIN KEELEY MARSHALL

FAITH STEP: *Read John 15 and then memorize John 15:5. Ask Jesus to help you remain in Him.*

SUNDAY, FEBRUARY 8

Watch what God does, and then you do it, like children who learn proper behavior from their parents. Mostly what God does is love you. Keep company with him and learn a life of love. Observe how Christ loved us. His love was not cautious but extravagant. He didn't love in order to get something from us but in order to give everything of himself to us. Love like that. Ephesians 5:1–2 (MSG)

I HAVE A HARD TIME loving our cat, Rooney. He's really my daughter's, a feral kitten found in a Korean alley and eventually shipped to the United States where we picked him up at an O'Hare freight terminal in a snowstorm. We took care of him until my daughter and her family moved here. When they went back and couldn't afford to reverse the process, we ended up with Rooney.

He's an odd cat with a funny mustache. He doesn't like people but is very attached to an old blue blanket he drags around and sucks on as if it were his mother. He waits for our other cat to fall asleep, then sinks his teeth into Braveheart's thigh to begin their nightly fight. Also, when I'm annoyed about something, he weaves himself through my ankles, tripping me (and annoying me further). This is not a lovable cat.

Watching him one night, I wondered if he knew how I really felt about him. That made me sad so I asked God to help me love him. I immediately decided that was the number-one most ridiculous prayer I ever prayed—he's a cat! There have to be bigger things God wants to teach me.

Wait. Bigger than learning to love?

Loving someone who's interested only in himself and has nothing to offer but need? Like Jesus did when he died for us?

I'm in. Use a cat if you want, Jesus, but teach me to love.

There's nothing bigger. —SUZANNE DAVENPORT TIETJEN

FAITH STEP: *You may not have an eccentric cat, but I guarantee that someone in your life needs love. Jesus loves way better than we do. Ask Him to love someone through you today.*

MONDAY, FEBRUARY 9

*Grace, mercy, and peace, which come from God the Father and from
Jesus Christ—the Son of the Father—will continue to be with us
who live in truth and love. 2 John 1:3 (NLT)*

I PULLED THE HOT PAN from the oven and cut the buttermilk cornbread
into squares. It looked just right, golden brown on top and risen up just
high enough—the perfect partner to the beef vegetable soup I'd made this
winter evening. Several minutes later, my husband mentioned that the
cornbread "had a funny taste." I argued that it tasted fine. Of course, I'd
slathered so much butter on mine that it was all I tasted.

A few bites later, I had to agree. Something wasn't quite right, but we
couldn't figure out why the cornbread tasted "off." I read the recipe over
and over to see if I'd left out an ingredient. No, that wasn't it. Then I
saw the measuring spoons sitting on the counter and it dawned on me.
Instead of a quarter teaspoon of baking soda and one teaspoon of baking
powder, I'd reversed the amounts and put in a full teaspoon of soda.

Anyone who cooks has probably had similar experiences. Blame it on
multitasking or a wandering mind, but when we forget an ingredient or
don't measure correctly, the end result isn't what we were hoping for. Getting the ingredients right is even more important when it comes to our
life. We can go along looking fine on the outside, but if something in our
spiritual life is "off," we won't be pleased with the finished product.

Some days I don't take time to talk to Jesus, to read and meditate on His Word, or to worship or praise Him. As a result, I miss the
full measure of His grace, mercy, and peace that I could enjoy. And
no wonder, I've left out the most important ingredients of my day.
—DIANNE NEAL MATTHEWS

FAITH STEP: *Has any area of your life seemed a bit "off" lately? Make sure you're
including the right ingredients to enjoy grace, mercy, and peace each day.*

TUESDAY, FEBRUARY 10

Your faithfulness extends to every generation. Psalm 119:90 (NLT)

I HEAR THE WORDS FREELY spoken by all ages of people, but especially the older generation: "We live in a different world. Things are not the same as they once were. People have changed. Times are harder. Less respect. More violence." Teens love to challenge parents' rules with the changing times argument. Pastors, school principals, and even psychologists may echo those thoughts. And if we park there, life can seem fairly depressing.

Are they right? Yes. And no. The world has changed. Sidewalks no longer teem with kids. Playing without adult supervision or riding to school alone—things many of us enjoyed in years past—have disappeared. Simple communication, like letter writing, has been replaced with less personal technology. Too many changes to name.

But have people really changed? Has violence truly increased? Or have our modern communication tools and social media outlets merely opened the floodgate to our awareness of the "real" world.

We'll never lack for bad news. The good news is that some things have never changed, one thing in particular. From the beginning of time and the words, "Let there be light!" spoken by the Creator Himself, to the last "Amen" at the end, one truth will always remain: in every generation, no matter how good or bad things are perceived, Jesus and His faithfulness will never change. That faithful character "extends to every generation." Jesus is the same as He's always been: yesterday, today, and forever (Hebrews 13:8, NIV).

Now that's good news. —REBECCA BARLOW JORDAN

FAITH STEP: *Make your own chart. On one side, list all of the changes, good or bad, that have happened in your lifetime. On the other side, list the things that never change—and thank Jesus that He and His faithfulness are one of them.*

WEDNESDAY, FEBRUARY 11

Be alert and of sober mind. Your enemy the devil prowls around like a roaring lion looking for someone to devour. 1 Peter 5:8 (NIV)

AFTER SPEAKING AT A LOCAL convention to a group of men with addiction problems, small groups formed for prayer. The group I was in was a diverse one with addicts and their family members, including children. As we stood in a circle and shared prayer requests, one of the young men confessed, "The battle is in the mind."

How young this man was (especially compared to me) and yet how right he was!

When I'm feeling a little sick or tired, I have to be extracareful. For that's when I have to fight the hardest. Temptations to doubt or envy or worry seem to hit me at those times. Sometimes I have to stop whatever I'm doing and recite those passages that remind me that my ill feelings are due to an ill thought.

Help us, Jesus, in our weakness. Help us not to sugarcoat those areas in which we need the most help. —ALICE J. WISLER

FAITH STEP: *What areas do you struggle with? How do you protect yourself from letting them take over and consume you? Jot down ways in which you can remain positive and focused on Jesus in a world where temptations to doubt and to become discouraged are rampant.*

THURSDAY, FEBRUARY 12

He saith unto him the third time, Simon, son of Jonas, lovest thou me?
. . . And he said unto him, Lord, thou knowest all things; thou knowest that
I love thee. Jesus saith unto him, Feed my sheep. John 21:17 (KJV)

ON THE CAMPUS WHERE I teach, there's an organization called BCM, short for Baptist Collegiate Ministries. When the group was forming, they asked me to be the faculty sponsor and we had a meeting in which pastors and other leaders in the area brainstormed on how to minister most effectively to the needs of students. I told them I thought one way would be to provide a free meal once a week because a lot of our students live in poverty and I know many of them don't eat during school hours.

Location seemed to be a problem till we contacted the Seventh Day Adventist Church that is very near campus. They graciously allowed us to start using their fellowship hall and now, every week, members from Baptist churches all over our area provide a free, home-cooked meal to hundreds of students and faculty. It has been a phenomenal success, and I love it for so many reasons, not the least of which is that people didn't let differences in church doctrine and beliefs get in the way of spreading the gospel of Jesus.

The greatest thing about it, though, is that the endeavor meets a basic need people have—to eat. We see this in the ministry of Jesus over and over in the Bible. Whether it was touching a leper or blind man, or feeding the five thousand, He went about meeting basic needs and concerns of people, reaching out to them in love and drawing them to Himself. As His disciples, I believe we need to follow this example.
—GWEN FORD FAULKENBERRY

FAITH STEP: *Gandhi said, "There are people in the world so hungry that God cannot appear to them except in the form of bread." Look around you. What needs do you see that you can meet in your community in order to share Jesus with others?*

FRIDAY, FEBRUARY 13

Live wisely. . . . Let your conversation be gracious and effective so that you will have the right answer for everyone. Colossians 4:5–6 *(NLT)*

ONE WORD TO DESCRIBE THIS verse? *Convicting!* When my talk isn't laced with grace, I'm not living the way I should. And it isn't just that I'm not; it's that I can't. I can't live wisely if I don't control my speech. The bugger of it is, I can't control my speech if my heart isn't filled with grace.

I'm not a very loud person. It's common for me to feel like I'm talking loudly, but others often ask me to repeat myself. Unfortunately, my "quiet" mouth has gotten me in trouble a time or three. A while back a speaker at church asked us, "Do you ever catch yourself saying that one more thing, that thing you probably should have kept to yourself?" As a matter of fact, yes, I sure do. I recall several of those cringe-worthy moments.

Our mouths are headstrong organs. At times I've felt nearly fearful of my ability to communicate clearly without causing confusion or injury. It isn't only my specific words, but my tone, body language, expressions, and even my level of stress energy that accompanies those words.

I believe Jesus's Word warns us frequently about controlling our tongue because our mouths function from the overflow of our hearts (Matthew 12:34 and Luke 6:45). Words that fly out willy-nilly reveal the state of our heart, whether it's filled with purity that uplifts or debris that divides.

When I take time to be with Jesus, to study His Word, listen for Him with a genuine heart, and submit to His Spirit, my entire being relaxes in His grace. And I speak effectively. It's the most fabulous experience, and you'd think I'd stay in that connected place with Him always.

But no. I am human, so I have to draw near to Him again so I can live wisely. And, Lord willing, may my regrettable comments be mistakes of the past. —ERIN KEELEY MARSHALL

FAITH STEP: *Memorize Matthew 12:34.*

SATURDAY, FEBRUARY 14

One night the Lord spoke to Paul in a vision: "Do not be afraid; keep on speaking, do not be silent. For I am with you, and no one is going to attack and harm you, because I have many people in this city." Acts 18:9–10 (NIV)

DANGER FOLLOWED PAUL LIKE A hunter stalking prey. He could have opted to appease his abusive enemies with silence, never sharing the good news of Jesus. But Paul refused to choose the easy way out.

When he experienced trouble in the city of Corinth on one of his missionary journeys, Jesus appeared to him in a dream, encouraging him, and assuring him of His protection. Jesus told Paul he would not work alone. He had prepared those ahead: "many people in this city" who would lend their support and keep Saul safe.

And He did. Paul stayed in that city a year and a half, enlarging his audience to include Gentiles.

Just as for Paul and all believers, Jesus prepares His "angels" on earth—not just heavenly ones—to help protect us. We don't need to fear those who might oppose our efforts—sharing about Jesus, the One we represent. The message is so strong, and Jesus is so faithful, that we are covered.

That doesn't mean we won't suffer for the cause of Christ. In His lifetime Paul experienced shipwreck, stoning, hunger, imprisonment, and eventually death. But Jesus kept providing both heavenly and earthly protection until His work for Paul was finished.

He'll do that for us too. The good news of Jesus is too powerful and too precious for us to keep silent. —REBECCA BARLOW JORDAN

FAITH STEP: *Thank Jesus for His protection around you daily. Think of someone who needs to know about Him, and ask Jesus to show you how you can demonstrate His love to that person soon.*

SUNDAY, FEBRUARY 15

But one thing I do: Forgetting what is behind and straining toward what is ahead, I press on toward the goal to win the prize for which God has called me heavenward in Christ Jesus. Philippians 3:13–14 (NIV)

MOVING OUT OF A HOUSE we'd lived in for twenty-three years proved to be a real eye-opener. I couldn't believe all the unnecessary "stuff" we'd accumulated in closets, cabinets, drawers, and the garage. We saved the worst for last: the attic. Crawling over the patches of flooring, I discovered items I thought we'd gotten rid of long ago. We made several trips to donate items at Goodwill and drove away from a huge pile for the garbage collectors to pick up. *Never again,* I vowed.

Yet three years later I found myself once again preparing to move. Although nothing like the previous experience, I was still surprised by how much I had to purge from our belongings. But hanging on to old papers, unused makeup, and home decor that doesn't fit anymore isn't my worst problem. I also have a hard time letting go of past mistakes, hurts, and disappointments. Whenever I talk about what "should have been" or "could have been," my daughter says, "You gotta let it go, Mom. Just let it go."

Dwelling on negative aspects of the past paralyzes me. It keeps me from growing into the person Jesus wants me to be and prevents me from being a blessing to others. It's important to review our failures to see what lessons we can learn. But once we've been forgiven and restored, it's time to put the guilt and shame behind us and press on toward what Jesus has in store for us. It's time to "just let it go." —DIANNE NEAL MATTHEWS

FAITH STEP: *What "old stuff" do you need to purge from your life so you'll be free to move forward and live the life Jesus intends for you? Jot down your list, pray over it, then destroy it.*

MONDAY, FEBRUARY 16

Jesus replied, "The truth is, no one can enter the Kingdom of God without being born of water and the Spirit." John 3:5 (NLT)

JESUS ALWAYS SPOKE THE TRUTH when people asked Him questions, and the truth wasn't something they expected—or necessarily wanted. Sometimes His answer seemed irrelevant to the question. Nevertheless, it was important for them to hear because it would change their lives if they heeded Him.

On one occasion, Nicodemus asked Jesus how a person could be born again. The prospect of an old man reentering his mother's womb seemed ludicrous to him, and rightfully so. Jesus's answer about being born of water and the Spirit may have sounded equally strange, but it was the life-changing truth.

On another occasion, a crowd waited on a shore to see Jesus. When He arrived, they asked, "How did you get here?" He answered, "The truth is, you want to be with me because I fed you, not because you saw the miraculous sign" (John 6:25–26). What? The people may have wondered if He misunderstood what they'd asked.

Of course Jesus didn't misunderstand. But He knew their hearts, and He knew speaking truth to them mattered more than how He landed on the beach.

People nowadays need to hear truth, too, but we might hesitate to speak it lest we offend somebody. The point is, we're responsible to speak up if we see someone heading for trouble. Perhaps a loving warning (not a tongue-lashing) will change somebody's choices and have long-lasting results.

We also need to be willing to accept truth when others speak it in our lives. It might not be something we expect or even want to hear, but it might change us forever. —GRACE FOX

FAITH STEP: *When was the last time someone spoke truth into your life? Was it something you expected or wanted to hear? How did you respond? Thank Jesus for godly friends who care enough to speak up when necessary.*

TUESDAY, FEBRUARY 17

A song of ascents. I lift up my eyes to the mountains—where does my help come from? My help comes from the Lord, the Maker of heaven and earth. He will not let your foot slip—he who watches over you will not slumber; indeed, he who watches over Israel will neither slumber nor sleep. Psalm 121:1–4 (NIV)

THIS MORNING I WOKE UP to find Addison tucked up against me. He is a cuddler. I know at some point the cuddling will stop so I am going to take it while I can get it.

I remember when I was a little girl waking up on warm summer nights to huge thunderstorms with cracking lightning. Usually, all four of us kids would end up in my parents' bed where we knew we were safe. We were with Mom and Dad.

I think Addison feels the same way. Any fears melt away when he snuggles down between Scott and me. He feels safe. We all want to feel that. In moments of fear or suffering, when we are scared or hurting, we know who we can run to. It's Jesus. We know the One Who keeps us safe and holds us close. We know that our help comes from the Maker of heaven and earth. He doesn't let up in His caring for us, in His healing of us, in His leading. Jesus did all that He could to be close to us. When we run to Him, He doesn't think, "Why don't they go bother someone else?" He is like me when I hear Addison coming down the hall and I throw back the covers and say, "Get in here." He wants to comfort us and let us know that we are loved and that we are protected by the One Who laid out the universe. And that is a beautiful thing. —SUSANNA FOTH AUGHTMON

FAITH STEP: *Snuggle up on the couch in your favorite blanket. Feel Jesus wrap you in His love. And remind yourself that He watches over you with an everlasting love and He will never let you go.*

WEDNESDAY, FEBRUARY 18

"No, I tell you, but unless you change your hearts and lives,
you will die just as they did." Luke 13:3 (CEB)

MY MIDDLE SON WAS QUICK to seek forgiveness when he did something wrong. In that respect he fit the mold of a middle-child personality wanting to make things right between us as soon as possible.

But he was a child. And human. So he had plenty of opportunities to put that into practice.

On one particularly "Mommy's had enough" day, he came to me with his traditional "I'm sorry" for a familiar infraction.

Without thinking of the consequences the words would have as they resonated in my own soul, I said, "Honey, if you were really sorry, you wouldn't do it again."

That was the day I understood the true meaning of repentance. It's not a word on a billboard. Not a ritual at the beginning of Lent. Not a puppy's tail between his legs, head-hanging-low heart response for our mess-ups.

Repentance, as Jesus described it, is a change of heart. It's honoring what Jesus wants more than the pull of a temptation, changing our way of thinking about what we're entitled to, what we deserve, if that runs contrary to what the Bible teaches. It's a transformation from one way of thinking—one mind-set—to another that is not only spiritually healthy but God-pleasing.

The ashes of Ash Wednesday represent repentance, a symbol of grief over our sins, sins that sent Jesus to the Cross. But commemorating grief stops short if it doesn't commemorate true repentance, the change of heart that marks us for life.

My son had a vast reservoir of "I'm sorry's." The day eventually came when he didn't need them so often. He'd had a change of heart. —CYNTHIA RUCHTI

FAITH STEP: *At the beginning of these forty days of Lent, purchase a charcoal or gray notebook (or recover another notebook with gray or charcoal cloth or paper) and record the ways you've had a change of heart in how you think about yourself, others, and Jesus.*

THURSDAY, FEBRUARY 19

"I do know that the Messiah is coming. When he arrives, we'll get the whole story."
"I am he," said Jesus. "You don't have to wait any longer or look any further."
John 4:25–26 (MSG)

IN THEIR BOOK, *SACRED ROMANCE*, Brent Curtis and John Eldredge say we all have a continual story, a Sacred Romance calling to us every moment of our lives. That voice awakens in us a "yearning for intimacy, beauty, and adventure," a deep desire for someone to know us, while inviting us to know them, and a longing to be part of something larger than ourselves.

The authors talk about arrows, like Cupid's aiming at unsuspecting victims, and how all of us experience "arrows" of pain and suffering that leave holes, turning us away from the very intimacy we crave.

The woman at the well experiences that when Jesus goes out of His way to offer her a sacred relationship. One by one, Jesus uncovers her defenses and excuses, leaving her open and vulnerable. She sees impossibility, too many differences. But that doesn't stop Jesus.

The woman's wounds run deep: loneliness, misunderstanding, and fear of exposure. Jesus knows and gently reveals her past—and it's not pretty.

This woman doesn't understand that Jesus is the Living Water, the One Who can meet her soul's deepest needs for a lifetime. But to her credit, she accepts His offer—and the truth that Jesus is the Messiah, and the author of her sacred romance.

When we listen, we'll hear Jesus calling us to a sacred relationship too. It's the greatest love story of all. And when we make it our own, it's a match made in heaven. —REBECCA BARLOW JORDAN

FAITH STEP: *Draw a heart in your journal for today, and place an arrow running through it. Express your thanks to Jesus through your writing and your prayers for offering you His sacred romance.*

FRIDAY, FEBRUARY 20

I have hidden your word in my heart that I might not sin against you.
Praise be to you, Lord; teach me your decrees. With my lips I recount all the laws
that come from your mouth. Psalm 119:11–13 (NIV)

MY YOUNG CHILDREN HAVE RECENTLY joined a program where they are encouraged to memorize Scriptures. It's so adorable for them to work so hard to memorize the words. Maybe they're doing it because they remember that they'll get a sticker or a piece of candy for each one they know. Maybe they work so hard because they see the smile on my face and the joy in my eyes as they try. Recently, I found my six-year-old daughter trying to teach her brother John 3:16, "For God so love the princesses that He gave His only begotten Son." I corrected her, but I had to smile. Yes, Jesus died for the princesses too.

I know that my children are working hard for immediate rewards, but I also know that they will receive other, more long-range rewards too. How do I know? Like them, when I was little I memorized Scripture verses so that I could pick out pink plastic rings and miniature chocolate bars from Miss Margo's treasury box. Those treats were soon broken, lost, or eaten, but the words remained, and in my teen years when I was living far from Jesus, those words returned to me, and they brought me back to Him.

Psalm 37:31 (NIV) says, "The law of their God is in their hearts; their feet do not slip." There are many things of this world that will cause us to tumble, but the words of Jesus will be like stepping stones on a slippery path.

It's a wonderful thing for us to hide God's Word in our heart. And if we get a sticker, it's a bonus. But we are never too young—or too old—to work to plant His Words deep. —TRICIA GOYER

FAITH STEP: *Choose a verse to memorize this week. Psalm 119:11 is a great one to start with!*

SATURDAY, FEBRUARY 21

If you give up your life for Me, you will find it. Matthew 10:39 (NLT)

I'M NOT ONE TO GIVE up easily. This quality has served me well in some situations. In others, however, I may have needed to give up long before I did. It's worth examining. Especially since in this verse, that's exactly what Jesus says to do: *Give up. Give up your life* in order to *find it.* What does He mean by this?

I believe it has something to do with our willingness to surrender all we have—and all that we are and dream of—to Him. Some of us may have a strong desire for things. The goal to get things can be all-consuming. Jesus invites us to give up the chase for things and enter into something better, something deeper—life in Him.

Others may not focus on things. We may have carved out a life we find comfortable and want to cling to it too tightly. I once knew a man who had a good job and a perfectly normal life with his family in the suburbs. He felt Jesus said to him one day, "This is not the life I have for you. Give it up for Me and you will find out how to really live." They took off to join Youth With A Mission and became missionaries.

Still others may have dreams—even dreams they believe God has inspired—and they will do anything they can to make them come true. I believe sometimes Jesus says to us, "Are you willing to give up that dream if I ask you to? In order to find your life?" This is the one I have struggled with the most. I've had to learn in my life that sometimes we must let things die in order to live in His peace. In some cases, when we've done all we can do, we need to give up. To trust Him, and find our peace again.

—GWEN FORD FAULKENBERRY

FAITH STEP: *Take a personal inventory of what consumes your attention. Is there anything you need to give up in order to find your life in Jesus? Write down these items and ask Jesus to help you give them up willingly.*

SUNDAY, FEBRUARY 22

Furthermore, because of Christ, we have received an inheritance from God,
for he chose us from the beginning, and all things happen just as
he decided long ago. Ephesians 1:11 (NLT)

A FAMILY FRIEND WAS DIAGNOSED with diabetes several years ago. Newly married, she and her husband had hoped to have children someday, but doctors warned that she'd be considered a high-risk pregnancy. The couple took their disappointment to Jesus and sought His guidance. They felt His nudging them to apply for adoption rather than risk her health.

The adoption process took several years, and then one day they received a phone call. "Are you willing to take four siblings?" the caseworker asked.

Four? They'd planned on one, or maybe two, kids joining their family. Four would change everything. They'd need a bigger house, a larger vehicle, beds, dressers, clothing, bikes, and toys. What's more, only two of the children were school age. Our friend would have to quit her job to stay home and provide stability as everyone transitioned into being a family of six.

The couple said yes without hesitation. Perhaps their instant acceptance came from understanding firsthand the value of providing a good home for children. You see, both were adopted as youngsters.

Today the family is flourishing. Christ's purpose—ordained for them long ago—is being fulfilled. It's beautiful to behold.

What's Christ's purpose for your life? Nestle, don't wrestle. He will make all things happen to fulfill it, and it, too, will be beautiful to behold.

—GRACE FOX

FAITH STEP: *How has Jesus worked in your life to fulfill His purposes? Make time to write the story, including details that show His presence and power. Tell that story to your family—doing so will help them rest in the knowledge that He'll accomplish His purposes for them too.*

MONDAY, FEBRUARY 23

Don't be afraid of those who want to kill your body; they cannot touch your soul. Fear only God, who can destroy both soul and body in hell. Matthew 10:28 (NLT)

ON A RECENT VISIT, I was playing with my granddaughter while my daughter-in-law prepared supper nearby. The baby wasn't speaking yet, but she communicated clearly through gestures. When she heard music she loved, she'd bob her head and wriggle, doing a gleeful "baby boogie."

My daughter-in-law turned on the blender and the baby started dancing. She apparently considered the blender to be music. I was still laughing at her antics when her mom pulled out a box grater and began shredding a sweet potato. My granddaughter's face fell, then she tugged on my leg and started to cry.

"She always does that when I use the grater," my daughter-in-law informed me. "We haven't figured out why it upsets her."

I marveled at the logic of the baby brain. Why would she dance to the blender and be terrified of a much quieter grater?

We all fear the wrong things sometimes, don't we? I'm often afraid of the opinions of other people . . . when it's much more important to seek to please Jesus. Or I worry about my children, forgetting that Jesus holds them secure in His hands. Or I fear poverty, accident, or illness instead of remembering that the details of my life are under His authority.

When Jesus tells us to "fear God," it's actually an invitation to stop being afraid of all the wrong things. When we recognize the awesome strength and power of God, other things lose their power to terrify because we know He is in control. —SHARON HINCK

FAITH STEP: *Picture three things you fear alongside the might of God and see them shrink in power.*

TUESDAY, FEBRUARY 24

For no one can lay any other foundation than what has been laid down. That foundation is Jesus Christ. 1 Corinthians 3:11 (HCS)

WHEN MY HUSBAND AND I went house-hunting last year, one thing I learned: just because a house looks good online doesn't mean it's the right one. One afternoon I requested our Realtor show us a home that appeared to have everything we were looking for. The home featured a large yard with landscaping and mature trees, something at the top of my list. It also met my husband's top priority: it was new enough that it shouldn't need repairs or updating right away.

The house turned out to be cozy and inviting, but as I walked across the family room, the floor felt a bit odd in one spot. Stepping into the first bedroom, I could tell that the floor in front of the closet was not level. And one look at the floor in the hallway revealed a definite sloping.

We eventually decided to go with new construction. As the builder's mom listed the advantages of homes built by her family, she mentioned getting a "good slab" laid down. I didn't understand the specifics about "Concrete 3000 psi" or 24-by-12-foot beams or five-eighths of an inch rebar. But I could certainly grasp the importance of a good slab after seeing the house with the sinking floors.

It's important to make sure our life is built on the solid foundation of faith in Jesus Christ and obedience to His teachings. All of our daily decisions, actions, and attitudes should reflect that. Other lifestyles or belief systems may look good from the outside, but they won't stand the test of time; eventually they will start to shift or crumble. No matter what troubles come our way, we'll never be in danger of sinking if we have the right foundation. —DIANNE NEAL MATTHEWS

FAITH STEP: *Are you building on Jesus as the foundation of your life? How do your actions and attitudes reflect that?*

WEDNESDAY, FEBRUARY 25

I keep asking that the God of our Lord Jesus Christ, the glorious Father, may give you the Spirit of wisdom and revelation, so that you may know him better.
Ephesians 1:17 (NIV)

I'VE LIVED IN ARKANSAS LONG enough to know a few of its claims to fame. For instance, Arkansas is the only state where people can mine for diamonds. Visitors travel to the Crater of Diamonds State Park in hopes of unearthing these elusive treasures from an ancient volcanic crater.

The Uncle Sam diamond, a 40.23-carat whopper that is the largest found in the United States, was discovered there in 1924. Hillary Clinton wore the 4.25-carat Kahn Canary on loan to her husband's 1993 and 1997 inaugural balls to honor their home state, where the diamond was found. And recently an Oklahoma teen found a 3.85-carat canary diamond at the park, which averages several hundred finds per year.

Diamond fever sets me thinking about another treasure that seems just as mysterious: wisdom. Wisdom is one of those higher-level gifts we regular folk long for. It's linked with history's heavy hitters like King Solomon. Unreachable. Inaccessible.

Well here's a game-changing tidbit I discovered: If we're the Lord's, we can ask for His Spirit of wisdom. All of His power is at our disposal, including wisdom.

Wisdom isn't only for the supersmart or aristocratic. Wisdom is accessible to all who need it, young or old, educated or not, healthy or sick, rich or poor. You and me. The world may claim to be wise, but wisdom's pure form comes from our Maker, who sent His Son to tell us about it.

When we study Jesus's life in His Word, when we seek to understand His heart and purposes, we see the contrast between the world's version and Jesus's untainted wisdom.

Jesus offers us His power to live as wisely as He did, when we seek Him as our treasure. —ERIN KEELEY MARSHALL

FAITH STEP: *Read Proverbs 8:11–12 and Romans 11:33 for more about wisdom.*

THURSDAY, FEBRUARY 26

"Because [He] knows how we're made, [He] remembers we're just dust."
Psalm 103:14 (CEB)

THE WALLS BETWEEN CHANGING ROOMS in the charity discount store aren't thick. And although the doors are solid, there's a good foot or more of space between the bottom edge of the door and the floor.

So it wasn't my fault that I could hear the conversation going on in the room next to mine. A young dad was trying on shirts while attempting to herd his toddler children in the room with him. No easy feat for any parent. It was obvious from his tone of voice that it had been a long day already, and this wasn't their first stop.

I listened as his voice rose, then he caught himself and turned his sentence into something as patient as possible, under the circumstances.

I tried to envision what the little ones were doing, trying to open the locked door, crawling on the floor, playing hide-and-seek behind the clothes hanging from the hook on the wall, trying on Dad's shoes...

I couldn't help but smile because my kids were grown and capable of taking care of themselves.

At the end of his parenting rope, the dad finally lost his grip on patience and said, "Why can't you kids act like normal people?"

Did he hear me chuckling next door? Kids act like kids. And even "normal" people wouldn't solve his problem. That's why Jesus came, because normal is selfish, sometimes unkind, impatient, rude, unthinking, oblivious to the needs of others.

Dad, don't hope for normal. Thank the Lord for children who can climb, run, and talk. And pray for Jesus-kids with Jesus-hearts who will rewrite society's idea of "normal." —CYNTHIA RUCHTI

FAITH STEP: *Focus on one attribute of Jesus's character today: His love, joy, faithfulness.... Make choices that reflect His "normal," especially as it relates to that specific character trait.*

FRIDAY, FEBRUARY 27

God did not lead them through the land of the Philistines, although that was the most direct route from Egypt to the Promised Land. The reason was that God felt the people might become discouraged by having to fight their way through, even though they had left Egypt armed; he thought they might return to Egypt. Instead, God led them along a route through the Red Sea wilderness.
Exodus 13:17–18 (TLB)

"I SNAGGED AN EARLIER FLIGHT!" Our daughter's call caught us off guard, but we dropped everything so we could arrive at the airport on time. That day was a perfect storm: one traffic detour after another. When the creeping detours took three times longer than expected, we grumbled the entire way.

The Israelites didn't like detours either. Finally freed from Pharaoh after four hundred years, they didn't take the easy path to their "Promised Land." Instead, God took them on what seemed like a wild goose chase into the heart of the Red Sea wilderness. And did they ever complain!

What they didn't know, however, was that discouragement could have enslaved them more than the Egyptians if they had tried to fight their way prematurely through a land of giants and gigantic obstacles.

None of us like wilderness wanderings or "character-building" experiences. We may question or misunderstand God's whys. Maybe He wants to protect us from a moral disaster, or help us to avoid a physical accident. He may design a detour for discipline, patience, trust, or joy in all circumstances.

Jesus's followers thought His death detoured their hopes and dreams. Who would free them from Roman rule, if not Him? But Jesus's death and Resurrection provided the way, not a detour, to greater—and permanent—freedom.

And did I mention trust and joy—in all circumstances?
—REBECCA BARLOW JORDAN

FAITH STEP: *What character-building detours have you experienced in your life? Share with someone this week one positive thing you learned from a detour.*

SATURDAY, FEBRUARY 28

Therefore do not worry about tomorrow, for tomorrow will worry about itself. Each day has enough trouble of its own. Matthew 6:34 (NIV)

THERE ARE PEOPLE WHO THINK we're crazy, for just when we had three children grown and out of the house, we adopted three more. Another cycle of chore charts and manners. Another cycle of T-ball and piano lessons. Another cycle of conjugating verbs and multiplication tables.

I have to admit that sometimes I think we're crazy, too, and worries sift in. *We're older now; are we going to be able to keep up? What about the cost of college? Will they want to search for their birth parents? How will that go?* I have to remind myself that those aren't things that I need to think about. Instead, I only need to consider today.

"No man ever sank under the burden of the day," wrote George MacDonald. "It is when tomorrow's burden is added to the burden of today that the weight is more than a man can bear. Never load yourself so."

Yes, there are things that are troubling. When our kids first came home we had to deal with emotional and behavioral issues that were brought on by the neglect they endured. It wasn't as if we never wanted to worry, but Jesus also told us where to take those worries—to Him in prayer.

"Do not be anxious about anything, but in every situation, by prayer and petition, with thanksgiving, present your requests to God."

"Don't worry," Jesus tells us. "And when you do, present your requests to God." Jesus knows that both are the right answer, and He gives us two options. But both options are a confession that He is in control. He can take care of everything better than we can, so why don't we turn it over and let him get to work on that! —TRICIA GOYER

FAITH STEP: *For the next week place a heart around that day's white square on your calendar and let Jesus know that you aren't going to get stuck in worries beyond today. And then offer up even those daily worries to Him in prayer.*

SUNDAY, MARCH 1

By this all men will know that you are My disciples, if you have love for one another. John 13:35 (NAS)

I'M A UNIVERSITY PROFESSOR, AND my campus is a few blocks from where my kids go to school. We get out of classes about the same time, they ride the bus over to my office every day, and then we go home. It fills me with joy to see each of them walk through my office door: Harper, the fifth-grader, with his camouflage backpack; Grace, in seventh, with her stack of books; and Adelaide, my first-grader, with her owl lunch bag.

Our schedules are similar, but they usually go back to school from a break a bit sooner than I do. On my first day back with students, Adelaide rushed through the door first. "Did you have a good day, Mommy? Did you like all of your students?"

She came around my desk and sat in my lap.

I kissed her on the cheek. "Yes, I did."

"Good. I prayed for you during my moment of silence."

My heart was touched that my little girl, in her classroom with all of her classmates around, thought of me during the moment of silence they observe after saying the pledge of allegiance. In fact, she used this time to talk to Jesus about me. And He answered.

One thing this taught me was not to worry much about the lack of prayer in schools. Prayer happens whenever and wherever a heart turns toward God, regardless of any man-made law. The other thing was more of a reminder: love is what matters most in life. It's simple, and it's what counts. Furthermore, it identifies us as followers of Jesus. It doesn't have to be loud or showy. But to a world that is watching, it is the thing that sets us apart as His. —GWEN FORD FAULKENBERRY

FAITH STEP: *What simple act of love has been lavished on you lately? Thank Jesus for it. Then, pay it forward.*

MONDAY, MARCH 2

"I tell you the truth, you can say to this mountain, 'May you be lifted up and thrown into the sea,' and it will happen. But you must really believe it will happen and have no doubt in your heart. I tell you, you can pray for anything, and if you believe that you've received it, it will be yours." Mark 11:23–24 (NLT)

ONE SUNDAY AFTERNOON WHEN I was a little girl, I climbed up on the roof of our chicken shed and stood on the edge, trying to muster enough courage to jump off. That morning our pastor had preached a sermon on Jesus's words about moving mountains. Blame it on Peter Pan, but at that age I had an obsession with flying. I could not imagine anything more wonderful than soaring over the woods at the edge of the farm. And according to Matthew 11, if I just believed hard enough, I could do it, right? What I wanted couldn't be more difficult than moving a mountain.

Thankfully, I never found the nerve to step off that roof before I grew older and wiser. Later I learned that Jews often spoke in hyperbole, and that "moving a mountain" was an expression for doing something considered impossible. Now I understand that Jesus's promise doesn't apply to just any whim or desire, but to prayer that fits guidelines laid down in the Bible: a request that aligns with God's will, prayed by a believer who has godly motives and a forgiving spirit toward others.

Jesus taught that when we ask for something in prayer, we need to have faith that we will receive it. But that doesn't mean I can claim a specific verse as a guarantee that I'll get whatever I want. I need to also invoke Jesus's prayer just before His Crucifixion: "Yet I want your will to be done, not mine" (Mark 14:36). —DIANNE NEAL MATTHEWS

FAITH STEP: *Do you have a "mountain" you want moved? Evaluate whether your request fits scriptural guidelines, then get in the habit of ending your prayer with "Your will be done."*

TUESDAY, MARCH 3

Those who trust God's action in them find that God's spirit is in them—living and breathing God! Obsession with self in these matters is a dead end; attention to God leads us out into the open, into a spacious, free life. Focusing on the self is the opposite of focusing on God. Romans 8:5–7 (MSG)

I REMEMBER THE MOMENT MY childhood ended. I was in seventh grade and had what today they call high self-esteem. When school let out, an excited friend talked about what we were going to do. I said, "Oh, that sounds like fun!" assuming that the "we" in her statement included me.

It did not. I can still see her stop and turn toward me, a puzzled expression on her face. "But you're not coming."

Surprised not to be invited, I just stood there while she walked away. What was wrong with me? I'd never been on the outside—I hadn't really been aware until then that an outside existed. I wondered why I'd been excluded. I couldn't think of a thing.

I struggled with self-consciousness after that. I watched myself, as if from outside, wondering how I looked to other people. I anticipated disapproval and changed my behavior to head it off. I left the naturalness of childhood behind. Whatever I'd done, I wasn't about to do it again.

I went to Sunday school and church but I confused the "be good" message I heard there with another requirement for acceptance. It was many years before the words of a children's song shifted my focus from myself.

Jesus loves me, this I know, for the Bible tells me so.

I believed it. I didn't need to be afraid Jesus would reject me. He already loved me. Nothing I did would make Him love me more.

Jesus said we must accept God's kingdom simply, like a child, to enter in. Eyes on Jesus, take that step. —SUZANNE DAVENPORT TIETJEN

FAITH STEP: *Self-consciousness is paralyzing. Ask Jesus for childlike faith and joy. Try doing something you liked as a kid—go to the park, swing on the swings! Worship.*

WEDNESDAY, MARCH 4

"Jesus said, 'You have seen him. In fact, he is the one speaking with you.'"
John 9:37 *(CEB)*

IMAGINE MEETING THE ORGAN DONOR who saved your child's life. Imagine a face-to-face meeting with the heroic fireman who pulled you from the flames. Imagine meeting Jesus after He healed your lifelong blindness.

A man born blind didn't realize what was happening when Jesus made mud and smeared it on the man's eyes, and then sent him to wash in the pool of Siloam. The man did as instructed—*who wouldn't want to wash mud from his eyes, blind or not?*—and when he returned, he could see.

The press—the Pharisees and other Jewish leaders—peppered him for details, questioning whether he had ever had a problem. Was he even the same man reported to have been blind? If so, what did he know about this Jesus?

The man answered their incessant questions in a way that revealed he was beginning to understand. His faith grew as he talked about what had happened to him and declared there was no other explanation than that Jesus was from God.

Rather than welcome the now-sighted man back into their social circles and their religious community, the leaders expelled him for being a smart aleck! "You were born completely in sin!" they said. "How is it that you dare to teach us?" (John 9:34). They excommunicated him.

Jesus found him and asked an all-too-familiar question. "Do you believe in the One Who healed you?" The once-blind man answered the stranger, "I want to believe. Who is he?" After being ridiculed, shamed, and expelled, the man still defended the truth and sought to know more.

It's then Jesus revealed who He was. What a moment! What a beautiful, two-person worship service. —CYNTHIA RUCHTI

FAITH STEP: *We don't have to understand everything about Jesus or every nuance about the Bible to defend Him, bravely speak our own story of an encounter with Him, and watch our faith grow in the process. Watch for an opportunity today to share what Jesus has done for you.*

THURSDAY, MARCH 5

"No one who has left home or brothers or sisters or mother or father or children or fields for me and the gospel will fail to receive a hundred times as much in this present age: homes, brothers, sisters, mothers, children and fields—along with persecutions—and in the age to come eternal life. But many who are first will be last, and the last first." Mark 10:29–31 (NIV)

WHEN MY BIBLE STUDY TEACHER took a business law class in college, he said the professor first arranged the class in alphabetical order. But after the first graded test, he rearranged the seating chart, placing the highest-scoring students in the back and the lowest scorers at the front. He would then address the students in the back, hoping that the exchange of ideas would be pounded into the brains of the lower-scoring students.

I can only imagine that those students sitting near the front must have felt inadequate, to say the least. Or maybe they felt...special.

There's another way to look at that picture. In our culture, at times we tend to unconsciously place the "not so smart," the "not so fortunate," or the "lesser" at the back of the room. The talented, the smart, and the successful earn spots at the head of the class.

But that professor's system, though his reasons differed, mirrored what Jesus will do one day when the world takes its final breath. He will rearrange the seating: the first shall be last, and the last, first. But not so they can learn. He does it because they did learn—what Jesus meant about leaving everything to follow Him.

My teacher said his professor placed him in the third or fourth row of his class. And he took the class three times.

Does that matter in Jesus's scheme of things? Hardly. Humility and love will always triumph over the world's grading system.

—REBECCA BARLOW JORDAN

FAITH STEP: *How have you valued others? What have you left to follow Jesus? Take time to demonstrate Jesus's love and humility to someone this week.*

FRIDAY, MARCH 6

Through Jesus, therefore, let us continually offer to God a sacrifice of praise—the fruit of lips that openly profess his name. And do not forget to do good and to share with others, for with such sacrifices God is pleased. Hebrews 13:15—16 (NIV)

WHEN MY SPIRITS ARE LOW, spending time praising Jesus is a sure way to allow His peace and joy to fill me again. It can feel like a sacrifice—an effort that costs something—to form words that focus on His greatness when I'd rather remind Him of everything wrong. I'm grateful that He invites us to be real with Him, to pour out our hurts and concerns. However I also know that it's important to spend time professing His name, and acknowledging the truth.

The other day I was stuck in bed dealing with a lot of pain and weakness. I tried to offer praise, but couldn't keep focused long enough to string thoughts together. "Lord, thank You for creating the world and..." My mind wandered away from any specifics. "Jesus, You are so loving and..." I'd shift my position and lose the last part of the sentence. I wanted so much to praise Him with my whole heart and soul and mind, but floundered.

Then I remembered the alphabet game. On long car trips, we'd look around for objects starting with the letter A, then when we'd run out of ideas, we'd move on to B. I wondered if I could use that same tool to help me praise. "Lord, I'm so grateful for the flavor of apples. Thank You for creating them. For my friend Amy. For the authority You have over this world. For authors whose books have nourished me. You designed butterflies and beaches and You are bountiful and full of blessings." As I worked my way through the alphabet, my heart grew more peaceful and I drifted off to sleep. —SHARON HINCK

FAITH STEP: *Praise Jesus for His qualities and His gifts, using the alphabet tool.*

SATURDAY, MARCH 7

Let me see your face; let me hear your voice. For your voice is pleasant,
and your face is lovely. Song of Solomon 2:14 (NLT)

I LOVE ASKING PEOPLE WHAT their favorite Scripture verse is. Why? There is usually a story behind it—a time when God's Word touched their heart in a meaningful way. When they think of their favorite Scripture verses it's as if they can travel back to a specific time and place where they heard or read those words and something resonated.

Personally, my favorite verse is Zephaniah 3:17 (NIV), "The Lord your God is with you, he is mighty to save. He will take great delight in you, he will quiet you with his love, he will rejoice over you with singing."

Why does this verse mean so much to me? Growing up I didn't know my biological father, and I wasn't very close to my stepfather. I felt as if something was wrong with me. I longed to be loved. As I grew older, it was easy for me to focus on my failures, instead of realizing the depth of Jesus's love and forgiveness. When I came upon this verse a flood of emotion filled my soul. I can picture where I was sitting when I read those words and when truth sank deep in my heart. A truth that said that Jesus, the Lord of the Universe, takes delight in me. He longs to hear my voice and see my face. He sings over me, and wants his love to quiet my worries, fears, and feeling of inadequacy. Those words are personal to me, and every time I read that verse—or hear it quoted—I can't help but smile!

As I read those words I pictured His voice—perfect, calming, lovely. I pictured it sinking deep, soothing my heart and stilling my heart and mind. And when I focus on Jesus's love, nothing else matters. And that's exactly what a favorite verse should do! —TRICIA GOYER

FAITH STEP: *Ask two people what their favorite Scripture verses are, and then ask to hear the stories behind why those verses mean so much to them.*

SUNDAY, MARCH 8

Like newborn babies, you must crave pure spiritual milk so that you will grow into a full experience of salvation. 1 Peter 2:2 (NLT)

As a society, we're pretty proud of our accomplishments. We've halted many diseases, developed technology that links us to the world, delved into space, written countless self-help books, and stocked our grocery-store shelves with convenience products we "can't do without."

We're pretty smart.

But sometimes we miss the forest for the trees. With all the resources at our disposal, it's easy to start thinking we're self-sufficient. Once we fall for that lie, pride grows and convinces us we're capable of—no, entitled to—define truth. And then we're in real trouble.

Sometimes it's good to go back to the beginning for a reset. This verse scatters contemporary theories about how to thrive in this life and reminds me of the source of simple, pure nourishment.

To be honest, my heart craves a lot of things: love, health, financial stability. But when it comes to faith, which directs all of life whether we say we have faith or not, we need to be like brand-new people who crave pure nourishment more than we pursue anything else that promises fulfillment.

When I'm pressured to do more, be more, accomplish more . . . I just want to hide away in my Savior's arms and let Him nourish me with His love, truth, and power.

None of this world's theories of fulfillment are going with us when we leave earth. I want to leave here filled up with what I can take with me. I want to meet Jesus fully stocked with His Spirit's produce, nourished by His tender mercies, and guided by His faithful hand.

Lord, make me thirsty for Your nourishment. —Erin Keeley Marshall

Faith Step: *Ask Jesus to simplify for you what He wants you to fill up on. Memorize 1 Peter 2:2 and meditate on it throughout the day.*

MONDAY, MARCH 9

"Don't store up treasures here on earth where they can erode away or may be stolen. Store them in heaven where they will never lose their value, and are safe from thieves." Matthew 6:19–20 (TLB)

ALL DAY LONG I'VE BEEN wishing I had a stapler. Why don't I just go out and buy one? Because we already own six staplers. There's the really nice big one I bought for our family room and the pretty pink one for my home office. I keep a tiny stapler in a basket where I pay bills in the evenings. Plus, my husband has three old staplers in his dresser drawers. Unfortunately, all of them are in a storage facility several hours away.

Since the moving company stored our possessions in a vault along with other families' furniture, it would be extremely difficult for us to access our stuff. It would also be extremely expensive. While the movers were packing at our old house, I tried to figure out what we would need in our temporary apartment, and how much would fit in our car. But every day, I think of something I wish I had. Like a cookie sheet or my rain jacket. Like rubber bands or running shoes or the big television...

Deep down I know I spend too much time thinking about what I have in storage, and too little time thinking about what I have stored up in heaven. Money can be lost; material possessions can be damaged or stolen. But every sacrifice I make for Jesus and every act of obedience is an investment in heavenly riches. That's the kind of wealth that will last forever. And that's what Jesus wants me to have in storage waiting for me.

—DIANNE NEAL MATTHEWS

FAITH STEP: *Jesus said that wherever our treasure is, there our heart will be also. (Matthew 6:21). Ask Him to show you if your heart is focused more on earthly gain or on things that have eternal value.*

TUESDAY, MARCH 10

Then he said to them, "Watch out! Be on your guard against all kinds of greed; life does not consist in an abundance of possessions." Luke 12:15 (NIV)

WHEN MY YOUNGEST WAS IN grade school she used to come home from friends' houses and say, "They're rich."

"How do you know?" I'd always ask.

"They have a basement," she replied one time. Sometimes her answer differed. "Because they have three cars." One time it was, "Because we got to order pizza *and* chicken wings at their house."

I wish that it was only the years of childhood that made us look at others and envy them. In other words, I wish we could outgrow that behavior. But adults can be more envious and jealous of others than children can be.

How do we detach ourselves from wanting what others have? How do we love others without looking at their possessions or talents or experiences and not letting envy consume us?

We are made for so much more than having or not having. We are in relationship with the Giver of Life, the Creator and His Son. Why do we lower our standards and focus on that which is petty in comparison to the vast love and fellowship of Jesus? Do we doubt that our needs are of concern to our Father? —ALICE J. WISLER

FAITH STEP: *Pray for those you envy. Pray for the rich blessings of Jesus to pour upon them and for them to know His love more deeply.*

WEDNESDAY, MARCH 11

Then Andrew, Simon Peter's brother, spoke up. "There's a young boy here with five barley loaves and two fish. But what good is that with this huge crowd?"
John 6:8–9 (NLT)

ANDREW'S QUESTION SEEMED PERFECTLY LOGICAL considering the circumstances. Thousands of men, women, and children had listened to Jesus teach for hours. Now they were hungry and had no immediate access to food. How in the world would five little barley loaves and two small fish feed them?

The idea of serving supper seemed ludicrous to everyone except Jesus. Doing so was *His* idea, and He knew exactly how to make it happen. He took the loaves, gave thanks to God, and passed them out to the people. He repeated His actions with the fish. Everyone ate until they were satisfied, and then the disciples gathered twelve baskets of leftovers.

Can you see Andrew scratching his head in amazement? He could scarcely believe what he'd witnessed. How did such a small portion stretch so far? The secret was this: Jesus, the Almighty, took the meager offering and infused His power into it. The same miracle plays out today when we give Jesus our humble offerings for His service.

Perhaps you play piano but the fear of inadequacy hinders you from doing so in public. Offer your ability to Him and see what happens.

Perhaps you feel your manual labor skills aren't as spiritual as other peoples' eloquent prayers or teaching abilities. Give your skills to the Lord and allow Him to use them for His glory.

Perhaps you feel too young, too old, or too inexperienced to contribute much to God's kingdom. Ask Jesus to infuse His power into you. Little is much when placed in His hands. —GRACE FOX

FAITH STEP: *What can you give Jesus for His service? Visualize your "five loaves and two fish" in your cupped hands and offer them to Him. Ask Him to multiply your offering and use it to bless the masses.*

THURSDAY, MARCH 12

He got you out in the nick of time; He put your feet on a wonderful road that took you straight to a good place to live. So thank God for his marvelous love, for his miracle mercy to the children he loves. Psalm 107:6–8 (MSG)

MY FIRST ATTEMPTS AT WRITING, over thirty years ago, included greeting-card verses. When others asked me to describe my work, I'd reply, "I'm a 'Band-Aid dispenser.'" To me, greeting cards are like Band-Aids. They temporarily comfort the hurts with laughter or consolation until the recipient finds more permanent help.

If you've ever put a Band-Aid on a child's scraped knee, you know there's magic in that covering. The Band-Aid doesn't heal the wound. But to a child, it's like magic. And the fancier and more fun the Band-Aid looks, the more magical the healing. Whether it's your own little girl, a student, or someone else's child, you are often rewarded with her butterfly kisses.

Taking the time to speak a kind word or to do a small act of kindness for someone else may seem like a Band-Aid to you. It may bring temporary relief, but certainly not the magical kind of patch from childhood days. Yet when offered in the name of Jesus, it can point a person to the One Who can change lives forever.

Sometimes Jesus uses our simple Band-Aids to hasten the process of healing: loving the unloved or accepting the outcast. He may even equip us with wings like earthly angels, impressing us to visit and bring cheer to someone, unaware of a depressed, even suicidal state.

How He answers in the nick of time is up to Him, but what a butterfly kiss when Jesus enlists us to share in this magical kind of transformation.
—REBECCA BARLOW JORDAN

FAITH STEP: *What "Band-Aids" have others offered you through the years? Thank Jesus for using His earthly angels to accomplish His work.*

FRIDAY, MARCH 13

*And the God of all grace, who called you to his eternal glory in Christ, after you
have suffered a little while, will himself restore you and make you strong,
firm and steadfast. 1 Peter 5:10 (NIV)*

MY FRIEND CHAWNA GAVE ME a flowering plant. She explained that it was
a cyclamen, and even after the plant appeared to die off, I should keep it
because it would resurrect and bloom again. I thought that was a lovely
metaphor for life. I enjoyed the cheery pink blossoms for many weeks.
Eventually all the blooms faded, the leaves dried up, and the plant looked
completely dead.

I identified with the sorry-looking plant. In recent weeks, illness had
kept me from the flow of life, and loneliness left me feeling as empty as
the bare stems. Still, I kept it, wondering if restoration was possible.

A month or two later, new blossoms appeared. However, the stems were
long and spindly. The plant still had no new leaves, and it looked like
some sort of alien...long tendrils with tiny bright colors on the ends. It
had survived and returned, but without its original vigor or beauty.

At some point in our lives, we all face trials that wither us down to
dust, until we feel there is no life inside us anymore. Sometimes suffering
changes us so much, we wonder if we can survive. Or if we do endure,
whether we'll become like my little cyclamen: a warped shadow of who
we are meant to be. Yet Jesus, Who understands suffering and suffered
for us, is able to restore us. In fact, because of His glory that He shares
with us, He can bring us through suffering and make us strong, firm, and
steadfast. —SHARON HINCK

FAITH STEP: *Do you feel withered and dormant from current or recent trials? Ask
Jesus not only to help you revive, but also to restore you to full beauty of spirit as only
He can.*

SATURDAY, MARCH 14

"He must increase, but I must decrease." John 3:30 (ESV)

WHEN MY HUSBAND AND I planned a trip to northern California years ago, we looked forward to stopping at the Redwood National Park. We did a little reading ahead of time about the redwood trees' size (as tall as 360 feet!) and life span (up to two thousand years!). We marveled at the online pictures of the three "Drive-Through" trees located on the coast.

All this information did not prepare us for the actual sight of the giant redwoods. Surrounded by the huge trunks, I craned my neck to try to see the tops soaring toward the heavens. I almost toppled over backward. The sheer majesty of the redwoods made me feel like a little bug on the forest floor.

It's not always a bad thing to feel small. Some of John the Baptist's disciples complained that everybody had started flocking to Jesus instead of to them. Rather than feel disgruntled, John was happy to hear of Jesus's growing popularity. That meant he had done his job of preparing people's hearts to receive the Messiah. Now that Jesus had come, John would gladly decrease in importance.

Feeling insignificant can help us more fully appreciate the majesty of Jesus. It can flood us with a sense of wonder that Jesus considered us worth dying for despite our sins, shortcomings, and frailties. An awareness of our weakness sets the stage for Him to display His strength and power in our life. That's important because our goal is to point people to Jesus, not shine the light on our own talents and achievements. Once we become willing to decrease in importance, then the evidence of Him in our life will become greater. We will have done our job of pointing others to the Messiah. —DIANNE NEAL MATTHEWS

FAITH STEP: *The next time you're feeling small and insignificant, use it as an opportunity to magnify Jesus. List His qualities that sustain and empower you. Thank Him for surrounding your life with His greatness.*

SUNDAY, MARCH 15

"Do you want to get well?" John 5:6 (CEB)

JESUS ASKED A QUESTION THAT stopped me in my Bible reading today. A man had been sick for thirty-eight years. "When Jesus saw him lying there, knowing that he had already been there a long time, he asked him, 'Do you want to get well?'"

Talk about your rhetorical questions! If the word "duh" had been popular in biblical times, we can imagine it would have been the sick man's gut-level response. "What do you mean, do I *want* to get well? Are you kidding me?"

Early in His public ministry, Jesus already knew that some whom He addressed would rather wrap their illness around them like a security blanket. Sickness, they knew. Health was an unknown. Despair, they recognized. Hope was unfamiliar territory. Addiction made sense; it had shaped their lives for years. Freedom felt like a dream too dear and peppered with uncertainty.

Following yet another probation violation, a young man confessed to me, "Jail is familiar to me. The routine, boring and endless as it is. Three meals. A bed. No responsibilities other than to do what you're told." The "outside world" we know as freedom was the scarier choice for him... until the day he wised up and let Jesus walk him through the cell doors and into a new life.

Do we want to stay mired in the equivalent of our sickness? How will we respond when Jesus asks us, "Do you *want* to be healed?" —CYNTHIA RUCHTI

FAITH STEP: *Has Jesus extended hope and healing to you, but you've pushed His hand away, refused His offer because hopelessness in that area is too familiar, too life-defining? Search your heart for any places where your forward momentum is stuck because your answer to His question wasn't "Yes, I want to be healed," but "Let me think about it."*

MONDAY, MARCH 16

The angel replied, "The Holy Spirit will come upon you, and the power of the Most High will overshadow you. So the baby to be born will be holy, and he will be called the Son of God." Luke 1:35 (NLT)

WHEN I WAS A CHILD, life seemed full of wonder and possibilities. Getting older meant being able to make more choices for myself. But when I encountered the reality of life, I was faced with a stream of negatives like "That's not possible" and "That is not going to happen" and "Life isn't fair."

It seemed that more often than not, life got in the way of my hopes and dreams. It was discouraging at best.

But something I have found as I've grown up is that when life is at its worst, Jesus is at His best. He likes the odds. It seems like the more we can't do, the more He can do. When the angel is explaining to Mary that she will give birth to Jesus even though she is a virgin, he tells her in essence, "What you think is impossible is possible. Just ask your cousin Elizabeth." Elizabeth never thought she would have a baby.

But the impossible was happening. A miracle was in the works. Her greatest dream was coming true. The same can happen for us. It doesn't matter if we can figure out how it can work, when Jesus is in the picture nothing is impossible. Possibilities, miracles, and dreams coming true are an option. And that is fantastic news. —SUSANNA FOTH AUGHTMON

FAITH STEP: *Find a flower in your garden or in a nearby park. Study it and its amazing workings. Know that Jesus Who designed this miraculous flower has an equally miraculous design for you.*

TUESDAY, MARCH 17

Blessed are those whose strength is in you, whose hearts are set on pilgrimage.
Psalm 84:5 (NIV)

WHEN MY HUSBAND AND I were in our twenties, we decided that we wanted to raise our three children in a quieter, slower place than bustling California. Our eyes were set on Montana, a place of old-time values and plenty of breathing room. Our hearts were set on pilgrimage. We packed up all our earthly possessions, knowing there was no turning back.

When we moved we had no job prospects, yet we had an inner knowing that Jesus was directing our path. After all, He owned the cattle on a thousand hills. When we got there, Jesus provided a rental house and my husband got a great job—better than he had in California. It was a miracle, and it showed us that when we sought Jesus He did have our best interest in mind.

Have you set your heart on pilgrimage in your Christian walk? Even though we never have a guarantee of an easy journey, Jesus has a good place reserved for each of us. Sometimes we'll get a glimpse of it on earth, but sometimes we'll have to wait until eternity.

When we choose to follow Jesus it sometimes means leaving behind what seems safe. It may mean leaving the known for the unknown. Setting our mind on pilgrimage means having an undivided heart: "Teach me your way, Lord, that I may rely on your faithfulness; give me an undivided heart, that I may fear your name" (Psalm 86:11, NIV).

Jesus may not ask you to move to a new land (although sometimes He will), but Jesus will always ask you to offer up an undivided heart. A heart set on His path, and a heart that seeks His strength. And as we walk along, we'll have a glimpse of eternity with Jesus by our side. —TRICIA GOYER

FAITH STEP: *Make a reservation at your favorite restaurant, and as you journey there with your spouse or a friend discuss what following Jesus with an undivided heart means to each of you.*

WEDNESDAY, MARCH 18

*With all these things in mind, dear brothers and sisters, stand firm and keep
a strong grip on everything we taught you both in person and by letter.*
2 Thessalonians 2:15 (NLT)

PAUL, SILAS, AND TIMOTHY WROTE a letter to the persecuted believers in Thessalonica. They encouraged them to persevere through their hardships. They also told them to hold fast to the spiritual teachings they'd received in the past. Doing so would enable their faith to flourish even in the midst of tribulation.

Holding fast to the spiritual lessons learned in the past is wise advice nowadays too. We live in a world where voices clamor constantly for our attention and affection. Standards of behavior shift, and moral values decline around us. If we're to remain steadfast in our faith, then it's crucial to cling to the never-changing truth we've been taught.

I attended Sunday school throughout my childhood. One of my teachers was a plump, gray-haired grandmother. She loved Jesus and His Word, and she loved teaching it to impressionable youngsters. She'd seen the truth proven right in her lifetime, and she wanted us to understand how it applied to us in our childhood.

I later attended youth group at my church. For several years, the sponsors encouraged participation in Bible quiz competitions. We formed teams, studied the assigned book of the Bible verse by verse, and memorized Scripture. No doubt the truths learned guided decisions I made then and as a young adult. Those truths remain in my mind and heart today.

Biblical truth we've learned in the past never grows old. It's as relevant now as it was two thousand years ago. Cling to it, for it's vital to effective Christian living. —GRACE FOX

FAITH STEP: *Think of someone who has taught you truth. This may be a pastor, Sunday school teacher, summer camp counselor, authors of faith-based books, worship leaders, or others. Write a thank-you note for her or his influence in your life.*

THURSDAY, MARCH 19

For we are God's handiwork, created in Christ Jesus to do good works,
which God prepared in advance for us to do. Ephesians 2:10 (NIV)

I DON'T KNOW ABOUT YOU, but when I get up in the morning, I don't feel like a piece of artistry. With my hair sticking out in all directions like a mad scientist, dark circles under my eyes, and teeth that feel like they are wearing wool sweaters, I look in the mirror and know I've got a ways to go to make myself presentable before I can ever show my face at work.

Did you know that we are God's handiwork? We are His artistry. Like the verse says, He created us in Christ Jesus to do good works. I believe what that means is that He created each one of us, and gave us special gifts in order to do the good things He has planned for us. And we don't have to do anything to make ourselves presentable. He's already done all of the work. Consider this: you are a toolmaker. You want a certain job done, so you design a tool that is perfect for that work. Nothing else will do. Or you are a sound-mixer. You want a song to sound a certain way, so you put in a little bass here, drums there, and a little of that one certain other instrument till it sounds just right. That's what God did when He designed each one of us. We were created for the purpose of good works, and good works He has ordained for us—in advance—to do.

That means He knows what you are going to face today. He knows who needs your special touch, your honesty, your integrity, your sense of humor, your way with words, whatever. Maybe it's your baking skills, your sewing, your leadership, or you're your mechanical prowess. Whatever it is, trust the One Who made you in Christ Jesus to lead you into the good works He's prepared for you today. —GWEN FORD FAULKENBERRY

FAITH STEP: *Pray this prayer: Lord Jesus, I want to be a tool in Your hands today. Use me in whatever good work You have planned for me. I am all Yours.*

FRIDAY, MARCH 20

"Peace I leave with you. My peace I give you. I give to you not as the world gives. Don't be troubled or afraid." John 14:27 (CEB)

A FRIEND OF MINE LIKES to take familiar phrases and tweak one little element to turn them into morphed but poignant thoughts. Conversation-starters. Thought-provokers. Sometimes devotion-prompts.

"Sticks and stones may break my bones...but words cut deeper than that. Much deeper."

"Slow and steady wins the race, unless someone else is faster *and* has learned endurance."

"If you can't say something nice, don't post on Facebook. Please."

"A bicycle built for tutus." Okay, her word twists don't all make sense.

My friend might turn "I'll give you a piece of my mind" into "I'll give you a peace of my mind."

What would happen to our relationships if we continually gave people a "peace" of our mind? Could that idea have been in Jesus's mind when He told His disciples—and us by association—that He was giving us His peace? Not just peace, but *His* peace?

From Jesus's perspective, peace doesn't mean the absence of war, or a mere paper truce. Another passage of Scripture tells us, "He is our peace." This is no ordinary peace He promises. It's a peace that surpasses understanding. That deep. That unexplainable. That generous. That rare in value but abundant in volume. That remarkable.

What the world wouldn't give for peace like that...

The world *couldn't* give it. Only Jesus could. Only Jesus did. And He offered it freely to us. He gave us a peace of His mind. —CYNTHIA RUCHTI

FAITH STEP: *Fill out a card with this statement: "Because of His peace—not an ordinary peace—I will not be afraid of _____." Add as many blanks as you wish, reflecting the truth applied to your life.*

SATURDAY, MARCH 21

When someone has been given much, much will be required in return; and when someone has been entrusted with much, even more will be required.
Luke 12:48 (NLT)

"I'M NOT SURE THEY'LL HAVE a bathtub."

My kids and I were shopping the dollar section to fill boxes for overseas children in need. One of them came across some tub toys that prompted my response. The toys revealed the gap between a third-world existence and ours. *Wow, what a small part of this globe I live on,* I thought.

I've seen extreme poverty in Honduras and Mexico. Whenever I've witnessed how the other nine-tenths live, I'm drawn to ask God why. I am no millionaire, and I work hard for sure. But there's nothing about me that makes me entitled to more than someone else. They work hard too. We give of our resources to help others, and I think that's all good and necessary. But my spirit says there's more truth to uncover.

When I look deeper into my heart, I wonder whether my lifestyle reflects my greatest riches, that is, the abundant forever I look forward to because of Jesus. How invested am I in sharing that wealth, the only kind that never loses its value and ensures eternal payoffs? Am I thriving from dividends of joy, peace, love, gratitude, Christlikeness, and hope? Am I committed to giving away this wealth?

Anyone can enjoy the riches of Jesus's saving grace. Those of us who've already received that abundance need to take seriously His command in Luke 12:48. Giving doesn't refer exclusively to material wealth. The joy and hope and love of Jesus's abundance that is ours for the taking is meant to be given away with abandon. There's no limit to His riches, if only we'll take fully to heart the reality of how rich we are in Him. —ERIN KEELEY MARSHALL

FAITH STEP: *Are you enjoying your spiritual wealth? Find a way to share it today.*

SUNDAY, MARCH 22

Because you have done this, you and your children and your children's children will suffer from Naaman's leprosy forever. When Gehazi left the room, he was leprous; his skin was white as snow. 2 Kings 5:27 (NLT)

GEHAZI HAD BEEN A FAITHFUL servant to Elisha until the day greed consumed him. He'd seen Elisha command Naaman's healing from leprosy, and he'd heard the grateful military leader press the man of God to accept his thank-you gifts. He'd also heard Elisha refuse.

Elisha was wrong, thought Gehazi. *He should have accepted those gifts. Oh well—he may not have wanted them, but I do.* And off he went, chasing Naaman. Then he lied to him, saying Elisha needed silver and clothing after all. He returned to his house with the goods and stashed them inside.

Gehazi was caught and he paid grievous consequences. Trouble was, he wasn't the only one those consequences affected. His family suffered too.

The choices we make—even seemingly small ones—carry results. Depending on their nature, those results can be wonderful and rewarding. They can also be destructive.

Selfishness is often at the root of those destructive choices and the consequences they bear. It creates in us a desire to satisfy lust, a longing for power or prestige, and an appetite for something that's not rightfully ours. Our actions reap consequences, and we often end up hurting those we love.

Conversely, good choices can bless many people. Christ chose to give His life for mankind, and millions of men and women have known the freedom of forgiveness and the hope of eternal life as a result.

How do our choices affect others? Let's model Christ, not Gehazi.
—GRACE FOX

FAITH STEP: *Strive in your heart to make choices that affect other people for the good. Ask the Lord to remove any shred of selfishness that might tempt you do otherwise.*

MONDAY, MARCH 23

The hopes of the godly result in happiness, but the expectations of the wicked come to nothing. Proverbs 10:28 (NLT)

THE OTHER NIGHT, WE TOOK the boys out to dinner at a favorite burger place. We were crammed into a booth, and I was chatting across the table with Scott when Addison spilled his full cup of cold ice water in my lap. It was a rude awakening. I jumped up and said, "Addison Aughtmon!" The look on my face must have been fierce since Addie quickly, said, "I'm so sorry, Mom." While our oldest son, Jack, who was sitting next to Addie, looked at me and said, "I am Legion. We are many."

Sometimes I wish the children didn't know their Scriptures so well. It's never good when they compare you to a demoniac. Jack's comment brought me around. I scooped up Addie, who was remarkably dry and said, "I know you didn't mean to, buddy…Mommy was just a little surprised."

Just a little. I tend to have high expectations. That is not always good because, on a regular basis, my life doesn't meet up to my expectations. There is some chaos and disappointment and spilled ice water. Jesus has been teaching me over many years that my joy can't come from expecting a perfect life. Mostly, because a perfect life doesn't exist. Real joy comes from placing my hopes in Him. Chaos may still reign on occasion but I have decided to choose Jesus and joy instead of unmet expectations and disappointment. I think it's a good trade. —SUSANNA FOTH AUGHTMON

FAITH STEP: *Listen to "I'm Trading My Sorrows for the Joy of the Lord" online as many times as you need to until the joy of Jesus begins to fill you up.*

TUESDAY, MARCH 24

"As long as the earth exists, seedtime and harvest, cold and hot, summer and autumn, day and night will not cease." Genesis 8:22 (CEB)

THE DAY THE FIRST SEED catalog of the year arrived in the mail, it was twenty below zero with a biting wind chill. My first thought was, *That's just cruel.* Pulling my wool sweater tighter around me, I stared out at the snow-covered ground, the garden stiff and lifeless. The seed catalog cover made me sigh. It would be many months before I'd see color like that in my garden.

The season of hibernation, not the season of growth. Too many gray days made me resistant to the joy-potential the seed catalog held.

"Plant a future seed." The idea came as soft as a summer breeze. Instead of mourning the contrast between my current circumstances and what the catalog promised, I could plant a virtual seed.

I spent the next hour plotting what new flowers I'd add to my garden in the spring. What would my vegetable raised beds hold? A new variety of an old favorite? Should I try cabbages again and find a more efficient way to fight off the cabbage-loving chipmunks?

My view out the window showed the same bitter, stark, cold whiteness. The view in my heart sported all kinds of anticipated color, dewy, sun-drenched magenta blossoms and fragrant herbs.

Jesus knew we'd be prone to getting mentally stuck in our current circumstances without a nudge from Him to think ahead to the joys that lie before us. The spring at the end of the winter. The lush garden of answers to replace our barren seasons. The heaven that awaits.

Winter to spring. Illness to health. Stress to peace. Broken to mended.

It might be time for me to plant a few more seeds. —CYNTHIA RUCHTI

FAITH STEP: *Have you planted seeds, mapped out a garden, envisioned what it will be like when this season of life passes? When the medical crisis abates? When the prodigal comes home? When you make it through the financial upheaval? Plant a faith seed today.*

WEDNESDAY, MARCH 25

Therefore encourage one another and build each other up, just as in fact you are doing. 1 Thessalonians 5:11 (NIV)

I DON'T ALWAYS REMEMBER, BUT one of the first questions I like to ask Jesus when I wake up each morning is, "How can I encourage someone today? And who?" He's always faithful to answer, often through His Word.

One morning after asking that question, I read from Isaiah 35:3–4 (NLT) and found a practical answer. First, "strengthen those who have tired hands." That might include teachers, hair stylists, moms, writers—and all who use computers, which includes most of us—missionaries, pastors, and parents who spend time "lifting up" the burdens of others.

Next, the passage mentions encouraging those who have "weak knees." I envisioned grandparents and senior citizens, veterans, and even athletes with wear and tear on their bodies. But the last category, the "fearful," could probably include everyone. These needed to hear the words, "be strong, and do not fear."

Sometimes I can offer an encouraging response to a needy e-mail request or blog comment from my Web site. Other times, my phone will ring, and the caller needs a cheerful word. And who can forget neighbors or our family members, who need a hug or a kind word?

Even through my prayers, especially as I turn Scriptures such as Ephesians 3:16–19 or Colossians 1:9–12 into heavenly petitions for others, I can pass on His encouraging truths, trusting Jesus to make those prayers a reality.

For me, finding people to encourage is not a problem. Remembering to listen and to follow through with Jesus's answers is where I need work. And the amazing thing is, when I try to lift up someone else, I'm the one who ends up encouraged. —REBECCA BARLOW JORDAN

FAITH STEP: *Ask Jesus to help you encourage someone today. Invite Him to speak through you, and be prepared for His answers.*

THURSDAY, MARCH 26

We capture every thought and make it give up and obey Christ.
2 *Corinthians* 10:5 (NCV)

DO YOU EVER HAVE TROUBLE with unwanted thoughts? Maybe it's temptation you struggle with, or regrets, or fear. I remember listening to Kay Arthur talk about this verse one time. She said when any thoughts come to our minds we have to "frisk them at the door." Like a police search. And if they're not thoughts that belong there, we have to send them away. She said if we do that as a habit it will become easier and easier. I think it's a good practice.

I have a dear friend who has a bad past. She knows God has forgiven her but she has a lot of trouble forgiving herself. Things can be going well and then it's almost like she feels guilty, as if she doesn't deserve happiness because of what she has done.

Hebrews 8:12 (NIV) tells us He forgives us *and remembers [our] sins no more.* I know we don't have the supernatural ability to forget things like God does. But I believe there's something to knowing that He forgets—truly forgets— and doesn't hold our past sins against us anymore. Perhaps that can free us not to hold them against ourselves?

Max Lucado writes, "In the cellar of your heart lurk the ghosts of yesterday's sins. Sins you've confessed; errors of which you've repented; damage you've done your best to repair....Do yourself a favor. Purge your cellar. Exorcise your basement. Take the Roman nails of Calvary and board up the door. And remember...He forgot." Going back to our verse, maybe this is how we make those thoughts give up. By taking them back to the Cross. He paid the price for us to be free. Any thoughts we have that would steal our freedom need to give it up. We need to put them to death at the Cross. —GWEN FORD FAULKENBERRY

FAITH STEP: *As they come to mind, make a list of your unwanted thoughts. Then take them to Jesus in prayer. Lay them down at the Cross and leave them there.*

FRIDAY, MARCH 27

"What's more, your relative Elizabeth has become pregnant in her old age! People used to say she was barren, but she has conceived a son and is now in her sixth month. For nothing is impossible with God." Luke 1:36–37 (NLT)

MY FRIENDS JERRY AND SARAH faced heartache that shook them to the core. After years of knowing they could not have biological children they were chosen to adopt a newborn boy. The paperwork went through without a problem until months later. It was then that the birth father—unnamed on the birth certificate—showed up. Many court dates later, the judge decided in favor of the birth father, and after nearly two years of living with Jerry and Sarah, their son went to live with a man he didn't know. Yet recently Jesus did the impossible and brought Jerry and Sarah a new baby, also through adoption. Daily I look at their photographs online, not because I don't believe it. Instead, I want to rejoice at what Jesus has done.

When Mary is told about the son she will bear, the visiting angel speaks of another miracle: her cousin, Elizabeth—well along in years—will have a son. Within days of the angel's visit, Mary heads to Elizabeth's house to confirm her cousin's destiny. She went to rejoice. And to see what she dared to believe in.

Upon Mary's arrival Elizabeth proclaimed: "You are blessed because you believed that the Lord would do what he said" (Luke 1:45, NLT). Sometimes we have to see something before we believe it. In Mary's case she believed, and then it was confirmed with what she saw! When I see Jesus at work in the lives of my friends, I rejoice at His work in my life too.
—TRICIA GOYER

FAITH STEP: *Have you seen Jesus do the impossible in the life of a friend? Send a short note relating how Jesus at work in her life has helped you rejoice at what Jesus is doing in your own. Thank her for helping you to "see" what you believed to be true.*

SATURDAY, MARCH 28

I pray for them. I am not praying for the world, but for those you have given me,
for they are yours. . . . My prayer is not for them alone. I pray also for those who
will believe in me through their message. . . . Father, I want those you have given me
to be with me where I am, and to see my glory, the glory you have given me because
you loved me before the creation of the world. John 17:9, 20, 24 (NIV)

"I'VE BEEN PRAYING FOR YOU."

The loving words arrived in a brief e-mail. Simple words, but they warmed me all the way to my bones, like a fireplace on a cold winter day. My friend didn't know I was having a rough day. She didn't know the details of my need. But she cared.

Many mornings, my husband holds my hand and prays for me. His words strengthen and comfort me. I often call my friend Patti and we pray for each other. Hearing her ask our Creator for the help I need renews my hope.

And another Friend also gives us the loving gift of prayer on our behalf: Jesus.

His petition was not only for the disciples who sat around Him, but for those who would come later. When we read the full chapter of John 17, we discover that He asked for protection, joy, sanctification, and unity for His followers. What a thrill to know Jesus has asked the Father for those blessings for us!

Then Jesus expresses His love in even deeper measure. We witness the longing of His heart as He asks that one day we would be with Him where He is, and see His glory. When I read these words I feel cherished. He wants us to be with Him.

When life seems overwhelming, and courage fails, we can take comfort in His beautiful expression of love. And we know His prayer will be answered. —SHARON HINCK

FAITH STEP: *Pray with a friend or family member today.*

SUNDAY, MARCH 29

They said with a loud voice: The Lamb who was slaughtered is worthy to receive power and riches and wisdom and strength and honor and glory and blessing!
Revelation 5:12 (HCS)

WHEN JESUS ENTERED JERUSALEM TO celebrate Passover, it was the only time He ever publicly presented Himself as the Messiah. Jesus rode the colt of a donkey, fulfilling the exact timing and details predicted in Zechariah 9:9 centuries earlier. The crowds pouring into the city with Him included eyewitnesses of His raising Lazarus from the dead and pilgrims from Galilee who were familiar with His ministry. They spread their cloaks on the ground before Him and waved palm branches, shouting "Hosanna! Blessed is the King of Israel!"

Jesus accepted the people's praise, but He also knew what lay ahead. Before the week ended, He would stand before a crowd shouting, "We have no king but Caesar!" and "Crucify Him!" Jesus understood His identity as the Lamb Who would atone for the sins of the world; He knew it was God's long-ordained plan to have Him sacrificed on Passover.

Thinking about Palm Sunday and the events that followed prompts me to examine my commitment to Jesus. I find it easy to acknowledge Him as my King when life seems pleasant and things are going smoothly. But what about those other days? When I don't like what's happening, or when my human nature urges me to go my own way rather than submit to His leading. Days when I don't feel like waving a palm branch.

Despite the ups and downs of life, and the highs and lows of my emotions, Jesus deserves more than superficial devotion. The Passover Lamb Who was slain for my sins always deserves to be honored, obeyed, and adored. And the fact that He loves me in spite of my fickleness gives me all the more reason to praise Him. —DIANNE NEAL MATTHEWS

FAITH STEP: *Is your commitment to Jesus weakened by negative circumstances or emotions? This Easter season, memorize Revelation 5:12 and be determined to change that.*

MONDAY, MARCH 30

After he has gathered his own flock, he walks ahead of them, and they follow him because they know his voice. They won't follow a stranger; they will run from him because they don't know his voice. John 10:4–5 (NLT)

I RECENTLY RECEIVED A CALL that left me feeling very uncomfortable. When I answered the phone, a man said, "Hey, Grandma—how are you?"

"Who is this?" I asked.

"Aw, Grandma, don't you recognize my voice?" he replied.

I have a cousin who loves practical jokes. *Perhaps it's Todd,* I thought. *It sounds a bit like him. He might call me Grandma just for fun.*

Before I could respond, the man said, "Grandma, I need to talk with you about something I've done. I'm not proud of it." That's when I hung up. This person was a stranger to me. He was likely a scammer, and I wasn't about to listen to him.

Scripture says Jesus speaks to those who have placed their faith in Him. He leads them along as a shepherd leads his flock. They follow Him because they recognize His voice and know they can trust Him.

Other voices beckon us too. Society seeks to entice us to follow its values even though they are often contrary to Christ's teachings. We're encouraged to follow our hearts even if we break a few hearts in the process, pursue happiness at all cost, and accumulate material possessions at the risk of going into debt.

How should we respond to voices such as these? We ought to refuse to listen. Hang up. Run. The only voice we ought to heed belongs to Jesus Christ. —GRACE FOX

FAITH STEP: *How do you respond when voices whisper to you, telling you to do something contrary to Scripture? Do you lend an ear, or do you shut them out? Ask the Holy Spirit to give you the ability to identify and reject those voices without hesitation.*

TUESDAY, MARCH 31

We love because he first loved us. 1 John 4:19 *(NIV)*

THE OTHER DAY, SCOTT CAME and sat next to me on the couch while I was writing. Sometimes the day can fly by without our actually having a real conversation. A real moment when we connect. I slipped my hand into his and he squeezed it. I looked him in the eye and said, "I'm glad you are mine." He said, "I'm glad you are mine."

And we meant it. Those words hold some weight. We have been married almost two decades. Love tends to change and shift over the course of twenty years.

My dad likes to say that "love" is an accordion word. It can mean anything and nothing. I love peanut butter. I love football. I love you. But that is because we see love as a feeling. Feelings are changeable. Love isn't so much a feeling as it is a choice. We choose what we love. Or we choose not to love. Some days I am great at loving Scott. Other days…not so much. But those choices shape our lives. How we love each other determines who we are and who we are becoming.

At the beginning of time, Jesus chose to love us. He chooses the same choice over and over again each day. He loves us in spite of ourselves. And at some point in our history, we chose to love Him back when we decided to follow Him. Some days we love Him really, really well. Other days…not so much.

But the thing is, when we keep at it, when we choose to love Him and follow Him and obey Him, day in and day out, we get better at it because His love starts to rub off on us. His goodness. His mercy. His grace. Not a day goes by that I am not thankful that He chose to love me first.

—SUSANNA FOTH AUGHTMON

FAITH STEP: *Have a real conversation with Jesus. Tell Him how glad you are that He chose to love you and why you love Him so much.*

WEDNESDAY, APRIL 1

Every morning you'll hear me at it again. Every morning I lay out the pieces of my life on your altar and watch for fire to descend. Psalm 5:3 (MSG)

I HAVE A MORNING RITUAL at the Lake House where I write. I start a fire in the little woodstove. Here in northern Michigan, I need to take the chill off on all but the warmest days.

I have no problem starting the fire. I was a Girl Scout (and know the secret of heart pine or fat lighter). After the flare of the match (just one), the sticks sizzle and flames curl around the logs. Soon the blaze brightens the room through the stove's glass door.

My problem is keeping the fire going. I forget to tend it when I settle down to pray or study. I end up deep in thought in front of the computer.

Fires are like children in this sense—if you don't hear anything, you need to go check on them. It may already be too late.

I can lose my focus on Jesus just as easily. Checking e-mail, Facebook, or the status of an eBay bid first thing in the morning doesn't work for me. I end up distracted, spending my energy on everything but my work. Everyone's different—you'll have your own pitfalls to avoid.

Come back to that fire, look for a glowing ember and blow gently to fuel it with fresh oxygen. Get the poker and rearrange the charred, now-cold logs.

Nothing? It's no defeat to strike another match.

Starting over is okay.

Better still to stay with the fire until you're sure it's taken hold. We can come to Jesus every morning. We have the privilege of laying out our concerns and requests before Him. Instead of leaving it at that, we can wait, expecting a response. For the fire to descend. —SUZANNE DAVENPORT TIETJEN

FAITH STEP: *Start your day with calm instead of chaos. Set your alarm, find a quiet corner, and be still. Talk to Jesus about the things that are on your heart. Then wait.*

THURSDAY, APRIL 2

*Then he poured water into a washbasin and began to wash the disciples' feet. . . .
When Jesus came to Simon Peter, Peter said to him, "Lord, are you going
to wash my feet?" Jesus replied, "You don't understand what I'm
doing now, but you will understand later." John 13:5–7 (CEB)*

No ONE LIKES TO HEAR that a friend is going to die, so naturally, the disciples
were devastated. Jesus was talking strangely, saying things about death and
rising after three days. They didn't get it. They'd been with Him for years,
traveled with Him, saw Him perform miracles and talk with God. Now He
had gathered them into a room where He took out a basin and bent down
to wash their feet.

Later He asked them to stay awake and pray, but it had been such a long,
confusing couple of days that they all fell asleep. When the soldiers came
to arrest Jesus, Peter wanted to stop the madness and took matters into his
own hands, by raising his sword and cutting off one of the soldier's ears.

What was happening was not "right." The disciples didn't expect Jesus to be
taken away. He was supposed to rise and be king. They didn't understand that
it wouldn't happen. Why couldn't he overthrow all those who opposed Him?

Not yet. First there had to be death, because Jesus's death was the only
way for the disciples to have life, and then would come the Resurrection.

Even today, with the Scriptures available to us and the Holy Spirit as a
comforter, we don't understand it all. Most days our faith seems tiny, our
confusion large. *What are you doing, Jesus? This is not how I thought my life
would be. This was not in my plans.*

Even though we have a hard time with our inability to grasp all that
Jesus is, all that we are in Him and all that He has planned for us, can we
trust the One Who was humiliated and put on a Cross to die so that
we might live with Him in eternity? —ALICE J. WISLER

FAITH STEP: *Help me to trust enough so that I can reach out to You, Jesus. May my prayer
be to practice the discipline of trust even when my circumstances overwhelm me. Amen.*

FRIDAY, APRIL 3

While Jesus was here on earth, he offered prayers and pleadings, with a loud cry and tears, to the one who could deliver him out of death. And God heard his prayers because of his reverence for God. So even though Jesus was God's Son, he learned obedience from the things he suffered. Hebrews 5:7–8 (NLT)

WE CANNOT FATHOM WHAT JESUS felt in the hours preceding His Crucifixion. In earnest, He knelt and prayed to His heavenly Father, begging Him for mercy and for a way to escape the inevitable. Inner anguish gave way to tears, mingled with sweat drops of blood.

God saw Jesus's anguish, but He turned His face away. Why? Because He knew that Jesus's suffering was a necessary part of His plan to bring salvation to all mankind. And so, Jesus obeyed the Father's will. He endured beatings and ridicule, became sin, and then died a criminal's death.

Jesus deserves our heartfelt gratitude. He also deserves recognition for teaching us how to respond to suffering. In those dark hours prior to His arrest, He poured out His heart to God, asking Him to take the cup of pain and death from Him. When God refused, Jesus obeyed with no trace of anger or self-pity. As a result, "God qualified him as a perfect High Priest, and he became the source of eternal salvation for all those who obey him" (verse 9).

Jesus understands how we feel when we suffer. He empathizes with our desire to forgo it, but He also knows when it's part of a divine plan. He desires our willing obedience, and He will not waste it. As was true for Him, our most effective ministry often flows from our deepest pain.
—GRACE FOX

FAITH STEP: *Set aside a few minutes today to ponder Christ's suffering on your behalf. How might your life be different if He'd refused to embrace the pain? Thank Him for what He did, and ask Him to make your ministry to others more effective through the suffering you've already experienced.*

SATURDAY, APRIL 4

We all, like sheep, have gone astray, each of us has turned to our own way; and the Lord has laid on him the iniquity of us all. Isaiah 53:6 (NIV)

A LOT OF US FEEL uncomfortable about the excruciating pain that Jesus endured on our behalf. We don't like the thought of the darkness of the grave or the stone covering the tomb. But we only truly honor Jesus when we realize that our freedom, our joy, our hope, our peace, comes at the cost of His pain and His death.

To skim over His suffering and His days and nights in the tomb diminishes the power and the breadth and the depth of what He did. He knew we couldn't set ourselves free. He knew we were stuck in sin, headed toward a lonely path of our own destruction. It's what we do when left to our own devices... we ruin ourselves. He knew we were a mess, inside and out. He knew that only He could do what needed to be done. He could bridge the chasm between a sinful people and a holy God. *He poured out his life unto death and was numbered with the transgressors.* Death was coming one way or another. It was either us or Jesus.

Holy Saturday seems like a terrible day—to know that Jesus is dead in the tomb. Yet it was the day that the gap was breached between heaven and hell. Jesus relinquished everything...His power, His will, His last breath, so that we could have life and have it to the full. Without Holy Saturday, there is no Easter Sunday. Because of His willingness to die, we have a chance to live. To love Him back with everything that is within us. Heart. Mind. Soul. And Spirit. Let's not, today, of all days, hold anything back. —SUSANNA FOTH AUGHTMON

FAITH STEP: *Write a Holy Saturday prayer in your journal thanking Jesus for loving you enough to die for you and praising Him for your new life.*

SUNDAY, APRIL 5

"They will call him Immanuel" (which means "God with us").
Matthew 1:23 (NIV)

THE FIRST EASTER. IT HAD been thirty-three years since Jesus was born, of a virgin, just like the angel said. It had been hundreds of years since Isaiah first spoke this prophecy that Matthew quoted (Isaiah 7:14). All of that was two thousand-plus years ago.

And Jesus, Immanuel, is still with us.

The promise of His birth was only the beginning of the blessing Isaiah foretold; it would have been incomplete had Jesus not followed through with Good Friday and Easter. The promise of Immanuel, first revealing itself in a manger in Bethlehem, was fulfilled one joyful day outside Jerusalem when Jesus rose. One empty tomb, many confused people, and one Immanuel who returned to be with us.

The celebration of Immanuel is associated with Christmas. But I've been thinking how much more Immanuel means because of Easter.

Immanuel's birth ushered in thirty-some years of Him walking the earth alongside people, but Easter ushered in eternity with Him. During the three decades after His birth, He healed lives, raised the dead, upended whole patterns of thinking. It was wonderful. Yet Easter's gift brought unending perfection. He came to be with us for a lifetime so that we could go to be with Him forever. In the meantime, we need him here and now. And so He is through His Spirit, who lives in us who call Him Lord.

I'm awed to think of God coming to earth as a man. I'm thunderstruck to consider that He died and rose for me. But is my daily life transformed to the degree that Immanuel abiding within me warrants?

—ERIN KEELEY MARSHALL

FAITH STEP: *Does the reality of Immanuel awe you? Ask Him to make the promise of His presence transforming to you right now and always.*

MONDAY, APRIL 6

For God so loved the world that he gave his only Son, so that everyone who believes in him will not perish but have eternal life. John 3:16 (NLT)

OKAY, I CONFESS. I FIND the depth of God's love for mankind and for me, individually, a bit difficult to fully grasp. I sing about the deep, deep love of Jesus. I discuss it in my weekly Bible study. I even quote Scriptures about it. And yet its scope escapes me.

One morning recently I picked up my Bible and plopped into my favorite leather loveseat to enjoy quiet time with the Lord. I began that time with a prayer: "Father, would You please give me an evidence of Your love today?"

I half-suspected the answer would appear in the form of an unexpected delight—a phone call from a long-lost friend, a word of encouragement from someone I respect, or a check in the mail, perhaps. My suspicions proved wrong.

A thought, like a quiet voice, popped into my mind the moment I ended my prayer: *I've already shown you in the best way possible. Remember? I sent my only Son to die on your behalf.*

I sat in silence for a few minutes. My thoughts focused on Calvary and the dark day Jesus gave His life so that I might live. An intimate, unforgettable God-moment that was, one I'll cherish for the rest of my life.

God displays His love for us daily in myriad ways. Sometimes they arrive as delightful surprises. Other times, I suspect, we take them for granted. But sending Jesus to die for us so that we might have abundant and eternal life tops all. Our present understanding is limited, but someday we'll "get" it. What a day that will be! —GRACE FOX

FAITH STEP: *Take a few minutes to reflect on Christ's love. List five ways in which you have experienced it, and then thank Him for His goodness.*

TUESDAY, APRIL 7

And when they had come to the place called Calvary, there they crucified
Him, and the criminals, one on the right hand and the other on the left.
Then Jesus said, "Father, forgive them, for they do not know what they do."
Luke 23:33–34 (NKJV)

I LIKE MALCOLM GLADWELL, AUTHOR of the best-selling book *Outliers* and, most recently, *David and Goliath*. Raised in a Christian home, he left the church for a time but returned. In an article for *Relevant* magazine called "How I Rediscovered Faith" he explains that he came back to Jesus after witnessing God's power through forgiveness.

Gladwell tells the story of meeting the Derksens, a Canadian couple whose daughter Candace was kidnapped by a sexual predator and murdered. He was interested in their story because of their response to the tragedy. When reporters at a news conference after Candace's funeral asked the Derksens how they felt about the person who killed their daughter, they responded in love and forgiveness. Gladwell could not wrap his head around that. He writes that he had never seen such weapons of the spirit—"the peculiar and inexplicable power that comes from within"—and concludes, "But I've seen them now, and I will never be the same."

The Derksens found their example in Jesus, and their relationship with Him is what gave them the power to follow His example. Their response was not normal, but it was biblical. (See the opening verse.) When Jesus was crucified, His response was forgiveness. Inexplicable love.

The reason we can't wrap our minds around this is that it is not a matter of the mind, but of the heart. Intellectually, love like this makes no sense. It is not humanly possible, but with Jesus all things are possible. His strength is made perfect in our weakness. And as we, His people, demonstrate His love to the world, the world will never be the same. —GWEN FORD FAULKENBERRY

FAITH STEP: *If you are going through a battle right now, consider the weapons of the spirit that are at your disposal. Ask Jesus to help you wield them for His glory.*

WEDNESDAY, APRIL 8

Blessed are those whose help is the God of Jacob, whose hope is in the Lord their God. He is the Maker of heaven and earth, the sea, and everything in them— he remains faithful forever. Psalm 146:5–6 (NIV)

ONE NIGHT AT BEDTIME I gathered my three littlest children, ages six, three, and three around me to practice their memory verse. "My help comes from the Lord, who made heaven and earth!" Psalm 121:2 (NLT). After they got it down pretty well, I told them that we were going to pray. But first we were going to think of things that we could pray about and ask Jesus to help us with. The first things they mentioned were spiders and fire.

"Yes, we do want God to help us with those things," I told them, "but have you thought about asking Jesus to help you be kind to your brother or sister? Or asking Him to help you obey Mom and Dad?" All of them sat there in stunned silence. My six-year-old's jaw dropped. No, they obviously hadn't thought of that before. But when they prayed, they prayed for obedience and kindness.

Listening to their soft breaths as they drifted off to sleep, I realized how often I was just like them. I trusted that Jesus would be with me with "big" stuff, but I often forget He's there to help me with ordinary, daily stuff too. Or with heart stuff, that seems so hard to overcome.

We are blessed when we turn to Jesus for help. He can meet a soul-need just as well as he can provide a few extra dollars until payday or offer encouragement from a friend at just the right time. Do you worry that Jesus won't answer when you pray? Why don't you test Him out? Then you can teach your children with confidence that Jesus is our help.
—TRICIA GOYER

FAITH STEP: *Pick a Scripture to memorize with a young person in your life. Then when you both have it memorized, celebrate in a special way, like with ice cream!*

THURSDAY, APRIL 9

*When I was a child, I spoke and thought and reasoned as a child. But when
I grew up, I put away childish things.* 1 Corinthians 13:11 (NLT)

LAST WEEKEND WE BROKE OUT the family movies. We didn't subject
relatives or friends to hours of our memories, but as for Steve, Paxton,
Calianne, and me, reminiscing did our hearts good.

The kids got a kick out of seeing themselves as infants and toddlers.
They giggled over their baby pudge and attempts at walking and talking,
and they howled with laughter when their diaper-clad selves sang and
danced to the "potty song." Steve and I oohed and aahed, and I think
Steve's eyes welled up a time or two. I know mine did.

I was awestruck by how much Pax and Cali are still who God created
them to be, albeit with several more years' growth and maturity behind
them. Paxton's eyes still hold the same depth that looked at us through the
lens. Calianne's face has the same chubby-cheeky-baby sparkle with a few
more years on it. And their personalities are still recognizable as *them*.

I wonder how I look to Jesus as He watches me grow. I still have the
same innate characteristics as when I was a new believer. I still struggle
with patience and faith and resting instead of fretting. I still let my type A
frailties overtake His Spirit's work in me.

But does he see growth in me? Although my kids' chubbiness was adorable, "spiritual baby fat" of judgmentalism, hypocrisy, ungraciousness,
anger, self-righteousness, and pride—to name a few—are areas to grow
and tone as we mature in Christ.

Someday when I get to heaven and get the replay of my spiritual devel-
opment, I pray that these years on earth will yield healthy growth and the
images will be ones to smile at with my Savior. —ERIN KEELEY MARSHALL

FAITH STEP: *Consider how you've grown the past year. Ask Jesus to show you areas of
"spiritual pudge" that He wants to mature.*

FRIDAY, APRIL 10

"I've said these things to you so that you will have peace in me. In the world you have distress. But be encouraged! I have conquered the world."
John 16:33 (CEB)

I WAVED AT MY FRIEND across the restaurant. She walked toward my booth on the way to the one she'd picked out to share with her eight-year-old son.

"How are you doing?" I asked, trying to avoid focusing on the nine-month bulge under her coat.

"Oh, you know. I'm still here. Still haven't delivered." She sighed the sigh of the overdue.

I resisted telling her that one of my babies had been two weeks overdue and my middle child topped that at sixteen miserable days overdue, and instead told her how beautiful she looked. And she did. Beautiful, uncomfortable, and convinced her pregnancy would never end.

Empathy came easily because of my own experiences years earlier. But I knew her anxiety that the baby would never come was unfounded. So I could smile as she waited. No matter what it felt like to her, it was clear to me that the baby would eventually make his or her appearance.

How often Jesus must feel that way with us! He knows the end from the beginning. He calls all afflictions temporary, even momentary. He understands our human nature, but must shake His divine head when we rant that something's "impossible to tolerate" or "endless" or "never going to let up."

Trusting the wisdom of His assurance that "Nothing is impossible with God" eases us into a different attitude. It's as if trust and rest are companion terms. We relax into the process, no matter how long it takes, when we trust what Jesus says in the Word. —CYNTHIA RUCHTI

FAITH STEP: *What's the most trying trauma in your life? Picture yourself falling back into the embrace of Jesus, who knows the truth about what you're enduring and how long it will last. Rest in that embrace.*

SATURDAY, APRIL 11

"Watch and pray so that you will not fall into temptation. The spirit is willing, but the flesh is weak." Matthew 26:41 (NIV)

IN MID-APRIL, MY HUSBAND HEADED to work, only to come back a half-hour later. The roads were so congested no traffic was moving at all, because of several inches of snow.

We Minnesotans are used to long winters and lots of snow. But even up here in the north country, a huge snowfall is a surprise if it arrives in mid-April.

In the same way, temptation can hit me out of the blue like an April snowstorm. There are times I know I'll face temptation. Perhaps I'll be at a gathering where there's an acquaintance who is annoying. I know I'll be tempted to be unloving—to avoid the person or not listen to what he or she shares. So I prepare my heart ahead of time and enter the situation aware of my own tendencies, aware of the potential danger, and calling on Jesus for help.

But when I'm taken by surprise, when I'm not alert, sin can grab hold of my thoughts and emotions with icy fingers. Last week some writer friends were chatting about an upcoming writers' conference. Happy memories rose up as I thought about the experiences I'd enjoyed attending and teaching at conferences. Then as if covered by a blizzard of snow, the happy memories were buried under envy, self-pity, and coveting. I wanted to go, too, and couldn't. The selfish desires rose up and swirled long after my friends had left.

No wonder Jesus tells us to "watch and pray." Temptations can bury us when we least expect them. I'm so grateful He knows our struggles, and that the One Who successfully faced and conquered every temptation now lives in us. —SHARON HINCK

FAITH STEP: *List a few of the situations where temptations most often snag you. Today, make a decision to avoid those situations, and ask Jesus to protect you from the unexpected temptations that may try to blindside you.*

SUNDAY, APRIL 12

For to me, living means living for Christ. Philippians 1:21 (NLT)

RECENTLY, I READ SOME OF the saddest words in the Bible I think I've ever seen, when King Jehoram died. As king of Judah, Jehoram was also the son of King Jehoshaphat and grandson of King Asa (both good kings). He started wearing the crown at age thirty-two and ruled in Jerusalem for eight years. His story is told in 2 Chronicles 21.

But the words that struck me were these: "No one was sorry he died" (2 Chronicles 21:20, NLT). If those words had been spoken over godly parents passing away in their nineties, they might carry a deeper meaning—especially if those loved ones had endured long illnesses. What waited for them in heaven was far better than languishing here: joy, cessation of pain, the presence of Jesus—and so much more. In that sense, we could express happiness, not sorrow, at their death.

But the absence of sorrow here had nothing to do with longevity or prolonged illness, but to prolonged evil. King Jehoram, unlike his godly ancestors, lived a life totally apart from His Maker, setting up idols and promoting anti-God ways of living. Greed and power seized him, and he even murdered his own brothers and several leaders of Judah (verse 24).

Passages like that sadden me, because I realize how easily that could happen today. Maybe that's why I usually include the phrase, "Live for Jesus. That's what matters most!" on every birthday card to my grandchildren.

Stepping from this world into their real home, prepared for them by Jesus, is truly a joyful occasion for Christ followers. Still, none of us want King Jehoram's epitaph.

No matter how old I am, I hope mine reads, "She lived for Jesus. That's what matters most." —REBECCA BARLOW JORDAN

FAITH STEP: *What would you like for someone to say at your funeral? How would you like to be remembered? How would your epitaph read?*

MONDAY, APRIL 13

We're all like sheep who've wandered off and gotten lost. We've all done our own thing, gone our own way. And God has piled all our sins, everything we've done wrong, on him, on him. Isaiah 53:6 (MSG)

IT SEEMS SAFE TO SAY that we don't understand sacrifice as people in biblical times did. Our churches don't smell of blood. We don't hear the cacophony of penned animals in the parking lot. If we think of lambs at all, we picture cute, woolly creatures. They don't carry the connotation of death like they did when John introduced Jesus as the Lamb of God. Anyone listening would have made the connection, especially when John added the descriptor, "who takes away the sin of the world."

God made this sacrifice personal. Every year at Passover good Jews chose a flawless lamb on the tenth day of the month, one for each family. They separated the lamb from the rest of the flock and took special care of it. For most of a week, it was penned and pampered, fed and watered, often by the children, until the evening of the fourteenth day when each family killed their lamb, smeared its blood on their doorposts, and then roasted and ate it. Little children knew what would happen to the lamb they cared for that week. They grew up knowing that sin required sacrifice.

We need to realize it too. Too often, we act as if we can earn God's mercy. As if through trying harder, we might deserve to be forgiven.

We can't. We're broken. We sin. Like sheep, we wander. Robert Farrar Capon said, "The finding, the saving, are all in his hand—the sheep do nothing but get lost. It's all grace."

Jesus, the Lamb of God, the perfect sacrifice, took our sins on Himself. For us. Grace. —SUZANNE DAVENPORT TIETJEN

FAITH STEP: *God knows who you are and what you're made of. Accept the fact you're flawed and need a Savior. Today, thank Jesus for loving you just the way you are and coming to be a sacrifice for you.*

TUESDAY, APRIL 14

As Jesus started on his way, a man ran up to him and fell on his knees before him.
"Good teacher," he asked, "what must I do to inherit eternal life?"
"Why do you call me good?" Jesus answered. "No one is good—except God alone.
You know the commandments: 'You shall not murder, you shall not commit
adultery, you shall not steal, you shall not give false testimony, you shall not
defraud, honor your father and mother.'"
"Teacher," he declared, "all these I have kept since I was a boy."
Jesus looked at him and loved him. "One thing you lack," he said. "Go, sell
everything you have and give to the poor, and you will have treasure in heaven.
Then come, follow me."
At this the man's face fell. He went away sad, because he had great wealth.
Mark 10:17–22 (NIV)

THE HYMN, "I SURRENDER ALL," takes me back to my time of teaching at the refugee camp in the Philippines. It was always an offering song, played when the collection plate was passed around at the modest little building where worship services were held. The refugees had been through devastation in their homelands, many losing family members to political unrest. They were so glad to be alive and looked forward to their new lives in the USA.

Years later, this hymn is sung in our church in North Carolina. I can't get the words out. Surrendering all? That's asking a lot. Can I sing these words? And mean them? What would surrendering all look like?

In our Western culture things—material stuff—easily comes between us and Jesus. Most of the time we don't realize how important some possession is to us until we lose it. We don't see that our things that we worship come in packages like education, social standing, travel, beauty, and fame.
—ALICE J. WISLER

FAITH STEP: *Pray for freedom so that Jesus can work in your life to show you both the tangible and intangible things you need to surrender to Him.*

WEDNESDAY, APRIL 15

Bless the Lord, O my soul: and all that is within me, bless his holy name.
Psalm 103:1 (KJV)

THE OTHER DAY I WAS caught off guard when Addison began to pray for the food at dinner. He started his prayer by saying, "Dear Jesus, I pray that you have a good day today...." I couldn't even listen to him after I heard him say that because it was like Addie was talking to a real friend that he was concerned about.

And of course, Jesus is a friend in the truest sense of the word. But I rarely think of Him in those terms. (I bet the disciples did.) What would it have been like to be Jesus's friend on earth? What would have been like for me? What if I had sat next to Jesus and held His hand in prayer and ate snacks with Him and heard His laughter fill the room? What if I had seen Him heal the sick and suffer on the Cross?

I think my prayers would be different. I think they would be like a real conversation. I think they would be full of hope because I knew that if anyone could answer my prayers, it would be my friend, Jesus. They would be full of thanks for all the amazing miracles He had done and continues to work in my life. They would be full of stories of how my boys are doing, and how I love Scott and how I want to follow in Jesus's ways even when I mess up. And then I would want to bless Him like He always blesses me. I think I would say, "And Jesus, I miss You and I hope You are having a really, really great day." Sometimes kids get it absolutely right. —SUSANNA FOTH AUGHTMON

FAITH STEP: *Have a conversational prayer with Jesus as if you were talking to a friend that you truly care about. Remind yourself that He is, in fact, your very best friend who loves you more than you can imagine.*

THURSDAY, APRIL 16

The heavens proclaim the glory of God. The skies display his craftsmanship. Day after day they continue to speak; night after night they make him known. They speak without a sound or word; their voice is never heard. Yet their message has gone throughout the earth, and their words to all the world. Psalm 19:1–4 (NLT)

EVER SINCE I WAS A child I have loved to gaze at clouds. When they're billowy like cotton, I pick a place in them where I'd love to sit for a while. When my daughter told me a couple of years ago that she wanted to sit on a cloud, I knew she was mine!

Something about letting my dreams linger in their depths moves me to envision the bigness of the Lord. When I look at the vastness above me, I love imagining my Savior bigger than the sky; I believe that's exactly how He wants us to see Him. That is, after all, how He sees Himself.

Jesus shares His glory with us through His creation, and that creation can inspire us to praise Him more. The sky is huge; how much greater still is the One Who formed it, redeems it, and holds it in His hand?

When we struggle to see hope in our circumstances, or when the days feel loaded with too much stress, too much that drains us, we can bask in Jesus's glory all around us. In fact, we can be inspired to ask for more of His glory. Because He loves to shine upon us, we can ask Him to send down His glory over everything that troubles us (Romans 8:18).

If we aren't asking Him for more of Himself, for more of His glory, why not? That's one prayer He will answer yes to, and the more we look for more of Him, the more we will experience all that He is.
—ERIN KEELEY MARSHALL

FAITH STEP: *What qualities about creation speak to your heart? Let their beauty move you to worship the Savior.*

FRIDAY, APRIL 17

Jesus replied . . . "My time hasn't come yet." John 2:4 (CEB)

IN THE BIBLE, WE SEE glimpses of Jesus as a newborn, at eight days old, two years old, twelve, and then not again until the years between thirty and thirty-three.

What was he like at sixteen? Twenty-nine and a half? What was Jesus thinking and doing during the six months prior to His appearance on the scene for the launch of His ministry that began at the Jordan River?

Was He impatient to begin His healing, teaching, disciplining work? Did He find the hours He spent in the carpentry shop boring, annoying, a waste of time? Did He practice healing on a small scale like a young boy might practice wheelies on his bike before letting anyone else see?

Tradition fills in some of the blanks. But for the most part, we don't know.

We know He observed life around Him. Important, since He'd draw from those observations about farmers and birds and houses with poor foundations during His public ministry. He knew the recorded Scriptures well, often quoting from them when making a point. So He must have been a lifelong student of the Word.

But Jesus may well have been completely content, unhurried, patient about the timetable of the Father God's ultimate plan for Him. At the wedding in Cana, when His mother pressed Him to "do something" about the lack of wine, He tried to shush her, saying His time had not yet come.

Within His core was beating a pulse that said, "Wait for it. Wait for it . . . " until "the fullness of time had come." —CYNTHIA RUCHTI

FAITH STEP: *If you're in a waiting season right now, consider keeping a penny jar as a visual reminder of spiritual discontent. Toss in a penny for each time your frustration over having to wait takes center stage in your thoughts or conversations. Then give those frustrations over to God and ask Him to help you rest in Him.*

SATURDAY, APRIL 18

Do not be anxious about anything, but in every situation, by prayer and petition, with thanksgiving, present your requests to God. And the peace of God, which transcends all understanding, will guard your hearts and your minds in Christ Jesus. Philippians 4:6–7 (NIV)

THE MORNING WAS GLOOMY WITH torrents of rain, making it a challenge to get up. My muscles ached; the stomach bug from the day before was still present. Ugh.

Immediately, I was faced with the mail carrier bringing me a certified letter that needed attention, an e-mail from a child's teacher (*Oh no, was my son skipping class again?*) and from there the circumstances went from bad to worse. The weather certainly wasn't helping.

Suddenly I recalled the words to a sermon about the need to protect our hearts and minds. When we are faced with something unpleasant, the pastor had said, quickly bring to mind passages of Scripture about Who Jesus is and how He is near to us and over all things. By doing this, you will put things into perspective. There is a fine moment of choice—to become completely unraveled by the current circumstances, or to guard our hearts and minds.

"I will keep him (her) in perfect peace whose mind is stayed on thee," I said out loud. Adding to that, I began to praise Jesus for Who He is— Friend, Brother, Redeemer, Conqueror, and King. He is greater than anything that tries to steal His joy from my day. —ALICE J. WISLER

FAITH STEP: *Find a verse that depicts the authority of Jesus, write it on a note card, and memorize it for future challenges that are sure to come. It's all about being equipped!*

SUNDAY, APRIL 19

For we do not have a High Priest who cannot sympathize with our weaknesses, but was in all points tempted as we are, yet without sin. Let us therefore come boldly to the throne of grace, that we may obtain mercy and find grace to help in time of need.
Hebrews 4:15–16 (NKJV)

THE OTHER DAY MY SON Harper was in trouble from the moment he got out of school. He behaved badly in the car, annoying his sisters, and when we got home it was more of the same. Complaining about gathering eggs. Arguing over which game to play. All of this culminated in a spanking and a trip to his room for some quiet time. I was ready to pull out my hair!

When my husband drove up after work, Harper ran out the front door. He'd been in his room long enough, so I didn't think much of it. The doorbell rang, which seemed oddly timed, but I stopped what I was doing in the kitchen and went to answer it.

There stood Harper, his face glowing, with his hands behind his back. "I love you, Mommy!" He produced a bouquet of beautiful flowers.

My husband explained how Harper planned all week and sent his own money with Daddy to pick up the flowers.

I hugged Harper to me and cried a little, thanking him for his thoughtfulness. The flowers spread their fragrance over both of us.

Later I thought about the irony of Harper's behavior. In trouble one moment, acting like a fiend. The next moment presenting me with a lavish gift that had cost him a lot, one he'd planned and saved for, just because. How can both of these things co-exist within one little boy?

The same way they exist within all of us. Some days I'm in love with Jesus, other days I'm sadly in love with self. It's a constant battle to walk in the spirit and not the flesh. But my heart longs to rise above. Thank goodness Jesus understands, and never gives up on me. —GWEN FORD FAULKENBERRY

FAITH STEP: *Do you feel like giving up on someone? Perhaps even yourself? Jesus understands our weakness. Ask for His grace to help you carry on.*

MONDAY, APRIL 20

"Woe to you, teachers of the law and Pharisees, you hypocrites! You give a tenth of your spices—mint, dill and cumin. But you have neglected the more important matters of the law—justice, mercy and faithfulness. You should have practiced the latter, without neglecting the former." Matthew 23:23 (NIV)

I GROW DILL IN MY garden. I love the delicate fronds, and the flavor it infuses into my pickles, soups, or salmon dishes. I can't help but giggle when I read Jesus's words about the Pharisees tithing their dill and other herbs and spices. Can you imagine counting out a tenth of tiny green bits of herb? I wonder what the usher would think if I put a bunch of dill into the offering plate on Sunday. Jesus's sense of humor shines as He points out these extremes.

But I'm not as different from the Pharisees as I'd like to be. Today I wrote up a long "to do" list and took great satisfaction in crossing out finished items. I even added a few things to the list that I'd already completed, just for the fun of checking them off.

The problem with focusing on my activities—whether it's meticulous tithing, or any other accomplishments—is that I begin to rely on my own supposed goodness instead of depending on Jesus. When I start feeling smug about my activities, it's a sure sign I need Jesus to remind me of His priorities. Justice, mercy, and faithfulness matter more—and those only grow in my heart as I allow Him to take over my life. —SHARON HINCK

FAITH STEP: *Cook with some herbs today, and as you hold the tiny plants, ask Jesus to show you if you've been obsessing about small matters and missing a bigger heart priority.*

TUESDAY, APRIL 21

In one of these meetings as he was eating a meal with them, he told them, "Do not leave Jerusalem until the Father sends you what he promised." Acts 1:4 (NLT)

JESUS APPEARED TO HIS DISCIPLES and talked to them about God's kingdom several times after His Resurrection. On one occasion, immediately prior to His ascension to heaven, He told them to stay in Jerusalem until they were baptized by the Holy Spirit. He said this would happen "in just a few days" (verse 5).

Waiting for God to do what He'd promised in His timing was essential. Had the disciples disregarded Jesus's command, they would have missed a world-changing experience. And so, they practiced patience. This didn't mean they sat and twiddled their thumbs until the appointed time. Rather, they prayed continually (verse 14) and they prepared for further ministry (verses 21–26). Their wait period was productive and prepared them for what was to come.

Sometimes Christ tells us to wait too. Perhaps we want to sell our house and buy another, but He says, "Not yet." Maybe we plan to serve Him overseas, but He says, "Not so fast." Perhaps we want to start a family, but He says, "Now's not the time. Wait."

In the disciples' case, they knew their wait would be short—just a few days. At least they were given that information. Lucky guys. Oftentimes we have no clue how long the wait might last.

Our tendency might be to balk or rush ahead, but doing so means missing the growth and blessings a waiting period can bring. Our role is to sit tight but not idle. We ought to follow the disciples' example—use the wait time to pray and prepare for whatever lies ahead. This response ensures Christ's blessing on our lives and our opportunity to be part of His purposes on earth. —GRACE FOX

FAITH STEP: *Recall a situation when Jesus asked you to wait. How did you respond? What lessons did you learn? How did you grow from this experience? What would you do differently if you had to do it again?*

WEDNESDAY, APRIL 22

But now, Lord, what do I look for? My hope is in you. Psalm 39:7 (NIV)

THIS MORNING IN THAT HALFWAY haze between sleep and wakefulness, I was mulling over all of the things that have been weighing on me. Work. Writing. The boys. Summer plans. New opportunities. Relationships. I'm a ponderer. Or if I am honest, a worrier.

You should know that the blessing and the curse of a writer's brain is an overactive imagination. When uncertainty arises, I can tend to think the worst might happen…when in fact the best could happen. Last night, talking with Scott over the things I have been worried about, he looked at me with compassion and said, "Sue, you have got to start telling yourself the truth. You have got to start telling yourself a different story." The man is a rock. Let's just be honest. In the face of problems or fear, he brings truth and usually some comic relief. Because he loves me. He wants me settled in a place of peace. Mostly, because he knows if Mama ain't happy…ain't nobody happy. It is to his advantage to have me embracing truth and laughter.

So back to my pondering this morning. The words of the Psalmist ring true even now. What are we looking for in this life? What do we need that can't be found in the one that loves us most? Where do we find our hope? Jesus, in His mercy, reminds us again where our hopes belong. In Him. So I have decided to mull that over, instead of worrying about things that are out of my control. Because He loves me. And He wants me settled in a place of peace. That is enough to make me happy…and hopeful.
—SUSANNA FOTH AUGHTMON

FAITH STEP: *Write out the word "HOPE" in big block letters. Under it, list all the ways that Jesus has given you hope.*

THURSDAY, APRIL 23

I want you woven into a tapestry of love, in touch with everything there is to know of God. Then you will have minds confident and at rest, focused on Christ, God's great mystery. Colossians 2:2 (MSG)

MY FRIENDS CAN'T UNDERSTAND WHY I spin yarn and weave it into fabric with tools Moses would've recognized. But weaving fills my senses and calms my heart. I lose myself in it and (usually) gain something beautiful. Along the way, I've learned about more than cloth.

God gave specific directions for the tabernacle (complete with visual aids) to Moses on Mt. Sinai. He filled Bezalel with the Holy Spirit and every gift needed to complete the work.

Many of the hangings and curtains were pictorial tapestries. They provided a sense of place, protection from the weather, and a beauty that spoke without words. In tapestry weaving, the lengthwise threads (or warp) form a strong, uniform base, holding the work together. Absolutely necessary, they are unseen, hidden by the crosswise weft threads.

Tapestry weft threads are anything but uniform. Different lengths of blue, purple, scarlet—even beaten gold—zigzagged across the warp, linking through other pieces before u-turning. Before hanging, the weaver fulled the yarn so it would relax and cling to the warp.

This is why I weave. It soothes my senses, while showing me a metaphor for Jesus, the core, uniform and perfect, who holds all things together. He draws us; then places us among all these other cranky, proud, irritating folks He's chosen as well.

We, a bunch of ragtag, multicolored, meandering lengths of yarn, form the tapestry of His Church. The world looks at us—flawed but loved—and we show them something more than we are. God's great mystery. Christ in us—the hope of glory. —SUZANNE DAVENPORT TIETJEN

FAITH STEP: *You may never know the part you play in God's plan. Relax. Offer yourself, your weakness, as a unique contribution. Let Jesus work through you.*

FRIDAY, APRIL 24

Every good and perfect gift is from above, coming down from the Father of the heavenly lights. James 1:17 (NIV)

MY FRIEND MARIAN LOVES A great deal. If there's a yard sale in the area, she arranges her Saturday morning to fit it in. Today she stopped by and treated me to a Jesus-moment when I was convinced, once again, that our Savior loves to love us uniquely.

"Have I told you about my bushes?" she asked.

I responded no, so she told me about two small bushes in her yard that had died. She looked for replacements but couldn't find the same variety anywhere, and she didn't know its name.

She figured she'd just remove the dead ones and plant something else or leave two empty spots among the other identical bushes.

Well, one day while running errands, she drove by her bushes lying at the roadside. Not *her* bushes exactly, but two of the same kind, roots and all. Yep. Just sitting there looking abandoned and forlorn (drama and all).

She pulled up to the house and rang the doorbell. The owners said, "Sure, go ahead and take them. We're redoing our landscape and getting rid of those."

Marian has big faith that trusts when Jesus shows up. If there ever was doubt whether Jesus cares about the smallest—even fairly insignificant—desires of our hearts, this story ought to ring with promise. Two rare bushes just like the two my friend needed. The added gift was that they were free, a sweet bonus that spoke personally to my frugal friend's heart.

Jesus knows what matters to you. Thank Him today for the gifts of love He may send when you're least expecting them. —ERIN KEELEY MARSHALL

FAITH STEP: *Why not begin a remembrance garden in a corner of your yard? Start with one rock and ask Jesus to grow your garden of faith. Add a rock to it each time He shows you He sees you and knows your heart.*

SATURDAY, APRIL 25

Dear friends, do not be surprised at the painful trial you are suffering, as though something strange were happening to you. But rejoice that you participate in the sufferings of Christ, so that you may be overjoyed when his glory is revealed.
1 Peter 4:12–13 (NIV)

MY YOUNGEST DAUGHTER CAME HOME from college on spring break with an appointment to have four wisdom teeth removed. Not a fun way to spend a vacation, but it was the only time that fit her schedule.

We stocked up on comfort measures: ice packs, sherbet, and DVDs of a favorite TV show to watch while she recovered.

But she had another treat that helped her look beyond the pain. Shortly before coming home, she'd won tickets to a Christian concert, including VIP passes to a meet-and-greet with the artists. Focusing on the excitement of the glorious concert ahead helped her endure.

Suffering is no fun, but the truth is that life includes pain. Peter reminds us not to be surprised by it. Even as followers of Christ, we aren't immune. We may confront physical pain, like having wisdom teeth pulled, or the emotional pain of loss or loneliness, or the spiritual pain of doubt and guilt. Having something wonderful to look forward to can help us endure.

Just as my daughter had an upcoming music event to think about, we have an exciting gathering around the corner. The promise in this verse hints of a coming time when joy will be so huge, it will overshadow even our memories of pain. One day, we will see the glory of Jesus fully revealed. What a healing concert of praise that will be! —SHARON HINCK

FAITH STEP: *Look at your calendar. Do you have an approaching event that you're excited about? Thank Jesus that He has an even better event planned for your future reunion with Him, and spend a few extra minutes today savoring His glory.*

SUNDAY, APRIL 26

Elijah replied, "I have zealously served the Lord God Almighty. But...I alone am left, and now they are trying to kill me, too." 1 Kings 19:10 (NLT)

ELIJAH WAS A TREMENDOUS MAN of God, but he plunged into despair after Queen Jezebel threatened his life. He lost perspective and eventually assumed a sense of entitlement. We can paraphrase his words like this: I've worked so hard for You, Lord. But now I'm the only prophet left, and I'm on the enemy's hit list. This is what You give me in return for serving You?

I don't condone Elijah's attitude, but I understand how easily it can overtake us. My husband and I were missionaries in Nepal in the eighties. Our son, Matthew, became deathly ill a few days before his first birthday. The nearest hospital was a three-hour drive away. The only vehicle available to go there was an ancient van with a broken clutch.

I recall cuddling my son's limp body as we lumbered down the road. These thoughts ran through my mind: *We've worked hard for You. We've sacrificed conveniences, family, safety, and health for Your sake. And now this? This is what You give us in return?*

That's when I heard a quiet whisper—a Jim Elliot quote, actually: "If Jesus Christ be God and died for me, then no sacrifice I make can be too great for Him." Elliot was a missionary martyred in South America in the fifties.

My sense of entitlement vanished and my perspective returned.

Jesus died for you and me. He owes us nothing more. We, however, owe Him everything in exchange. He's the entitled one. May He guard us from thinking we're entitled to more, and may He grant us grateful hearts for all He's done on our behalf. —GRACE FOX

FAITH STEP: *Do you sometimes feel as though you've done much for Jesus but He's short-changing you in return? If so, ponder Jim Elliot's quote. Ask Jesus to embed the meaning in your heart and give you a sense of deep gratitude for what He's done.*

MONDAY, APRIL 27

"Keep on asking, and you will receive what you ask for. Keep on seeking, and you will find. Keep on knocking, and the door will be opened to you."
Matthew 7:7 (NLT)

IT'S HOPELESS, I TOLD MYSELF. I'll never find what I'm looking for. My agent had agreed to guide me through the process of launching my out-of-print book as an e-book. I'd updated statistics and other information in the manuscript, tweaked some of the devotions, and replaced a handful with fresh ones. I'd also written a new introduction along with new back-cover copy. Now only one element was missing.

All I had to do was find a suitable photo and an art designer would adapt it for the front cover. For days I searched Web sites offering royalty-free and low-cost images. Nothing even remotely resembled the picture I had in mind. After scanning thousands of images, I wished I could afford to hire an artist. Sighing, I opened up my laptop and went to yet another Web site. And then it popped up: a scene with early morning light sweeping across a green meadow with a solitary tree greeting the new day. It was perfect for the book cover, and better than the image in my mind.

One of my character flaws is a tendency to give up too easily; I'm sorry to say that sometimes I let that weakness spill over into my prayer life. That's why I desperately need to hold on to Jesus's words about persistence in prayer. Jesus encourages us to keep on asking, seeking, and knocking. Even when nothing seems to be happening. Especially when we feel the situation is hopeless. If we don't give up, He promises that the answer will come at just the right time. And who knows, it might even be better than what we had in mind all along. —DIANNE NEAL MATTHEWS

FAITH STEP: *Do you feel like giving up on a prayer request that's close to your heart? Talk to Jesus about it anyway, asking Him to give you renewed faith that the answer will come.*

TUESDAY, APRIL 28

If we confess our sins, he is faithful and just and will forgive us our sins and purify us from all unrighteousness. 1 John 1:9 (NIV)

SCOTT AND I LIKE TO call living in the Aughtmon home "happy chaos." We are happy. We live in chaos. What else can you expect from living with a crew of three young boys? There is a lot of love. A lot of wrestling. A lot of fighting. And a lot of blaming. After all, it is so much easier to blame one's brother than to yield and say, "Oops. I made a mistake." It's much more convenient to throw your sibling under the bus and say, "He kicked me in the knee" than to say "I bit his elbow first."

But the problem is that the argument or the brawl is rarely solved unless someone actually admits to doing wrong. Until that happens, nothing can change. A while ago, I overheard Jack say to his brother, "Will, is there something that you want to say to me that rhymes with "I'm florry?" I had to laugh. I'm not sure Will was ready to ask for Jack's forgiveness but Jack was ready to give it.

Forgiveness is the most powerful life-changer in the world. Jesus knows that we are going to mess up. It is our human condition. But His divine condition is that if we bring those mess-ups to Him, He is always ready to forgive us. He will give us a new start. New mercies. New grace. A new way of thinking. A new way of acting. He takes our mess and clothes us with His righteousness. From my way of thinking, we get the better end of the deal. —SUSANNA FOTH AUGHTMON

FAITH STEP: *Write out the words "I AM FORGIVEN" in big block letters in your journal. Then imagine yourself standing clean, white, and clothed with His love and righteousness...because you are.*

WEDNESDAY, APRIL 29

"When you pray, don't pour out a flood of empty words . . . (People who do) think that by saying many words they'll be heard." Matthew 6:7 (CEB)

THE LAST OF THE PLATES reached their destinations at the restaurant table that seated ten friends. As each order was placed, the tableful of people expressed their appreciation for how delicious the food looked and smelled, for the tasteful plating, and generous portions.

"Who would like to pray over the meal?"

The ten of us gazed around the circle to see if anyone else volunteered. Jokingly, our leader pointed to one individual and said, "Not Charlie. Our meals will be cold before he finally says amen."

An undercurrent of light laughter soon settled, and a not-longwinded person asked the blessing over the meal.

We'd laughed, but my thoughts turned to how easily we slip into thinking that the value of prayer is in its length (or brevity) rather than its depth.

Jesus told us not to pour out a flood of empty words when we pray. Immediately after that, He gave us instructions on how to pray. We know that passage as the Lord's Prayer. It takes up half a column in my Bible. Plenty of words. So what was Jesus saying?

His point may have been, "Make it mean something," whether short or long. Make it come from the heart, and express the Father's will.

What gives prayer its meat and meaning? Through the verses that follow, Jesus tells us it lies in acknowledging Who God is, expressing our longing for His kingdom, lobbying for His will both on earth and in heaven, thanking Him for providing, asking His forgiveness, and seeking spiritual protection so we can live in a way that pleases Him. —CYNTHIA RUCHTI

FAITH STEP: *What's one prayer concern you often bring before Jesus? Rather than begging Him to provide a larger home or reconnect your wayward son with faith or help you land a better job, thank Him for how He's already at work behind the scenes.*

THURSDAY, APRIL 30

Don't become so well-adjusted to your culture that you fit into it without even thinking. Instead, fix your attention on God. You'll be changed from the inside out. Readily recognize what he wants from you, and quickly respond to it. Unlike the culture around you, always dragging you down to its level of immaturity, God brings the best out of you, develops well-formed maturity in you.
Romans 12:2 (MSG)

I REMEMBER MY FATHER TEACHING me to ride my bicycle. He ran alongside, holding the back of the seat. Before letting go, he told me, "Look straight ahead—not off to the side. Where you look is where you're going to go."

I proved that with many a skinned knee. It's as true for anyone—driving, even walking—as it was for me peddling furiously down the rocky roads of our neighborhood. Anything longer than a glance to the side had me veering toward the curb.

The direction of our gaze affects our Christian walk as well. Jesus calls us to follow Him, but where are we looking? At celebrity culture or reality shows? At our neighbor with the bigger house or better car? At our coworker with the new promotion?

Who are we watching?

We can't follow Jesus if we're looking somewhere else.

We may think it'd be easier to follow Jesus if we could see Him with our own eyes. Possibly, but even with Jesus right there, the disciples struggled and failed.

We can see Jesus more clearly by reading the Bible, hearing wise counsel, and praying. Stay open to finding Him in unexpected places. Fixing our eyes on Jesus will transform us into the people He intends us to be.
—SUZANNE DAVENPORT TIETJEN

FAITH STEP: *Picture Jesus alongside you today. Imagine His concern for you in every situation that arises. He promised to be with us always.*

FRIDAY, MAY 1

*Therefore, since we are surrounded by such a great cloud of witnesses,
let us throw off everything that hinders and the sin that so easily entangles.
And let us run with perseverance the race marked out for us, fixing our eyes on
Jesus, the pioneer and perfecter of faith.* Hebrews 12:1–2 (NIV)

FROM MY CHAIR ON THE patio I watched a goldfinch flit past the garden
and into a nearby tree. Unfurled irises bobbed in a light breeze, showing
off shades of blue and purple. Lush ferns lined the edge of the yard. The
beauty filled my chest like a deep breath.

Then as dusk approached, a few gnats found my spot in the backyard.
I tried to wave them away, but they kept swarming around my head. I
squinted and changed my focus so I could see what I was batting at. As I
zeroed in on the tiny bugs, the rest of the world blurred out of focus. All
the details and beauty I'd been savoring faded into a vague background as
long as I stared at the gnats. I couldn't focus on both at once.

Some days, life feels full of gnats—problems, annoyances, frustrations.
Traffic jams, telemarketing calls, broken appliances. Little conflicts buzz
and swarm and irritate. When those draw my focus, all Jesus's blessings
blur into a hazy backdrop that I'm no longer able to see clearly. His grace
is constant, but my focus is inconsistent. It's only when I fix my eyes on
Jesus that the beauty of the life He gives us is clear.

With His help, I can see the big picture again. —SHARON HINCK

FAITH STEP: *Go outside and fix your eyes on a distant point. Notice how everything
else around it fades into the background. Then ask Jesus to fix your heart on Him with
that same intensity of focus.*

SATURDAY, MAY 2

I have been crucified with Christ; and it is no longer I who live, but it is
Christ who lives in me. And the life I now live in the flesh I live by faith in the
Son of God, who loved me and gave himself for me.
Galatians 2:20 (NRSV)

SOMETIMES IT SEEMS WHAT WE do is so little. I feel it when I am folding clothes, washing dishes, tying my baby's shoes, doing homework with my six-year-old, and packing my husband's lunch. I feel it when I pray for my eleven-year-old on his spelling test, when I send my teenager a text of encouragement before her game. I feel it when I play the piano for a church of seventy-five members and teach a class of twenty-five students.

The hope for all of these things is in the story of the little boy with his loaves and fishes. He offered what he had. Not much. But Jesus took his small offering and increased it. He does the same with us.

John writes, "Unless a grain of wheat falls into the ground and dies, it remains alone; but if it dies, it produces much grain" (12:24, NKJV). We may feel like we're constantly falling short, but even Jesus seemed to fall short at the Cross. All of His efforts met with apparent defeat. Yet three days later He rose from the grave.

The greatest theme of the story of Jesus is this—redemption. Life out of death. When we are "crucified with Christ," putting self to death, we are also raised with Him, to walk in newness of life. It is Jesus Who lives His life in us and through us. This turns all of our "little things" into things that matter, deeds with divine purpose, seeds that fall to the ground only to produce a harvest beyond our wildest dreams.
—GWEN FORD FAULKENBERRY

FAITH STEP: *Lord Jesus, help us to remember that everything Your spirit ordains for us to do, no matter how small it may seem, is of great value in the kingdom of heaven. Help us to work for You today.*

SUNDAY, MAY 3

*Jesus replied, "The truth is, you want to be with me because I fed you,
not because you saw the miraculous sign." John 6:26 (NLT)*

To WHAT MIRACULOUS SIGN WAS Jesus referring when He spoke these words? The feeding of more than five thousand men, women, and children. He'd taken a little boy's offering—five barley loaves and two fish—broken the food, blessed it, and then fed the masses. Everyone stuffed their tummies, and twelve baskets of leftovers remained. The crowds were amazed and exclaimed, "Surely, He is the prophet we've been expecting!"

The same crowds gathered on the shore the next morning to wait for Jesus. When He arrived, He wasted no time exposing their reason for being there. Their motive, He said, was merely to satisfy their physical appetite—they were hungry again and wanted Him to provide breakfast. Their spiritual appetite—their desire to be with Him simply because of who He was—sorely lacked.

I wonder if Jesus felt used, like a lottery winner suddenly surrounded by new "friends" hoping to benefit from His wealth and generosity but not truly interested in having an honest-to-goodness relationship. And I wonder what Jesus would say to you and me individually if we were part of that crowd.

Do we want a relationship with Jesus because we hope He'll give us a coveted position at work, restore our marriage, or heal a loved one? Do we regard Him as our personal genie in a bottle Whose purpose is to grant our whims and wishes? Or do we follow Him because we truly believe He's the Son of God and long for intimacy with Him?

What would Jesus say to us about our reason for following Him?
—GRACE FOX

FAITH STEP: *Read this sentence and then fill in the blank: I follow Jesus because
_____. Ask Him to give you an unquenchable desire for intimacy
with Him.*

MONDAY, MAY 4

"If a fellow believer hurts you, go and tell him—work it out between the two of you. If he listens, you've made a friend." Matthew 18:15 (MSG)

POLITICIANS, PASTORS, WRITERS, SPEAKERS—ANYONE who's ever made a public statement or written a published piece—know the sinking feeling of being misunderstood. We've all seen the havoc wrought by one sentence, one phrase, one word written or spoken without careful editing.

I coauthored my first book with my husband: *Marriage Toners: Weekly Exercises to Strengthen Your Relationship*. When our publisher first sent out the publicity blurbs, this is what showed up in the letters: "Sexercise your way to a healthier relationship!" Fortunately by the time we called them, they had already caught their misprint and repaired the damage. It was an innocent, humorous mistake.

But with serious misunderstandings people often choose knee-jerk reactions. "What did you mean by that? And you call yourself a Christian?" Media can embellish the blunder, blowing it into outlandish proportions. Both Facebook followers and bloggers love to weigh in, which can add even more fuel to the fire. Anyone can fall into that trap without thinking.

Jesus encourages us to take the right steps when we've misunderstood someone or have been offended. Rather than jumping on someone first, we can ask for clarity. We can look at his or her entire life or ministry—or the entire article or book—and respond without reacting or judging. And we can go to others privately when they've offended us, or if we sense an error in judgment. If that doesn't work, Jesus gave follow-up steps in the remaining passage in Matthew 18.

When I've applied these steps, or others have approached me that way, the results have usually been positive. I'd rather make a friend than an enemy. Wouldn't you? —REBECCA BARLOW JORDAN

FAITH STEP: *Read the rest of Matthew 18. The next time someone offends you, or you misunderstand, work through these steps, asking Jesus to give you wisdom and a gentle spirit.*

TUESDAY, MAY 5

Let us therefore make every effort to do what leads to peace and to mutual edification. Romans 14:19 (*NIV*)

IT WAS ONE OF THOSE mornings. Multiple spills, tears of shame, cross words, too-busy schedules, unfinished homework, looming deadlines, and worn nerves ganged up on our family.

I watched my husband and daughter hold hands as they left for "Donuts with Dad" at her school and I dropped my son off at his. One happy family, tra-la-la. My heart ached knowing that none of us were feeling fulfilled just then. Fortunately no one's feelings were injured permanently, but it wasn't the peace-filled send-off we seek.

However, the light in this fog is an area of growth that redeemed the morning from being a total liability. As the stress was mounting and Steve and I were trying to get everyone going, I sensed in both of us the higher calling to care rather than to bark everyone into submission. My heart is lifted in the understanding that Jesus did indeed reign in that way.

I think about the times I haven't prioritized hearts over harried moments, and I am grieved. Too often my countenance hollers *Get it done now!* rather than *It can wait; you're doing great.* Too often my heart-stress creates tension for those I love rather than edifies them in an atmosphere of peace.

To be sure, we'll have more spills, more irritations, more reasons to want to yell at the ceiling. And I'll never enjoy those things.

But I thank the Savior Who takes His time with me and lets me hurt over tearing down a soul He died to rebuild. —ERIN KEELEY MARSHALL

FAITH STEP: *Memorize 1 Corinthians 13:13. Ask Jesus to help you radiate His love during stressful times.*

WEDNESDAY, MAY 6

He [Christ] is the one who made us acceptable to God. He made us pure and holy, and he gave himself to purchase our freedom. As the Scriptures say, "The person who wishes to boast should boast only of what the Lord has done."
1 Corinthians 1:30–31 (NLT)

MINISTERING IN EASTERN EUROPE ALLOWS me to hear testimonies from men and women who have discovered the difference between being deeply religious and having a relationship with Jesus. They tell of growing up in families where church attendance was non-negotiable. Confessing sins to the priest was a necessity. Celebrating various rites and rituals was the norm. They speak of striving to meet God's standards but falling short, and of longing for assurance of salvation but finding none. Then they speak of discovering Jesus.

Every summer, I have the opportunity to give Bibles to Eastern Europeans who have not yet heard of Jesus. Most have never held a Bible. Their eyes light up when they hear salvation does not depend on their human efforts. Christ has accomplished the work on their behalf, and they simply need to place their faith in Him.

A man who's become a close family friend says, "For decades I believed salvation was something I must earn so I became profoundly religious and tried to do all the right things. Then I learned about Jesus and what He'd done for me, and the pressure to perform ended." What a life-changing realization! And it applies to us too:

Jesus bought our freedom.

Jesus makes us holy.

Jesus makes us acceptable to God.

Jesus satisfied God's requirements through His sacrifice on the Cross. Ponder these truths today, and celebrate them! —GRACE FOX

FAITH STEP: *Jesus is sometimes called the "Rose of Sharon." Buy a single long-stemmed rose today. Place it in a vase on your dining room table. Each time you look at it, thank Jesus for making you acceptable to God through His death and Resurrection.*

THURSDAY, MAY 7

Gracious words are a honeycomb, sweet to the soul and healing to the bones.
Proverbs 16:24 (*NIV*)

THIS PAST WEEK I HAD the opportunity to speak at a mom's group. I love speaking to moms. They are my people. I talked about expectations and joy and how sometimes our unrealistic expectations can keep us from enjoying the life God has given us. It seemed to resonate with the women. I know it resonated with me. I am usually speaking to myself when I give talks. We laughed together and asked Jesus to help us place our hopes in Him, not in our circumstances.

I got a chance to talk to a few of the ladies before leaving, but as I was heading out the door, one of the leaders of the group pressed a stack of cards into my hands. She said, "This is a little something for you to take with you." When I got to my car, I glanced through the cards and found they were cards of affirmation. Each person in the group had taken the time to write a note to me about how they enjoyed my talk. I began to cry a little. They were good tears. All that love and encouragement caught me off guard. It was unexpected. It takes so little for someone to lift my spirit. An encouraging note. Small arms wrapped around my leg in a hug. A kiss from Scott. A friendly smile from another parent at my kids' school. A prayer spoken over me on the phone.

We have the power to lift each other up with kindness. Jesus lived this out daily. His words brought light and life wherever He went. Sincere affection and words of hope give wings to the soul. Those women made my day. I couldn't stop grinning all the way home.
—SUSANNA FOTH AUGHTMON

FAITH STEP: *Write notes of encouragement to three of your favorite people that you will see today. Hand deliver them. Know that Jesus is glorified each time you use your words to lift up others.*

FRIDAY, MAY 8

"This is why he can completely save those who are approaching God through him, because he always lives to speak with God for them." Hebrews 7:25 (CEB)

I'VE DRIFTED AWAY FROM A ministry I'm now determined to reinstate: Mug-of-the-Day.

My day starts with coffee but soon moves to tea. A self-confessed mug snob, I consider the vessel for the beverage almost as important as the drink. Significant size. Interesting shape. Keeps the beverage hot. And must, must, must have a handle that fits four fingers comfortably. The grip is key.

My collection of pottery mugs includes souvenirs from vacations and speaking event locations, mug-messages—*Hope Always, Write Anyway, A Mom Is..., Inspire*—and gifts from friends. I bought look-alike mugs for a friend of mine so we'd think of each other when drinking our tea.

For a season, I used whatever mug I'd chosen as a prayer reminder that day. If the mug was a gift from a friend, I'd pray for that friend throughout the day. If the mug sported a camp logo, I prayed for the camp's ministry and staff. My *Hope Always* mug reminded me to pray for those struggling to keep their hold on hope. Even a souvenir mug could remind me to pray for those who live in that area.

I regret having let up on that practice. It's been too long since I looked at my tea mug as more than a container for a beverage. Jesus would never neglect an idea like Mug-of-the-Day. The Bible tells us He "ever lives to make intercession" for us. *Lives* for it! Unceasingly praying for His children. Constantly talking to God the Father about us and our needs.

The thought fills me with awe. He needs no reminders. He doesn't have a prayer list. He has a heart that remembers. —CYNTHIA RUCHTI

FAITH STEP: *Our humanity makes us susceptible to forgetting. Consider your own Mug-of-the-Day reminders to pray for the people, topics, and ministries that matter to you... and to Him.*

SATURDAY, MAY 9

He is the Rock; his deeds are perfect. Everything he does is just and fair.
He is a faithful God who does no wrong; how just and upright he is!
Deuteronomy 32:4 (NLT)

LAST YEAR MY HUSBAND AND I adopted two young children from the foster care system, making us parents of three children over the age of twenty, and three children under the age of seven! I jokingly say that the first three were the "test set" and now we know what to do as parents. There is some truth to that, but the "doing" part is much harder than the "knowing what to do" part.

Even though I'm the mom and know better, sometimes I'm the selfish one. I've changed the kids' clock in their room so they'd think it was time for bed before it really was. I've eaten the last cookie. I've allowed myself to get angry over silly things. In fact, if I ever want to know how much I still need Jesus's transforming power at work in my life, I just need to spend a few hours with my kids!

I'm thankful that Jesus is not the same way. He is just and fair. His deeds are perfect. As Psalm 18:30 (NLT) says, "God's way is perfect. All the Lord's promises prove true. He is a shield for all who look to him for protection."

Jesus doesn't expect me to be a perfect mom, and no matter how much I know how to do, I can't do it all in my own strength. Whenever I need help, wisdom, guidance, or patience, I can turn to Jesus for help. He's promised to be there for me in everything and in every way...and that includes parenting! Jesus will never give up on me as a person or a mom, and I'm thankful for that. —TRICIA GOYER

FAITH STEP: *Do you know a mom who is struggling with her kids? Think of a small thing you can do for her, such as taking over some frozen pizzas or offering a listening ear. It'll make a big difference!*

SUNDAY, MAY 10

The word of Christ must live in you richly. Teach and warn each other with all wisdom by singing psalms, hymns, and spiritual songs. Sing to God with gratitude in your hearts. Colossians 3:16 (CEB)

"TEACHER," A VIETNAMESE STUDENT SAID to me, "I am going to America tomorrow."

Her face was bright, her expression filled with hope. She had been in the Philippine Refugee Processing Center for six months and, at last, it was time to leave for her destination—a new life in the USA. "Thank you, Teacher," she said and then for emphasis, she thanked me in Vietnamese for teaching her English and about life in America.

She and her family had little, but they were so gracious to me. I had been the recipient of many sweets and soda they had bought for me as I taught in the dusty and hot classroom while rats scurried across the rafters.

Over two decades later, when I think of gratitude, my refugee students and their families come to mind. These political refugees had suffered under a communist regime, and been torn from their homes, many of them escaping on crude boats in the South China Sea. They had little but were gracious and thankful. I was humbled by their gratitude.
—ALICE J. WISLER

FAITH STEP: *Create your own psalm of praise to Jesus for being in your life. Start it off with the line: How thankful I am for Your love.*

MONDAY, MAY 11

So all of us who have had that veil removed can see and reflect the glory of the Lord. And the Lord—who is the Spirit—makes us more and more like him as we are changed into his glorious image. 2 Corinthians 3:18 *(NLT)*

MOST OF US HAVE LOOKED in the mirror at one time or another, asking the familiar fairy-tale question: *Mirror, mirror on the wall…?* As a young teen, I'd look at my peers and complain, "Mirror, mirror on the wall, why'd you make me so tall?"

The thing about mirrors is, they never lie. What you see is what everyone else sees, at least physically. And sometimes, all our best efforts to accentuate the positive and downplay the negative still leave us discontented with our looks.

But Jesus never lies either. It's just that He sees things differently than we do. He gauges our "looks" by a different mirror. We're not too short, too tall, too big, or too small. He doesn't measure us by a wooden yardstick, or compare us to our peers. He knows we are uniquely made, one of a kind, a creatively designed child of His. And He looks at our hearts, not at our outward characteristics (1 Samuel 16:7).

Unfortunately, we see ourselves through a veil. Jesus wants to remove that veil so we can view His mirror, not ours. As His followers, what He wants us to see is His reflection daily. And the more we look into His mirror and what He says about us, the more we'll come to believe—and reflect—His image. When we look into His mirror, we'll see what Jesus sees: "beautiful," "loved," "redeemed," "Mine." —REBECCA BARLOW JORDAN

FAITH STEP: *The next time you look into your mirror and are tempted to complain, remember how Jesus sees you. Thank Him, not only for making you unique, but for creating you in His image.*

TUESDAY, MAY 12

Then I saw heaven opened, and there was a white horse. Its rider is called Faithful and True, and He judges and makes war in righteousness. His eyes were like a fiery flame, and many crowns were on His head. He had a name written that no one knows except Himself. He wore a robe stained with blood, and His name is the Word of God. Revelation 19:11–13 (HCS)

FROM BEGINNING TO END, THE Bible is about Jesus. Old Testament prophecies and symbolism picture His life and His mission to save people from their sins. In the New Testament, we first see Him as a helpless baby born in a stable. As a twelve-year-old boy, He submitted meekly to His earthly parents' authority. As a man, Jesus spent three years traveling and preaching with, as He said, "no place to lay [my] head" (Luke 9:58).

During the final week of His life, Jesus rode into Jerusalem on a donkey's colt, signifying peace. He submitted to His betrayal by Judas, His unlawful arrest, and His trials. Jesus allowed Himself to be mocked, tortured, and crucified. In order to fulfill God's plan, Jesus set aside His divine rights and privileges, but only for a time.

The book of Revelation paints a different picture of Jesus. The next time He steps on the earth, He will come for the purpose of judging and making war against God's enemies. This stern, fierce portrayal of Jesus used to make me uncomfortable; it seemed to contradict His name, Prince of Peace. Now I see things differently.

Some days it seems as though evil is winning over goodness, especially when I watch the news. But when Jesus returns, He will right all wrongs and end the turmoil and chaos caused by sin. That image of His strength and power comforts me and helps me remember that His war against evil will usher in peace and righteousness. —DIANNE NEAL MATTHEWS

FAITH STEP: *The next time you see evil triumph over good, read Revelation 19 to remind yourself that Jesus will take care of it all one day.*

WEDNESDAY, MAY 13

And this is his command: to believe in the name of his Son, Jesus Christ, and to love one another as he commanded us. 1 John 3:23 (NIV)

MY HUSBAND AND I WERE chatting with friends about the upcoming college graduation of our youngest. Suddenly my husband punched the air and grinned. "No more filling out FAFSA forms!" For well over a decade he'd been dealing with complicated financial aid forms and all the paperwork involved each year one of our children was in college.

Paying taxes has also become ridiculously complicated. Tax codes are thousands of pages, with a maze of rules and loopholes guaranteed to cause migraines. I usually feel fairly intelligent, but staring at an IRS form with various schedules and "if/then" boxes, I'm quickly overwhelmed.

When it comes to spiritual matters, it's no wonder we expect the way of truth to be just as complex. Yet Scripture sums it up more concisely than the shortest 1040EZ tax form:

Believe in Jesus Christ.

The work of our salvation is His. Faith in Jesus is not just the first page of a list of regulations. There is no fine print. No complicated added schedules or supplemental forms.

Yes, the Bible gives us examples of what our lives will look like as Jesus lives in us. But when I take Scripture as a series of laws and use them to try to earn God's favor, I'm missing the point. I begin to focus on my own efforts instead of the love of Christ. Before long, I'm wilting under the burden of a perfection I can't reach, and trudging along in fear of making mistakes, rather than walking in the joy of forgiveness. I'm so grateful that Jesus interrupts my attempts to be my own little god, holds out His hand, and says simply, "Believe." —SHARON HINCK

FAITH STEP: *Has following Jesus felt overly complicated lately? Ask Him to help you stop striving in your own power. Ask Him for faith to simply believe in Him.*

THURSDAY, MAY 14

How precious are your thoughts about me, O God. They cannot be numbered! I can't even count them; they outnumber the grains of sand! And when I wake up, you are still with me! Psalm 139:17–18 (NLT)

LAST WEEK, I WENT WITH my son Addison on a class field trip to the beach. It was a perfect day. As soon as the kids hit the sand they flung themselves to the ground, making sand angels. I took my cue from them and lay down on the sun-warmed sand. With the cries of the gulls and the laughter of the kids surrounding me, I let handfuls of sand funnel through my fingers.

My thoughts immediately turned toward the Psalms. It would have taken me hours to painstakingly count each tiny grain of sand in my palm. I couldn't imagine even trying it. But Jesus loves me so well and so much that His thoughts about me outnumber those grains of sand.

Sometimes I get caught up in worrying about life. About the hard things that are taking place. About the struggles I face or the sins that keep coming back around. And I wonder if Jesus sees me. If He is listening to my prayers. If He knows me at all. The enemy of my soul would like me to think I am alone. The Lover of my soul would like me to know that He can't stop thinking about me. Jesus wants me to know that His thoughts about me would fill hundreds of beaches, thousands of oceans, millions of sand dunes. He loves me completely and is interested in every subtle nuance of my life.

As I let the warm sand sift through my fingers, I realized that Addie wasn't the only one who was learning something on his field trip that day. —SUSANNA FOTH AUGHTMON

FAITH STEP: *Fill up a jar with sand and set it on your kitchen counter. Know each time you see it, that Jesus knows you and loves you inside and out.*

FRIDAY, MAY 15

"Pursue the goal of peace." Hebrews 12:14 (CEB)

SHE MADE IT! A FRIEND of mine returned to college at the age of fifty-five for her graduate degree. She felt the pull to take another step in her education, a step that would prepare her to pursue a second-chapter career in a field for which she'd been divinely created.

We cheered her on as she tackled reading and homework, exams, practicals, and dissertations. She graduated with honors and stepped into a new job with all the challenges and joys she expected.

It's easy to imagine what it means to pursue an education, or a dream, or a mate-in-waiting. We pour our energies into that goal, doing whatever it takes to advance, focused on reaching what it is we're chasing.

The idea of pursuing peace appears in a Scripture passage that talks about running the race of faith, about leaning on Jesus as our example.

Hoping for peace and longing for peace are far different from this biblical challenge. My friend could have hoped for a new career, could have longed for an advanced degree. Nothing would have changed for her until she actively pursued it, signed up for classes, paid the fees. Her pursuit required hard work, diligence, attentiveness, intentionality.

Will peace and holiness arrive on my doorstep because I long for them? Thought they'd be nice to have? How do I actively pursue peace at a family gathering? In the workplace? Online? Should I speak my mind or pursue peace? Correct someone or pursue peace?

The teaching Jesus gave us in the book of Hebrews through the Apostle Paul makes it clear that peace doesn't come naturally. It's elusive. But it can be captured, if pursued. —CYNTHIA RUCHTI

FAITH STEP: *Before the day is over, you'll no doubt have an opportunity to make a peace-pursuing choice as a reaction to an incident. Will you take it a step further and intentionally set the stage for peace?*

SATURDAY, MAY 16

[Christ's] love was not cautious but extravagant. He didn't love in order to get something from us but to give everything of himself to us. Love like that.
Ephesians 5:1–2 (MSG)

MY HUSBAND AND I RECENTLY celebrated our tenth anniversary in Banff, Canada. No words can describe the grandeur; the mountains were beyond big. I remember looking way up, trying to focus on a tree or slope, tiny in the distance. Just when it appeared that an elevation had run out of height, it gave way to a sheer rock wall that shot straight upward, as if the land sought to point to the heavens.

The landscape could have appeared to loom and threaten. In fact, we rode a gondola up the side of one mount, and my smallness and lack of control made my stomach churn as the compartment swayed.

But for all the mountains' power to intimidate, I couldn't help viewing them from Jesus's perspective. Our Creator formed them with His very hand. One touch from Him could flatten them.

As all of nature does, the mountains give a glimpse of Jesus's glory. They reflect His expansive, extravagant love. He doesn't give Himself cautiously. He's all in. He went to the Cross, no holds barred, no dragging Him there necessary. He offered His whole self for us, knowing we have nothing comparable to give in return.

His love makes me want to love in a similar way. When I feel like holding back a part of myself for fear of rejection or weariness, His majestic heart inspires me to love outward, upward, for the good of others instead of my own. —ERIN KEELEY MARSHALL

FAITH STEP: *How can you love extravagantly this week? Love doesn't always have to show itself in grand ways; sometimes consistency and faithfulness are the most needed forms of wholehearted giving.*

SUNDAY, MAY 17

The Lord is not slow in keeping his promise, as some understand slowness. Instead he is patient with you, not wanting anyone to perish, but everyone to come to repentance.

2 Peter 3:9 (NIV)

"HOW MUCH FARTHER?" I SQUIRMED in the van's front seat, trying to find a comfortable position. My husband's lips twitched as he drove, undoubtedly remembering countless family road trips where choruses of "Are we there yet?" rang from the backseats.

We were on our way to Chicago for our daughter's college graduation, and even though we were stocked with snacks and CDs to listen to, the hours on the road seemed endless.

I've never been good at patience. My impatience shows up when traveling, when waiting for a slow computer program to boot up, or when standing in line at a store checkout. I'm eager to dig in my garden before the snow is even gone each spring. And my greatest impatience rises up when I return to Jesus with a long-term prayer request. "Come on, fix this problem already!"

This verse reminds me to trust that when His answer seems slow in coming, He has a reason. The reason isn't because my need is unimportant to Him, or that He doesn't feel compassion for my struggle. His reason is shaped by His great love and wisdom.

Whether we're praying for healing, for the salvation of a family member, for restored relationships, or for financial provision, we can be reassured that Jesus knows our needs, cares about our longings, and will fulfill His promises to us. We can also know that if the answer feels slow in coming, He is using that time to form a better answer than we could imagine.
—SHARON HINCK

FAITH STEP: *Think of a request you've prayed where Jesus seems slow to answer. Thank Him for knowing the perfect time to fulfill His plans.*

MONDAY, MAY 18

Let your unfailing love surround us, Lord, for our hope is in you alone.
Psalm 33:22 (NLT)

SEVERAL HOMEOWNERS IN MY NEIGHBORHOOD have erected chain-link fences around their yards recently. The fences are nearly six feet tall, the type often seen on school property.

I haven't asked these folks why they're putting up the fences, but I can guess. Maybe they're trying to protect their dogs or small children from running into the street. Perhaps they don't want peddlers coming to the door. Maybe they've experienced trespassers dropping litter on the lawn. Or maybe they've been robbed in the past and they think a fence will prevent a recurrence. Their reasons for erecting chain-link fences may vary, but I have a hunch they all want more security.

I want security, too, for my spiritual, mental, and emotional well-being. I want protection from "enemies" such as envy, fear, doubt, pride, and negative thinking. From where does this protection come? From Christ.

"Many sorrows come to the wicked, but unfailing love surrounds those who trust the Lord," says Psalm 32:10–11. "So rejoice in the Lord and be glad, all you who obey him! Shout for joy, all you whose hearts are pure!"

Like an impenetrable fence around our souls, Christ surrounds those who love Him and walk in right relationship with Him. He gives us wisdom to prevent us from making foolish choices. And He gives us His Holy Spirit to help us walk in truth.

Surrounded by Jesus and His unfailing love—there's no safer place to be. —GRACE FOX

FAITH STEP: *Draw a stick figure of yourself inside a circle. Outside the circle, write the names of several things you consider personal enemies. Now draw an arrow pointing to the circle and label it, "Christ's unfailing love." Thank Jesus for surrounding and protecting you.*

TUESDAY, MAY 19

"...Of God our savior and of Christ Jesus our hope." 1 Timothy 1:1 (CEB)

MY FOURTEEN-YEAR-OLD GRANDDAUGHTER and I shared dinner together at a restaurant not long ago. She's a trivia buff, so facts and odd tidbits of information flowed. Shortly before I asked for the check, we talked about any homework she had yet to finish that evening.

"I have a quiz in health class tomorrow."

Middle school health classes. I remembered them well. "What topic?"

"Depression and suicide."

She didn't flinch. I did. "Oh, honey. I so wish you didn't have to discuss that topic at your age."

"But, Grammie, it's so important. A lot of my friends are really stressed out. Some of them think about hurting themselves, or worse. We *have* to be willing to talk about it."

My granddaughter serves as a peer counselor, her God-given compassion stepping to the plate no matter how unnerving the subject. I discovered a new reason to pray for her that evening.

I left our dinner together with a broken heart, aching for those who try to stumble through life without hope. Hope isn't an idea, an elusive dream, a commodity some feel is beyond their grasp. It is a person. Jesus.

"Christ Jesus our hope" is the phrase Paul used when writing to a young person of his day—Timothy. Many chapters follow that salutation at the beginning of Paul's letter. Perhaps these four words were the most important: "Christ Jesus our hope." —CYNTHIA RUCHTI

FAITH STEP: *When you pray today, consider using a term of endearment and courage like Paul used. "Christ Jesus our hope, I'm coming before You on behalf of young people who are hurting..."*

WEDNESDAY, MAY 20

Make them holy by your truth; teach them your word, which is truth.
John 17:17 (NLT)

I'M AMAZED AT HOW FAR e-mail scams and online hoaxes have come. Everyone has probably received a plea from a supposedly wealthy Nigerian promising a huge reward for assistance in getting his money out of the country. Now I'm seeing more subtle and sophisticated scams designed to gain access to my personal information and steal my identity. Recently I received notice that one of my online accounts would be deactivated unless I updated my information. The e-mail looked legitimate. But a couple of minor grammatical errors caught my attention; then I remembered that I use a different e-mail address for that account.

So far I've never clicked on a link that took me where I didn't want to go. Unfortunately, I'm not always as careful to recognize and avoid scams from a different source. Jesus warned that Satan is "a liar and the father of lies" (John 8:44). Every day Satan tries to gain access to my mind so he can plant lies there. He uses subtle deceptions designed to make me doubt my identity in Jesus. He wants to steal the joy of that relationship and replace it with fear, confusion, discontent, or rebelliousness.

Jesus prayed that His followers would be made holy by the Word, or "truth" (John 17:17). Daily time in the Bible will shape what I believe and how I act. Jesus also said, "I am the way, the truth" (John 14:6). His life shows me how to live in a godly way and proves His love for me, if I'm ever tempted to doubt it. Thank goodness I have these two sources to evaluate what I hear or think, because falling for one of Satan's scams has far more serious consequences than clicking on a suspicious computer link. —DIANNE NEAL MATTHEWS

FAITH STEP: *Are you in danger of falling for one of Satan's scams? Ask Jesus to direct you to the appropriate Bible verses to help you choose truth over lies.*

THURSDAY, MAY 21

As Moses and Elijah were starting to leave, Peter, not even knowing what he was saying, blurted out, "Master, it's wonderful for us to be here! Let's make three shelters as memorials—one for you, one for Moses, and one for Elijah." But even as he was saying this, a cloud overshadowed them, and terror gripped them as the cloud covered them. Luke 9:33–34 (NLT)

I LOVE READING ABOUT THE apostle Peter, probably because he depicts our own human tendencies so well: bold faith enough to move mountains one minute, a blundering fool with "foot in mouth disease" the next. His experience of Jesus's transfiguration is one example.

When Peter awoke on the mountaintop with Jesus and two other disciples, he witnessed the divine appearances of Moses and Elijah along with Jesus's transformation in His shining glory. Peter was so awestruck that he blurted the first thing that came to his mind: "Let's make three shelters!" He wanted to worship and remember this momentous occasion.

But the next minute fear filled his heart as a cloud overtook them all. A voice from heaven must have both terrified and comforted them as it affirmed Jesus as God's Chosen One.

When we experience the awesome presence of Jesus, true worship releases—and yes, maybe even requires—a response. That response might mirror Mary's reverent one as she pondered all the things (birth of Jesus) that had happened to her (Luke 2:19). Some might act like David, who couldn't restrain his exuberant joy, dancing over the return of the Ark of the Covenant, the symbolic presence of the Holy One (2 Samuel 6:14). Still others might cry out like Isaiah with emotions of unworthiness and humility. (Isaiah 6:5).

But however we respond, one thing's for sure: Jesus deserves our worship and a response that is both unique to us, and honoring to Him. —REBECCA BARLOW JORDAN

FAITH STEP: *How have you responded when you've experienced Jesus's presence? In your own unique way, worship Him today.*

FRIDAY, MAY 22

Jesus turned and said to Peter, "Get behind me, Satan! You are a stumbling block to me; you do not have in mind the concerns of God, but merely human concerns."
Matthew 16:23 (*NIV*)

RECENTLY MY HUSBAND WAS TEASING me, saying that we needed to buy a second microwave because he was having to wait three minutes to heat his leftovers while I was heating mine. We both had to laugh at his words. We have a term for comments like this. We call it our "first-world problems." While people in third-world countries are wondering if they can get enough water for the day, we are stressed because we have to wait to use the microwave, or because our shoes and belt don't match, or we're out of coffee creamer. These things frustrate us, but they should not hinder our souls.

It's easy to focus on what we can hold and taste and feel, while missing out on the spiritual side of us that matters forever. After all...we are human! Yet, as Colossians 3:2 (*NIV*) says, "Set your minds on things above, not on earthly things." How do we do this? Concern ourselves with the things of Jesus. What we focus on is what's going to get the most attention. Don't become distracted with things that won't matter in eternity. Yes, there are things we need to care for, but these should not consume us. Realize that Jesus is quick to point out areas where we have our mind on the wrong concerns, just as He did with Peter.

No one wants a reprimand, but sometimes we need it. Sometimes it takes a stern word from our Savior for us to realize we've been paying far too much attention to human concerns, and not enough to heavenly ones.
—TRICIA GOYER

FAITH STEP: *On a note card write ten earthly concerns that have been consuming too much of your time. Pray and turn them over to Jesus. Rip up the note card and every time you start to worry about those concerns, remind yourself that you have already put them in Jesus's hands.*

SATURDAY, MAY 23

For God so loved the world, that he gave his only begotten Son, that whosoever believeth in him should not perish, but have everlasting life. John 3:16 (KJV)

I MEMORIZED JOHN 3:16 AS a child, back when faith was so simple and life made more sense. I remember kneeling by the couch with my mother and asking Jesus to come into my life, believing He saved me from my sins, and walking down an aisle to tell the preacher the next Sunday. I was baptized soon after. The wonder of it all amazed me then, and looking back it amazes me now.

Although Jesus has never left me, the Christian life has had its ups and downs. I've had a few intellectual crises, seasons of extreme doubt, and plenty of times when I've questioned why certain things are allowed to happen in a universe where a loving God is in control. I hope I'm not jaded, but as I've matured it is not as easy for me to trust as it used to be.

And yet, a few Sundays back, I was sitting at my post at the piano during the invitation at church. As we sang "Only Trust Him" I saw out of the corner of my eye a little blonde-haired girl tug at her mother's sleeve. They talked for a moment and then slipped out of their seats and walked the aisle together. They knelt to pray with the preacher, and as the service ended, he announced that the little girl had accepted Jesus. She was positively beaming.

In the next few weeks I learned that the little girl was sharing her experience with her friends at school. She talked to her grandpa about being a missionary, and decided to give away her birthday presents to the poor. And I thought, *This still happens. Jesus is still happening to people.* I was challenged to open my heart a little wider, to trust like a child, and let Him happen to me all over again. —GWEN FORD FAULKENBERRY

FAITH STEP: *How long has it been since Jesus "happened" to you? Open your arms of faith like a child and receive all He is for you today.*

SUNDAY, MAY 24

O Lord, I am calling to you. Please hurry! Listen when I cry to you for help!
Psalm 141:1 (NLT)

MY SON AND HIS FAMILY came for a visit one Sunday afternoon. We sat in the living room while the grandkids played nearby. All was well until toddler Luke wandered into the kitchen and, seconds later, let out a cry of pain. He'd opened a drawer filled with cookbooks. The weight caused it to slide shut automatically, pinching his teeny fingers in its grip.

We jumped from our seats and ran, nearly tripping over each other in our haste to help him. Why? Because we love this child. We want to protect him. We care for his well-being. There's no way in the world we would have stayed on the sofa and ignored his pleas.

So it is with the Lord. He's attentive to His children's cries for help. The psalmist's words remind us of this truth, and they bring comfort to us when we're desperate for His aid. Sometimes we experience immediate relief, but at other times our pain lasts much longer than we wish. "When are You coming, Lord?" we cry. We might wonder if Jesus is ignoring us, if He's distracted by bigger concerns, or if He even cares about our hurts.

Rest assured, He does care. But He also cares about our growth and maturity. His rush to our aid is always right on time from an eternal perspective even when we might feel it's delayed.

Today, call out to Jesus. Tell Him your concerns. Ask Him to help you. Believe He'll respond, and then watch for His answer. —GRACE FOX

FAITH STEP: *I live near a hospital where helicopters land to pick up or deliver patients in crisis. Whenever I hear a chopper, I pray for the comfort and safety of those involved. Today you might hear a rescue vehicle siren. Pray that the Lord will help everyone involved.*

MONDAY, MAY 25

Together, we are his house, built on the foundation of the apostles and the prophets. And the cornerstone is Christ Jesus himself. Ephesians 2:20 (NLT)

MY FIRST MISSION TRIP WAS leading a group of teens, working with Christians from a different country, and trying to share Jesus with people who spoke broken English. I felt very weak, unsure, and limited! The more time we spent there, the more I realized how very different our culture and beliefs were. For Czechs discussing spiritual things was a private matter, but we were there to do that very thing! I longed for deeper connections.

Things began to change during our first morning devotion. As our team gathered with members of the Czech church we knelt in prayer. In English and Czech our prayers lifted up. They could understand only part of what our team was saying, and we couldn't make out more than a few words of their prayers, but Jesus's presence was strong. For the first time I truly understood the body of Christ. Together we are Jesus's house and Jesus's church—not just the Christians from different denominations in the United States, but around the world.

Only a handful of apostles and prophets set out to share the good news of Jesus, and from their humble efforts Jesus, the Word, spread. Those first believers faced the very same things I had—trying to share the Good News of Jesus with people very different from them. They did it by focusing on the key foundation—the cornerstone.

1 Corinthians 3:9 (NLT) says, "For we are both God's workers. And you are God's field. You are God's building." The church of God is made up of people from all around the world, with different traditions and worship styles, but in the midst of it all is Jesus, our cornerstone. —TRICIA GOYER

FAITH STEP: *Go outside and find a small rock to signify the cornerstone of Christ Jesus. Put it in a prominent spot. Every time it catches your eye, say a prayer for Christians—your brothers and sisters in Christ—around the world.*

TUESDAY, MAY 26

Christ is the visible image of the invisible God. He existed before anything was created and is supreme over all creation, for through him God created everything in the heavenly realms and on earth. Colossians 1:15–16 (NLT)

FACEBOOK HAS DELIVERED SOME SAD news to me lately. Through it I have discovered three people who've been battling serious illnesses. I went to school with two of them and met the third after college. Disease has already claimed the life of one, and it appears to be winning again. The third person is undergoing chemotherapy.

All three have young children who need their mom or dad. Some of those kids won't remember their parent and will grow up missing important history together.

I want to holler *NO!* Death never was supposed to be part of our human story. We were created by the Ancient of Days to share life with Him and the other members of the Trinity, Jesus and the Holy Spirit.

More and more I find myself looking at Jesus's big picture for comfort. Because of Him, all is not lost. At least two of those people have a vibrant, soul-saving faith in their Savior. They are promised life, despite the grief of earthly separation. Their spouses and children have hope through their shared legacy of faith. I am not sure about the third person, but I know my Jesus enough to trust that He spoke powerfully to her in the months of her sickness.

The Savior of the world has been Lord of ancient history from eternity past, and He is not ever going to relinquish that role. He went to the greatest lengths to offer life by dying on the Cross, and He certainly will continue drawing hearts to Himself as our earthly days fade.
—ERIN KEELEY MARSHALL

FAITH STEP: *Talk to Jesus about your feelings regarding death and an eternal future of life with Him. If you haven't accepted Him as your Savior, talk to Him about what's stopping you; then ask Him to meet you there with His answers.*

WEDNESDAY, MAY 27

When the people were full, Jesus told his disciples, "Gather the leftover pieces so that nothing will be wasted." John 6:12 (GW)

SEVERAL YEARS AGO MY HUSBAND and I attended the wedding of one of his coworkers. After the couple exchanged vows, they faced each other as a recording played of the bride singing, "Bless the Broken Road." Not being a country music fan, I'd only heard of the title. I couldn't help wondering at their song choice—until I listened to the lyrics. The bride and groom had both gone through divorce; they chose to focus on how their pasts had brought them to this point.

Every long lost dream led me to where you are
Others who broke my heart, they were like Northern stars
Pointing me on my way into your loving arms
This much I know is true
That God blessed the broken road
That led me straight to you.

We all have aspects of our past that we'd like to forget. Maybe we often imagine how much better our life would be now if we hadn't made that mistake or foolish decision. But what appears to be wasted years of our life may be exactly what shaped us into someone Jesus can use in a powerful way. It's usually our brokenness that leads us to Jesus in the first place and draws us into a relationship with Him.

And Jesus doesn't want to waste the broken pieces of our lives. All of our previous hurts, poor choices, and failed relationships can be used to make us more compassionate and equip us to minister to others in similar situations. They also help us become more dependent on the One Who walks our broken road with us. —DIANNE NEAL MATTHEWS

FAITH STEP: *Invite Jesus to gather up the broken pieces of your painful past experiences and use them all for His purposes. Then release your guilt and regret.*

THURSDAY, MAY 28

Don't be so naive and self-confident. You're not exempt. You could fall flat on your face as easily as anyone else. Forget about self-confidence. It's useless. Cultivate God-confidence. 1 Corinthians 10:12 (MSG)

IT'S HARD TO DEPEND ON God. I say I do. I want to. But too often I depend on myself, my judgment, my opinions, my decisions. Some of this is cultural, but I suspect it's common to all humans. We want our own way.

I take a problem to Jesus. Lay it out before Him. Sometimes I suggest a solution to the Creator of the universe. I ask for wisdom. For Him to change people's hearts. Sometimes I remember to ask Him to change my own. I say "Amen," but before too long I'm considering angles. Figuring out what to do. Coming up with a solution. More often than not, I implement it.

It rarely works.

What's wrong with this picture? Why, after praying, do I act as if it's still up to me to fix things? And where is God in the process?

The Apostle Paul warned the Christians at Corinth not to get caught up in wanting their own way and never to try to get God to serve them rather than the reverse. It's a classic mistake, trusting ourselves instead of Jesus, and it's one each of us is capable of making. I make it when I try to be the answer to my own prayers. Because, deep down, I don't trust Him.

But Jesus can be trusted. We can't (and shouldn't try to) control Him. He isn't a talisman we add to our lives. He can't be reduced to that. He made the world. He holds everything together. And Jesus, at great cost, brings us unto Himself.

He's got this. Believe it. —SUZANNE DAVENPORT TIETJEN

FAITH STEP: *The next time you pray, spend more time listening. Ask for the mind of Christ. Ask Jesus how to pray. Share your heart. Ask Him to share His with you.*

FRIDAY, MAY 29

But those who hope in the Lord will renew their strength. They will soar on wings like eagles; they will run and not grow weary; they will walk and not be faint.
Isaiah 40:31 (NIV)

ADDIE BROUGHT HOME A PICTURE of an eagle that he had colored at school yesterday. It had bright blues and greens in the feathers. On it was written the words, "God will help Addison Aughtmon soar like an eagle. He will carry Addison on his wings." Addison had written his name in a large declarative scrawl.

As I pinned it up on the refrigerator, I couldn't help blinking back some tears. Because that is my prayer for all my boys. That Jesus will carry them and give them wings to soar. That He will lift them up and keep them safe. That they will know that real living happens when we trust Jesus and He fills them with His goodness and His grace.

I don't know if Addison took all that in while he was coloring his eagle picture. I don't know if that Scripture filled him with the sense of joy that it filled me with as I read it. I don't know if at seven years old you understand all that Jesus has done for you. I don't know if you understand all that Jesus has done for you at seventy years old. But each year that I am alive, I realize the truth of this more and more. When I put my hopes in Jesus, things are different. When I trust the One Who calms seas and breathes life into us, it buoys me up. When I lean into His strength, I get to be more than I could ever be on my own. And those are the things that give me wings to fly. —SUSANNA FOTH AUGHTMON

FAITH STEP: *Watch a video of an eagle in flight. Notice how he soars with confidence, finding the best currents of wind. Ask Jesus to help you lean into Him today and draw strength from Him.*

SATURDAY, MAY 30

"Make straight paths for your feet so that if any part is lame, it will be healed rather than injured more seriously." Hebrews 12:13 (CEB)

WHEN I CROSSED THE COUNTY road in front of our house to get the mail today, I looked both ways first—basic rule of safety. I lingered at the edge of the road, marveling that I could look a quarter of a mile to my left, straight up a hill, and see no traffic. To the right, the ribbon of highway stretched at least a mile.

As a teen, I learned to drive on roads far different. The rolling hills of southwestern Wisconsin, where our family lived at the time, made for highways that twisted and contorted, dipped and dropped, curved and swerved. Imagine learning how to pass a car on roads with more double yellow than a Crayola factory on Canary Day.

Part of the teachings of Jesus included what one of the biblical writers talked about in the book of Hebrews—removing hazards in our faith journey, making the path straight for our feet. This verse in Hebrews 12:13 adds another dimension. A straight path aids healing for the lame and prevents further, more serious, injury.

Straight paths prevent emotional injuries that can cripple us. Straight paths keep us from faith injuries where we get tripped up in our thinking if we follow a direction contrary to God's Word. Straight paths smooth regret injuries that still sting. Straight paths—holding to the course Jesus charts for us—prevent relationship injuries or reinjuries.

Healing isn't a passive activity. We influence our healing by making straight paths, clearing the clutter, and eliminating blind corners, so we don't risk reinjury, incur fresh hurts. —CYNTHIA RUCHTI

FAITH STEP: *What are you consistently tripping over, stubbing your toe on, or dodging— spiritually or relationally? Why is it still in your way? Take one step today to drop that habit or repair that relationship.*

SUNDAY, MAY 31

It is useless for you to work so hard from early morning until late at night, anxiously working for food to eat; for God gives rest to his loved ones.
Psalm 127:2 (NLT)

LIVING IN A NEPALESE VILLAGE for two years meant immersion in that culture. Some aspects of life there fascinated me. Others not so much. Take, for example, the villagers' practice of planting themselves on my doorstep for hours. Occasionally they wanted to visit, but often they passed the time sitting in silence.

Can't they see I'm busy? I wondered. *How can they afford the time to just sit?*

I was in my midtwenties then. Time and age have matured my perspective. Hindsight tells me my neighbors knew something I didn't—they worked hard, and they understood their need for rest.

So did Jesus. Mark 6:6–13 tells about the workload He and His disciples faced. They traveled, taught, preached, cast out demons, and healed the sick. No doubt they grew weary physically, emotionally, and mentally. One day, when the disciples returned from a ministry tour, Jesus said, "Let's get away from the crowds for a while and rest" (verse 31). They climbed into a boat and sought a quiet place. Unfortunately the crowds found them, and Jesus—feeling compassion for them—began to teach again.

Jesus—God in flesh—understands our human limitations; therefore He commands us to stop and rest. That's often easier said than done in our rush-rush world. We might have to learn to delegate. We may have to say no (without feeling guilty). We may need to release a current obligation.

We're not machines programmed for endless duties. We're humans, formed from dust with mortal bodies. Let's learn from the Nepalese and make time to rest as we ought. —GRACE FOX

FAITH STEP: *Memorize Matthew 11:28 (NLT)—"Then Jesus said, 'Come to me, all of you who are weary and carry heavy burdens, and I will give you rest.'" Thank Jesus for the invitation and ask Him to give you His rest.*

MONDAY, JUNE 1

The Lord answered, "If you had faith even as small as a mustard seed, you could say to this mulberry tree, 'May you be uprooted and thrown into the sea,' and it would obey you!" Luke 17:6 (NLT)

"LOOK, MAMA! A BOOTIFUL FLAH-LER!"

As a mom, I do my best to update my children's baby books. It's hit or miss depending on the busyness of the season, but "flah-ler" definitely made it into Calianne's book. Flah-ler and callapitter. At five years old, she still mispronounced that one, and I wasn't too eager to give it up and correct her. All in good time.

We all begin small. But look at how a baby grows. From complete dependence and inability to do anything but sleep, snuggle, cry, drink, and fill a diaper, a child tackles rolling over, crawling, real food, walking, running, talking, and any number of "Me-do-it!" skills—and that's just in the first year or two.

We must never underestimate the power of small. Jesus values small things. Just reread today's verse or Google "Jesus and children."

Jesus adores meager beginnings. Take the mustard seed. You've heard this verse in some form or another. A tiny faith can move Jesus's hand to move mountains.

If we don't trust that He can do mighty things through our faith in Him, then we need to ask Him to grow the seed we do have. If we wonder whether we have a seed at all, He'd love to start there with us.

Embrace your faith, no matter what its size, and offer it to the Lord. Take Him up on the challenge and ask Him to move whatever mountains He wants to through your trust in Him. —ERIN KEELEY MARSHALL

FAITH STEP: *On a piece of paper, draw a picture of your faith, as if it were a seed. Put the drawing in a drawer, ask Jesus to grow it, and see if you draw a bigger seed six months from now.*

TUESDAY, JUNE 2

Then he said to the crowd, "If any of you wants to be my follower, you must turn from your selfish ways, take up your cross daily, and follow me." Luke 9:23 (NLT)

EVER SINCE HIGH SCHOOL, I have struggled with my weight. Although I was able to mostly maintain a healthy size for years, when I had my children I became overweight and could not seem to establish better eating and exercise habits with any consistency, no matter how hard I tried.

By the grace of God, that has changed. After trying every diet in the world and failing, there is one thing I have learned to do, and I believe it has made all of the difference for me. It's simple, and probably obvious to anyone who has changed a bad habit: I take it one day at a time.

A week ago I had a very stressful few days. On a couple of them I could not exercise and I ended up overeating, and eating the wrong things. In the past this would have destroyed my whole plan. I would have felt like a failure and thrown up my hands, deciding to quit. It was tempting to feel that way in this situation, but instead I let it be what it was: a bump in the road. And then I got right back to business.

I think this principle is biblical. When Jesus tells us to take up our Cross daily, I believe He knew how hard it would be, and how weak our flesh is even though the spirit is willing. The whole journey can seem daunting. But one day at a time, we can bear that Cross. Pretty soon we're a long way down the road of faith and we can see how far He's led. One day at a time, He'll get us where He wants us to go.
—GWEN FORD FAULKENBERRY

FAITH STEP: *Is there an area of your life that is overwhelming to you? Commit it to Jesus today, and do what you can. Then get up and do the same thing tomorrow.*

WEDNESDAY, JUNE 3

For this reason I bow my knees before the Father. Ephesians 3:14 (NAS)

I AM A MOTHER OF six children, three who are grown, and three little ones whom we've adopted in the last three years. I've always known it's important to pray for my kids, but I pray for them more than ever these days. Why? I've seen how prayers for children when they are little turn into heritages of faith when they get big. Seeing how my prayers were answered for my first three fuels my prayers for the younger three.

I prayed for godly spouses for my children, and my oldest son married a wonderful young woman whom I adore. I prayed that my children would have servant hearts and would be bold in sharing the good news of Christ, and my oldest daughter is currently a missionary in Central Europe. I prayed that my children would discover the unique gifts that Jesus planted inside them, and my third son is finishing his first novel at age nineteen. Did my prayers make a difference in their lives, in their futures? Yes. In the strange way Jesus works, it's our prayers that help mold our children's futures.

Author and pastor Mark Batterson writes, "Prayer turns ordinary parents into prophets who shape the destinies of their children, grandchildren, and every generation that follows." When we pray, we submit our will to Jesus's. When we pray, our hearts are transformed, too, and our deeds follow the desires of our hearts for our children.

What do you wish most for those around you? Pray for those things. Your prayers invite Jesus to work in the lives of young people. Your prayers today will mold generations. If you have children and grandchildren, nieces or nephews, today is the day to pray for them, and in many tomorrows others will reap the rewards. —TRICIA GOYER

FAITH STEP: *Buy a journal for each of your children and grandchildren and start writing out prayers for them as Jesus puts them on your heart. Save the finished journals for a special, future gift.*

THURSDAY, JUNE 4

*And because of their unbelief, he couldn't do any mighty miracles among them
except to place his hands on a few sick people and heal them. And he was
amazed at their unbelief. Mark 6:5–6 (NLT)*

THE THOUGHT OF JUMPING OFF the high diving board terrified me when I
was eight years old. Thankfully my swimming instructor was tenderhearted. He treaded water below and encouraged me to muster my courage.
"Everything's okay, Grace," he said. "I'll catch you. Trust me."

I chose to believe my teacher. I closed my eyes, plugged my nose, and took
the plunge. *Kersplash!* Miracle of miracles, I not only survived but I actually
enjoyed myself. I walked home later feeling like an Olympic gold medalist.

My success that day had nothing to do with my instructor's capability;
he was strong and able regardless. It depended on whether or not I believed he could protect me from drowning. When I chose to believe that
was true, I experienced his strength and skill.

Jesus's friends and family in Nazareth faced a similar crisis of belief.
Unfortunately, they doubted His abilities. *He's just a carpenter's son,*
they reasoned. They "were deeply offended and refused to believe him"
(Mark 6:3). The result? They failed to experience His power.

We face the same crisis of belief today each time we carry a concern
about our health, money, the people we love, or our ability to accomplish
a God-given task. The truth stands: Jesus is omnipotent God and wants
to demonstrate His power in and through us. Do we believe He's able or
do we limit Him with our failure to believe?

Let's not repeat the same mistake that Christ's friends and family made.
Let's respond in a way that expresses faith in Him. Let's amaze Him with
our belief. —GRACE FOX

FAITH STEP: *Name at least one concern about which you're praying today. Now
tell Jesus that you believe He's able to resolve that concern in ways that exceed your
imagination. Invite Him to leave you in awe at His answer.*

FRIDAY, JUNE 5

And when you stand praying, if you hold anything against anyone, forgive them, so that your Father in heaven may forgive you your sins. Mark 11:25 (NIV)

CHURCH FIGHTS HAVE BEEN GOING on since there have been churches. Two thousand years ago, Paul urged two churchgoers in Philippi, Euodia and Syntyche, to reconcile. They'd worked with Paul to spread the Gospel, but something went wrong. Feelings got hurt. Grudges were held. They chose not to forgive. Paul asked a friend to remind the two women that Jesus could come back and find them at odds.

We don't know how it turned out, but we've probably seen something like it in our own churches or maybe in our own lives. Because it's familiar, we may have lost the sense of urgency Paul felt. Forgiveness is not optional—it's essential.

Forgiving and being forgiven are connected. We say this every time we pray the Lord's Prayer—*Forgive us our trespasses as we forgive those who trespass against us.* We are asking to be forgiven the way we forgive others. This should be a scary thought for many of us.

Still, we may feel justified. We call it righteous anger and think God will take our side. We can't understand why He wouldn't.

It may not be that He won't, but that He can't. God respects our free will. He doesn't force us to say "I'm sorry," and shake hands like children. By refusing to forgive, we block the channel through which forgiveness flows to us. Unforgiveness hurts the one who won't forgive.

Jesus spells out a better way. He says to love, to do good, and to pray for our enemies. It's better to allow ourselves to be wronged than take the chance of wronging someone else. When we react to pain with love, we are like our Father in heaven. —SUZANNE DAVENPORT TIETJEN

FAITH STEP: *You may feel unable to forgive. Ask Jesus to make you willing. Or ask Him to make you willing to be willing. Bitterness will hurt you. Jesus will help you lay it down.*

SATURDAY, JUNE 6

"And be sure of this: I am with you always, even to the end of the age."
Matthew 28:20 *(NLT)*

YEARS AGO I ENJOYED PLAYING hide-and-seek with my children; now I have an excuse to indulge in the game with my grandkids. But toddlers don't always grasp the concept of hide-and-seek. That was made clear when I tried to play one-on-one with my grandson who was two years old at the time. As soon as I announced, "Ready or not, here I come!" Roman always responded with "Here I am, Nana!" When it was my turn to hide, he finished his counting with the question, "Where are you, Nana?"

I have to admit there are days when I feel like crying out, "Where are You, Jesus?" It might be because I'm weary of bringing the same prayer request to Him over and over with no sign of an answer. Or maybe I don't see any evidence of His working out a problem or troubling situation in my life. During those times it's tempting to wonder where He went or why He seems so distant from me.

Jesus never plays hide-and-seek with us. Before He ascended to heaven, He promised to always be with His followers, even to the end of this age. That's a promise I can surely count on, regardless of my feelings or my circumstances. Disobedience and unconfessed sin will diminish my fellowship with Jesus. Loneliness, fear, and troubles may cause me to doubt His presence in my life. But I never need to ask Him, "Where are You?" Deep down I know the answer: He is always right here with me.
—DIANNE NEAL MATTHEWS

FAITH STEP: *Sit down in a quiet spot and invite Jesus to fill your soul with a sense of His presence. Sing a hymn or praise song, read a favorite Scripture, or just sit quietly as you focus on His promise to always be with you.*

SUNDAY, JUNE 7

In Christ, we, though many, form one body, and each member
belongs to all the others. Romans 12:5 (NIV)

I AM TOLD THAT MY generation is leaving the church in droves, and I certainly understand disillusionment with any sort of organized religion. Just the other day someone who is a believer but doesn't attend church anywhere asked me about my own experience. I think she was surprised to find out that I go to a little country church that has about seventy-five members. I'll admit it surprises me too.

I could have told her all of the things that are wrong with my church. None of our problems are unique nor would they be surprising to an outsider. They are true of most churches, I am sure. I'm not talking about gross abuses that have to be addressed. I'm talking about everyday stuff. Problems are not hard to find when you get a group of human beings together.

What I told her instead is that even though I have issues with organized religion too, I have embraced the fact that I need my church. I need my brothers and sisters in Christ. Like the verse says, we belong to each other. That means I belong to the ultraconservatives in my church just like they belong to me, even though we don't always agree. I belong to the nonmusicians even though I'm a musician. And I belong to the people who have known Jesus longer than I have as well as the ones who are just beginning.

At its best, church is not utopia. Instead, it's a place where we get to practice all of the things Jesus taught us: loving our neighbors, being patient, kind, tenderhearted, forgiving. It's not a place where we're all the same. In fact, we need have nothing else in common if we have the main thing: Jesus. He is the glue that holds us together—in all of our differences—as His body. —GWEN FORD FAULKENBERRY

FAITH STEP: *What kind of "body-building" exercises have you been doing lately? Think of one you can implement today.*

MONDAY, JUNE 8

Therefore, as God's chosen people, holy and dearly loved, clothe yourselves with compassion, kindness, humility, gentleness and patience. Colossians 3:12 (NIV)

GOD, GIVE ME PATIENCE...and I want it right now!

We are an instant society. We've been conditioned to live with speed. From fast food to our microwaves, we are used to getting things quickly. My pastor says that while waiting for a page to download on his computer, he can get impatient.

Perhaps the hardest time we have exercising the gift of patience is as we wait for prayers to be answered. *How long, O Lord?* We are tempted to doubt that Jesus has our best interests in mind. We let Him be our king, but when He takes so long, we are eager to be in control. It's hard to be patient that Jesus will answer, and we have to remind ourselves, *In His time.*

In the fall when the leaves change, we admire their colors. But in order for the leaves to produce such an array of reds and golds, the leaves must die.

Winter sets in. It can appear a bleak season—lifeless. But with the onset of spring, we realize that nature was working undercover to produce the new growth of April and May.

Patience requires living each day even when it doesn't look like anything is growing or improving. There was a season when I cried out the same prayers over and over for my kids to get along better with their stepdad. Would it ever happen?

Even when we give up on Jesus, Jesus doesn't give up on us.
—ALICE J. WISLER

FAITH STEP: *What a friend we have in Jesus! Sing this familiar hymn today and thank Him for bearing your burdens and patiently carrying them for you.*

TUESDAY, JUNE 9

Consider the ravens: They do not sow or reap, they have no storeroom or barn;
yet God feeds them. And how much more valuable you are than birds!
Luke 12:24 (NIV)

NATURE DOCUMENTARIES FASCINATE ME. I'M endlessly grateful to the photographers who spend years in the ocean depths or on the rainforest canopy capturing intricate details of the enthralling wildlife that God has created. Whether I'm noticing squirrels chase each other across the backyard, or watching a film about snow leopards in Tibet, the time spent appreciating nature always teaches me new things about our Creator.

I'm reminded that He is imaginative, that He has built a universe rich with endless variety. When my daily problems seem to be an impossible mess, the God who solved the challenge of creating life that can exist at the South Pole will have no trouble showing me a creative solution.

The created world also shows me He has a plan. All the parts work together with unique qualities and purposes. I'm reassured that when my life experiences seem convoluted, one day they will make sense, and I'll understand the value of even strange twists and turns.

Studying nature also reminds me of the lavishness of God's love. From the iridescent dragonfly's wings to the odd and beguiling silhouette of a seahorse, everything He made overflows with improbable and unnecessary beauty. At times when I wonder where I fit, I can remember that He has made a world that celebrates uniqueness, and that He cherishes me.

When Jesus reminds us to notice how wildflowers grow, how our heavenly Father watches even tiny sparrows, or how mustard seeds transform, He's reminding us that God cares about the intimate details of our lives, and we can trust Him. —SHARON HINCK

FAITH STEP: *Watch a nature documentary today, and thank Jesus for these reminders of our Father's love.*

WEDNESDAY, JUNE 10

Be happy with those who are happy, and weep with those who weep.
Romans 12:15 (NLT)

As a young believer, I searched for answers to give grieving family members: some verse of Scripture, some "magical" words that would ease their pain. But futile attempts always left me—and I'm sure, them—feeling inadequate and still hurting. An answer to their "whys" seemed distant, and impossible.

When I began writing greeting cards, I found words that seemed to convey what I could not verbally, usually expressing simple empathy, but pointing toward Jesus, our true Comforter. Still, words alone can't fill empty arms and aching hearts.

Through the years as I matured, walked with Jesus a few decades, and experienced sorrows of my own, I stopped trying to find answers and perfect words. Trite phrases from those early years disappeared. In time, Jesus brings good from our losses (Romans 8:28) and healing to get past the grief. However, some holes in our hearts won't be completely filled this side of heaven.

Only Jesus can turn our mourning into dancing (Psalm 30:11). We can't do that ourselves. No one can shortcut the process of grief for another. Thankfully, because of Jesus, we don't grieve as those who are without hope (1 Thessalonians 4:13).

Jesus is truly our burden-bearer (Psalm 68:19). But as a pastor reminded us recently at the funeral of a sweet sixteen-year-old, Jesus has also given us the responsibility of caring, of empathizing, and yes, of helping to bear the burdens of others (Galatians 6:2). Sometimes the best thing we can do, including our hands-on acts of love and service, is to be there, to hurt with them, and to "weep with those who weep."

Burdens were never meant to be shouldered alone.

—Rebecca Barlow Jordan

Faith Step: *Think about those you know who have lost loved ones or experienced sorrow in some way. Ask Jesus to help you find sensitive ways to help bear their burdens.*

THURSDAY, JUNE 11

Now all glory to God, who is able, through his mighty power at work within us, to accomplish infinitely more than we might ask or think. Ephesians 3:20 (NLT)

As soon as I stepped through the door, it caught my eye. My granddaughter Lacey had set a tiny plastic potted flower on the windowsill of her bathroom. The yellow bloom moved from side to side, back and forth, while the two green leaves waved up and down. That little flower seemed so full of joy and excitement, as though it might burst at any moment. I assumed there was a battery in the pot, until that evening I walked in and found the flower perfectly still. That's when I knew it was a solar-powered flower.

I felt a bit sad seeing the flower not moving, but I understood the spiritual lesson it offered. Just like that plastic flower, I need to stay close to my source of power. I can't live out a godly lifestyle through my meager human strength; I need Jesus's divine power to work *in* me, *on* me, and *through* me. He will enable me to choose the Christlike response to people and situations rather than a response based on emotions or my self-centered nature. He will provide the strength I need for daily living and for carrying out the kingdom work He assigns me.

My granddaughter's solar-powered flower loses its ability to move once the sun goes down, or if it's removed from the windowsill. Thankfully, I have Jesus inside me all the time. I can draw strength and joy from Him through prayer, Bible study, praise and worship, or simply meditating on what His presence in my life means. And that's enough to get me to wave my "leaves" up and down for joy any day. —DIANNE NEAL MATTHEWS

FAITH STEP: *Have you been too far away from the Son lately to operate in His supernatural power? What do you need to do today to get closer to Jesus so He can work through you in miraculous ways?*

FRIDAY, JUNE 12

"He fell on his face at Jesus's feet and thanked him." Luke 17:16 (CEB)

SOMETIMES I WONDER HOW PEOPLE without children in their lives learn things. Nieces and nephews, offspring, grandchildren, a Sunday school class, a team to coach, a nursery, babysitting, childcare, adopting, fostering…We learn so much by being around children.

Over coffee the other day, young parents told me the story about their two-year-old daughter learning how to pray. They'd videotaped one of her first attempts at praying as she knelt beside her toddler bed. In essence, this is the transcript from her lyrical, little-girl prayer:

"Thank You, Jesus, for my friends. And…thank You, Jesus. Jesus, thank You. And…Jesus, thank You so much. Thank You soooooo much, Jesus. (Deep breath.) Jesus, thank You. Thank You, Jesus. Thank You, Jesus, for my friends. Thank You so much. Jesus, thank You. Thank You, Jesus." That wasn't the end. But by this point in the video, the parent holding the camera could hardly stay still. Suppressed laughter shook the camera.

How precious! And how precious it must be for Jesus, on the receiving end of such a prayer. He must have observed that scene and thought, *Finally! Finally someone gets it—how to really pray.*

Simply thanking Him. Nothing fancy. Expressing gratitude in childlike but loving exuberance.

What well-crafted prayer could compare to a sincere heart expressing its gratitude. "Jesus, there's really nothing more to say beyond 'Thank You.'"
—CYNTHIA RUCHTI

FAITH STEP: *Spend at least a portion of your prayer time today, if not all of it, saying your heart's version of "Thank You so much, Jesus." Don't be surprised if you hear a whisper from heaven that sounds like divine joy.*

SATURDAY, JUNE 13

Keep your servant also from willful sins; may they not rule over me. Then I will be blameless, innocent of great transgression. Psalm 19:13 (NIV)

THE OTHER DAY MY MIDDLE son, Will, was begging to stay home with his older brother, Jack, while I took the youngest son, Addison, to the store with me.

The following conversation ensued.

Me: If I leave you with your brother while I go to the store, will you promise me no violence?

Will: We can't promise you that.

Me: That's what I was afraid of.

Jack: Don't worry, Mom. If he doesn't do what you ask, I'll beat him up.

Me: Everybody get in the car.

I loved Jack's and Will's honesty. They know their weaknesses. Pounding each other.

I don't tend to struggle with pounding people as much. But I have a lot of other sins. Pride. Coveting. Ungratefulness. To name a few. Luckily, Jesus loves me anyway. He is changing my heart daily. And He is the One Who can keep me from sinning.

Just like I loaded up Will and Jack in the car to keep them from injuring each other, Jesus offers me a way to escape my weaknesses. By inviting Him into my life, my thoughts, and my actions. When I come to Him with my struggles, I invite Him into the areas in my life where I am weak. When I ask for His help, He is willing and able to give it. When I share the areas in my heart that are dark, He is able to flood my life with His light.

He doesn't expect me to be strong on my own, He only expects me to invite Him into my life. He does the rest. And that is the best news yet.

—SUSANNA FOTH AUGHTMON

FAITH STEP: *Write the sins you struggle with on smooth pebbles and take them to a creek. As you fling them in the water, ask Jesus to keep you from sinning so they won't rule over you.*

SUNDAY, JUNE 14

Where can I go from your Spirit? Where can I flee from your presence?
If I go up to the heavens, you are there; if I make my bed in the depths,
you are there. If I rise on the wings of the dawn, if I settle on the far side
of the sea, even there your hand will guide me, your right hand
will hold me fast. Psalm 139:7–10 (NIV)

WHEN OUR GRANDDAUGHTER WAS ABOUT a year old, I sat on the floor with her and played a game she created. She pulled a blanket over her head and waited for me to say, "Where did she go? Oh no! I can't find her." She giggled, swayed, and waited for an impressive length of time to build the suspense. Then with a flourish, she pulled the blanket off her head and appeared while I squealed in delight and hugged her. We played that game about fifty times in a row.

In her little mind, with that blanket over her head she was invisible.

There have been times I've slipped into that same childish understanding of Jesus. Recently I was irritated at someone. I didn't want those feelings. I especially didn't want Jesus to know I was so impatient and unloving. So instead of bringing Him the problem of my heart, I just avoided talking to Him. Subconsciously, I imagined that if I didn't look at Him, He couldn't see me.

Not only is it ridiculous for me to play "peek-a-boo" with Jesus, it also keeps me away from the One Who can heal my heart, give me grace to forgive others, and teach me how to overcome. Jesus was already well aware of the battle in my attitude. Once I pulled the blanket off my head and remembered He saw and knew me—and loved me anyway—He helped me respond more kindly the next time I was with that difficult person. —SHARON HINCK

FAITH STEP: *Talk to Jesus today about the parts of your heart you most want to cover.*

MONDAY, JUNE 15

Every moment you know where I am . . . You both precede and follow me. You place your hand of blessing on my head. Such knowledge is too wonderful for me, too great for me to know! Psalm 139:3–6 (NLT)

I SETTLED INTO MY SEAT on a Boeing 747 bound for Romania and sighed. Every weekend for two months prior I'd traveled in Canada for speaking engagements. I'd logged several thousand miles and was about to log a few more, this time across the Atlantic.

The plane taxied and took off. I closed my eyes and pondered Psalm 139: "I can never escape from your spirit! I can never get away from your presence! . . . If I ride the wings of the morning, if I dwell by the farthest oceans, even there your hand will guide me, and your strength will support me" (verses 7, 9–10).

I rested during the flight, and I reveled in the assurance these words brought. No matter where I traveled, I was not alone. Christ—omnipresent, omnipotent, omniscient God—went with me. What better companion could I wish for?

Christ promises His presence to His followers no matter where we go. He's with us whether we fly across an ocean or ride the subway. He's with us whether we descend the stairs into our basement or ride an elevator to the top floor of a towering skyscraper. He's with us whether we work from home or commute. We can talk with Him and count on Him as we would a best friend who never leaves our side.

We're never alone. Never.

The Psalmist wrote, "That knowledge is too wonderful for me." I feel the same way. The reality of Christ's ever-presence leaves me in awe. How about you? —GRACE FOX

FAITH STEP: *Matthew 28:20 records Jesus's words to His disciples before His ascension into heaven. He said, "And be sure of this: I am with you always, even to the end of the age." What difference does this knowledge make for you today?*

TUESDAY, JUNE 16

He must become greater and greater, and I must become less and less.
John 3:30 (NLT)

THIS PAST YEAR I'VE BEEN on an odyssey in healthy eating and exercise and I've lost almost one-hundred pounds. When people see me, especially if they've known me only since I've been overweight, the reactions are hilarious. *You're wasting away to nothing! You look like a different person!* And my personal favorite: *My goodness, Gwen! There's hardly anything left of you!*

I was joking about this with one of my friends the other day and I told her how happy I was that I've decreased in size. Later, though, the whole scenario got me thinking about the above verse, which in another version says, *He must increase, but I must decrease.* (KJV)

As I've lowered my weight, it's as if layers have practically peeled off. You can see the contours of my face a lot better now, my cheekbones and jawline, and you can also see the wrinkles on my forehead. I have basically no upper body strength, but where my arms were rather plump before, now you can see the outlines of muscles. Even my feet have gone down a size.

What does it mean to become less and less that He may become greater? I think it's a similar process. As we peel off layers of self, more of Jesus is revealed. Anger melts into forgiveness. Weakness gives way to strength. Pride is replaced by meekness, and bitterness succumbs to peace. All we are lacking is swallowed up in love. What a huge compliment it would be in that sense for others to say, *My goodness! There's hardly anything left of you! All we can see is Jesus!* —GWEN FORD FAULKENBERRY

FAITH STEP: *Pray and ask the Lord to show you what qualities need to decrease in your life that Jesus may increase in you.*

WEDNESDAY, JUNE 17

"Yes, I am the vine; you are the branches. Those who remain in me, and I in them, will produce much fruit. For apart from me you can do nothing." John 15:5 (NLT)

GROWING UP ON OUR SMALL family farm in Tennessee meant spending all summer working in the cotton fields. Chopping down weeds with a hoe was exhausting work. But it was also difficult for my preschool brother to spend the long, hot day at the edge of the field entertaining himself. One morning, Phillip became captivated by the masses of morning glory growing near the field. Their trumpet-shaped flowers dotted with dew were a vivid blue, his favorite color. He must have spent a couple of hours pulling branches off the vines to take home. Later that morning, the rest of us joined Phillip in the shade to take a break and sharpen the hoes. We found him distraught. The back of our station wagon was filled with drooping branches with withering blossoms.

Perhaps the connection I feel with Jesus's teaching in John 15 can be traced back to that childhood memory. The analogy of the vine and branches provides the perfect picture of life in Christ. I'm already united with Jesus since I accepted the gift of salvation made possible by His death on the Cross. Still, it's vital for me to stay closely connected with Jesus through prayer, Bible study, worship, and obedience to His commands.

Being connected with Jesus the Vine is an unspeakable privilege and joy. But it also carries the responsibility to nurture that relationship. Only then will I draw spiritual nourishment from Him that leads to a fruitful life. Only then will my faith and my life bloom in ways that will never fade or wither. —DIANNE NEAL MATTHEWS

FAITH STEP: *Think of at least one step you can take this week to stay more closely connected to Jesus. Write it on a slip of paper to keep in your Bible as a reminder.*

THURSDAY, JUNE 18

---

*Yet what we suffer now is nothing compared to the glory
he will reveal to us later.* Romans 8:18 (NLT)

MY HUSBAND AND I RECENTLY finished our state's foster-care training to be respite workers at a nearby foster facility. This facility includes home environments for these precious kids, who can heal and be loved by dedicated house parents. We'll help out while those house parents go on date nights.

I feel blessed to be part of the healing for these kids who have lost so much. But I am also sobered to be what they'll need for the few hours I'll spend with them every month or two.

Lately I've been feeling generally at a loss regarding loss. How do we deal with huge sorrows on earth? How do we alleviate suffering from the death of dreams or connections or loved ones or promises made and broken?

If it weren't for the hope of wholeness and joy in heaven, this life would become too much. Even with hope in mind, the blessings yet to come through Jesus don't remove heartaches that can last oh so long on earth.

Take Job, for instance. He lost his first ten children, and even though the Lord blessed him with ten more children, he lived his remaining years without those first unique people he loved as a father. What exactly does Jesus's healing cover?

I don't have all these answers, but I have to fall back on what I do know and trust about the greatness of my Savior and our heavenly Father.

This life is temporary. This pain is temporary. An eternal focus on the One Who was and is and is to come will more than make up for every wound on earth.

Someday there will be no loss for those who call Jesus Savior, and I believe that He will wipe away every tear. Hope in that promise makes celebrating today a possibility, even in loss. —ERIN KEELEY MARSHALL

FAITH STEP: *What losses have you grieved? List them, and commit each one to Jesus to cover and heal. Memorize Revelation 21:4.*

FRIDAY, JUNE 19

Simon Peter said, "You're the Christ, the Messiah, the Son of the living God."
Jesus came back, "God bless you, Simon, son of Jonah! You didn't
get that answer out of books or from teachers. My Father in heaven,
God himself, let you in on this secret of who I really am."
Matthew 16:16–17 (MSG)

WHEN MY CHILDREN WERE SMALL, they often asked questions about Jesus. "Did He really wear a beard? How did He travel? When He comes back, will He ride on a camel?" In their childish minds they couldn't picture Jesus except from some artists' imaginations in Bible storybooks.

Jesus gave the disciples ample opportunities to know what He was like. After all, they lived with Him for three years. He taught them by example and through His teaching. One day Jesus asked Peter point blank: "Who do you say that I am?"

Surprisingly, in spite of Peter's misconceptions and blunders, he replied, "the Christ, the Messiah, the Son of the living God."

Jesus knew that even with Peter's limited understanding and experience, he got it. But books and knowledge hadn't revealed Jesus's true identity as the Messiah to Peter. That took a divine transaction.

It's the same way for us. Like children, we can't wrap our minds around Who Jesus really is, though Bible studies and teachers can point the way to Him. But through Jesus's divine nature as God, He opens our eyes and shows us His true identity. —REBECCA BARLOW JORDAN

FAITH STEP: *If you have a personal relationship with Jesus, when did you first realize Who He really was? Celebrate that divine transaction today by writing briefly your own story and thanking Jesus for revealing Himself to you.*

SATURDAY, JUNE 20

"One of the disciples, the one Jesus loved dearly, was reclining against him, his head on his shoulder." John 13:23 (MSG)

A QUIRK IN MY SCHEDULE had me traveling five hours away to a metropolitan area four different times within three weeks. At the peak of construction season. Every alternate route seemed destined to be included in the construction fury. Weaving through concrete barriers and twenty-five mph speed limits on the superhighway on the first trip convinced me I could make better time on the second trip if I took the scenic route through small towns and suburbs.

Although I was introduced to towns I'd never met before, the slogging pace of speed-up/slow-down and the incessant voice of my phone's navigation guide telling me to "turn here, turn there, make a U-turn" changed my mind about the scenic route saving me from the construction bottlenecks.

Trip number three had me back on the superhighway, requiring more than twice as much time as it should have taken to travel that distance. Concrete barriers narrowed the highway even further and large signs shouted, "Warning! No shoulders!" I gripped the wheel and focused on maneuvering through the treacherous, endless construction zone. Shoulders would have helped. They always do.

Comfort comes from having a strong shoulder to lean on in chaos. A trusted friend. A spouse. A mentor. As I think back on what the "Warning! No shoulders!" sign did to my driving experience, I hear an old familiar song stirring: "Leaning on Jesus. Safe and secure from all alarms."

That favorite invitation of His resonates through history: "Come. Lean on Me. I'll get you through this. I have Shoulders with a capital S."
—CYNTHIA RUCHTI

FAITH STEP: *You may be trying to navigate a path that seems to have no shoulders, no border between you and the concrete dangers of life. Even before your circumstance changes, make it a point to thank Jesus daily for providing a strong, steady, dependable, unfailing shoulder to lean on.*

SUNDAY, JUNE 21

I will say of the Lord, "He is my refuge and my fortress, my God, in whom I trust." Psalm 91:2 (NIV)

I HAVE A VIVID MEMORY of when I was a little girl on summer vacation with my family. We had gone to visit the historic city of Boston. My sisters and brother and I followed our parents through the city, trekking on the freedom trail, taking in the Old North Church, Paul Revere's house, and a ship where we could reenact the Boston Tea Party.

We were having the time of our lives when the dense humidity gave way to a summer downpour, sending us scurrying to a little alcove with an overhang as we waited out the storm. I remember being hunkered down with my shirt plastered to my skin. I wasn't scared. I wasn't impatient. I knew we were safe and we just had to wait.

The moment that we invite Jesus to be the Lord of our lives, He becomes our safest place. Our retreat. Our refuge. He is the one we can run to when life breaks out in a downpour.

He doesn't promise that crazy things won't happen to us in life. Or that we won't have struggles before us. I keep hoping for that. But what He does offer us is a life hidden in His. A life that is secure in Him when everything else is going nuts. We can take our hopes, our fears, our hurts, and our dreams, and trust Him. He will never leave us or forsake us. Even when life is stormy. —SUSANNA FOTH AUGHTMON

FAITH STEP: *Walk around your house. Notice how it protects you from the elements outside, whether it is cold, hot, sunny, raining, or snowing. Thank Jesus for shielding you and being with you in life's storms.*

MONDAY, JUNE 22

Therefore God has highly exalted him and bestowed on him the name that is above every name, so that at the name of Jesus every knee should bow, in heaven and on earth and under the earth. Philippians 2:9–10 (ESV)

MY DAUGHTER HOLLY INTRODUCED ME to Words with Friends several months ago, and now I'm hooked. This Scrabble-like game has taught me a few things, though. In one of my first games, I began to feel a bit cocky since I was so far ahead. Then Heather, my opponent, earned ninety-five points with a single word! I didn't know that was possible, but I learned that she got extra points for using up all her letters in one move. No way could I catch up after that.

On the other hand, there are times when I don't expect to win because of my low score. Then I see how I can combine a triple word space with a double letter space or two, and, suddenly, I'm back on top. As Holly likes to remind me, "Just one word can make all the difference."

I've also learned that one powerful word can make all the difference in my day. That word is "Jesus." Meditating on Jesus and all that He has done for me transforms my mood instantly. It changes my perspective from an earthly one to a heavenly one. It encourages me to live as a winner regardless of my circumstances.

When I'm lonely, His name reminds me that He promised never to leave me. If problems are getting me down, I can think about the perfect eternal home that He's preparing for me. When I'm feeling unloved, unworthy, or inferior, I remember that Jesus thought I was worth dying for. The name of Jesus does make all the difference—in my attitude, in my day, and in my life. —DIANNE NEAL MATTHEWS

FAITH STEP: *Spend a few moments meditating on what the name of Jesus means to you. Write out your thoughts and use them as a prayer, thanking Him for His presence in your life.*

TUESDAY, JUNE 23

*Love is patient, love is kind. It does not envy, it does not boast, it is not proud.
It does not dishonor others, it is not self-seeking, it is not easily angered,
it keeps no record of wrongs. Love does not delight in evil but rejoices with
the truth. It always protects, always trusts, always hopes, always perseveres.*
1 Corinthians 13:4—7 (NIV)

WHEN MY FIRST BABY CAME along almost twenty-four years ago, I decided that I could be the world's best mom. I wouldn't make the mistakes my parents had or treat my child as I've seen harassed mothers do, scolding their children in the grocery store. I was smart, I was gifted, I could do this job of parenting.

Then one day my children showed that they were human and, worse yet, I realized I was human too. Faulty, sinful, in need of grace. There were times I had no answers. There were times I felt everything I was doing was wrong. And yes, I even yelled!

I have always said that a mother's love is the closest thing to God's love. A mother's love nurtures, believes, and hopes.

Still, I am humbled by how lacking it is, for it is not a perfect love as is Jesus's love for us.

May our prayer be: Help us not to withhold our love toward children, no matter what their behavior is or what path they're on. Help us to see that Your love, Jesus, for our children is far greater than our love will ever be. Amen. —ALICE J. WISLER

FAITH STEP: *What can you do to encourage your children and/or those you are close to who are struggling with parenting?*

WEDNESDAY, JUNE 24

*From the time the world was created, people have seen the earth and
sky and all that God made. They can clearly see his invisible qualities—
his eternal power and divine nature. So they have no excuse whatsoever
for not knowing God. Romans 1:20 (NLT)*

LAST SUMMER MY FAMILY TOOK a two-thousand-mile road trip from our
home in Arkansas to visit family in Montana. There isn't much to see
along the way. There are few large cities on this path. Small towns dot the
landscape. There are rolling hills and sprawling prairies. Mostly there is
sky—lots of sky. And, amazingly, it's the sky that we still talk about most.

There were lightning storms that danced and flashed in Wyoming.
In Kansas we almost got caught in a tornado. We looked up and dark,
ominous clouds were spinning above us like a washing-machine drum.
Thankfully, they didn't funnel downward. And in Montana we saw the
largest rainbow we've ever seen. It stretched like an arching, colorful highway to heaven—so close we felt as if we could drive up to it and onward
into the clouds. My preschoolers still talk about that rainbow and about
how Jesus gave it to us that day.

Sometimes in life we get so used to staring up at the same sliver of sky
that we forget how expansive the sky truly is. Driving for dozens of hours
and thousands of miles reminded us how big the sky is…and it's a good
reminder of Jesus's eternal power and divine nature.

When we take time to wonder at the marvels of Jesus's creation, our
hearts fill with awe. There is something inside us that views the vast, wonderful sky and can't help but declare, "He is here!" And then we see that
we have no excuse except to lift up a chorus of praise! —TRICIA GOYER

FAITH STEP: *Take a drive in an area that you aren't very familiar with, and allow
yourself to marvel at the sky that continues to stretch outward. Thank Jesus for His
eternal power and divine nature as you drive.*

THURSDAY, JUNE 25

I can do all things through Christ who strengthens me.
Philippians 4:13 (NKJV)

A FEW YEARS AGO, MY husband and I went through a terrible season in our marriage. It was a time when keeping promises was hard, and I honestly didn't know if we would come out together on the other side. All I knew is that in my heart I felt it was right to try. For the sake of our family, our commitment to God, and the life we had built together, we had to try.

There were moments when it seemed impossible. The hurt seemed too much to bear. When a person is happy, family life is still not always easy. When one is falling apart inside, it's downright excruciating. You want to work through personal stuff but it feels like there is no time. You want to protect others. You want to provide stability and security, but at the same time you feel these have been taken from you. You have nothing left to give. You can't breathe.

I can see from the experience why so many homes are crumbling. I can see why people can't handle it, why they give up. Life chews you up and spits you out sometimes. I'd have never been able to handle it without Jesus.

Looking back over that experience I can say that I lived Philippians 4:13. There were things I thought I'd never have to do, things I certainly never wanted to do, things I thought I'd never be able to do. But I did them through Jesus. He strengthened me.

I can't tell other people *what* God wants them to do. We must study the Scriptures, pray, and listen to the Spirit for guidance. But when you know what He wants you to do, I can tell you that He will give you the strength to do it. You can count on Jesus, no matter what.
—GWEN FORD FAULKENBERRY

FAITH STEP: *What is the hardest thing you are facing right now? If you know what God wants you to do, gird up your loins and do it. You can do all things through Christ Who gives you strength.*

FRIDAY, JUNE 26

For you were continually straying like sheep, but now you have returned to the Shepherd and Guardian of your souls. 1 Peter 2:25 (NAS)

AS A YOUNG ADULT, I met other Christians with amazing stories of salvation and dramatic change: a woman who fled a cult and now served Jesus; a drug addict who turned to Christ and was freed from bondage; an angry rebel who met Jesus through a quiet conversation at a coffeehouse and was set on a new road.

I never tired of hearing the testimonies of those who were rescued by Jesus. As I spoke about my faith to others, I sometimes wished for that sort of story. But I soon realized that my Shepherd's efforts in my life are also tireless and powerful.

We are all continually straying. Like sheep we are lured off course by a choice bit of greenery, or frightened by a shadow, or swept along by the herd. Despite my determination to listen to my Shepherd, I often find myself knotted in the thorns of faithless worry, or stranded on a ridge of broken relationships, or stalked by wolves of doubt and despair. My prayers must sound like pathetic bleats sometimes—wondering how I got so turned around, and crying out for a protector.

What a gift to know that our Shepherd hears us! He rescues us, gathers us into His arms, and returns us to wholeness. He guards our souls against the predators that threaten. Whether our story is one of the Shepherd snatching us back from the edge of destruction, or His daily coaxing us back from our wandering, we can rejoice in the beautiful experience of returning, of knowing we are safe in His arms. —SHARON HINCK

FAITH STEP: *Think about where you are prone to wander, and ask for the Shepherd to return you to His arms.*

SATURDAY, JUNE 27

When I was a child, I spoke and thought and reasoned as a child. But when I grew up, I put away childish things. 1 Corinthians 13:11 (NLT)

MY MOM SEWED MANY OF my clothes when I was a child. For years I remember seeing stacks of colorful material folded in her closet or sewing area. As soon as the pile diminished, a new stack replaced it. Mother shopped the fabric sales for bargains continually. So I did too.

She taught me the basics, and in school, I also learned the art of sewing. Only, my finished products looked childish (to me) compared to my mom's professional touch.

After I married, I continued to buy fabric on sale, which I stored out of sight in plastic tubs. Occasionally, I'd attempt an outfit for myself or my daughters, or something creative for a craft sale. And I'd keep buying material. The stacks grew larger—mostly unused. I was spending on autopilot.

Eventually, writing and ministry consumed my time, so I reduced the fabric stacks and sold the machine.

I asked my mother one day why she always bought so much fabric. She said during the war years, supplies were rationed. When they could buy, she learned to stock up at sales—and continued to do so for years.

I chuckled, realizing I had copied a practice that profited me little. Important for her, but not for me. And I wondered how many other thoughtless "autopilot" activities or habits I could label as childish.

Jesus reminds us through the apostle Paul that childish practices are expected—for children. But when we're adults, it's time to put away anything childish, including whatever drains our pocketbooks, our time, or our growth in Christ. —REBECCA BARLOW JORDAN

FAITH STEP: *Make a list of childish behaviors that slip into your life. Ask Jesus to help you replace those with meaningful, wise habits that will help you to become like Him.*

SUNDAY, JUNE 28

I reflect at night on who you are, O Lord, and I obey your law because of this. Psalm 119:55 (NLT)

HAVE YOU EVER STAYED AWAKE at night when your brain wouldn't slow down despite your body feeling exhausted? I have. I often lie awake for hours on the night before an early morning flight too. A nagging doubt says I'll sleep through my alarm, so my subconscious reacts as though I've injected it with caffeine.

Insomnia wracked my body for nearly four months following leg injuries. That period provided opportunity to pray during the night. It also tested my ability to control my thoughts when I couldn't sleep. This was critical, for allowing dark thoughts to run amuck would have meant drowning in a pool of self-pity, fear, or even anger.

Hour after hour, night after night, I had to reel my thoughts into a positive place—focused on the Lord. I meditated on Scripture verses, stopping to ponder key words and visualizing what they meant. I prayed for my husband, kids, grandkids, and extended family members. I prayed for friends far and near, for the Church, for our country, and for missionaries.

Conversing with the Lord during those sleepless nights deepened and sweetened my faith. So did fixing my mind on the character of Christ. Thinking about His attributes, such as holiness, compassion, boldness, and wisdom, caused me to realize afresh how marvelous He is, and that He deserves all my affection and praise.

The next time sleep evades you, embrace it as an opportunity to focus your undistracted thoughts on Christ. Meditate on Who He is and trust Him to deepen your faith as a result. —GRACE FOX

FAITH STEP: *What character quality do you admire most about Christ? Find a Scripture that extols this quality. Write it on a recipe card (for spiritual nourishment) and then put it on your nightstand so you will have easy access to it the next time you can't sleep at night.*

MONDAY, JUNE 29

But because Jesus lives forever, his priesthood lasts forever.
Therefore he is able, once and forever, to save those who come
to God through him. Hebrews 7:24–25 (NLT)

As I WRITE THIS, MY jaw is still sore from dental surgery. I recently had my fifth procedure done within four years—on the same tooth. It started with a root canal. A year later, that root canal had to be redone. The next year, an apicoectomy. When that didn't solve the problem, the endodontist tried something else. He warned me that if the infection came back, the tooth would have to come out. But several months later, he persuaded me to have a second apicoectomy. Only time will tell if this last-ditch effort can save the tooth, or if it's time to give up on it.

I'm so grateful that Jesus never gives up on anyone, and that He has the power to save completely, once and for all. In contrast with the Old Testament priests who had to offer sacrifices over and over, Jesus offered a one-time atonement for sin. By willingly laying down His life, Jesus paid the penalty for my past, present, and future sins. Nothing more needs to be done. He simply asks me to believe in Him as Savior and Lord and accept His gift of forgiveness and eternal life.

I don't need to worry about being good enough or working hard enough to earn Christ's favor. I don't have to wait until this life is over to find out the eternal destiny of my soul. Jesus settled that with His supreme act of love on the Cross. And I can only be amazed that He considered me worth saving, and that He will never give up on me.
—DIANNE NEAL MATTHEWS

FAITH STEP: *Are there days when you don't feel worthy of Jesus's sacrifice or you struggle with doubts that Jesus has truly saved your soul? Meditate on John 3:16 and let its wonderful message sink into your heart and mind.*

TUESDAY, JUNE 30

"Jesus said to him, 'Get up! Pick up your mat and walk.'" John 5:8 (CEB)

I'M IMPRESSED BY SMALL DETAILS—THE way topstitching jazzes up a leather glove, the fine hairs on a newborn promising eyebrows soon, the silky feel of the fluff-parachute on milkweed seeds...

At least two of the stories of Jesus healing lame men included an unusual detail. For the man let down through the roof by his friends and the man who lay lame beside a pool of supposedly healing waters, Jesus didn't just say, "Be healed." He told both men to pick up their sick beds and haul them away.

The "pick up your mat" detail for the man by the pool is repeated three times in the retelling. The man lame for thirty-eight years wasn't told to dance a jig or to run around the block to prove he'd been healed. The instruction was, "Pick up your mat and walk."

It could have been a test of faith. By Jewish law, it was illegal to move a bed on the Sabbath. Was the lame man going to follow the law, or follow Jesus?

It could have been a test of strength. Jesus may have been saying, "Roll up your mat and carry it on your shoulder. Only well people can do that."

It could have been a test of obedience. "I don't care how weak you think you are," Jesus might have left unsaid. "I'm telling you you're healed."

It could have been a sign that the sickbed was no longer needed. "Get rid of that mat. It's been your home for thirty-eight years, your prison. You're free now because of Me."

Eternity will be too short to hear all the stories-behind-the-stories. But knowing Jesus was intentional about that detail—among others—keeps me reading and looking for clues. —CYNTHIA RUCHTI

FAITH STEP: *In your alone time with Jesus, do you rush past the small details? Take a deep breath. Carve out a larger spot of time. And linger today over the unabridged versions of Bible stories you know well.*

WEDNESDAY, JULY 1

Now we see things imperfectly as in a poor mirror, but then we will see everything with perfect clarity. 1 Corinthians 13:12 (NLT)

THE SEATTLE CHILDREN'S MUSEUM PROVIDES hours of enjoyment for little people. Against one wall rest "magic" mirrors. Their concave and convex surfaces portray kids' images as anything but normal. Contorted, they are—short and stubby or long and pencil-thin.

On a recent visit there, my preschool-age grandsons stood before these mirrors. The boys twisted and turned, stretched and squatted. Their imperfect reflections drew delighted giggles and more antics.

Scripture says that we see our circumstances imperfectly. The reflection rarely evokes laughter and delight. It often appears unfair, harsh, or painful.

I experienced this when my dad died in Canada while I was ministering in Eastern Europe. Circumstances made it impossible for me to return for his memorial service. I felt alone during the days following his death. I wondered why God, in His sovereignty, allowed this timing. I struggled with feeling as though serving Him required too great a sacrifice.

Seven years have passed since that experience, and I still don't see God's purposes clearly. But this I know—someday Jesus will set it right. "All that I know now is partial and incomplete, but then I will know everything completely, just as God knows me now" (1 Corinthians 13:12 NLT).

Maybe you, too, have experienced heartache or puzzling circumstances. Gazing into the mirror of your situation only yields a contorted image of what's really happening. Doubts arise. Questions abound. Hope struggles to survive.

Take heart. Jesus knows the end from the beginning. Trust Him. Someday everything will become clear. —GRACE FOX

FAITH STEP: *Are you facing a situation that leaves you with more questions than answers? Tell Jesus how you feel, and resolve to trust Him in the midst of uncertainty. Thank Him in advance for promising to clear your vision someday.*

THURSDAY, JULY 2

God, my shepherd! I don't need a thing. You have bedded me down in lush meadows, you find me quiet pools to drink from. Psalm 23:1–2 (MSG)

IT WAS A HOT DAY in Central Illinois and lambs ringed the galvanized tank, panting like puppies. They were quiet, waiting for water—and trusting that someone would provide it.

The larger sheep, resting in the shade, had drunk enough that the lambs couldn't reach the water's surface. Nearly empty, the tank was rimmed with algae. The green gunk seemed to come back overnight this time of year.

I tipped the tank over, scrubbed it and hosed it out. The lambs were noisy now, smelling fresh water. I lowered the hose in front of one of the ram lambs. He approached. Then retreated. I coiled the hose in the bottom of the tank. The water level rose but, even without splashing, the hose created a current that circled the tank. Lamb after lamb leaned in to drink only to back away.

Why? Because sheep can't drink from moving water. They don't lap water like dogs; their noses are immediately above their mouths. To drink, they place their lips on the water and suck, much like we drink through a straw. If the water isn't still, they either can't make a seal or they get water up their noses (or both). Shepherdless, they'd die of dehydration next to a rocky stream or get sick from stagnant puddles.

Why should we care? Because God does.

David called the Lord his Shepherd, who knows, loves, and cares for us in ways we, like my sheep, can't begin to comprehend.

Thank God, we don't have to.

We have a Good Shepherd, Jesus, who laid down His life for His sheep.

May we, like my lambs that hot day, trust Him to provide what we need.

—SUZANNE DAVENPORT TIETJEN

FAITH STEP: *Do you have to understand in order to trust? Sheep don't know what the shepherd is thinking. They just know the Shepherd. And follow Him. You can too. Try it today (even if you don't understand).*

FRIDAY, JULY 3

My heart says of you, "Seek his face!" Your face, Lord, I will seek.
Psalm 27:8 (NIV)

LAST WEEK MY HUSBAND AND I spent some vacation days on the north shore of Lake Superior. We enjoyed seeing a full moon over the vast expanse of water, hiking beside waterfalls in pine and birch forests, and reconnecting with the peace that we find "up north." One of our favorite activities is to walk along pebbly coves on the shoreline looking for agates. We aren't actually very good at finding them, but we collect any stone that looks interesting to us, whether it's valuable or not. I'm fascinated by the variety of colors and textures of the stones. I also love the thrill of searching for beauty.

When we returned home, I filled a glass vase with some of our recent finds. Each time I look at them, I remember the sound of water lapping the shore and the hint of spruce in the air.

The stones also remind me that each day I'm on a hunt even more exciting than the search for agates.

Sometimes Jesus is easy to spot. A praise song on the radio may speak to my heart and comfort me in a place where I've been grieving. Or a friend may e-mail me a note of encouragement, and I hear the breath of Jesus in the words. Those moments shine like precious gems that sparkle along the edge of the water.

Other times, I have to squint, dig, or shift my focus to a new angle to find the blessing of His grace. Still, it's always worth the search. Jesus is involved in our lives, and each day we have an opportunity to watch for His blessing, His guidance, and His presence. —SHARON HINCK

FAITH STEP: *Find a rock, stone, or pebble today that has hidden beauty—perhaps in its color, form, or texture. Put it in a place where you'll see it often, as a reminder to seek the beauty of our Lord's face.*

SATURDAY, JULY 4

Then He who sat on the throne said, "Behold, I make all things new."
Revelation 21:5 (NKJV)

WHEN MY SON HARPER WAS a baby, he suffered from severe acid reflux. We took him to several doctors, tried a million different things, but not a lot helped in his case. He was in a great deal of pain, and let us know it. The worst times were at night.

In order to try to relieve him, I would sit upright in a recliner and hold him while he slept. I got very little sleep, and this went on for months. Besides not sleeping, I was deeply concerned for him, and felt helpless. This was a somewhat dangerous combination of troubles, and I became depressed.

During those times I felt my life had become consumed by Harper's illness. The doctors who told me he'd grow out of it seemed cruel. Night after night as I faced that chair with my crying baby I remember feeling it would never get better. I could not see any light at the end of our tunnel.

John Eldredge writes that one of the most poisonous of all Satan's whispers is simply, "Things will never change." That lie kills expectation, trapping our heart forever in the present. To keep desire alive and flourishing, we must renew our vision for what lies ahead.... Jesus has promised to "make all things new."

One day the pain was gone. The miracle of becoming more upright, sitting, standing, and walking, had apparently changed Harper's digestion to the point where his esophagus healed. This meant I could start sleeping more and quit being so worried about his well-being. I remember being almost shocked to lie down in my bed again and forgo our more difficult routine.

That experience taught me the importance of perspective. We must always hold on to the promise that Jesus makes all things new. No matter how dark things are, nor how long the night seems, morning is coming.
—GWEN FORD FAULKENBERRY

FAITH STEP: *Are you going through a valley of shadows right now? Cling to the promise that Jesus makes all things new.*

SUNDAY, JULY 5

You are precious in my eyes, and honored, and I love you.
Isaiah 43:4 (ESV)

WE'VE ALL FACED THE LOSS of an important relationship at one time or another. It stings, sometimes badly and for a long time.

When I was grieving a friendship that had faded, the loss struck my confidence. Life had taken us in different directions, but I still felt abandoned, unimportant, and forgotten. And I struggled with unworthiness. I couldn't shake off wondering why my friendship wasn't worth holding on to. Or more honestly, why wasn't *I* worth it?

I had made the last few efforts to communicate, and eventually I had to admit that any desire for friendship had become one-sided. I couldn't help second-guessing whether it always had been that way.

I felt let down, but I also questioned my value as a friend and even as a person. Sure, I know Jesus loves me for me, but who am I irreplaceable to on earth?

Our relationships are tied to our personhood, for better or worse. They have the power to get to our deepest insecurities, and oftentimes relationships create those self-doubts. If we don't solidify whose opinion matters most about us, then we are forever at the whim of others' acceptance or rejection of us.

I am still working through some lingering feelings about missing this friendship, but the core of who I am has been strengthened by today's verse. My Savior thought I was worth sacrificing everything for, and I am still on His mind—24–7. —ERIN KEELEY MARSHALL

FAITH STEP: *Write a letter to Jesus about your relationship losses. Go deep on this, because admitting your hurt comes before you can really feel His healing.*

MONDAY, JULY 6

Therefore confess your sins to each other and pray for each other so that you may be healed. The prayer of a righteous person is powerful and effective.
James 5:16 (NIV)

"THANKS FOR BEING AUTHENTIC AND real," a friend said to me the other day.

Truth is, I wasn't always this way. I used to keep all my problems to myself, thinking that if I shared them, others would see me as weak.

Then my son Daniel died. My husband spiraled into mental illness and left the home, wanting a divorce. I was thrown into raising three young children on my own.

Then came a new marriage, my kids having to adjust, lack of adequate employment, financial chaos, health and relationship issues within the home, and countless other struggles.

All of these brought me to my knees. I couldn't keep silent anymore. I couldn't pretend all was well when it clearly wasn't. I had to share. I knew that I needed others who had experienced the heartache of life.

When I seek the listening ears of others in similar situations and learn to trust them with my problems, Jesus opens the door for them to feel comfortable and safe to share their difficulties with me. The result has been rich friendships and truth. —ALICE J. WISLER

FAITH STEP: *Ask God to give you friends to be authentic with. Pray for authentic believers within your church.*

TUESDAY, JULY 7

To them God has chosen to make known among the Gentiles the glorious riches of this mystery, which is Christ in you, the hope of glory. Colossians 1:27 (NIV)

THE ARK OF THE COVENANT was the most sacred object in the tabernacle, but 1 Samuel 4 records a time when the Israelites treated it as a charm to help them achieve a military victory. Instead, the Philistines easily defeated the Israelite army. When Eli, the high priest, heard that his two sons had been killed and the Ark captured, he died. When Eli's daughter-in-law learned of the deaths and the fate of the Ark, she went into labor. Although the Israelites considered the birth of a son a great blessing, she named her baby Ichabod ("Where is the glory?"). Just before she died, she declared, "The glory has departed from Israel, for the Ark of God has been captured."

There may come a time when we feel as though the glory has departed from our life. Failures in business, relationships, or ministry can make us long for "the good old days." Age, health problems, or disability may force us to live with limitations that keep us from serving God in ways that we used to. Instead of growing despondent and wondering if He can still use us, we need to grasp the truth of Who lives within us, infusing our life with strength, power, and glory.

To think that Jesus Christ lives in me! Colossians 3:4 promises that when He appears, I will share His glory. Although I don't fully understand what that means, I'm certainly looking forward to it. His indwelling presence right now and His promise for the future encourage me to shine for Him regardless of what's going on around me. It also assures me that I never have reason to feel like the glory has departed from my life.
—DIANNE NEAL MATTHEWS

FAITH STEP: *If you sometimes feel as though your life doesn't reflect God's glory as much as it used to, memorize Colossians 2:7 and 3:4.*

WEDNESDAY, JULY 8

They do not fear bad news; they confidently trust the Lord to care for them.
They are confident and fearless and can face their foes triumphantly.
Psalm 112:7–8 (NLT)

ONE MONTH HAD PASSED SINCE my husband's biopsy. Now we sat alone in the doctor's office, waiting for the physician to appear and give us the results.

"Do you have a sense about what he'll say?" I asked.

My husband shook his head. "I haven't got a clue. But I'm sure of one thing—our future rests in God's hands. He's got everything under control."

Thirty minutes later, we left the office having received the diagnosis: cancer. Now we face oncology appointments, treatment options, and a future filled with question marks. Uncertainty looms for us, and—humanly speaking—we have every reason to feel scared. After all, we've lost several close friends our age to cancer in the past two years.

Perhaps your story is similar to ours. Bad news concerning your finances, health, marriage, or a family member has hit home, and you have no clue what the future holds. If so, I want to encourage you with this truth: Jesus is aware of your circumstances and cares deeply for you.

Together let's declare that Christ's wisdom, sovereignty, faithfulness, love, and power rule over every detail of our situations. Let's keep our eyes focused on Him and His promises, and let's thank Him for walking our journey with us. Let's remember that no foe can stand in His presence. According to Psalm 112:7–8, doing so will make us confident, fearless, and triumphant. Bad news might change our lives, but the good news about Christ and His trustworthiness remains our constant. —GRACE FOX

FAITH STEP: *Write today's key verse on a recipe card. Now add Psalm 118:6 "The Lord is for me, so I will not be afraid." Post the card where you'll see it often. Memorize the verses, and meditate on them as you fall asleep at night.*

THURSDAY, JULY 9

This is a large work I've called you into, but don't be overwhelmed by it. It's best to start small. Give a cool cup of water to someone who is thirsty, for instance. The smallest act of giving or receiving makes you a true apprentice. You won't lose out on a thing. Matthew 10:41–42 (MSG)

I SAT AT MY COMPUTER one morning, reading the latest news. Tears streamed down my face as I watched a video of the Philippines typhoon and its aftermath. Villages disappeared. Families lost. Businesses destroyed. The task of rebuilding, of finding survivors, of restoring the devastation would be monumental. I grieved for the people and the losses.

When Jesus sent His disciples out two by two, they must have felt overwhelmed at Jesus's instructions: "Bring health to the sick. Raise the dead. Touch the untouchables. Kick out the demons" (Matthew 10:8, MSG). Entire villages were lost in sin and hopelessness. The lame, the leper, the blind, and the sick all needed Jesus.

Their work was huge, seemingly impossible. Not only that, they would often face opposition. But Jesus gave them His power and authority, knowing the difficulty of their assignment.

As a writer and a minister's wife through the years, I've often been overwhelmed by the magnitude of ministry needs. Where do I start? How can I possibly make a difference with such a tremendous task? But Jesus gives the same encouragement to me as He did to His own disciples. "Don't be overwhelmed. Start small. The smallest act of giving makes you a true apprentice."

Ministering to others, whether to Filipino typhoon survivors, friends or family members, or your next-door neighbor requires the same thing: a dependence on Jesus's power. He will multiply our smallest efforts into huge kingdom results. —REBECCA BARLOW JORDAN

FAITH STEP: *Thank Jesus for His available power to accomplish whatever tasks He gives you. Write down one small thing you can do to make a difference in someone's life today.*

FRIDAY, JULY 10

*But Moses protested to God, "Who am I to appear before Pharaoh?
Who am I to lead the people of Israel out of Egypt?" God answered,
"I will be with you. And this is your sign that I am the one who has sent you:
When you have brought the people out of Egypt, you will worship
God at this very mountain." Exodus 3:11–12 (NLT)*

WOULDN'T IT BE EASY IF Jesus guided us by way of signs? "Lord, show me the man I'm going to marry by having him wear a red polka-dot shirt on our first meeting." Or, "Lord, let me know if this is the right job for me by having the interviewer clear his throat as he introduces himself." It would be easier, don't you think, to know exactly what Jesus is asking you to do?

In the Bible Jesus was gracious enough to lead some people by signs, but it's not normally the way He works. In Exodus, God told Moses He was going to give Him a sign, and it most likely wasn't what Moses expected. In Exodus 3:12, God tells Moses that the "sign" would be his success. God wasn't going to give Moses something to look at now, but rather something he'd experience later...when the job was done.

As an author, I find that Jesus's spirit often speaks to my heart, "I see the finished book on the shelf." To the worried mom who's concerned about her pregnancy Jesus may whisper to her heart, "I see you snuggling your child to your chest." We want something to cling to now—a tangible hope—yet Jesus points us to a fulfilled future. He asks us to trust Him, trust He can see the future, and to take the first step. —TRICIA GOYER

FAITH STEP: *Find a 3-by-5 card and write:* Action is where faith becomes real. *Below that write down one step of faith that Jesus is asking you to take.*

SATURDAY, JULY 11

I urge you to pray for absolutely everything, ranging from small to large. Include everything as you embrace this God-life, and you'll get God's everything. Mark 11:24 (MSG)

As A FORMER SHEPHERD, I feel qualified to answer the question, "Can a sheep pray?" My answer: *mmm*, no—not really.

The members of my flock knelt, but not in prayer. They didn't speak in words. They occasionally concentrated—when they were in labor or expected a treat. They looked thoughtful when ruminating—but who knew what was going on in their minds?

Whole books are written about prayer. Jesus taught His followers how when they asked Him. Praying can seem difficult. But it isn't, in its essence. Prayer is talking to God—conversation with the Creator.

My sheep got their point across. They bellowed their desire for grain when they caught sight of me near feeding time. They protested during shearing, and leaned sociably against my leg when I paused in the pasture. And they called for help when they got in trouble.

We used electric woven wire fencing and trained the sheep to avoid it. When we presented our yearly refresher course on electricity, we left the windows open and kept an ear out for entangled sheep.

Yes, it's a stretch to say my sheep were praying when they bleated out their panic, but Jesus was right when He called us His sheep. The connection between the cry of a distressed lamb and a prayer of desperation would've been very clear to His contemporaries.

And just like I opened my windows and tuned my ears to my sheep, He stands ready to hear us. We have only to ask.

—SUZANNE DAVENPORT TIETJEN

FAITH STEP: *Jesus urges us to pray, like He did, for everything. Too often, I pray as an afterthought or when I've exhausted other options. Today carry your concerns, your hopes, to Jesus first. Watch for the difference.*

SUNDAY, JULY 12

"Jesus said to them, 'When I sent you out without a wallet, bag, or sandals, you didn't lack anything, did you?' They said, 'Nothing.'" Luke 22:35 (CEB)

WHAT WAS JESUS TRYING TO teach His disciples by instructing them not to take a wallet or luggage or even spare sandals when they traveled with Him? Was He showing that He was all they ever needed? Did He want them to learn that their dependence had to be on Him alone? Was He instructing them in the humility of accepting help from others—a bed for the night, a meal, a borrowed coat when temperatures dropped?

Did He hope they'd realize they could get along on fewer belongings than they imagined? Or that their success depended on their traveling light? Or that they'd be safer from thieves along the journey if they had nothing worth stealing?

Was it focus that Jesus cared about most? With nothing in their hands, nothing to distract them, would the disciples cling more diligently to Jesus's words and to the ministry of caring for the people's physical and spiritual needs?

The more I think about it, the more value I see in the "no baggage" directive. What if I walked into my day conscious of a "no baggage, no wallet, no extra sandals" mentality, intensely focused on Jesus, on His words, on His mission, the mission He passed on to us? What if I measured success not by how much I accumulate but on how little I need to survive, if I stay close to Jesus?

What would I lack? Nothing. —CYNTHIA RUCHTI

FAITH STEP: *Is an accumulation of things holding you back from what Jesus is asking you to do? Is there anything you own that is beginning to "act" as if it owns you? Are you willing to take a step toward the freedom of no baggage?*

MONDAY, JULY 13

Walk in the light, as He is in the light. 1 John 1:7 (KJV)

AT THE BEGINNING OF EACH semester, I assign Zora Neale Hurston's essay *How it Feels to Be Colored Me* in all of my classes. We read it, discuss it, and then the students have to write an essay about how it feels to be them. I love this exercise because it is so life-affirming.

Hurston describes her life as a young African-American growing up in Florida in the early 1900s, and how she comes to realize that people look at her differently because of the color of her skin. There's this great moment when she writes that in spite of the difficulties, the injustice, the pain, she refuses to be *tragically colored*. She goes on to write, *I do not weep at the world, I am too busy sharpening my oyster knife.*

In class we talk about this choice and how it is really one that transcends race. It's a choice we all must make. I look out at my classes and see people my parents' ages who have lost their jobs. Single mothers, immigrants, people battling disease, others living in poverty. Whatever our backgrounds, we all have reasons we could weep at the world. And just like Hurston, we must make a choice.

I believe the choice is spiritual—light or darkness. We can choose to see ourselves as victims, to be bitter, to be angry, to feel sorry for ourselves. The truth is we all probably have legitimate reasons, if in varying degrees. It's empowering to know that we can choose to walk in the Light, to view the world as an oyster ripe for the opening, rather than to weep at it in regret.

Walking in the Light as Jesus is in the Light is a daily choice. Sometimes for me it is moment by moment. But, like Hurston, I know it is worth it. It's the difference between life and death. —GWEN FORD FAULKENBERRY

FAITH STEP: *Instead of walking unthinkingly through your day, make the choice to walk in the Light, putting your focus on Jesus to guide you into all truth.*

TUESDAY, JULY 14

And everyone who calls on the name of the Lord will be saved. Joel 2:32 (NIV)

WHAT'S IN A NAME? A LOT.

I recently heard of a young woman who'd worked as a summer intern at a local business. Her proficiency earned her the business owner's respect. When the summer ended and the woman prepared to return to university for her final year of classes, the owner thanked her and said, "You're welcome to apply for a job here after graduation. Feel free to use my name as a reference."

Did the woman land the job? Of course.

Good names carry influence and can open doors for us in amazing ways. They also challenge us to make a difference. Names such as Mother Teresa, Nelson Mandela, or Rosa Parks, for instance, motivate us to live for a higher cause than simply meeting our personal needs and wants. They inspire us to exercise courage and set aside our comfort for the sake of others.

A good name carries influence and inspiration. But one rises above all others known to mankind. It does what no other name can do. That name is Jesus.

Mocked and scorned, Jesus's name brings peace to those in pain, power to the weak, and hope to those in despair. Best of all, it offers us forgiveness of sins and grants eternal salvation. Whether whispered in private or proclaimed in public, the name of Jesus—acknowledged as the answer to our heart's deepest needs—changes our lives now and purchases a place in heaven for us when we place our saving faith in Him.

Names come and go over time. But Jesus's name—powerful and life-giving—remains forever. —GRACE FOX

FAITH STEP: *Prayerfully whisper the name of Jesus several times. In an attitude of worship, invite Him to teach you more about the power of His name. Ask Him to show you what it really means to end prayers with, "In Jesus's name, amen."*

WEDNESDAY, JULY 15

His divine power has given us everything we need for a godly life through our knowledge of him who called us by his own glory and goodness. 2 Peter 1:3 (NIV)

OUR TWELVE-YEAR-OLD SON, JACK, KEEPS hacking my husband's e-mail account, sending me messages that look like they are from Scott. This morning I received this e-mail: "Hey, should we give the kids fifty dollars now or later?" For a moment I actually thought, "Did we talk about giving the kids fifty dollars?" And then I realized that I was dealing with Jack. I had to laugh.

Our kids are tremendously creative when it comes to getting what they want. However, what they need and what they want are two different things. Scott and I do a good job of providing them with everything that they truly need. But they tend to think that they need a lot more money, candy, and video games than we do.

We can't blame them. We are pretty similar in how we approach Jesus in prayer. We keep hinting at what we really want, telling Him what would best improve our lives and how we would like to be blessed. But Jesus knows what we truly need.

What is even more remarkable is that He has already given us everything we need to live out the life He designed for us. Sometimes we forget that.

What we need is His divine power flooding our lives. His power to forgive. His wisdom. His clarity. His strength in our current situation. Jesus loves us so much. He wants to give us all that we need physically, emotionally, and spiritually. When we lean into Him and His power, we tend to find that what we really want, we can only find in Him. And that is even better than fifty dollars. —SUSANNA FOTH AUGHTMON

FAITH STEP: *Make a needs list in your journal and ask Jesus to meet those needs. As He meets the need, mark the date in your journal, reminding yourself of His faithfulness.*

THURSDAY, JULY 16

"I want to study the way of integrity." Psalm 101:2 (CEB)

PEOPLE-WATCHING IS A LIVING CLASSROOM. Jesus told stories because He knew we would learn best by watching or listening to examples.

We observe the twenty-dollar bill that floats to the ground in the grocery store parking lot, and the teen boy who picks it up and runs to return it to its owner. Integrity.

We watch the friend, who's struggling with finances, tell the server about the error on her lunch tab, an error that costs her more money. Integrity.

We see what it costs a coworker to admit he was the one who messed up the project. He humbled himself to not only admit it, but to do everything he could to help resolve it. Integrity.

We watch a child tell the truth about why his school assignment is late, no excuses. Integrity.

We observe the woman of God who is the same at home as she is at church, the same under pressure as she is at rest, the same gracious person whether sick or well, disappointed or elated. Integrity.

Jesus, the Living Word, is at it again. He's not content to have me comply with what He teaches. He wants me to comply thoughtfully. Not brain-dead obedience, not self-blinded obedience, but *intentional* obedience that comes from studying what it means to walk through life—and in my home, as Psalm 101:2 adds—in integrity. Love-obedience. Integrity-obedience that radiates from a core understanding of the truth.

Jesus, make me a student of integrity who passes all the pop quizzes of life! —CYNTHIA RUCHTI

FAITH STEP: *Sometimes integrity means not making more work for someone else, owning up to personal responsibility. Sometimes it means cleaning up someone else's mess without complaint. Watch for opportunities today to bolster your education as a student of integrity.*

FRIDAY, JULY 17

---

*You know my thoughts even when I'm far away.... You know what I am
going to say even before I say it, Lord. Psalm 139:2, 4 (NLT)*

BEING MARRIED FOR OVER FOUR decades gets a little scary sometimes.
My husband or I will say something, and the other will respond with,
"I was just about to say the same thing." It's like we know what the other
is thinking, because years of being up close and personal have planted
similar thoughts in our heads.

But even as long as we've shared life together, I sheepishly admit my
inadequacy. I'm not a mind reader, and there are still ample times when
I feel clueless. At least we can laugh now about how opposite we really
are in so many ways—even in our thoughts. Love and forgiveness have
played a huge part in covering the clueless areas of our lives, just as they
do in any relationship.

Jesus is never oblivious to our thoughts. In Matthew 9, Jesus healed a
paralyzed man and forgave his sins. The teachers of the law formed unspoken questions like, "Who does He think He is, God?" And of course,
yes, He was God incarnate. Jesus knew their thoughts, and as He often
did, confronted them with questions of His own.

Realizing Jesus has intimate knowledge of us, including our thought
life, might seem a little intimidating at times. Unnerving. Downright
embarrassing! Our thoughts are not like His (Isaiah 55:8) and can often
be as far away from Jesus as the East is from the West (Psalm 103:12).

On the other hand, even though He knows us so thoroughly, He chooses
to love us intimately. His love and forgiveness cover a multitude of clueless
patterns in our lives. Jesus longs for a close relationship with us. And He
wants us to feel the same way about Him. —REBECCA BARLOW JORDAN

FAITH STEP: *Thank Jesus for His intimate knowledge of you. Review Psalm 139 to
see how many times Jesus thinks about you.*

SATURDAY, JULY 18

The apostles gathered around Jesus and reported to him all they had done and taught. Then, because so many people were coming and going that they did not even have a chance to eat, he said to them, "Come with me by yourselves to a quiet place and get some rest." Mark 6: 30–31 (NIV)

I NEVER KNOW HOW MY day will start—I can be thrown into needing to respond to an urgent e-mail, or heading out to the store if the toilet paper has run out. Some days everything I had planned changes.

In our American culture, being busy is made to look like a virtue. We rush, we complain, we scurry from one thing to the next.

The other day while I was working toward a deadline, a sparrow tapped against my windowpane. At first I ignored him, but he wanted my attention. He flew to the next window in the room and tapped some more. Then he just stayed there, against the screen until I stood and took a close look. He had gotten my attention and with that, he flew to a nearby tree.

Today, take time to notice the simple and the beautiful. Take time to fuel your soul by being still, listening, praying. —ALICE J. WISLER

FAITH STEP: *Today listen to that quiet voice, and hear the simple words Jesus speaks: Trust Me. It's an invitation. Come, sit beside Me, get to know the feel of My hand in yours. I love you. I am your hope. Wait upon Me. Let Me renew your strength.*

SUNDAY, JULY 19

Trust in the Lord with all your heart and lean not on your own understanding; in all your ways submit to him, and he will make your paths straight.
Proverbs 3:5–6 (NIV)

I FOUGHT AGAINST JESUS FOR many years. I thought that following Him was too restricting. I wanted to date the guys I wanted to date. I wanted to watch the movies that were popular, even though the content wasn't wholesome or uplifting. And I was miserable.

Even after I asked Jesus to forgive my sins and make me a new creation in Him, there were times I still struggled. I wanted to write Christian fiction, and I pushed and pushed to make it happen. Every time I heard of a genre that publishers were interested in I tried to write that—no matter if it wasn't what I was drawn to write (or even drawn to read). I found no success.

Finally, I gave up trying. I told Jesus that I'd do whatever He wanted me to do. I told Him I would stop fighting Him. He led me to help start a crisis pregnancy center. He led me to mentor teenage mothers. I found joy in both those things that I hadn't expected. I also followed Him toward stories that He wanted me to tell... and I found success in publication too!

I've heard it said that the secret of an unsuccessful life lies in an unsurrendered will. The opposite is true: the secret of a successful life is in a surrendered will. Your success may not be what the world views as success: money, fame, popularity, but the success Jesus gives is even better. His success comes as peace, joy, friendships, purpose, and a fulfilled mission. Those are the things so many people search for and never find. And it all starts with surrender. —TRICIA GOYER

FAITH STEP: *Is there a desire that you've been fighting for, striving for? If so, get on your knees and surrender your will to Jesus. Ask Him to make His desires for your life your desires.*

MONDAY, JULY 20

Jesus said to her, "I am the resurrection and the life. He who believes in Me, though he may die, he shall live. And whoever lives and believes in Me shall never die. Do you believe this?" John 11:25–26 (NKJV)

I HAD THE SAME PIANO teacher for twelve years growing up. She was a huge influence on me in music, and more important, in my Christian life. We have always stayed in touch.

This past year I learned she was dying. I took my family and went to see her one last time. She seemed a shadow of her former self as she lay there in bed, emaciated. Her hair was white and her skin translucent. The hands that once marched up and down the piano playing "Onward Christian Soldiers" trembled so much that I had to look away. Still, she was practical about the whole matter.

"I've had a great life," she said. "And dying is not so bad. I keep very busy reading and praying here in my bed. But I see no reason to prolong it. To be absent from the body is to be present with the Lord."

Her life, as I've observed it, has been a resurrection story. I've seen her lose loved ones, lose her health, die personal deaths I'd never wish on anyone. I've seen her stressed out. I've seen her cry. But mostly what I've seen is that she believes in Jesus as the Resurrection and the life. Because of this she walks through it all in victory. "I've had a great life," she reaffirms. Even now, on her deathbed, she inspires me.

Perhaps a great life is not measured in how many places you go, how much fun you have or what you accomplish. It's not measured by how much tragedy you manage to avoid. The lesson Gail has taught me is that a great life is a life of trusting Jesus and believing that He brings life out of death. Over and over until He takes you home.

—GWEN FORD FAULKENBERRY

FAITH STEP: *What lesson is your life teaching others? Write out what you want it to be and then ask Jesus to help you live it.*

TUESDAY, JULY 21

He will take these weak mortal bodies of ours and change them into glorious bodies like his own, using the same mighty power that he will use to conquer everything, everywhere. Philippians 3:21 (NLT)

PHYSICAL CHALLENGES HAVE PLAGUED MY husband and me in the past twelve months. First, I partially ruptured my left Achilles tendon. The opposite knee required surgery several weeks later. Those combined injuries landed me in a wheelchair for three months. Two weeks after I resumed walking, I developed shingles. Most recently, my husband contracted a blood infection from a biopsy procedure. Unfortunately, the biopsy proved positive.

I would never have chosen these circumstances, but they've deepened my relationship with Jesus. For that reason alone, I wouldn't trade them for anything. They've also given me a greater appreciation of good health. I know many people whose physical struggles far outweigh ours, and some are on the brink of despair. Compared to their lot, I consider us fortunate.

Our human bodies, weak and mortal as they are, fall ill and suffer injuries. They're also prone to weight problems, congenital birth defects, and mental challenges. And yet there's hope. Someday Jesus will take these exterior shells in which we dwell and transform them into glorious bodies like His.

Imagine! We'll no longer struggle with issues surrounding chronic pain, cancer, migraines, birth defects, learning disabilities, and injuries. Even our weight concerns will become past tense. Jesus, using His divine power, will speak health and wholeness into our bodies. No more pills, blood tests, X-rays, ultrasounds, surgeries, or hospital stays.

Glorious bodies await us. The physical limitations we face now will not exist in eternity. *Wahoo!* May this reminder bring hope and inner strength until the day Jesus makes us new. —GRACE FOX

FAITH STEP: *Each morning you awake means you're one day closer to possessing your glorious new body. In the meantime, ask Jesus to help you properly care for your present body. What's one new thing you can do to treat it with respect?*

WEDNESDAY, JULY 22

Take the helmet of salvation and the sword of the Spirit, which is the word of God. And pray in the Spirit on all occasions with all kinds of prayers and requests. With this in mind, be alert and always keep on praying for all the Lord's people.
Ephesians 6:17–18 (NIV)

THERE AREN'T MANY EXPERIENCES MORE moving to me than watching my children's faith in action.

When we pass an emergency vehicle with its lights on and siren blaring, if I listen closely I can hear my five-year-old daughter asking Jesus to watch over whoever is in trouble. One summer at a water park I watched my son, six at the time, climb to the top of the high dive and pause on the end of the board. My stomach dropped in anticipation . . . until I saw his mouth moving, and I wondered if he was praying. He tells me he prays when he needs help in school, and I know both kids talk to Jesus at night when their rooms look dark and shadowed.

My heart leaps for joy at these discovery moments, and I feel like shouting, "It's working! They're getting it!"

They need to build their prayer-warrior muscles to live strong and true throughout life. They'll face challenges like all of us, and they'll need these verses in Ephesians. They'll also need to remember 2 Corinthians 10:4 (ESV), which says, "The weapons of our warfare are not of the flesh but have divine power to destroy strongholds."

Earth is loaded with strongholds, barriers erected by unseen forces to twist truth, to break us, and to keep us separated from Jesus.

But the weapon-gift of prayer changes lives. When a Jesus follower enters the Holy of holies on behalf of a need on earth, the throne room ignites into action. Strongholds better beware, because they cannot stand forever against the forces of heaven that are unleashed by a faithful prayer warrior.

Will she be you? —ERIN KEELEY MARSHALL

FAITH STEP: *Read Psalm 18 and imagine the Lord's action in response to your prayers.*

THURSDAY, JULY 23

When they saw the courage of Peter and John and realized that they were unschooled, ordinary men, they were astonished and they took note that these men had been with Jesus. Acts 4:13 (NIV)

PETER AND JOHN WERE ARRESTED after healing a lame man in the name of Jesus and then urging the people to put their faith in Him as the Messiah. The next day the two men stood trial before the rulers, elders, and teachers of the law. This same council had condemned Jesus of Nazareth to death; now they were determined to stamp out the teaching being spread by His followers. How hard could it be to frighten two simple fishermen into silence?

Instead of being intimidated by the questioning from the highest Jewish leaders in the land, Peter and John displayed confidence and courage. Peter boldly testified to Jesus as the fulfillment of Old Testament prophecies and the only source of salvation. The leaders were astonished that these uneducated fishermen with no special training in the Scriptures spoke so powerfully and with such authority. And they noted that these men had been with Jesus.

We're all deeply affected by our friends, whether we realize it or not. Our mood, our behavior, and our attitudes will be influenced by those we spend a lot of time with. I have certain friends who lift my spirits and make me laugh, while others encourage me to think seriously. But Jesus is the One I want to have the greatest impact on me.

Spending time with Jesus through prayer, Bible study, or praise and worship should make a noticeable difference in my life. It will shape my character to become more like His. It will give me courage and boldness to share about Him as two fishermen did long ago. And people will note that I've been with Jesus. —DIANNE NEAL MATTHEWS

FAITH STEP: *Has your life been reflecting time spent with Jesus? How could spending more time with Him influence your decisions and actions today?*

FRIDAY, JULY 24

Now there are varieties of gifts, but the same Spirit; and there are varieties of service, but the same Lord; and there are varieties of activities, but it is the same God who empowers them all in everyone. 1 Corinthians 12:4–6 (ESV)

MY FAVORITE STRETCHY COTTON SLACKS had shrunk in the wash. I tugged and pulled, trying to lengthen them back into shape, but within minutes, they had become "high-waters" again.

Shopping isn't my favorite pastime, but it was time to invest in new pants. This time I'd look for a longer length, so even if they shrank a little, they would continue to cover my ankles. I headed to the sale rack in the back of one of the outlet stores I really like. The hangers held the style I liked, in a variety of beautiful colors. There were extralarge, large, medium, small, and extrasmall. There were lengths in petite and in tall. Yet after searching every hanger, I came up empty. None in the right combination of my size with a tall length.

Clothes shopping can be frustrating for anyone. There are so many variables. Finding the perfect fit seems impossible. Even when we do, sometimes our size and shape change and we need different clothes.

The experience reminded me of seeking a place to serve in the Church. Sometimes I've tried a way of service, and like my too-short pants, I soon learned it wasn't the place I fit. Other times I found a ministry where I belonged, but after several years, Jesus guided me in a new direction. I'm thrilled that in Jesus's kingdom He has gifts and callings and activities as varied as each of us. We may need to try on a few before we find the right match, and we may need the courage to try something completely new, but He can empower us in finding that perfect fit. —SHARON HINCK

FAITH STEP: *Choose something in your closet that no longer fits and give it away. Ask Jesus to show you if He has a new area of service for you.*

SATURDAY, JULY 25

"How can you say to your brother, 'Let me take the speck out of your eye,'
when all the time there is a plank in your own eye?" Matthew 7:4 (NIV)

AT DINNER LAST NIGHT, WILL looked at me and said, "*Um*...Mom...you've got a little something..." I started brushing my face for invisible crumbs..."Where, on my face?" "*Um*...in your hair." "My hair?" "Yep. It's gray." I looked at him and said, "Thank you, Will, for pointing out that I have gray hair. I'll make sure to take care of it right away."

There may have been some sarcasm in that statement. I did not mention to him that he has given me quite a few of those gray hairs. I didn't mention that he might want to work on his people skills in the area of tact and kindness. And I didn't mention that instead of pointing out my overgrown roots, he might mention how he appreciated the dinner I had made him. But I wanted to. I also wanted to make an appointment with my hairdresser.

It is way easier to point out other people's shortcomings than to take time to address our own. Jesus gets that. He understands that it is in our nature to extend grace to ourselves and judge others. But He doesn't let us off the hook. He suggests that we take care of our own business, our own sins, our own weaknesses, instead of pointing out the weaknesses of others. I am thinking that if we actually did this, we might have more grace for those struggling around us. Even for the people who have gray hair. —SUSANNA FOTH AUGHTMON

FAITH STEP: *Find a stick outside and put it near where you have your prayer time. Each time you find yourself wanting to judge someone, look at the stick, remember the log in your own eye and ask Jesus to help you extend grace.*

SUNDAY, JULY 26

Don't copy the behavior and customs of this world, but let God transform you into a new person by changing the way you think. Then you will learn to know God's will for you, which is good and pleasing and perfect. Romans 12:2 (NLT)

MY KIDS RECENTLY DISCOVERED THE fun of mimicking. For a while the game brought on giggles no matter who was the copycat, but after a while the novelty wore off and the repetition got old. The one being copied was hard pressed to shake off the sibling who hovered nearby.

Every now and then as a parent I think, *Yeah, I'll be glad when that phase is over.* No home needs a copycat; originals only, please.

I think that's what Jesus would like to say to us when we resort to looking and acting like those around us. Some trends are harmless, but not when it comes to the big deals of life that involve the special purpose we've been given life to pursue. When the Creator formed the first human beings, He took His time and shaped them one by one. Each one reflected His glory in his or her own way, and the Lord saw both as beautiful.

He still shapes each person individually. He has never made a copycat, and for good reason. When each one of the gazillions of souls He has created reflects His beauty in their own way, He is glorified bountifully.

Jesus showed us how to live set apart for the special purpose His Father gave Him. He wasn't afraid to forge His own path, to stand alone, or to do things differently when it meant pleasing His Lord with His unique best.

Live your creative, beautiful best and touch the lives around you as only you can, just the way the Lord intended for you.

—ERIN KEELEY MARSHALL

FAITH STEP: *Take five minutes to list several unique qualities about yourself. They may even be traits you've felt self-conscious about. Give them to Jesus, and ask Him to use those characteristics to bless someone.*

MONDAY, JULY 27

For the Spirit God gave us does not make us timid, but gives us power, love and self-discipline. 2 Timothy 1:7 (NIV)

RECENTLY I WAS ASKED TO write a book under a very fast deadline. It was a project about mothering that resonated with my heart, yet the writing would take place around the holidays. I was worried. Would I be sacrificing my family time in order to inspire and encourage other moms?

Even before he knew about this book possibility my father-in-law called me and told me that he was praying for me, and that my next writing project would bless a lot of people and it would not hinder my own family time. I knew then that as my father-in-law had prayed for me, the Spirit of Jesus spoke those words to him. With a new boldness and confidence I accepted the writing project and, amazingly, it got done during my kids' nap times, after they went to bed, and even as we traveled in the car on vacation.

The writing took self-discipline and prayer, but Jesus met me as I molded this message for moms. And I was reminded that the Spirit of Jesus gives us power. I could not accomplish this task, but Jesus could through me. When I looked to Him in trust, the fears vanished, just like He said they would.

"Peace I leave with you; my peace I give you," we read in John 14:27 (NIV). "I do not give to you as the world gives. Do not let your hearts be troubled and do not be afraid."

So many times we let fears and worries keep us from the tasks that Jesus is calling us to. Instead, we need to trust that what we can't accomplish in our natural selves, He can accomplish through us! —TRICIA GOYER

FAITH STEP: *Is there something you feel that Jesus is asking you to do? Write down your fears. Then cross out those and write down what Jesus can do through you as you walk in faith.*

TUESDAY, JULY 28

For the word of God is alive and powerful. It is sharper than the sharpest two-edged sword, cutting between soul and spirit, between joint and marrow. It exposes our innermost thoughts and desires. Hebrews 4:12 (NLT)

WHEN I WAS A CHILD, our church participated in "sword drill contests." Our "swords"—our Bibles—were not crafted by skilled metal artisans, but by the Master Craftsman Himself. The objective was to familiarize ourselves with Scripture, finding verses in the Bible quickly.

I remember spending hours practicing at church or with friends and family members calling out a Scripture reference such as Hebrews 4:12, then the words: "Attention. Draw swords. Charge!" The first one to find the Bible verse would step out, finger on the verse, ready to read. The competitions began at the local church, then advanced to a larger level, much like a spelling bee.

That simple, repetitious training helped me tremendously as a writer and Bible teacher, and it often gave me instant recall when I wanted to share what God's Word said about a particular verse or subject.

But that experience did even more. It embedded in my heart the importance of brandishing my sword in the face of my enemies: like worry, fear, temptation, discouragement. I learned to whip out that two-edged sword and use it to pierce through the heart of those unseen things that threatened to keep me from faith, trust, and dependence on Jesus.

The Bible exposes our foolish desires and our harmful thinking patterns. When I forget to use that sword and depend on less effective weapons, I suffer the consequences—and wounds—from temporary amnesia. But when I do remember the power of His Word, I can almost hear Jesus's encouraging words in my heart: "Attention. Draw swords. Charge!"
—REBECCA BARLOW JORDAN

FAITH STEP: *Practice using your sword this week. Write down several Bible verses and conduct a mock sword drill contest, even involving your family members.*

WEDNESDAY, JULY 29

I thank Christ Jesus our Lord, who has given me strength, that he considered me trustworthy, appointing me to his service. 1 Timothy 1:12 (NIV)

IN MY LATE TEENS, MY mom started a full-time job, but she still found plenty of time to do things for other people. Babysitting, cooking, sewing, volunteering at church—whatever anyone needed or wanted. It bothered me that people sometimes seemed to take advantage of her willingness to serve, especially when they planned something that used her day off from work. As years passed and our family expanded, the stacks of dishes grew higher after dinners my mom wanted to cook mostly by herself. I found it necessary to argue with her in order to help with the cleanup (no dishwasher) rather than leave them for her to do after everyone had left.

It took a lot of years for me to figure out that my mom has a servant's heart. She simply delights in doing things, often unasked, that bring comfort and joy to other people. For her, receiving thanks and gratitude in return aren't necessary, although they are nice. My mom knows that whenever she ministers to others, she is really serving Jesus. He once told His disciples that He "did not come to be served but to serve others and to give His life as a ransom for many" (Matthew 20:28).

As for me, I enjoy giving, volunteering, and doing things for others, but I find it hard when my efforts seem unappreciated or taken for granted. That's why I've decided to memorize 1 Timothy 1:12. That single verse reminds me that whether I'm ministering at church or meeting a neighbor's need, it's because Jesus considered me trustworthy and appointed me to serve Him in that capacity. The verse also promises that He will provide the strength I need to fulfill any assignment. I still have a long way to go in developing my servant's heart, but at least I'm making progress.
—DIANNE NEAL MATTHEWS

FAITH STEP: *Do you struggle with feeling unappreciated? Why not join me in memorizing 1 Timothy 1:12.*

THURSDAY, JULY 30

"He didn't need anyone to tell him about human nature, for he knew what human nature was." John 2:25 (CEB)

MY KRYPTONITE IS BEING MISUNDERSTOOD. It's my weak spot, the offense that bothers me more than others. Some days feel like a walk through a kryptonite minefield.

Jesus was misunderstood more than He was understood, it seems. Even those closest to Him repeatedly missed what He was trying to say.

One day, Jesus reminded His disciples that when He asked them to follow Him on His teaching/healing junket without wallets or luggage, they lacked nothing. Hours before His arrest, in an attempt to get the men mentally and spiritually prepared for what was about to happen, He said, "But now, whoever has a wallet must take it, and likewise a bag. And those who don't own a sword must sell their clothes and buy one" (Luke 22:36, CEB).

A couple of the disciples reacted with, "Lord, look, here are two swords!" Can you imagine the glee on their faces as they brandished the swords?

I picture Jesus slapping His palm against His forehead. How grossly they misunderstood what He was saying. "Enough of that!" (verse 38), He groaned, as if to say, "Guys! Not *real* swords! Get with the program!"

None of that caught Jesus by surprise. He understood human nature and its tendency to misread the holy in the middle of the mundane, to relate what the Son of God taught to their experiences as earth-dwellers, to see danger and think, "Swords!" rather than "Jesus, Messiah!"

Where do I shout, "I eagerly await heaven, where I'll see Him as He is, understand what I misunderstood on earth"? I'm well aware what a glorious relief that will be for me. Imagine what a relief it will be for Him.

—CYNTHIA RUCHTI

FAITH STEP: *Make it the cry of your heart today to grasp what Jesus is really saying, to hear His Word with ears unhindered and open to truth. Press in to know Him more.*

FRIDAY, JULY 31

I want your joy to be the fullest joy. . . . You are my friends. John 15:11, 14 (ICB)

WE TAKE TURNS SAYING THE prayer at mealtimes. It has been sweet to watch the children learn to talk to Jesus throughout the years. Now Stella, who is almost two, is taking her turn, much to the others' delight.

The first time Stella said the prayer we all held hands and bowed our heads, wondering what she would say.

"Dear God…" she began fervently. "Thank you…food. Thank you… family." There was a big pause. Then a hearty, "Amen!"

We all looked up at her, laughing, and clapped for a job well done. She gave us a gigantic grin, clasped her hands together, and declared, "God likes me!"

It was one of those moments when I wanted to freeze time. Not only because it was a happy moment in our family, but because it was a profoundly spiritual moment I want Stella—and all of us—to remember always. And yet I know how easily the lesson of the moment can slip through our fingers.

Why is it so hard to remember God likes us? Jesus calls us friends. And yet years of making mistakes can convince us to dislike ourselves, and to believe He doesn't like us. How could He, when we keep letting Him down?

I'm afraid church doesn't always help. From well-meaning fronts we hear the message that God is angry with us, disappointed, because of our behavior. And I don't want to oversimplify. Just like it hurts us when our loved ones misbehave, I'm sure the heart of God is hurt when He sees us making bad choices.

But I don't believe He ever stops liking us. Could I ever not delight in Harper's sense of humor? Will Stella's curls ever lose their charm for me? What about Grace's quirky ways? And Adelaide's penchant for creating silly songs? It is precisely because I am so crazy about them that I want them to make good choices. To follow Jesus with all of their hearts. —GWEN FORD FAULKENBERRY

FAITH STEP: *Do you ever feel like Jesus doesn't like you? Cling to the promise that he calls you friend.*

SATURDAY, AUGUST 1

"The light shines in darkness and the darkness doesn't extinguish the light."
John 1:5 (CEB)

WHEN MY GRANDCHILDREN HAVE A sleepover at our house, they always ask me to leave the guest room door open and the hall light on. That's understandable. It isn't only children who are uncomfortable sleeping in an unfamiliar room with no nightlight.

The door needs to remain open only a small crack for them to see well enough to know where they are, to be reassured, reoriented. As I narrow the door opening, I can hear their protests forming. But they soon realize the truth. It doesn't take much light to navigate in a darkened room.

Science tells us the human eye can detect the flame of a single candle from as far away as ten miles in otherwise complete darkness. Imagine. The circle of our inky crisis may seem to stretch ten miles in every direction.

A single candle flame means it's no longer abject darkness. A single flame can tell us we're not completely in the dark, not completely immersed in the anxieties and traumas. Our situation has not dropped us into a windowless cave with the opening sealed shut...as long as Jesus is there.

For good reason, Jesus is called the Light of the World. His presence is that inextinguishable flame of hope that changes utter darkness into a dramatic backdrop for light.

How dark a cancer diagnosis can seem. How dark the loss of a loved one. How dark a child's unwise choices. How dark an unexpected job loss. How dark the death of a dream. The dark loses its dominance in the presence of light. It only wins if it can snuff the light. And it can't.

There, in the darkness, the brilliant, darkness-dispelling light of Jesus changes everything. —CYNTHIA RUCHTI

FAITH STEP: *Do a Bible word search for passages that link Jesus and light. Linger over those verses as hope-givers for your next or current concern.*

SUNDAY, AUGUST 2

*The Lord says, "I will guide you along the best pathway for your life.
I will advise you and watch over you." Psalm 32:8 (NLT)*

OUR GROUP OF CAMPERS GAZED up at the night sky lit with stars too many to count. It was a mesmerizing sight, but what had our focus most was a paper lantern moving higher above our heads.

The night was still, hardly any wind to blow the globe, so it floated lazily toward the heavens. Along with my husband, our friends, and our collective kids, I *oohed* and *aahed* as the glowing object moved over the treetops and eventually beyond our vision.

Despite some rain that weekend, we all had a wonderful time making memories, canoe floating downriver, roasting s'mores, romping through the campground, and falling asleep to the sounds of the great outdoors.

But that moment in particular as I watched so many people I care about gazing upward, I breathed a prayer of thanksgiving that God's eye is ever on us. We lost sight of that lantern as it floated beyond our reach, vulnerable to the slightest pressure against it. How peaceful it also felt to trust that the God who created the mighty winds and expansive sky carries us tenderly, guides us faithfully, and shelters us constantly. His own are never truly at the whim of any other force. It may seem so at times, but the Lord is still sovereign and in control.

What a beautiful sight our hearts can enjoy when we envision ourselves and those we love being led along by the mighty hand of a loving God.
—ERIN KEELEY MARSHALL

FAITH STEP: *Buy a paper lantern and offer a prayer as you send it upward. Thank the Lord that He carries you.*

MONDAY, AUGUST 3

Since you call on a Father who judges each person's work impartially, live out your time as foreigners here in reverent fear. For you know that it was not with perishable things such as silver or gold that you were redeemed from the empty way of life handed down to you from your ancestors, but with the precious blood of Christ, a lamb without blemish or defect. 1 Peter 1:17–19 (NIV)

WHEN I GET FRUSTRATED WITH life here on earth, a gentle reminder comes to me: *You were created for more than this. This earth is not your home; you are only passing through.*

Having grown up overseas and lived in a few countries, I have often thought of myself as a pilgrim, a nomad, a woman without a home.

When I was little and my family and I would travel from Japan to the USA, my grandparents would say, "Welcome home!" But I knew nothing of the American culture and felt like a stranger. In Japan, my birthplace, I felt more relaxed, but was reminded daily that I was a foreigner.

Perhaps that's one of the reasons I look forward to that place where I will truly feel at home.

As we struggle with the evil in this world and with our own longings for something more, our eyes look upward to our heavenly home. Something stirs in our hearts and we know that only then will we find the full joy and comfort of being at home.

Earth is not our final destination. Don't get too comfortable. Be ready to move. We are being prepared for heaven, for glory. This life is only the preparation for greater things to come! —ALICE J. WISLER

FAITH STEP: *Rejoice today in the knowledge and anticipation of your heavenly home. Place your faith and hope there; does that change your perspective on life's circumstances?*

TUESDAY, AUGUST 4

Show me your ways, Lord, teach me your paths. Guide me in your truth and teach me, for you are God my Savior, and my hope is in you all day long.
Psalm 25: 4–5 (NIV)

MY HUSBAND AND I MET with our pastor. "We've been invited to spend a month serving a mission in Hong Kong. We believe this is a door Jesus has opened for us," I said.

"On the other hand," my husband added, "the company I was working for stopped meeting payroll, so we have no job and no savings. How do we know this is the Lord's guidance and not just our own inclination? Are we being saintly or stupid?"

Our pastor smiled. "Maybe a little of both. As sinful humans we can get it wrong. But that doesn't mean we let fear stop us. Whether you decide to tackle this challenge, or decide it's not the right time, Jesus loves you. Even if you don't raise the money in time, Jesus loves you."

Asking Jesus to guide us, we began planning for the trip. Our kids helped us bake cookies that we served during fellowship time at church. Friends contributed. Still, the day before we had to buy plane tickets, we were short five hundred dollars. Our church's mission board called and asked my husband to swing by and pick up their contribution—which we remembered hearing would be about fifty dollars. When he arrived home, my husband looked a bit stunned. "I guess it's time to buy the tickets."

Without knowing the amount we still needed, the mission board had readied a check toward the mission trip—for five hundred dollars.

In this case, Jesus showed us His path through supernatural provision. Other times He's guided by firmly closing a door. Either way, we can always trust Him. —SHARON HINCK

FAITH STEP: *Are you facing a decision? Ask Jesus to lead you, and watch for the ways He guides your path.*

WEDNESDAY, AUGUST 5

And you will seek Me and find Me, when you search for Me with all your heart.
Jeremiah 29:13 (NKJV)

MY DAUGHTER GRACE, THIRTEEN, HAS a unique way of seeing Jesus in daily life. The other day she showed me how the marshmallows lined up on top of her hot chocolate to form a cross. She delights in such things as a lighted cross on a hillside when we are driving on the interstate at night. For her these things are glimpses of Jesus, evidence that He is personally involved in the details of her days.

I have a couple of friends at work who are like this as well. One told me a story of how she was having a bad morning, nothing going right in her home or at the office. She looked down to see two rubber bands on the floor in the shape of a cross, and it reminded her Jesus was with her. She was able to find peace and carry on, hope restored.

I think I must be the meanest person alive when people tell me things like this. Because even though I would never show outward disrespect, inwardly I'm a doubter. I suppose it's because I never see Jesus this way. And if it wasn't my own sweet beautiful daughter sharing her heart with me, or a dear friend at work, I'd think it was crazy. I'd be tempted to judge. And I'd be wrong.

The Bible promises that those who search for Him with all of their hearts will find Him. And whether He aligns marshmallows or rubber bands for our benefit is really not the point. The point is the heart. Is my heart soft enough to see Jesus in a sunset? To feel His love in the kiss of the wind on my face? Is my office door open to Him? If I judge these things as nutty, I'm the one who is missing out. —GWEN FORD FAULKENBERRY

FAITH STEP: *Pray this with me: "Lord Jesus, I want to see You wherever You choose to reveal Yourself. Give me an open heart to recognize You wherever You are in my day."*

THURSDAY, AUGUST 6

So don't be afraid, little flock. For it gives your Father great happiness to give you the Kingdom. Luke 12:32 (NLT)

THE SHEEP ARE GATHERED IN a bunch, trembling, almost out of sight of the crowd seated on bright blankets and in bleachers to watch the working-dog trials. A man stands next to a post holding a staff, while beside him a black-and-white border collie waits—trembling too—anticipating the high-pitched whistle telling him which way to run.

The outrun is flawless. The dog cuts in behind the sheep just close enough so they walk toward the crowd without scattering. A perfect lift, difficult because the sheep see the dog as a predator. He leans to the right and the sheep head the other way. Through the first gate, then the second. Sheep are vulnerable and defenseless. They run, but not usually as fast as their pursuers. The dog keeps precisely enough distance to move the clustered woolies through the course until the handler leaves the post to grasp the rope that closes the gate once the sheep are penned.

These aren't the handler's sheep. That wouldn't be enough of a test. He's a stranger and they're more scared than usual, what with trailering, wolf-like dogs barking and people moving about.

Dog trials depend on the nature of sheep. Their default is fear. If they aren't timid by nature, their mothers teach them to be. It helps them survive. But familiarity overcomes fear. Bottle lambs, used to people and being handled, come running—in contrast to any mothered lamb that's on its feet when it spots you.

We aren't so different. Jesus was forever telling people not to be afraid. He knows what we're like. And he still loves us. Fear not, little flock.

—SUZANNE DAVENPORT TIETJEN

FAITH STEP: *Do you struggle with fear? You have a Shepherd Who loves you. Spend time with Him. Talk with Him. Become familiar with Jesus so that you will recognize His voice and draw near with confidence.*

FRIDAY, AUGUST 7

In the same way, let your light shine before others, that they may see your good deeds and glorify your Father in heaven. Matthew 5:16 (NIV)

ONE OF MY FAVORITE THINGS as an author is for my publisher to send me a potential cover design for one of my books. I love getting a glimpse of the characters who I've made up in my mind represented by models chosen for the photo shoot. I love the drama, or the tranquility, of the cover that reflects the story. A good cover lets the reader "see" what's on the inside. The same is true in our lives.

Not too long ago my husband sat down next to an elderly woman on an airplane. She asked if he had any children. John answered, "Yes, six." He then proceeded to tell her about our three biological children, and the three we adopted. He even showed her photos of them on his phone.

They hadn't been talking for more than three minutes when the woman interrupted him. "Son, you must have the love of Jesus in you, loving and caring for those children as you do." John hadn't mentioned that he was a Christian. He hadn't tried to share Scripture verses, but because of his deeds in adopting our children she saw Jesus in him.

John 15:8 (NLT) says, "When you produce much fruit, you are my true disciples. This brings great glory to my Father." Jesus gets the glory for the goodness in our lives!

So many times we feel as if we need to witness to people wherever we go. But sometimes we just need to do the work that Jesus has asked us to do and trust that others will see Him in us as we go along in our everyday lives. It's the easiest way to share Jesus, because we don't have to say a word! —TRICIA GOYER

FAITH STEP: *Think of someone who is living his or her ordinary life in an amazing way—a way where Jesus shines through them. Then take a minute and write that person a note, telling that person what you see.*

SATURDAY, AUGUST 8

Suddenly, a man in the synagogue who was possessed by an evil spirit began shouting, "Why are you interfering with us, Jesus of Nazareth? Have you come to destroy us? I know who you are—the Holy One sent from God!"
Mark 1:23–24 (NLT)

WHEN I FIRST BEGAN WRITING professionally, I exchanged a couple of e-mails with a very well-known author who wrote best sellers. I mailed her a copy of my first published book, and she sent me her latest novel. Some time later a close friend told me of her plans to attend a conference in a nearby city, headlined by that famous author. Jokingly, I told Kelsey that the author and I were best buds, and asked her to take my greetings along. After the conference, I was dismayed to learn that Kelsey had taken me seriously. When she got a chance to speak to the author alone, she had been sure to tell her that her "friend" said "hello."

There's a world of difference between knowing *about* someone and knowing them personally, isn't there? I find it fascinating that demons who encountered Jesus knew exactly Who He was. While most of the Jewish people failed to recognize the Messiah, fallen angels serving Satan acknowledged Him as the Holy One from God and submitted to His authority, albeit unwillingly. But they didn't have a personal relationship with Him.

This reminds me that believing in Jesus requires more than an intellectual assent to His identity. Knowing Jesus personally goes beyond the brain; it affects the heart and influences the attitudes and behavior of a believer. It means that I trust Him as my Savior with the eternal destiny of my soul. I willingly submit to His authority as Lord over my life. I can truly say I know Him as a close friend Who loves me, comforts me, and corrects me. And He knows me. —DIANNE NEAL MATTHEWS

FAITH STEP: *Take a few moments to examine your day-to-day life. Does it reflect a superficial knowledge of Jesus or an intimate relationship with Him as your Savior and Lord?*

SUNDAY, AUGUST 9

*It's in Christ that we find out who we are and what we are living for. Long before
we first heard of Christ and got our hopes up, he had his eye on us, had designs
on us for glorious living, part of the overall purpose he is working out
in everything and everyone. Ephesians 1:11–12 (MSG)*

MANY OF US MAY DESCRIBE ourselves by our weaknesses rather than our strengths. Our beliefs may cling to past accusations: "loser," "wimp," or "inadequate." We don't understand our true identity in Christ.

Neither did Peter. When Jesus chose this brash fisherman to follow Him, what did He see in him? For three years Peter walked with the Master, sat at His feet, and watched Jesus breathe new life—both spiritually and physically—into others. Then one day Jesus revealed to Peter his own God-given identity: "And now I'm going to tell you who you are, *really* are. You are Peter, a rock" (Matthew 16:18, MSG).

Not long after that Peter failed Jesus miserably, denying Him at Jesus's greatest point of need. His "rock-solid" identity turned to mush—he was a loser.

But not in Jesus's eyes. After His death and Resurrection, He met with the disciples on a familiar sandy beach and offered grace to Peter—as if Peter were still a rock-solid follower, commissioning him to "feed my lambs" (John 21:15). Peter must have finally accepted his true identity in Christ, because Jesus used Peter to change countless lives.

It's in Christ that we find our true purpose and identity. Our actions and attitudes may not always measure up to who Jesus says we really are. But as followers of Christ, the more we cling to our true identity in Him, the less we'll act on our old beliefs.

Jesus's grace will make the difference. —REBECCA BARLOW JORDAN

FAITH STEP: *Thank Jesus for your true identity in Him. Write Ephesians 1:11–12 on an index card and keep it in a place where you can review its truth daily.*

MONDAY, AUGUST 10

Jesus reached out and touched him. "I am willing," he said. "Be healed!"
And instantly the leprosy disappeared. Luke 5:13 (NLT)

DOES IT EVER GRATE ON your nerves how often God gets a bad rap? Many people, including many believers in Jesus, have the misguided idea that we have to beg our way into His Father's heart. Oftentimes this belief that God the Father is an angry withholder is based on the Old Testament era before Jesus came and offered grace.

However, think about these facts for a minute. Who sent Jesus to save us? *God.* Who made a plan for our salvation and recovery before Adam and Eve ever sinned? *God.* Whose words flow with emotive longing for the salvation of humankind throughout the Old Testament, even as His people turned from Him to do their own thing, even to the point of repeatedly choosing evil over His holiness? *God.*

When I say no to avoid spoiling my kids when they get the gimmes at a store, my heart still tugs with the desire for their happiness. But giving them everything they ask for would not be best for them.

Our Lord's longing for our fulfillment is immeasurably greater than any earthly parent's. However, He, being wiser than we are, sees the whole path that giving us everything we desire would lead us down. Even our good desires for healing and security in this life are not the end-all goal He has for our well-being. Sometimes He withholds what feels like necessity for a greater purpose.

But everything Jesus does comes from His Father's heart of love. He desires for us to be whole and holy, patterned after Himself. The heart that led Jesus to willingly heal the leper is Father God's heart.

He is willing. He wants good for you. Trust the One Jesus trusts.
—ERIN KEELEY MARSHALL

FAITH STEP: *Journal a letter to the Lord telling Him honestly how you view Him—whether as more of a judge or a Savior. Then ask Him for greater understanding of His loving heart that desires to provide what you truly need.*

TUESDAY, AUGUST 11

*So everywhere we go, we tell everyone about Christ... I work very hard at this,
as I depend on Christ's mighty power that works within me.*
Colossians 1:28–29 (NLT)

WHAT'S THE SECRET TO BEING most effective in fulfilling your life's purpose? Some folks might think training or experience makes the difference. Others believe networking and making valuable contacts hold the key. Some think being at the right place at the right time spells success.

While these factors matter to a degree, I believe the apostle Paul got it right. He knew God had appointed him to be an evangelist, to tell others about Jesus Christ everywhere he went. And so he did. He preached, taught, and warned so people would trust in Christ for salvation and then grow to maturity in their faith. And he saw results!

What was the secret of Paul's effectiveness? He worked diligently, and granted, he possessed impressive credentials. But more important—he trusted in Christ's mighty power at work within him to get the job done.

I believe my life's purpose involves connecting the dots between faith and real life for my audiences and readers. I work diligently, but ultimately I must trust Christ's mighty power in me to make me most effective. I need Him to help me understand the Scriptures and to teach me how to apply them. He alone knows the heart cries of those who will read my words, and so I need Him to show me what to write and speak. On my own, I'm like an archer shooting in the dark, hoping to hit the bullseye. But Christ's power changes everything.

Let Christ's power infuse you, too, as you pursue your life's calling.
—GRACE FOX

FAITH STEP: *When you rise each morning, offer your day's work—whatever it may be—to the Lord. Perform your tasks with excellence, but acknowledge your need for Christ to empower you. Invite Him to fill and control every cell and fiber of your being.*

WEDNESDAY, AUGUST 12

Make a clean break with all cutting, backbiting, profane talk. Be gentle with one another, sensitive. Forgive one another as quickly and thoroughly as God in Christ forgave you. Ephesians 4: 31–32 (MSG)

THE AUTO INSURANCE COMPANY'S REP assured me that he would be able to get the mother of the son who stole our car to pay the insurance deductible. He went on about how good he was at getting people to pay. But weeks later when the letter came from the insurance company, things didn't look good. The boy's mother had refused to pay. That was that. Case closed.

Anger filled me as it had periodically since this fifteen-year-old had robbed our house and stolen many of our possessions, not to mention our sense of security.

But at that moment I made a choice. I would let it go. I would release my anger and the hope that I once had that this mother would do as she'd been asked to do. I tore the letter into pieces, lifted them above my head and let them fall onto the kitchen floor. Over. Done with. I would not let anger reside in my heart any longer. —ALICE J. WISLER

FAITH STEP: *Go out on a walk and think of those you need to forgive. Ask Jesus to bring them to mind. Allow Him to replace your anger with His love. Remember to pray for your enemies.*

THURSDAY, AUGUST 13

He gave five bags of silver to one, two bags of silver to another, and one bag of silver to the last—dividing it in proportion to their abilities.
Matthew 25:15 (NLT)

I RECENTLY READ A BOOK that I loved. It was written by a woman who opened her home and offered her table to others. She told story after story about the food that she'd cooked, the conversations that she'd had. As I read the book I was reminded of the importance of sharing meals, but I also felt like I was falling short.

We all do this, don't we? We see or read about someone else's abilities and accomplishments, and we feel as if we've somehow failed. Yet as I considered my table, and the food shared there, images of family dinners came to mind. We gather as a family around the table on most weeknights, and we enjoy each other.

Jesus hasn't given all of us the same abilities. In the passage in Matthew 25, the master of the home gave his servants varied amounts of money to manage; one servant got five bags of silver, one got two bags, and one was given one bag. The first two doubled their investment, and the master's words for them were the same. "The master was full of praise. 'Well done, my good and faithful servant. You have been faithful in handling this small amount, so now I will give you many more responsibilities. Let's celebrate together!'" Matthew 25:21 (NLT).

The master called both the five bags and the two bags a "small amount." What Jesus gives us to manage is small in comparison to all our Master owns. My job isn't to compare how I use my small amount. My job is to manage what I've been given faithfully. And sometimes that's done over spaghetti and meatballs with family or friends. —TRICIA GOYER

FAITH STEP: *Come up with discussion questions for your next meal with family or friends, and set aside a time to have an inspiring conversation. Take time to simply enjoy being together.*

FRIDAY, AUGUST 14

"From his fullness we have all received grace upon grace."
John 1:16 (CEB)

HAS ANYONE EVER ACCUSED YOU of acting like the main character in the fairytale *The Princess and the Pea?* As a test of the princess's royal heritage and sensitivity, twenty mattresses and twenty featherbeds were stacked one or top of the other with a single hard, dried pea placed under the bottom mattress. In the morning, the privileged princess reported she'd been kept awake by an annoying discomfort. Despite the plentiful layers. Despite the tininess of the offending agent. The princess-seeking prince was thrilled. Her exquisite sensitivity proved her to be of royal blood.

Reading that story as a child, I looked for the moral to the tale and wasn't sure there was one. Apparently, Hans Christian Andersen's critics felt the same.

Today, though, I can see a point to the story, but it may not be what Mr. Andersen had in mind.

The Apostle John said that through Jesus, we have been given grace upon grace. Mattress piled upon mattress. And yet we still complain about the small irritants of life.

Grace upon grace. A lifetime—no, an eternity—of graces. Breath. Life. Health. Gifts. Opportunities. The favor of God. The joy of Jesus. His peace.

And we gripe about some driver who pulls out in front of us. On the phone, we find it unbearable to be kept on hold. We feel our blood pressure rising if the line at the grocery store is longer than two carts ahead of us. We send back a steak that isn't done to our preference.

We have all been given grace upon grace because of Jesus. I wonder if heaven would consider it a show of our royal heritage if, rather than complaining about the irritating pea, we expressed our gratitude for the many layers of mattresses. —CYNTHIA RUCHTI

FAITH STEP: *It's a given that expressing our gratitude to Jesus is a relationship-builder with Him. Consider the companion importance of confessing and repenting of our ingratitude.*

SATURDAY, AUGUST 15

"You're blessed when you get your inside world—your mind and heart—put right. Then you can see God in the outside world." Matthew 5:8 (MSG)

JESUS'S WORDS IN THE BEATITUDES may seem strange—and opposite from most philosophies we discover in life. Some think the words *blessed* or *happy* usually apply to those who have achieved great positions in life, such as scholars, presidents, CEOs, entrepreneurs, and the wealthy. Or at least those who have obtained some measure of success.

Others define happiness by the size of their possessions. If we're honest, we'd probably admit that new clothes, furniture, or kudos from others have nudged that blessed feeling into our hearts, even if only temporarily. I've shopped more than a few needless sales myself. There's nothing wrong with new things—or accomplishments—as long as they don't steal our hearts away from true kingdom living.

But Jesus redefines the spirit of blessedness. Congratulations go instead to the ones who experience things like sorrow, persecution, or despair, but whose lives also demonstrate humility, mercy, and a thirst for God in the midst of it all: genuine "be-attitudes." True happiness finds its source in the One Who has already provided everything we need.

Perhaps Jesus summed up the word "blessed" in verse 8. As believers, Jesus has already declared us blessed—and right with Him—both in this life, and in eternity. But we experience true blessedness when we let Jesus work through us, helping us to get our inside world right and see what kingdom living is all about through His eyes.

As we make His values our own, we'll understand the importance of those godly attitudes to "be" in. —REBECCA BARLOW JORDAN

FAITH STEP: *Take time to make a list of good attitudes you want Jesus to help you to be in. Thank Him for blessing you and for His help demonstrating them.*

SUNDAY, AUGUST 16

If any of you lacks wisdom, you should ask God, who gives generously to all without finding fault, and it will be given to you. But when you ask, you must believe and not doubt, because the one who doubts is like a wave of the sea, blown and tossed by the wind. That person should not expect to receive anything from the Lord. Such a person is double-minded and unstable in all they do. James 1:5–8 (NIV)

IN THE MIDDLE OF AN argument, I breathed a quick prayer, asking for wisdom. Instead of great words, what came to mind was an instruction in the form of one word: *breathe.*

Although it went against my nature, I stopped talking and let my husband speak. I was aware of my breathing, which calmed me down and soon I was able to listen fully to my husband. He wanted to be heard. That was important to him.

I love this passage about wisdom and memorized it as a teen. It fascinates me because it comes with a promise. If you lack, ask. The stipulation is almost as fascinating—don't doubt that you will get what you ask for. In other words, if you are going to ask for wisdom because you lack it, then believe it will be given to you. And who doesn't need the gift of wisdom?

I have learned that if you want to be wise, be in tune with the needs of others. I had to put aside my own frustrations and be willing to really listen to my husband. Wise conduct, wise in words, wise in understanding, are what we can pray for so that we can have more of the nature of Christ. —ALICE J. WISLER

FAITH STEP: *Memorize James 1:5–8 and see how it can equip you in your daily conversations and decisions.*

MONDAY, AUGUST 17

---

*"Anyone who welcomes you welcomes me, and anyone who welcomes me welcomes
the one who sent me . . . And if anyone gives even a cup of cold water to one of
these little ones who is my disciple, truly I tell you, that person will certainly
not lose their reward." Matthew 10:40,42 (NIV)*

I VIVIDLY REMEMBER THE YEARS of being a young mother of four. With
a new baby, a toddler, and two grade-school children, days and nights
passed in a blur of exhaustion. I longed to meet the needs of my children,
help them feel cherished and safe, and remind them daily of how much
Jesus loves them. However, I often felt buried by the sheer workload of
endless meals, laundry, and cleaning up yet another spill.

At the same time, I'd hear about other people's important service to
God's kingdom. A friend taught well-attended Bible classes, another traveled on mission trips, another organized food drives. I yearned to have
a special "ministry"—some activity I could point to where I was serving
Jesus. Instead, a sense of inadequacy dogged my steps as I filled sippy
cups, passed out crayons, and washed another load of diapers.

One bleary-eyed morning in my quiet time, I stumbled over this section of Matthew and understood Jesus's words in a new way. I was definitely giving cups of cold water to little ones. In fact, most days it seemed
as if that was all I was doing. In a rush of grace, I realized that as I kissed
jam-smudged faces, pushed a stroller around the block, or read *Runaway
Bunny* for the hundredth time, I truly was serving Jesus.

We often have an upside-down view of importance. Jesus reminds us
over and over about the value of the small act of love, the tiny step of obedience, the faithful service in hidden places. Each day as we welcome the
humble tasks Jesus gives us, we welcome Him. —SHARON HINCK

FAITH STEP: *Choose a small and humble task. Do it with an awareness of serving
Jesus.*

TUESDAY, AUGUST 18

On the contrary, we speak as those approved by God to be entrusted with the gospel. We are not trying to please people but God, who tests our hearts.
1 Thessalonians 2:4 (NIV)

I HAVE REALIZED A FEW things about myself: (1) I have a huge desire to please people; (2) people are changeable; (3) trying to please everyone all the time is impossible; (4) I still want to do it; and lastly, (5) this is a one-way ticket on the crazy train.

I have been known to make up scenarios and conversations in my head about what I believe people are thinking about me when I think I have disappointed them. I also like to reimagine conversations that I think have gone poorly. Conversation do-overs. Sadly, I am much more brilliant in my do-over conversations than I am in real-life conversations.

I am convinced that this is not the way that Jesus meant for me to live. Because that is not how He lived. Jesus only cared about what One "person" thought about Him. His Dad. Everything Jesus did revolved around what His Dad wanted, what He liked, what He valued, what He had asked Jesus to do. I am trying to follow His lead.

I'm stepping out of the "what ifs" and "I wonders" that swirl around in my brain and onto the firm truth of the Father's love. If I really want to spend my days worried about pleasing someone, shouldn't it be Him? If I am pleasing Him, if I am living for Him, if I am following His direction, than I don't have to worry about whether people like me or what I do or what I say. Because I am living out my life the way that it was meant to be lived. And that is an invitation to get off of the crazy train.

—SUSANNA FOTH AUGHTMON

FAITH STEP: *Tell Jesus, "You are the One I want to please with my life." Each time a people-pleasing thought enters your mind, remind yourself that you are pleasing an audience of one.*

WEDNESDAY, AUGUST 19

"Does anyone care, God? Is anyone listening and believing a word of it?" The point is: Before you trust, you have to listen. But unless Christ's Word is preached, there's nothing to listen to. Romans 10:16–17 (MSG)

FOR THE LAST THREE AND a half years I've been leading a teen moms support group in inner city Little Rock. The moms are young, and some have two or three children by the time they turn twenty. They live in poverty and make lots of unwise choices about jobs, money, education, and especially relationships. It's easy to get overwhelmed by all their needs.

At one of our support group meetings I'd decided to share a devotion about the wise men who sought Jesus. They traveled far, at great cost to themselves. I wanted to encourage the young moms to seek Him too. Yet once I started telling the story it was clear that nothing about Christ's birth was familiar to them.

"Born in Bethlehem, huh? Laid in a manger? What are you talking about? Born to a virgin? How in the world did that happen?" Their questions came one after another. Soon my talk about the wise men became a talk about the basics of Christ's birth.

I left that night realizing that I'd expected these young women to change—I'd wanted them to turn from their destructive ways to follow Jesus—yet I'd done a poor job of sharing even the basics. Raised in church, I expected everyone to know the story of Jesus's birth. It's hard to believe there are Americans who don't know, but those are wrong assumptions. Unless God's Word is preached how will they know? How will they change? How will they believe? I'm making it a goal to speak about Jesus more, and to start with the basics. —TRICIA GOYER

FAITH STEP: *In your city is there an organization that is reaching out to those in the inner city, or those who live in the lower-income parts of town? Contact them and find out ways you can support their efforts, whether it be through volunteering, financial assistance, or prayer.*

THURSDAY, AUGUST 20

"They got up right then and returned to Jerusalem." Luke 24:33 *(CEB)*

DUSK. THE INK OF NIGHT fast approaching. The end of a long, emotionally exhausting day. So much confusion. *Where do we go now? What do we do? What just happened?*

I've had days like that. Walking in the door after hours of arrangements at a funeral home. Pulling in the driveway after a sobering diagnosis. Sighing my way home after a hospital vigil.

Cleopas and another disciple walked a tortured path toward Emmaus, confused about what they'd witnessed—the death of Jesus. And what they'd heard—He was alive again. All their hopes rested in Jesus. Logic told them He was dead. Hadn't hope died on the skull hill?

As they walked and wondered, a man joined them. He made them see God's Word as never before. He radiated hope, so much that they felt as if their "hearts were on fire" when He explained the Scriptures to them.

When the man took a loaf of bread in His hands, blessed it and broke it, their eyes were opened and they saw who He really was—the Jesus of their hope.

This next bit is the detail that drilled its way into my heart the other day. "They got up right then and returned to Jerusalem." That was a walk of seven miles! In the dark. The joy of knowing the truth about Jesus, the very-much-alive Christ, pushed out all the weariness, all the uncertainty, all the anxiety, and got them moving again.

After a long afternoon at the funeral home. After a sobering diagnosis. After a hospital vigil. The truth about Who Jesus is—the Hope-giver—pushes out the weariness and uncertainty and gets me moving again.
—CYNTHIA RUCHTI

FAITH STEP: *Whatever anxieties dribbled over from yesterday into today, consider them dwarfed by the shadow of the Man Who conquered death to give you unshakable hope. Move forward—even through the dark—with your path lit by that Hope.*

FRIDAY, AUGUST 21

When he had said this, Jesus called in a loud voice, "Lazarus, come out!"
The dead man came out, his hands and feet wrapped with strips of linen,
and a cloth around his face. Jesus said to them, "Take off the grave clothes
and let him go." John 11:43–44 (NIV)

THE SCENE OF JESUS RAISING Lazarus paints a powerful portrait of Who He is and of our relationship with Him. Since Lazarus had been dead four days, the natural process of decay would have set in. But when Jesus called his name, Lazarus appeared at the opening of the tomb. His body had been so tightly bound that he probably couldn't have walked on his own. A supernatural power brought him out of the dark tomb. Jesus instructed the onlookers to remove the grave clothes so that Lazarus would be free.

When I answered Jesus's call and accepted His gift of forgiveness, it was every bit as miraculous as a formerly dead body coming out of a grave. I stepped out of darkness into light, from death into eternal life. But sadly, my way of living doesn't always reflect the new life I have in Jesus. Old sinful habits and attitudes can bind me as tightly as old-fashioned grave clothes. Worry about temporal things can hold me in an iron grip; getting too closely entangled with this world is sure to trip me up.

Jesus calls me to remove whatever restricts me from following Him more closely. He wants me to live in the freedom that comes with fully obeying His teachings and submitting to His leadership. He wants me to be clothed with the joy and peace that implicit trust in Him brings. Only then can I be "let go" to really live. —DIANNE NEAL MATTHEWS

FAITH STEP: *What "grave clothes" are binding you today? Ask Jesus to help you remove them so you can "let go" and fully live for Him this day.*

SATURDAY, AUGUST 22

He lifts the poor from the dust and the needy from the garbage dump. He sets them among princes, placing them in seats of honor. 1 Samuel 2:8 (NLT)

GROWING UP IN A FAMILY of collectors I frequently heard the phrase, "One person's trash is another person's treasure." I have fond memories of my mother's frequent garage sales and of my dad dragging home the "treasures" he rescued from a nearby Dumpster.

That phrase took on a new meaning last year when I read about Landfill Harmonic. Cateura, Paraguay, one of the poorest slums in Latin America, is located in the center of a huge garbage dump. The drug-infested, gang-filled area left few hopes for children growing up there. But that changed when a local garbage picker dragged home a piece of trash from the dump and presented it to a musician. Together, they birthed an idea that is changing the hopes and dreams of families into valuable treasures. Using recyclable discards from the dump, they crafted violins, flutes, drums, and other instruments and placed them in the hands of the slum's children—who, once discouraged and hopeless, suddenly found purpose and joy through music.

Now, after lessons and practice, their Landfill Harmonic orchestra has made headlines around the world.

Over two thousand years ago, Jesus entered a world filled with soul-sick poverty, hopelessness, and decay. He became a divine "garbage picker" as He walked the streets of humanity, rescuing and redeeming the "trash." Then He presented His findings to the Master Musician to fulfill a masterly plan, one that would change the world forever.

Why would He do that? Because one person's trash, in Jesus's eyes and in divine hands, becomes a beautiful treasure, filled with purpose and joy to be used by Him. —REBECCA BARLOW JORDAN

FAITH STEP: *This week create something useable from a garbage discard. Then display it in a central place to remind you of what Jesus did for you.*

SUNDAY, AUGUST 23

"Come," he [Jesus] said. Then Peter got down out of the boat, walked on the water and came toward Jesus. But when he saw the wind, he was afraid and, beginning to sink, cried out, "Lord, save me!" Immediately Jesus reached out his hand and caught him. "You of little faith," he said, "why did you doubt?" And when they climbed into the boat, the wind died down. Matthew 14:29–32 (NIV)

I'VE ALWAYS IDENTIFIED WITH PETER. I have that same enthusiasm that leads me to scramble out of the boat ready to take a risk to be with Jesus. The adventure of marriage? Yes, I'll dive right in. Venturing to grad school on a shoestring budget? Why not? Raising children? Of course! Mission trips? Sure. Arts ministry, career changes, public speaking? I've splashed into the water with reckless excitement and my eyes on my Savior.

However, also like Peter, I plunge first and then stop to look around. And when I do, my faith wobbles. Suddenly the risks seem too great, the storms too frightening, each step too hazardous and impossible. Relationships are more challenging than I expected, doors close, plans change, opposition knocks me over like salty waves. With Peter, my boldness changes to a simple plea: "Lord, save me!"

Recently, one word in this account from Scripture stood out to me that I hadn't noticed before: "Immediately." Jesus didn't wait until Peter had lungs full of water. He didn't stand off and watch Peter struggle. Jesus grabbed His floundering disciple at once.

We can pray that Jesus will continue to grow our faith so that we're not as easily frightened in following Him. But even when we put our focus on the wrong things and begin to sink, we can rejoice that Jesus loves us so much that He reaches out His hand to catch us—immediately.

—SHARON HINCK

FAITH STEP: *Is there a life circumstance where you feel like you're sinking? Reach up your hand and call out to Jesus, "Lord, save me!"*

MONDAY, AUGUST 24

Therefore, if anyone is in Christ, the new creation has come: The old has gone, the new is here! 2 Corinthians 5:17 (NIV)

YESTERDAY WHEN WE GOT TO church, we realized we had left a bin full of items that we needed back home. I got Will and Addie back in the car and headed back home.

The following conversation ensued:

Will: Mom, you shouldn't have made me go back home with you. Aunt Jenny wants me to be the main actor in her skit for kids' church.

Me: Oh, I'm sorry! Were you supposed to practice?

Will: Yes. I'm the leper.

Addie: *Awww!* I want to be the leper.

Will: No. You can't be the leper. I am the leper.

Addie: It's not fair. Aren't there ten lepers? Why can't I be a leper too?

Will: No. There is just one leper.

Addie: *Ooooo! Oooo!* I want to be Jesus. Can I be Jesus?

Will: Jesus isn't in this story. Just the leper. (FYI: The skit was about Naaman—an Old Testament Bible story.)

Addie: *Awww*, man. I never get to be the leper.

Poor Addie! Life is tough sometimes. I do love that my children enjoy church. I love that they get excited about Jesus. I love that they know that whoever gets to be the leper, won't be a leper by the end of the story.

Because that's what happens when Jesus shows up. Miracles take place. Lives are changed. Hope is restored. In some ways, we all are the leper. Then Jesus heals us. He restores us. He makes all things new when we yield our lives to Him. —SUSANNA FOTH AUGHTMON

FAITH STEP: *Find a plant, tree, or flower to study. Check out the dying parts and the new growth that is taking place. Remind yourself that when you invite Jesus into your life, new growth shows up in your life.*

TUESDAY, AUGUST 25

"I will remember the deeds of the Lord; yes, I will remember your miracles of long ago. I will consider all your works and meditate on all your mighty deeds." Your ways, God, are holy. What god is as great as our God? You are the God who performs miracles; you display your power among the peoples.
Psalm 77:11–14 (NIV)

RECENTLY I'VE BEGUN LEARNING ABOUT essential oils and how in ancient times God gave His people these healing oils to use for health. Aside from enjoying the scents and experiencing their healing power, I've been fascinated to read about the biblical basis for their use and the documented stories of their success.

I love history, but when something in the present reminds me that the Holy Hand that held life together thousands of years ago is the very hand of my Savior today—*Wow!* That's history to build on.

I am saddened to think of the millions who consider human heritage to be manmade, bubbling up from primordial sludge.

I've wondered before whether I would have believed as readily in Creation and salvation and eternity if I hadn't been taught it as truth from my early years. Would life and humanity's "advanced" wisdom have hardened the eyes of my faith? Would believing have been a struggle for me?

I can't say. But I do trust that Jesus's timing for each person is chosen ideally for them. He knows who will have a heart for Him, and He has been working throughout history for this very hour for everyone on earth now.

For my part, I can pray that His mighty deeds and miracles will speak His love into the hearts of those who need Him. —ERIN KEELEY MARSHALL

FAITH STEP: *Spend a few minutes recalling miracles you've heard about from the Bible, and ask Jesus to reveal Himself in history that continues to unfold today.*

WEDNESDAY, AUGUST 26

Three different times I begged the Lord to take it away. Each time he said,
"My gracious favor is all you need. My power works best in your weakness."
2 Corinthians 12:8–9 (NLT)

WE DON'T KNOW WHAT PHYSICAL ailment plagued the apostle Paul, but
we do know he begged the Lord to remove it three times. Three times the
Lord denied his request because He knew Christ's power could best be
seen if Paul had no strength of his own on which to rely.

Receiving a divine "No" must have been difficult for Paul, but eventually
he learned not to wish away his weaknesses. He chose instead to embrace
them as opportunities for Christ to be seen and honored in his life. That
perspective enabled him to develop contentment with his circumstances.

Often we consider our weaknesses as deficiencies. We want them fixed,
healed, removed. We beg. We plead. But God says no. We may be tempted to grow frustrated, angry, or disillusioned, but we need to remember
He sees life from an eternal perspective. He has purposes we can't understand. Are we willing to surrender and let God be God?

As disciples of Jesus Christ, let's ensure that bringing Him glory is our
ultimate goal. If that means learning to live in peace with so-called weaknesses, then so be it. Maybe our surrender will create curiosity within
those who would expect an alternative response. They may ask questions
about the reason for our hope, and then we'll have an open door to tell
them about Christ.

God's power works best in our weaknesses. Let's live as though we believe this is true. —GRACE FOX

FAITH STEP: *Identify something you consider a weakness in your life. How might
this allow you to experience Christ's strength? Invite Him to turn this weakness into an
opportunity for your faith to grow and for Him to receive honor.*

THURSDAY, AUGUST 27

Meanwhile, Jesus was in Bethany at the home of Simon,
a man who had previously had leprosy. Matthew 26:6 (NLT)

NOT LONG AFTER MY GRANDMOTHER had her third child she came down with an autoimmune disease. Sores covered her body, she lost her teeth, and she was hospitalized for months.

The doctor told her husband that he didn't understand what was happening, but he had no hope for her recovery. Even though she wasn't raised knowing about Jesus, she cried out to Him. She asked for Him to heal her. She prayed like she never prayed before, and Jesus met her there. He healed her. She walked out of that hospital and raised her three daughters and cared for her husband. She even worked outside the home for many years, and she was known for her cooking and hospitality. Now in her eighties, she is still a strong believer who turns to the Lord daily in prayer.

Jesus changes everything. He can turn those who are down-and-out, or on their death beds, into party hosts! And it was at Simon the Leper's party that one of the most beautiful displays of love for Christ was shown. "While [Jesus] was in Bethany, reclining at the table in the home of Simon the Leper, a woman came with an alabaster jar of very expensive perfume, made of pure nard. She broke the jar and poured the perfume on his head" (Mark 14:3, NIV).

When we turn to Jesus for help and healing, the impact extends far beyond ourselves. Simon's healing allowed him to open his home to others, transforming it into a gathering place for those who wanted to know Jesus more intimately. My grandmother's healing allowed her to become an important influence to many, especially me. Often we want healing for ourselves, but Jesus knows it will affect so many more. —TRICIA GOYER

FAITH STEP: *Do you need a specific healing in your life? Turn to Jesus in prayer. If you have been healed, offer yourself, and your home, to others. Throw a party!*

FRIDAY, AUGUST 28

For I was hungry and you gave me something to eat, I was thirsty and you gave me something to drink, I was a stranger and you invited me in, I needed clothes and you clothed me, I was sick and you looked after me, I was in prison and you came to visit me. Matthew 25:35–36 (NIV)

WHEN JESUS SAID THESE WORDS, He was describing a time of judgment when those who really knew Him would be recognized because they did these things. In later verses He says He will tell those who did not do them to depart from Him. I want to really know Jesus, but sometimes I feel small. When I hear about the suffering of women and children in Afghanistan, or see tragedy strike in faraway places, my impulse is to go, to give, but realistically, what can I do?

C. S. Lewis offers this advice: "I think each village was meant to feel pity for its own sick and poor whom it can help and I doubt if it is the duty of any private person to fix his mind on ills which he cannot help. This may even become an escape from the works of charity we really can do to those we know. God may call any one of us to respond to some far away problem or support those who have been so called. But we are finite and he will not call us everywhere or to support every worthy cause. And real needs are not far from us."

It is tempting to think that the big things are what matter most, and certainly they do matter. But the "least of these" are all around us. There are students in my classes every day with real needs I can address. There's a food bank in my town where I can donate groceries. My kids have friends who need coats. The hospital and nursing home are full of people who are sick. There's even a county jail. Lewis's directive reminds me that I can— and should—carry out the mission of the gospel in my own community.
—GWEN FORD FAULKENBERRY

FAITH STEP: *Ask Jesus to show you a real need you can help meet in your sphere of influence. Then commit to doing what you can, and do it!*

SATURDAY, AUGUST 29

Blessed are those who mourn, for they will be comforted.
Matthew 5:4 (NIV)

LOSING A LOVED ONE IS painful. When my son Daniel died at age four after eight months of vicious cancer treatments, I wanted to crawl into a hole and have the dirt cover me. I didn't want to live anymore.

While there were those who had no clue how to reach me, others were creative in their approach. Friends baked me bread, gave me gifts, took me on walks and out for lunches. They let me talk about my son; they listened. Those who had known him shared their stories of him. Those were all gifts for me. That kind of care and compassion was what I needed most.

On the other hand, what I didn't need were those who avoided me in the grocery store (I suppose it was because they didn't know what to say) or those who said things like, "God needed another flower for His garden and so He chose Daniel."

God is the Creator of comfort. He sent Jesus into this world to bring us comfort in a tangible way. Jesus lived among His disciples and in community with others. He had compassion for those who mourned.

When we meet others where they are and extend a heart of compassion, we become a healing balm for those in need. —ALICE J. WISLER

FAITH STEP: *Can you be the one to bring comfort to those who mourn? Can you change your plans and reach out to someone who is hurting?*

SUNDAY, AUGUST 30

He will not allow your foot to slip; your Protector will not slumber.
Psalm 121:3 (HCS)

AFTER I FINISHED LOADING THE groceries in my car, I drove out of the parking lot to turn left on the highway. The red light stopped me, but at least it gave me a chance to notice the beautiful sunshine. Staring at the light made the wait seem longer. I began to mentally rehearse all that I hoped to accomplish that afternoon. As soon as the light changed, I moved my foot from the brake to the accelerator. But for some reason, I seemed to be going in slow motion.

I felt a sense of oddness as I realized that I wasn't pulling out onto the road at my usual speed, yet I wasn't sure why. At the same time, I wondered if the driver behind me was annoyed at my snail pace. Those thoughts were interrupted when a large SUV zoomed down the highway right in my path, ignoring the red light for oncoming traffic. It wasn't until I got home that it finally sank in what would have happened to me if I had pulled out onto the highway at a normal speed in my smaller car, instead of pulling forward in slow motion.

Sometimes I wonder how many times Jesus has gotten me out of trouble, or even saved me from catastrophe, without my being aware of it. As I go about my daily routine, I'm so thankful to have Him as my Protector. He may choose to openly display His actions or He may quietly work behind the scenes. Either way, I have the comfort of knowing that Jesus is looking out for me. And when things in my life seem to be moving slowly, I need to remember that it might be because He's keeping me safe.

—DIANNE NEAL MATTHEWS

FAITH STEP: *Before you go to sleep tonight, review your day. Can you discern moments when Jesus kept you safe, even when you weren't aware of it at the time? Thank Him for being your Protector.*

MONDAY, AUGUST 31

"Dear brothers and sisters, when troubles come your way, consider it an opportunity for great joy. For you know that when your faith is tested, your endurance has a chance to grow." James 1:2–3 (NLT)

LAST NIGHT I WAS READING an article that focused on being grateful for the difficulties of life. The hard places. The struggles. The disappointments. They offer an opportunity for change, for overcoming, for a shift in worldview.

A Pulitzer-prize winning author who had been diagnosed with melanoma took the diagnosis as a sign to pour his life into helping others with melanoma by organizing runs for research. I read that and thought, "Huh."

Because mostly, I am thankful for the things in my life that are good, easy and uplifting. The hard things? Not so much.

But he says that the struggles are like the contrast in a painting that shows off the good in our lives. We can say, "This time was incredibly difficult. But I made it through. And look at the beauty that can still be found in my life." We may not welcome troubles but we can welcome what Jesus can do with them.

Here are a few hard things I am grateful for: the experience of having a broken heart...because it showed me how amazing real love is. The rejections that I got for my fiction children's books...they started me on the path of writing adult nonfiction. The downward spiral I fell into in my college years; it sent me running back into the grace-filled arms of Jesus. But mostly, I am grateful for the rock solidness of Jesus and the love of the people He has given me. I could have never gotten through the hard things without them. —SUSANNA FOTH AUGHTMON

FAITH STEP: *Write your own hard gratitude list. Thank Jesus for what He has taught you in the midst of your struggles.*

TUESDAY, SEPTEMBER 1

Finally, brothers and sisters, whatever is true, whatever is noble, whatever is right, whatever is pure, whatever is lovely, whatever is admirable—if anything is excellent or praiseworthy—think about such things. Whatever you have learned or received or heard from me, or seen in me—put it into practice. And the God of peace will be with you. Philippians 4:8–9 (NIV)

THE OTHER DAY WHILE OUT on a walk, I was steeped in thoughts about my financial deficit. I lamented, and the more I lamented, the more I realized how many other problems I had. I felt like crawling into a manhole and giving up. "Dear Jesus, I need help," I cried. "I am so weary. Give me some pep in my step."

Suddenly a butterfly on a bush caught my attention. I stopped to view her work as she fluttered around each flower. Her wings were a pattern of orange, black, and even violet. *Wow,* I thought, *I am rich.* And as I continued my walk and the sun shone through the blue sky and over the tops of the trees, I said, "I am rich because I get to walk on this beautiful early fall morning."

The bank doesn't think I'm rich. The world doesn't, and when there is no peanut butter left in the jar, my kids certainly don't think I am. But I know that richness is more than numbers in a bank account or what others think.

I am rich because I get to watch the sun rise. I am rich because I have seen forgiveness. I am rich because I know the Giver of Life. I am rich because I know my identity is in Christ Jesus. —ALICE J. WISLER

FAITH STEP: *List ways in which you are rich because Jesus walks daily with you in your life. Reflect on life-giving truths, and watch your steps increase with pep and your heart fill with His perfect peace.*

WEDNESDAY, SEPTEMBER 2

And without faith it is impossible to please God, because anyone who comes to him must believe that he exists and that he rewards those who earnestly seek him. Hebrews 11:6 (NIV)

MY FRIEND LESLIE IS AFRAID of clowns. My children think this is funny. They want to send her pictures of scary clowns. They take after their father. Other people's fears can seem funny to us. But our own fears? Not so much.

Lately, Jesus has been challenging my fears. I have a lot of them. A long list. Spiders, cicadas, or any other insect landing on me. Heights. Airplane turbulence. Saying the wrong thing in a conversation. Making a fool of myself. Being a failure. Being attacked in a dark parking lot (I *will* use my keys as weapons). Losing the people that I love. Being attacked by a large animal (I dreamed as a kid that I was eaten by a bear...and a giant crab). Not being able to write anymore. Going either bald or blind (I'm not kidding). Persecution. Letting down my friends and family. Missing out on God's will.

I could go on...but let's not. The thing is that when we follow Jesus, He calls us to a life of doing things that are impossible without Him. He calls us to a life of jumping out of boats and believing that He will do the rest. It's called faith.

The truth is that when I empty my life of faith, I empty it of possibility. When I let fear win...well, fear wins. And who wants that? When we decide to follow Jesus, we can move past our fears and trust that He, in His great mercy and creativity, will lead us on a journey that is more than we could ever hope for or imagine. —SUSANNA FOTH AUGHTMON

FAITH STEP: *Take a faith walk with a friend. Close your eyes and follow the sound of their voice. Know that just as your friend makes sure that you are safe, so does Jesus when you follow the sound of His voice.*

THURSDAY, SEPTEMBER 3

Now my heart is troubled, and what shall I say? "Father, save me from this hour"? No, it was for this very reason I came to this hour. Father, glorify your name!
John 12:27–28 (NIV)

MY FRIEND PAM REACHED FOR my hand. "They finally figured out what's wrong with me," she said quietly. "It's pancreatic cancer."

Her words slammed into me, and my stomach dropped. There had to be a mistake. A mixed-up lab report. Sitting beside her on the pew after church, I longed to do anything to save her from the road she was facing.

As we talked, she said, "I know Jesus can heal, and I'll pray for that and fight for that. I don't want to leave my husband and children. But whatever happens, I want to bring glory to Jesus."

In the following months, every conversation we had, each small group gathering with friends to pray and share, she continued to affirm the goodness of Christ, and her confidence in His love for her. When she died, with her family gathered around, it was with a prayer on her lips.

There are many times when I'm not sure how to pray. A circumstance is so frightening or overwhelming that I don't even know what to ask. At those times, I think of Pam's prayer, and Jesus's words here, to help shape my prayer. "Lord, I don't understand what's happening here, and I don't want to walk this road. But glorify Your name." —SHARON HINCK

FAITH STEP: *Think of one earnest prayer you've been praying in which you've been asking Jesus to change circumstances or another person. Today, pray a new way about that deep longing, asking that God will be glorified.*

FRIDAY, SEPTEMBER 4

"I, Jesus . . . am the bright Morning Star." Revelation 22:16 (NIV)

As I TYPE, THE PITCH dark outside is giving way to the sunrise. A medium-blue sky peeks over the neighbors' trees while I see next to me the outline of a sweet little girl sleeping in the dark.

Last night our family split up for separate adventures. The guys went to deer camp for Paxton's first hunt this morning, and my daughter and I pulled out the sofa bed for a movie night and slumber party in the family room. Fighting a cold, and unaccustomed to sleeping on the thin mattress, I awoke early and am enjoying the peaceful morning hush.

I love this kind of wake-up. It feels as if I'm sitting here waiting for Jesus to fill me with His heart for the day. There's something special about the morning, something spiritual.

It's easy to take for granted that the morning is just like any other time of day, but Jesus's Word speaks of gifts that come with the morning. When we wake up, He has new mercies to shed on us (Lamentations 3:22–23). The morning scatters the threats of darkness (Luke 1:78–79) and awakens us to His glory (Psalm 57:8). He even calls Himself the bright Morning Star.

The Creator did not have to form our solar system to rotate and revolve so we could experience refreshment and a new beginning every twenty-four hours. But He did. Could it be that His plan and provision for each new day was precisely so that we could be reminded of His care and hope and light so frequently? We need morning eyes to notice Him though.

The sky is light now. A new day has begun, filled with hope, soul-care, and awareness of His love if I'll be attuned to see Him in it.

Good morning to you. —ERIN KEELEY MARSHALL

FAITH STEP: *No matter the hour, ask Jesus to help you see Him today.*

SATURDAY, SEPTEMBER 5

"Jesus, Son of David, have mercy on me!" Luke 18:38 (NAS)

FREDERICK BUECHNER WRITES IN *WHISTLING IN THE DARK* that we erect walls around our hearts in order to hide from other people and from ourselves. He says we do this to keep pain out, but we end up creating our own prisons, where we become lonely and isolated. "Fortunately," he writes, "there are two words that offer a way out, and they're simply these: 'Help me.' It's not always easy to say them...but they're always worth saying. To another human being—a friend, a stranger? To God? Maybe it comes to the same thing. *Help me.* They open a door through the walls, that's all. At least hope is possible again. At least you're no longer alone."

I love Buechner's idea that reaching out to another human being, whether friend or stranger, may turn out to be the same thing as reaching out to God. Jesus embodied this idea by being Emmanuel—God with us. When the blind man Bartimaeus called out to Him, he was crying out for help, for hope. And Jesus responded by giving him sight.

How do you respond when people ask you for help? Do you turn away? Or, like Jesus, are you someone who listens and offers hope? Perhaps you're like me and the giving of help is not the difficult thing, but the asking for it is. We have our pride, after all.

The truth is, however, that we are all like blind Bartimaeus. We are all in need of Jesus and the hope He offers. The mercy. The new perspective. It's only in receiving from Him that we have anything worthwhile to offer others in need. The story continues that after Bartimaeus received his sight, He followed Jesus. The Bible says *He glorified God and when all the people saw it they gave praise to God.* —GWEN FORD FAULKENBERRY

FAITH STEP: *If you need a way out today, cry out to Jesus. Ask for help—from a friend or a stranger. Jesus is everywhere. And when your hope is restored, share your story with others so that they'll give praise to Him.*

SUNDAY, SEPTEMBER 6

*And he said: "I tell you the truth, unless you change and become
like little children, you will never enter the kingdom of heaven.
Therefore, whoever humbles himself like this child is the greatest in
the kingdom of heaven." Matthew 18:3–4 (NIV)*

BY EARLY SEPTEMBER, MY NINE-YEAR-OLD granddaughter's thoughts had already turned to trick-or-treating. "Well," Lacey announced one day, "I guess I could always be a princess for Halloween. But that seems so childish."

Her three-year-old-brother looked at her earnestly. "So what?" he asked with a puzzled expression. "You *are* a child."

Jesus used a child as an example of the Christian faith and what makes a person great in heaven's eyes. We may think we have to become a great theologian or accomplish great works to impress Him, but what Jesus values most is a humble, childlike spirit. We can only come to Him through our vulnerability and need, with no agenda of our own, trusting Him to work in our life. Once we realize our utter dependence on Jesus, then we can receive His greatest blessings.

Sometimes I get weary of trying to figure out things I'll never understand. I can knock myself out attempting to fix myself, other people, and every problem I see around me. That's when I need a reminder of the attitude that demonstrates genuine faith.

When her little brother pointed out the obvious, Lacey's response was, "Thanks a lot, buddy. You really lightened me up." How often my burdens would be lightened if I let go of my striving and unrealistic expectations, and simply remembered my identity. I am a dearly loved child who can always trust Jesus to take care of me. —DIANNE NEAL MATTHEWS

FAITH STEP: *In what ways are you growing in your childlike faith? What burdens would be lifted if you could develop that quality more? Ask Jesus to help you fully depend on Him and receive His blessings as a child.*

MONDAY, SEPTEMBER 7

"There is more than enough room in my Father's home. If this were not so, would I have told you that I am going to prepare a place for you? When everything is ready, I will come and get you, so that you will always be with me where I am."
John 14:2–3 (NLT)

MY HUSBAND AND I ENJOY traveling. We love visiting new places, learning about our nation's history, and drawing close to Jesus through God's beautiful creation.

In years past I often grieved when our vacation ended. I love my work, home, and family, but I wasn't ready to face busy schedules, daily routines, and less glamorous tasks. Couldn't we stay longer, tucked away from the demands of everyday life? No: time, money, and energy would eventually run thin.

Recently, however, I experienced something different on our planned getaway. We enjoyed the same things as always: beautiful scenery, rich history, new places. But on the last day of our vacation, I got homesick—tearfully homesick.

Maybe the 3,100 other passengers left me claustrophobic and eager for quiet, even though our ship provided a great temporary home away from home. Perhaps it's because as the years progress, my energies decrease faster. Daily excursions sapped my strength more than usual on that trip. At any rate, I couldn't wait to leave. I longed for the comforts and joys of my real home.

The older I get, the more homesick I grow for another kind of getaway: a permanent one, filled with glorious beauty, where history has no end or beginning, where time stands still and energy never wanes.

After Jesus's death and Resurrection, He ascended back to heaven and is now preparing a place for me. There, I won't be asking Jesus the question, "Could I stay a little longer?"

Forever is long enough. —REBECCA BARLOW JORDAN

FAITH STEP: *Do you ever grow homesick for heaven? Take time today to thank Jesus for the permanent "home away from home" He is preparing for you.*

TUESDAY, SEPTEMBER 8

And pray in the Spirit on all occasions with all kinds of prayers and requests.
With this in mind, be alert and always keep on praying for all the Lord's people.
Ephesians 6:18 (NIV)

THE NEWS SHOOK ME AND deep grief filled my heart. Tyreic, one of my son's friends, had been killed in a car accident. The boy was a senior with plans for graduation and college, and in one second, he had become distracted and that cost him his life.

Prayers were fervent for his family. On my daily walks, I agonized over this death and felt compassion for his father. Although I didn't know him well, I knew a lot about his new pain.

My sorrow in my heart—a perpetual hole—for the loss of my own son Daniel, caused me to be able to grieve as someone who knows. I wrote about Tyreic's life and death on one of my blogs, contacted his father and even wrote to the principal of the high school, thanking him for the way he handled the memorial vigil my son attended days after Tyreic's accident. For days, I was consumed with sadness.

I didn't fight it. I believe that God places on our hearts people to pray for. When He moves us to pray, we can't do anything else but obey. I suggested that those close to Tyreic's family would know how to best reach his father. —ALICE J. WISLER

FAITH STEP: *Has Jesus placed someone on your heart today? Be open to being moved to pray fervently for someone this week.*

WEDNESDAY, SEPTEMBER 9

Two by two they came into the boat, representing every living thing that breathes. A male and female of each kind entered, just as God had commanded Noah. Then the Lord closed the door behind them. Genesis 7:15–16 (NLT)

I LAY IN BED THINKING of how we could get some extra money. My husband was thinking too. Some friends of ours had alerted us to a business opportunity. A local, start-up Internet company was in talks with one of the big Internet search engines. They needed some capital to hold out till the documents were signed. Investors would get ten-fold their investment back.

"If we put in one thousand dollars, we'll get...ten thousand dollars back," I whispered to John.

"I know, but we don't have it." John sighed. "Jesus is closing the door on this one."

I prayed that Jesus would open the door for us, but it didn't happen. Our friends invested all the money they'd made on a recent house sale. But things didn't go as planned. The deal fell through, and their investment was gone. Looking back, what we saw as a closed door to a good investment was Jesus's hand of protection.

Do doors of opportunity seem to be closing? Look to Jesus. He alone sees the future, and He knows how to keep you safe. Sometimes we'll understand the reasons now. Other times we'll discover them in eternity. Because of Jesus's gift of salvation, one day His hand of protection will be completely known.

Jesus has your best interests in mind; He always has. Trust that every closed door means He has your best care in mind in the long run. —TRICIA GOYER

FAITH STEP: *Start an "investment" jar. Each night clean out the change from your wallet and move it into a jar. When the jar gets full, donate the money to an organization that is making an investment in eternity, such as a Bible society or outreach group.*

THURSDAY, SEPTEMBER 10

I want you to know me more than I want burnt offerings. Hosea 6:6 *(NLT)*

I WAS OFTEN OVERWHELMED AS a young mom with three preschoolers. My chore list never ended—laundry, cooking, cleaning, doctor appointments, potty training, and more laundry. I invested so much time and energy in serving my family that, ironically, I found it difficult to stop, sit down, and give them my undivided attention. No doubt they appreciated my labors of love, but they cherished time with me more.

Meaningful relationships don't just happen haphazardly. They need time to develop and deepen. This requires being intentional about spending time with those we want to know better. It also means engaging in two-way conversations, listening to each other as well as sharing our thoughts. It means applying the brakes of our crazy-busy lifestyles and stopping long enough to let a fellow human being know we truly care.

Jesus cherishes time with us too. He longs for a meaningful relationship with His followers, but that doesn't happen unless we're deliberate about it.

We might mistakenly think that attending church on Sunday mornings is enough to grow that relationship. We might even add an occasional prayer meeting to our schedule. Or volunteer on a church committee. Or do a short-term missions trip. We might cram our calendars with spiritual activities. But the service we do for Him can actually hinder our relationship with Him.

Let's keep first things first. Friendship with Jesus matters most. He's pleased when we serve Him, but He receives greater joy when we pursue knowing Him by spending time in His Word, conversing with Him, and practicing inviting His presence into our lives throughout the day. —GRACE FOX

FAITH STEP: *Because you're taking time to read this book, I know you value friendship with Jesus. Take a moment now to tell Him how much you love Him. Ask Him to give you an unquenchable thirst to know Him more.*

FRIDAY, SEPTEMBER 11

"I am the vine, and you are the branches. If any remain in me and I remain in them, they produce much fruit. But without me they can do nothing."
John 15:5 (NIV)

TODAY MY HUSBAND AND I had an unplanned state-of-the-finances talk. (Do those ever bring on warm-fuzzy feelings?) We usually do this about twice a year, and today the conversation jumped right up and smacked us. We realized that we'd been spending a little too freely in recent months.

While often not super-uplifting, financial gut-checks are beneficial just like taking the time to assess where we are in any area of life. It's easier to keep going with the status quo than it is to pause and consider whether the path we're on is the most fruitful.

Take our spiritual life, for example. We can easily get into a pattern of attending church, doing ministry, putting in a certain amount of time reading the Word and praying. We can go through the motions, but is the heart really seeking to know Jesus better through the time we invest in activities that appear spiritual?

If the things my husband and I invest our money in (aka spend it on) are not productive and useful for the long term, we may be wasting money and being too frivolous with the dollars we've been given.

Spiritually speaking, if we invest our spiritual energies without really considering the primary goal of knowing Jesus better, then we'll end up draining our spiritual resources just as we can drain our financial ones. If our spiritual life isn't deepening our connection with Jesus the Vine, then we, the branches, will dry up.

I think the next time I take out my credit card at a store, I'm going to cross-check my investments both financially and spiritually. How's that for checks and balances? —ERIN KEELEY MARSHALL

FAITH STEP: *Spend some time today investing in your relationship with Jesus.*

SATURDAY, SEPTEMBER 12

Therefore, since we are surrounded by such a great cloud of witnesses, let us throw off everything that hinders and the sin that so easily entangles. And let us run with perseverance the race marked out for us, fixing our eyes on Jesus, the pioneer and perfecter of faith. Hebrews 12: 1–2 (NIV)

THESE PAST THREE MONTHS MY sons, Jack and Will, have been playing basketball. I am highly invested in their games and tend to give a running commentary while they play.

The children have pleaded with me, "Mom, please be quiet." But I continue to yell out things like, "Get your rebounds!" and "Nice try!" and "Pay attention!" I also cheer loudly. Very loudly.

Scott asked them what else they hear me yell while they are playing. Jack piped up with, "Sweet mercy!" and Will followed with, "Oh, help him, help him!"

The thing is, I can't help cheering them on. I am rooting for them. I want them to focus on what is in front of them and to get everything out of the game that they can.

Jesus is the same with us. He wants us to throw off everything that gets us sidetracked and follow Him. It is His great joy to see us to excel and to succeed as we maneuver through life.

He doesn't want anything holding us back! He has made a way for us to have the best life possible and He is overjoyed when we turn our faces toward Him and follow in His footsteps. Our best days happen when we focus on Him! —SUSANNA FOTH AUGHTMON

FAITH STEP: *Take a walk that ends at your favorite coffee shop or friend's house. Remind yourself as you walk that when your life is focused on Jesus it determines the steps you take each day, and at the end of this life you will find the joy of being with Him.*

SUNDAY, SEPTEMBER 13

Then Peter said to Jesus, "Lord, how many times should I forgive my brother or sister who sins against me? Should I forgive as many as seven times?" Jesus said, "Not just seven times, but rather as many as seventy-seven times."
Matthew 18:21–22 (CEB)

WHEN I WORKED AT A group home for emotionally abused girls in Pennsylvania shortly after graduating from college, the girls were quick to bleat out obscenities, lie, and break any rule they could. As leaders, we had to watch them with eagle eyes. Yet I knew that they needed to be accepted and loved. I thought I understood about forgiveness and second chances, but the trying times with these girls taught me that I still had a ways to go.

We might boast about how we give our time or our money or even our forgiveness. But Jesus asks for more. More than we bargained for. More than we think is necessary. He wants us to be emptied of self, to weed it out like an overgrown garden, and be filled with Him.

Jesus asks us to come to Him and repent. Repent of our hardness of heart, our worries, the way we put ourselves before others, the bitterness we harbor. You might not think you can do this, but He believes in you and that with His help, you can. He wants to use you. He wants to mold you into a vessel where forgiveness flows freely for yourself and for others.
—ALICE J. WISLER

FAITH STEP: *Ask Jesus to reveal to you whom you need to forgive today. Pray for that person. Pray for his/her health, family, day-to-day struggles, and relationship with Jesus. Write down what you learn from Jesus about Himself after praying for this person.*

MONDAY, SEPTEMBER 14

So now there is no condemnation for those who belong to Christ Jesus.
Romans 8:1 (NLT)

I'VE ALWAYS HAD A PROBLEM with guilt. As a kid in school, I felt guilty whenever a teacher confronted the class about a problem—even if I had nothing to do with it. When I hear a pastor addressing sinful actions, I want to crawl under the pew even though I may not currently be struggling with what he's discussing. I always imagined that if the doctor slapped my bottom when I was born, I probably tried to say, "I'm sorry. I won't do it again."

Then there are the times when I fail and need to seek forgiveness from my Savior. Even after repenting and confessing my wrongdoing, I have a hard time letting go of the guilt and shame. Instead of putting the mistake behind me and moving on, I get mired down in reliving my failure over and over.

Sometimes I wonder why I struggle so much with guilt and why it's hard to accept the forgiveness that Jesus freely offers. Is it because I'm well aware of what I'm capable of doing? I have no idea where my excessive guilt comes from, but I know where it should go.

Jesus voluntarily offered His life as payment for our sins. His sacrifice took care of all of them—past, present, and future. He died to give us the gift of eternal life, but also so that we can live this earthly life free from guilt and shame. Each time we fail, Jesus stands ready to hear our confession and wash us clean with His forgiveness and mercy. The next time I'm weighed down with guilt, I need to remember to accept His lavish grace.
—DIANNE NEAL MATTHEWS

FAITH STEP: *Are you struggling with guilt over something that Jesus has already forgiven you for? Read Romans 8 and thank Him for the freedom He made possible through His death on the Cross.*

TUESDAY, SEPTEMBER 15

"Before he was taken up . . . in the power of the Holy Spirit, Jesus instructed the apostles he had chosen." Acts 1:2 (CEB)

PUTTING TOGETHER A TEAM IS a daunting task for anyone in leadership. Wouldn't it have been interesting to observe the thought processes Jesus went through when choosing the apostles?

"Okay, we need someone who will shake things up. How about . . . Peter? Feisty enough to keep managerial meetings from turning into a snore fest." Maybe that's why Jesus felt all the more disappointed by Peter's *somnia*—opposite of *insomnia*—in Gethsemane.

"We'll need someone to keep the books, someone good in math. Someone who knows how to stretch a buck. Integrity is key in this department. Judas Iscariot? Perfect!"

"Now, a couple of guys who know what it's like to live feast-or-famine. Who better than fishermen? Live-off-the-land kind of men. Bonus: anyone who can mend a net can probably sew on a patch too."

That may not be how Jesus chose His disciples. God's Word talks about Jesus informing those He loved about issues in their lives He'd "seen" before they ever came face-to-face. He knew what lay behind Judas's mask of integrity and Thomas's thin trust. He knew Peter's devotion would waver in the face of fear. But He chose them anyway.

Some of us can use what's in the pantry to feed fifty homeless people. Some can move a crowd to tears through storytelling. Others are skilled at counseling or expressing the Gospel in simple, gripping ways.

Jesus proved He could work with *anybody* when He chose that group of misfits. Whatever your gift or gifts, you're exactly what He is looking for. —CYNTHIA RUCHTI

FAITH STEP: *Give Jesus the entirety of your personality and skill-set and watch what He can do with them. He can change the world with no more than a heart fully devoted to Him.*

WEDNESDAY, SEPTEMBER 16

*Ever since I first heard of your strong faith in the Lord Jesus and your love for
God's people everywhere, I have not stopped thanking God for you.
I pray for you constantly. Ephesians 1:15–16 (NLT)*

PAUL'S ATTITUDE OF GRATITUDE AMAZES me. Several times throughout his
letters in the New Testament he mentioned "remembering" others and
giving thanks for them. The book of Ephesians is one of Paul's epistles
that records his frequent habit. Having spent two years in Ephesus previously,
Paul wrote this book in prison, possibly under house arrest.

Okay, maybe he did have more time to focus and remember in this
more isolated setting. But knowing Paul, he still spent time not only writing,
but also sharing about Jesus to anyone who crossed his path.

Paul didn't thank Jesus once for the beloved friends and new believers
he'd met, and then forget about them. He "never stopped." Obviously, he
had ministered to them. But they also touched his life. And then Paul did
more than just remember those people. He prayed constantly for them.

When Jesus spoke to Paul (then Saul) on the road to Damascus and
blinded him temporarily, He changed the former persecutor's life—
dramatically (Acts 9). That encounter not only resulted in a dynamic
missionary preacher, but a spirit of gratitude forever in Paul's life.

After reviewing Paul's letter I decided to top my new "thanksgiving" list
with the names of people Jesus has brought into my life through the years:
friends, family, church members, neighbors—whoever Jesus brings to mind.

Remembering so many may be challenging, and the list will keep growing.
But if I can simply ask Jesus to help me maintain a grateful heart, and review
that list of names often, that's a good start. —REBECCA BARLOW JORDAN

FAITH STEP: *Make a list of people who have influenced your life. Then write notes to
let them know how grateful you are, and that you are praying for them.*

THURSDAY, SEPTEMBER 17

And the Good News about the Kingdom will be preached throughout the whole world, so that all nations will hear it. Matthew 24:14 (NLT)

IN A SMALL CITY IN the Czech Republic there is an apartment not far from the town square where three young women room together. One is a Czech native who teaches high school and leads a local youth group. The second is from The Netherlands, working for a missionary organization for her second year. The third is a college graduate from the United States who shares Christ by teaching English classes for mothers and children, and who hosts a Bible study for international students. The third is my daughter.

My daughter told me that at the turn of the century, instead of using trunks, missionaries would have a wooden casket made for them, and then they would pack it with their things, knowing they would never return home. Today, I Skype with my daughter, text, and I post photos on Facebook of her younger siblings almost daily. Yet while the ways of communication with family at home have changed, the hearts of the missionaries haven't.

All over the world there are men, women, and families from all walks of life who have left the familiarity and comfort of home to share the Good News of the Kingdom—a message of reconciliation.

"For God was in Christ, reconciling the world to himself, no longer counting people's sins against them. And he gave us this wonderful message of reconciliation" (2 Corinthians 5:19, NLT).

Whether while strolling along on cobblestone or striding side by side through jungle trails, whispers about Jesus's love do their work penetrating native hearts. Ordinary men and women speak to other ordinary men and women and share that, through Jesus, we have a way to be forgiven and united with Him. And day by day, because of His followers, Jesus's prophecy is fulfilled over and over again. —TRICIA GOYER

FAITH STEP: *Do you know a missionary serving overseas? Pray especially for him or her today. Also, send a note of encouragement. It'll go a long way!*

FRIDAY, SEPTEMBER 18

Jesus replied: "'Love the Lord your God with all your heart and with all your soul and with all your mind.' This is the first and greatest commandment. And the second is like it: 'Love your neighbor as yourself.'" Matthew 22:37–39 (NIV)

I HAVE A FRIEND WHOSE love life has carried a theme of loss. He was divorced early in life, and thirty years later, after several dating experiences and a couple of serious relationships that ended, he finds himself alone. He would say that the right person just hasn't come along, and at this point I don't believe he has expectations of ever marrying again.

This friend is a man of many gifts, and I often think it regrettable that he has no soulmate to share them with. I was concerned when I heard he was retiring, afraid he might become isolated. He is a medical doctor, and tremendously successful. In that area, at least, he has been surrounded by people who appreciate him. But I shouldn't have worried—in retirement he decided to leave his practice in the States and travel with Doctors Without Borders, serving people in crisis situations all over the world.

Before he left on his latest mission, I was reading "Works of Love" in *The Essential Kierkegaard*. I came across this little gem that seemed to fit my friend perfectly, but I think it fits all of us who follow Jesus: *Whatever your fate was in erotic love and friendship, whatever your lack, whatever your loss was, whatever the personal disconsolateness of your life...the highest still remains: love thy neighbor!*

It's a beautiful thing that we have this command, because no matter what else happens in our lives, whatever we have or don't have, we can choose a higher calling. Our neighbors are everywhere. By using whatever gifts we have to love them, we participate in the mission of Jesus to bring about the kingdom of heaven on earth. —GWEN FORD FAULKENBERRY

FAITH STEP: *What gifts might you share with others in order to show Jesus's love? Someone needs your certain skills, prayers, financial means, or maybe just your time.*

SATURDAY, SEPTEMBER 19

"You are my witnesses," declares the Lord, "and my servant whom I have chosen, so that you may know and believe me and understand that I am he. Before me no god was formed, nor will there be one after me. I, even I, am the Lord, and apart from me there is no savior." Isaiah 43:10–11 (NIV)

MY HUSBAND AND I DATED in high school. Actually, dating might be too strong a word. We went to occasional school events together. But often the next day we'd pass each other in the halls and nervously look away from each other. Weeks might go by without him talking to me.

In the exquisite confusion of young love, I would analyze every glance, every silence, and endure hours of heartbreak, thinking he no longer liked me. Then out of the blue, he'd call and we'd talk about everything—all the things we couldn't share with anyone else.

Eventually I learned that he really did care about me. The awkward distance was simply caused by shyness and uncertainty. Still, when we didn't communicate regularly, it was easy for me to imagine the worst.

Sometimes I find myself doubting that Jesus really cares about the intimate details of my life. As with my high school romance, in the absence of regular communication my mind can play tricks on me. Does He really still care? Can I tell Him the deepest secrets of my heart? Will they seem silly to Him?

How wonderful that Jesus welcomes constant communion with Him. Instead of sitting beside a phone that doesn't ring, or watching for some signal in the hallway by my school locker, I can open His Word each day. I can allow the Holy Spirit to remind me exactly how much He loves me. I can savor the truth that Jesus desires to be known, believed, and understood. —SHARON HINCK

FAITH STEP: *On a small piece of paper write a note to Jesus telling Him you desire to know Him better. Tuck it somewhere you'll be sure to see it again.*

SUNDAY, SEPTEMBER 20

For every child of God defeats this evil world by trusting Christ to give the victory. And the ones who win this battle against the world are the ones who believe that Jesus is the Son of God. 1 John 5:4–5 (NLT)

MY FOUR-YEAR-OLD GRANDSON LUKE ENJOYS playing superhero. On one occasion, he asked his mom to tie a towel around his neck and drape it down his back to resemble a cape. Good sport that she is, Mommy also made a paper logo and pinned it to the cape to identify the tyke as Super-Luke.

Feeling bold and brave in his new uniform, Luke then picked up a stick and proclaimed, "Bad guys—you better watch out! I'm gonna get you. I'm gonna rescue the world!" He charged toward the family room, determined to accomplish his mission.

His imagination left me smiling, but it also reminded me of a spiritual truth. The world in which we live seems filled with evil. News reports tell of mass shootings, suicide bombs, domestic violence, and war. Immorality seems to be the norm in pop culture. Bullying hurts our kids.

Downright depressing, it is, if we focus on these evils. That's what Satan would love for us to do, but let's not allow him the pleasure. Let's fight for what's right by focusing on the truth. What does it say?

Scripture says we defeat this evil world by trusting Christ to give the victory. All who believe He's the Son of God are overcomers. Someday He'll return and wipe out wickedness forever. We know the end of the story already. But in the meantime, even if evil touches us now, it will not conquer us for Jesus can flip its harmful intent into something good when we allow Him to work.

Beware, evil one. The truth stands: Christ rules, and He's gonna get you! —GRACE FOX

FAITH STEP: *Today you might hear news that shows Satan's evil intent toward mankind. Pause for a moment to thank Jesus Christ for promising the victory over evil. Ask Him to unleash His righteous forces to vanquish the enemy's armies.*

MONDAY, SEPTEMBER 21

They were filled with joy when they saw the Lord! John 20:20 (NLT)

JOHN 20 IS SUCH A sweet chapter. I love it because I can imagine the sheer joy that plunked itself right in the midst of Jesus's followers whom He appeared to after His Resurrection.

But His appearing isn't all that I love, as if that weren't enough. I particularly love that He showed up in the middle of His followers' fears, and He replaced those fears with joy.

All who know Him as Savior will experience that transformation one day when He returns without warning to rescue His own. What a shift for the heart, to go from pain and fear to soar with the Lord of heaven and earth.

But in the meantime, He gives us His Spirit, Who is here for us now. Just as His disciples didn't have to be masters of faith to be worthy of His presence, we don't have to have it "all together" to earn His time either.

No matter how discombobulated I may be these days, no matter how crazy this day seems, my Jesus will show up for me, and His arrival will bring me joy and neutralize fear. I want more of that!

Later in that chapter, Jesus appeared to Thomas, who didn't believe Jesus was present until Thomas could see Him. To that, Jesus replied, "'You believe because you have seen me. Blessed are those who haven't seen me and believe anyway'" (verse 29).

I want more joy from Jesus's presence, but I also want His blessing for believing He is with me even when I can't see Him, even when fear hovers. Joy and blessing and freedom from fear...I'm going for the whole package. By His grace, I will trust Him when I can't see Him and I'll go ahead and feel the joy now. —ERIN KEELEY MARSHALL

FAITH STEP: *Ask Jesus to fill you with joy and blessing because you believe He is with you right now.*

TUESDAY, SEPTEMBER 22

This hope is a strong and trustworthy anchor for our souls. It leads us through the curtain into God's inner sanctuary.
Hebrews 6:19 (NLT)

I'D ALWAYS PICTURED AN ANCHOR as something a fisherman might toss over the side of his boat when he wanted to stay in one spot. Then I visited a lighthouse memorial in Oregon and met a *real* anchor, up close and personal. It was in the traditional shape that's so familiar, often used as a symbol or as a jewelry design. But it was huge! I couldn't begin to guess how many tons it weighed, or how many sailors it would take to manage the anchor and its chain. But I felt sure that this anchor would not have a problem in keeping a ship from drifting.

I love how the writer of Hebrews used the anchor, a popular symbol in the early church, as a metaphor for the hope we have in Jesus Christ. Life can sometimes resemble a stormy sea, with unexpected circumstances and raging emotions tossing us about. We wonder if our life will turn into a shipwreck. Even when life seems like smooth sailing, we may be in danger of drifting from the truth, blissfully unaware of the world's pull on us. During all of life's stages, we need to be anchored in Jesus. Our hope in Him is the only way to find stability for our life and security and peace for our soul.

No matter what troubles or heartaches this earthly life brings, I have the promise that Jesus is with me every step of the way. He will never stop loving me and will provide everything I need. One day He will welcome me to a perfect home where we'll live for all eternity. Surely that hope is enough to keep me from being tossed about or drifting off-course.
—DIANNE NEAL MATTHEWS

FAITH STEP: *The next time you face stormy seas, lay hold of your anchor in Jesus. Remind yourself of what it means to hope in Him.*

WEDNESDAY, SEPTEMBER 23

And now, dear brothers and sisters, one final thing. Fix your thoughts on what is true, and honorable, and right, and pure, and lovely, and admirable. Think about things that are excellent and worthy of praise. Philippians 4:8 (NLT)

I AM A GREAT FAN of letting things slide. Laundry. Dishes. Doctors' appointments. Flu shots. Washing the car. Washing the children. They don't seem to mind.

But sometimes this approach doesn't yield the results I long for. Like life with an empty kitchen sink and children that smell like roses.

But I think that letting things slide can be a great life strategy. I think I need to be strategic about what I let slide. Like wondering what people are thinking about me and focusing on the negative. Those things can slide. Irritability? Anger? Nagging? Whining? Worrying? Slide. And the things I can't afford to let slide? Laughing. Walking with my friends. Noticing the turning colors of the leaves. Finding more recipes with dark chocolate. Kissing my boys. Dating Scott. Loving Jesus. These are the things I should never let slide. These are the wonderful things of life that I want to focus on. I want to focus on the beauty of life and let the things slide that suck the joy out of my day.

Jesus has given us the great gift of life. He has given us these days to live out. We don't really get to choose what our days look like. But we can choose the lens that we look at them through. We can choose to focus on the beauty and goodness of our days and let the rest slide...or we can focus on the ugly things in life and get bogged down in the muck of negativity. —SUSANNA FOTH AUGHTMON

FAITH STEP: *Join me in letting things slide . . . and choose to see today through the lens of beauty. Tell Jesus all the things in your life that bring you joy and fill you with peace.*

THURSDAY, SEPTEMBER 24

"But [the crowd] objected strenuously, saying, '(Jesus) agitates the people with his teaching...'" Luke 23:5 (CEB)

JESUS AGITATES ME TOO. What He says doesn't always sit well. Sometimes it makes me feel light-headed. My skin crawls. My throat tightens. What He says sometimes brings me to tears.

Because He's right. Every word is faithful and true. The reason the crowd grew agitated over Jesus's teachings was because He was right. They didn't want to change, didn't want to have routines upended by living His way rather their own.

Would you imagine yourself having anything in common with the crowd that called for Jesus's Crucifixion? Not me. I picture myself as one of the mourners, one of the followers of Jesus who may have been confused over what was happening, but hanging in there anyway.

But here's what I have in common with the jeering crowd: I sometimes find His teachings disturbing. They convict me when I've not acted in love. They keep me awake at night when I've avoided what I know He wants me to do.

He lives within me by His Spirit, but I sometimes act as if I'm abandoned. He provides flawlessly for me, but I entertain a thought that I'm neglected. I justify a familiar sin, hearing the ridiculous in my words.

What if the agitated crowd had responded differently? What if they had confessed, "Yes, His teachings disturb us. We haven't been living the way God wants us to. That changes today!" Can you imagine the tears of joy on the face of Christ? Can you picture the ripple effect through history?
—CYNTHIA RUCHTI

FAITH STEP: *Are you agitated because you don't want to change, irked that God's Word pinpointed an area of weakness not yet surrendered to Him? It's not a call to guilt, but a call to "That changes today."*

FRIDAY, SEPTEMBER 25

There is no fear in love, but perfect love casts out fear. For fear has to do with punishment, and whoever fears has not been perfected in love. 1 John 4:18 (ESV)

As I SHARED MY FEARS over our household's financial woes, God led me to other Christian friends who had suffered through businesses that failed and financial struggles. They were still standing, still trusting in Jesus, and still hopeful. They had made it through the muddy waters.

If this is what you have for us, then give me the strength to deal with it, I prayed as I went on my daily walks.

Trying to capture my muddled thoughts, I spent time pouring out my uncertainties in the form of letters to Jesus.

What if this financial crisis is going to be a reality for the rest of my life? Hopelessness kicked in. I fought despair by memorizing verses that spoke of hope and the provision of God. I had never been in such a deprivation of funds in all my life.

I knew that with one sweep of His hand, Jesus could alleviate all of our debt, get us great-paying jobs, and even toss in a cruise to the Bahamas.

But that's not how it worked out.

Over the months, I changed my focus from the pit of fear to the love of Jesus. *If I truly believe that You love me,* I wrote in one of my letters, *can I learn better how to live each day? Can I bask in Your love, taking time to see how far it stretches, how constant it is?*

Pour that kind of pure love for others over me today. —ALICE J. WISLER

FAITH STEP: *Write a letter to Jesus, naming any fears you have. Ask Him to deepen your love for Him and to cast out those fears with His perfect love.*

SATURDAY, SEPTEMBER 26

As Jesus was walking along, he saw a man named Matthew sitting at his tax collector's booth. "Follow me and be my disciple," Jesus said to him. So Matthew got up and followed him. Matthew 9:9 (NLT)

JESUS COULD HAVE CHANGED THE world single-handedly. After all, He was the Son of God. Or He could have used ten thousand angels to do the job for Him.

In obedience to His heavenly Father, He entered the world as a baby, born of a virgin, by the power and miracle of the Holy Spirit. Then He used a simple method to share a world-changing message of love: multiplication—a divine and brilliant plan.

Jesus invested His life into twelve unlikely and ordinary disciples during His three years on earth. Peter, the brash fisherman; James and John, known as "sons of thunder"; and Matthew, the tax collector, to name just a few.

Paul used that same method everywhere he traveled: find a faithful few in each place who could lead a community of believers to maturity. Throughout his missionary journeys he established a few. Soon a church was born, and the message of Jesus spread throughout their world.

Jesus's strategy hasn't changed. His command to that small community of believers and to us is still "go...and teach all nations, baptizing them...teaching them to observe all things" (Matthew 28:19–20).

Instead of being overwhelmed with the daunting task of sharing that message single-handedly, I decided early on to add discipleship to my life's work: investing in new believers, struggling moms and couples, young writers, and even my own children and grandchildren through love and prayer.

You can do the math. After two thousand years, Jesus's plan still works. If all of Jesus's disciples would adopt His method, imagine what would happen. —REBECCA BARLOW JORDAN

FAITH STEP: *Think about the people in your circle of influence. How can you implement Jesus's plan of "multiplication" by investing in others? Write down one name and one way you will begin.*

SUNDAY, SEPTEMBER 27

"The woman said to him, 'Sir, you don't have a bucket and the well is deep.'"
John 4:11 (CEB)

THE RECIPE SAID, "PULSE IN food processor." *I don't own a food processor. Next recipe.*

"Pour batter into cast-iron skillet." *No cast-iron skillet here. Next?*

"Install sausage-stuffer attachment." *I have one of those!* "Prepare casings." *Oops. Next?*

I don't have an angel food cake pan, apple corer/peeler, pancake griddle, muffin/doughnut pan for baked doughnuts. Nor a juicer, springform pan, candy thermometer, or grapefruit spoons.

Unlike for me, hampered by missing utensils, for Jesus, not having a bucket with which to draw water served a high and holy purpose, especially on the day He met a Samaritan woman at a well.

The woman at the well recognized that Jesus wasn't wealthy. He wasn't befriending her to make her a charity case. She knew if He promised her water, there was more to the story. Living water? He didn't even have a bucket. He had nothing to offer but Himself. And the well was deep.

And that was the point.

The answer isn't in having the right equipment for the job. It's not about the bucket. The answer's in Him. More of Him.

If we have Jesus, it will show in what our lives produce and exude. He proved it to the woman at the well by showing His bucket list didn't even include a bucket. She expected a small drink that would refresh for a moment. What He offered her—and us—was a life so refreshing we'd never thirst again. —CYNTHIA RUCHTI

FAITH STEP: *Find an image of a person standing under a waterfall. Use that image as a stepping-off point in a prayer of gratitude for the way His Living Water flows over and through you without limits or hindrance.*

MONDAY, SEPTEMBER 28

As long as the earth remains, there will be planting and harvest, cold and heat, summer and winter, day and night. Genesis 8:22 (NLT)

LAST YEAR, MY HUSBAND AND I adopted two young children from the foster care system. When they came to us they'd already lived in five homes in six months. They were anxious, and they had large emotional swings. I started reading books to learn how to help them. We also visited a trauma therapist. An important first step was to establish a routine. For two children who didn't trust that they'd be living in the same place tomorrow, a routine gave them stability. They flourished as they became grounded in wake-up time, playtime, mealtimes, schooltime, and bedtime. When they asked me what would be happening that day—and I told them—I saw peace softening their little faces.

Sometimes we take for granted the peace that a routine brings. From creation, God set up earth in a natural pattern. "It was you who set all the boundaries of the earth; you made both summer and winter" (Psalm 74:17, NIV).

Winter may be hard, but we know spring is coming. Summer may be hot, but we anticipate autumn's cool breezes. In Genesis, Noah lived through a long year that included torrential rain, destruction, floating endlessly, and discovering a new landscape outside the ark window. As he emerged, God promised him the seasons and schedule would return.

Are you facing a hard time in life? Has darkness descended, or maybe the pressure is building and you're not sure if you can face the intensity much longer? Look outside your window, and remember that Jesus, too, works in seasons. What you face won't last forever. Jesus sets boundaries on the earth, and in your life. —TRICIA GOYER

FAITH STEP: *Get out your camera, step outside and snap a few photos of the season that you're in. As you do, pray and thank Jesus for the seasons in your life and faith walk.*

TUESDAY, SEPTEMBER 29

Create in me a pure heart, O God, and renew a steadfast spirit within me.
Psalm 51:10 (NIV)

I HAVE ALWAYS THOUGHT THAT fasting is for those who are holy. So clearly it was not for me. I have a lot of sins. But in the past few years, I have realized that fasting is not for the holy. It is for the desperate. For those who need Jesus to move and work and do miracles on their behalf. And that sounds a lot like me.

My brother-in-law, Van, says that fasting is a physical way of saying, "Jesus, I want what You want more than what I want."

Because let's just be honest. What I want is a chocolate bar. I don't fast perfectly. I tend to fast in fits and starts. I often put limits on Jesus with my prayers. I may even try to strong-arm Him a little to get what I want. I know that never ends well. I told you up front...I'm not that holy.

But really—most of the time—I don't want what Jesus wants more than what I want. I want what I want. I want healing or breakthroughs or miracles on my terms. I want what I want when I want it. I may shout, "Jesus, I want what You want!" But I usually end that shout with the whisper, "if it's what I want." I have known myself long enough to know that I can't change myself.

But I have known Jesus long enough to know that He can. And so I am taking a page from King David's playbook this morning. This is my prayer: *Create in me a clean heart, O God. And renew a right spirit within me.* This is what I would love Jesus to do in me. I think He is already working on it. Because it is what He wants too.
—SUSANNA FOTH AUGHTMON

FAITH STEP: *Pray King David's prayer for a clean heart. Ask Jesus to reshape your thinking and your desires so that you want what He wants in your life.*

WEDNESDAY, SEPTEMBER 30

Yet he commanded the skies above and opened the doors of heaven.
Psalm 78:23 (ESV)

MY KIDS LOVE TO SWING. Actually, I do too. Something about the fresh breeze, feeling as if I could launch and soar into the air, unencumbered by gravity...it thrills my heart.

I think a swing can draw a person closer to Jesus. That seems simplistic, I understand. But some of the best, most affecting truths come from unassuming sources, such as a piece of playground equipment most of us have enjoyed at one time or another.

Much as a swing pushes my heart to aim high, so does God's Word. Focusing on Jesus's promises of a future with Him helps me envision my real life that hasn't even begun yet: my someday life in heaven with my Savior.

Could it be that He wants my heart to soar with Him even now, buoyed with only the hope of the joys to come? Yes, I'm sure of it.

The reason Jesus's followers are still on earth is to bring glory to Him by shining His light in this world. When we aim high for Him, He can take us to greater heights than we could imagine.

The more we trust Him to take us beyond our finite scope, the greater the possibilities. This concept isn't just a pie-in-the-sky fairy tale; we are created to aim for more than what we can reach on our own. Every day the Lord wants to carry us higher, if we'll only set our sights on His realm, a whole world beyond this one. —ERIN KEELEY MARSHALL

FAITH STEP: *How big is Jesus's power in your life? Ask Him to help you aim for more of Him, and expect Him to amaze you with new views of Himself.*

THURSDAY, OCTOBER 1

There is no fear in love. But perfect love drives out fear, because fear has to do with punishment. The one who fears is not made perfect in love. 1 John 4:18 (NIV)

MY FRIEND STACY HAS A goldfish pond. Because we live in a northern climate, each fall her husband gathers the fish from the pond and brings them inside to survive the winter.

But the fish don't like the sight of the net. They dart away, try to burrow into the mud at the bottom of the pond, or hide behind plants. Occasionally one succeeds in escaping, and Stacy and her husband find its frozen corpse the next spring.

Our church recently went through a time of conflict—the sort of ugly disagreement in which people began to throw Scripture verses at each other like weapons. One morning when I sat down and reached for my Bible for my early quiet time, my hand stopped. I didn't want to open the Word. I was afraid to seek Christ, because I'd watched how people I cared about had twisted things in His name. My hurt ran deep, and made me want to avoid the very One Who could bring healing through His Word. Like a silly goldfish, I wanted to burrow into the mud so Jesus wouldn't have to see my doubts, hurts, and confusion. Eventually I opened the Bible and focused on His reassurances of love.

Jesus longs to save us from ourselves, but when He approaches, we often run away in fear. Because of the redeeming work of our Savior, we no longer have to be afraid of our heavenly Father. We can trust that the hands reaching toward us are hands of love—there to protect us, care for us, and guide us. —SHARON HINCK

FAITH STEP: *Are you hiding a secret hurt or doubt or fear? Journal about it and share it with Jesus instead of avoiding Him. He knows about it anyway, and is eager to rescue you.*

FRIDAY, OCTOBER 2

A merry heart maketh a cheerful countenance. Proverbs 15:13 (KJV)

OCTOBER HAS ARRIVED, AND DOWN here in northwest Arkansas the leaves are beginning to turn. There's a chill in the morning air, and it's time to put the fall decorations on the front step and by the street lamps.

About this time a few years ago, when Paxton and Calianne were tiny, we picked out a stand-up scarecrow from the grocery store. They're all over the place these days, and for seven dollars it has been a source of fun memories. Actually, the scarecrow isn't an "it," she's a "she," and she has acquired an identity of her own.

The kids dubbed her "Pumpkin Girl," and she's as cute as her name, even though she doesn't resemble a pumpkin at all. She's a scarecrow. Well, my husband pulled her down from the garage attic a couple of days ago, and I noticed her standing there this morning when I backed out to do the school run. Something about her smile has stayed with me. Who knew you could learn something about life from a raggedy scarecrow?

What I can't get out of my head is her unflagging look of peace and contentment. Granted, she's an inanimate object, but hear me out. She has weathered winds and rain, even some fierce storms over the years. She has been stuck where we put her, and her outsides show the wear and tear.

But her countenance has not faded. Her smile still lights the doorway to our home. I know that she cannot choose those characteristics, nor does she possess the life to care.

However, I can and I do. Am I choosing to wear Christ's joy on my face despite life's weather? Do I possess enough of Christ's life in me to care?

Long live Pumpkin Girl, and may my countenance light the doorway to Jesus. —ERIN KEELEY MARSHALL

FAITH STEP: *Memorize Psalm 89:15 (NLT): "Happy are those who hear the joyful call to worship, for they will walk in the light of your presence, Lord."*

SATURDAY, OCTOBER 3

Devote yourselves to prayer, being watchful and thankful. Colossians 4:2 (NIV)

DURING AN INTERVIEW ON A Christian radio station, the hostess confessed to me that her basic obligation each day was to spend time with Jesus. "We all have a list of what we want to accomplish every day, but when my feet touch the floor each morning, I want to look to see what Jesus has for me to do. That's where it's at. That's what matters most."

What if I tried that? I thought. So the next morning, I asked, "Jesus, what do You have for me to do today?" I hoped it would be something really dynamic. Maybe Dr. Phil would call and invite me to be a guest on his show.

I went about my daily routine, made a cup of Earl Grey and logged onto my social media accounts. I kept waiting. I worked on a few chapters of a novel I was writing, promoted an upcoming writing workshop, and waited some more.

Late in the afternoon, my friend Anna told me that her daughter was in the hospital after slitting her wrists. She poured out her anguish to me. Since my eldest suffers from mental illness, I could relate. My heart filled with compassion for Anna and her family. "Pray. I know you understand," Anna said.

Another friend wrote to tell me about her brother. After having gone missing three times over the past week, he had been admitted to the psychiatric ward. She wanted my prayers for her family.

At the close of the day as I settled into my chair to watch a movie with my husband and our two dogs, I realized that responding to the cries of my friends was the answer to my morning prayer. How rewarding it had been for me to be called upon to lift up others in prayer. —ALICE J. WISLER

FAITH STEP: *What a privilege it is to be able to come to Jesus and ask Him to use us for His glory. How can you best listen so that you can hear what He has for you to do today?*

SUNDAY, OCTOBER 4

"Come to Me, all of you who are weary and burdened, and I will give you rest."
Matthew 11:28 *(HCS)*

I WANDERED AROUND THE AIRPORT terminal, amazed at the variety of restaurant choices close to my gate. The little Irish pub tempted me since I'd never eaten at one but had always wanted to. As I concentrated on the menu posted by the open doorway, I heard a friendly voice: "Are you hungry, sweetheart?" My first impulse was to feel insulted that such a young man would address me like that. *Why, I'm old enough to be his...*

Then a young woman spoke up from several feet behind me: "No, just thirsty." "Well, come on in," said the young man. Watching the server escort the blonde girl in the short skirt to the bar, my second impulse was to feel insulted that he *hadn't* been speaking to me. I was standing right next to him, clearly interested in the restaurant. Yet he ignored me to reach out to someone at a distance, someone whose looks he liked better. I walked away, no longer in the mood for shepherd's pie.

I'm so grateful that Jesus is not like that. He reaches out to everyone, regardless of age, appearance, background, or baggage. When He walked the earth, He called out, "Come to Me, all of you who are weary, burdened, hungry, hurting, searching, scarred." Jesus still calls out today, inviting each one of us to accept His unconditional love.

I never have to worry about being judged less than desirable by Jesus. He stands ready to welcome me into fellowship with Him where my soul can be nourished and renewed. Thank goodness I can rest assured my Savior will never ignore me. —DIANNE NEAL MATTHEWS

FAITH STEP: *Picture Jesus stretching out His arms to you and saying, "Come to Me." Tell Him what you need most right now. Is it comfort, forgiveness, guidance, or reassurance of His love? Spend a few moments in His strong arms.*

MONDAY, OCTOBER 5

The Lord appeared to us in the past, saying: "I have loved you with an everlasting love; I have drawn you with unfailing kindness."
Jeremiah 31:3 (NIV)

LAST NIGHT, MY SEVEN-YEAR-OLD, ADDISON, tripped and fell at church, giving himself a bloody nose and a fat lip. These things happen. Regularly.

But at dinner, I noticed how puffy his top lip was and I said, "Addie, you have kissy lips." This is our family term for having a nice pucker. He answered, "So I can get the woman." His Aunt Jenny died laughing. He was smiling. Big. And I said indignantly, "The woman? What woman are you trying to get?" Without missing a beat, he said, "You." Good answer. I proceeded to kiss him. A lot. "Well, you did it. You got me." It's true. He has me. I love him. In fact, I can't get enough of him. I can't help it. He is mine.

And Jesus feels the same way about us. He really, truly loves us from the depths of His being. He can't help it. We are His. He draws us to Himself with His great love for us, with His kindness, with His grace. He stopped at nothing, not even death, to create a way for us to have a relationship with Him.

And something happens when we start hanging out with Him. When we read His Word and sit in His presence. His great love for us is addictive. He is out to get us with His goodness and mercy. He comes after us with His faithfulness and forgiveness.

And in the presence of so much love, we find ourselves unable to say anything but, "You did it! You win! You got me!" And the thing is, it just doesn't get any better than that. —SUSANNA FOTH AUGHTMON

FAITH STEP: *Read 1 Corinthians 13 and meditate on the amazing kind of love that Jesus has for you.*

TUESDAY, OCTOBER 6

"It's who you are and the way you live that count before God. Your worship must engage your spirit in the pursuit of truth. That's the kind of people the Father is out looking for: those who are simply and honestly themselves before him in their worship." John 4:23 (MSG)

THIS YEAR I WAS ASKED to be the guest speaker in two places that represent the broad spectrum of differences we find within the body of Christ. The fact that I am connected in some ways with both groups shows, I hope, that I am interested in different perspectives on the Christian life, and that I know I can learn from anybody. I was honored and thought it was very cool that they would both invite me to speak.

As I was preparing for the first event, I began to feel less excited, however, and more intimidated by the prospect. I realized, as I considered my audience, that everything I had to say would probably sound liberal to their ears. In my interpretation of Proverbs 31, by which I planned to deconstruct the idea of a "good Christian woman," I probably would be branded a feminist. They might decide I was dangerous and throw me out.

There was no comfort in turning to my preparation for the second event. For that one, I was supposed to talk about Lent, which we don't even officially practice in my denomination. *What could I possibly know about Lent?* Everything I could think of to say to that crowd seemed ignorant, naïve, decidedly unintellectual. Surely they would throw me out too. I began to consider declining both invitations.

That's when I heard Jesus speak to my heart. He said something like this: *I am what you have in common with all of these people, and I am all that matters. Just be yourself. Be who I made you to be, nothing more, and nothing less. I will be with you.* —GWEN FORD FAULKENBERRY

FAITH STEP: *Who needs to hear your unique voice today? Be who you are in Jesus.*

WEDNESDAY, OCTOBER 7

A vast crowd brought to him people who were lame, blind, crippled, those who couldn't speak, and many others. They laid them before Jesus, and he healed them all. The crowd was amazed! Those who hadn't been able to speak were talking, the crippled were made well, the lame were walking, and the blind could see again! And they praised the God of Israel. Matthew 15:31 (NLT)

IN MY TWENTY-FIVE YEARS of being a Christian there are two distinct times when I allowed Jesus to do a healing work in my soul. The first was when I was twenty-five years old, and I attended a Bible study for women who'd had abortions. The second was when close friends gathered around me to pray that I'd be healed from unhealthy relationships from my teen years.

In both cases, as I read the Scriptures, and allowed Jesus to enter the tender places of my soul, healing came. Jesus showed me that He loved me and He forgave me. He reminded me that His death on the Cross covered *all* my sins, not just the ones I deemed "not too bad."

And you know what? People saw the change: in my peace, in my joy, and in my desire to serve others. The healing wasn't physical, but it was noticeable. Those around me praised the God of Israel—in the same way that people praised Jesus when they saw Him healing the lame, the crippled, and blind.

Jesus heals to bring wholeness, but He also heals to build the faith of others. Seeing Jesus at work, they dare to say, "Maybe He can do that for me too."

Do you have an area in your life where you need healing—internal or external? Turn to Jesus. When healing comes He will get the glory, you will be made well, and others will have faith to turn to Him for their own brokenness, pain, and shame. —TRICIA GOYER

FAITH STEP: *Do you have pain from the past that you haven't fully healed from? Ask a few close friends to pray with you about that. Trust Jesus to forgive, to heal.*

THURSDAY, OCTOBER 8

But you have not honored the God who gives you the breath of life and controls your destiny! Daniel 5:23 (NLT)

KING BELSHAZZAR THREW A PARTY for a thousand nobles. During the gala event, he ordered his servants to fetch the silver and gold cups that his predecessor had taken from the Temple in Jerusalem. Then he and his guests, wives, and concubines filled the goblets with wine and toasted their idols. Not a good idea. Imagine the terror they felt when a human hand appeared from nowhere that very moment and wrote a message on the wall.

Belshazzar sought Daniel's wisdom to interpret the message. Daniel obliged. Bottom line, he said, the king and his company had not given God the honor He deserved. Instead, they'd praised idols, and God was most displeased.

We *tsk-tsk* Belshazzar, but we might easily fall into the same sins that caused his immediate demise—pride and idolatry. If not careful, we usurp Christ's position on the throne of our lives when we rely on our own wisdom and abilities rather than seeking His. We fall into idolatry when we invest more time, energy, and affection into hobbies, food, and friends than into Him. Not a good idea.

Jesus Christ gives us the breath of life. We literally cannot survive without His causing our lungs to fill and our hearts to beat. He controls our destiny. He equips us with skills and abilities needed to fulfill the tasks He gives us. He opens and closes doors of opportunity. He rules sovereignly over our circumstances, and nothing can thwart His purposes.

Let's read the writing on the wall: Jesus deserves our honor. Let's commit to giving Him our full devotion, every day and in every way. —GRACE FOX

FAITH STEP: *Ask the Holy Spirit to identify thoughts, words, or actions that dishonor Jesus in your life. Is there envy, jealousy, gossip, lust, selfishness, laziness, prayerlessness, or greed? Confess it as sin and then thank Jesus for His forgiveness.*

FRIDAY, OCTOBER 9

Beloved, if God so loved us, we ought also to love one another. No one has seen God at any time; if we love one another, God abides in us, and His love is perfected in us. 1 John 4:11–12 (NAS)

AS A PERFECTIONIST WHEN IT comes to my manuscripts, I strive to get my writing just right. When he cooks, my husband spends hours getting the seasonings in his dishes to come out just the way he wants them to.

*If I spent as much time loving others as I do on my novel's dialogue and scenes...*I thought one day as I was glued to my computer.

God loves us, giving us the gift of His only Son. It's awesome to think that within us God's love not only abides, it is perfected. How can I share this perfect love? How can I fully experience this gift of perfected love to others? What if I was a perfectionist about cultivating this love and freely giving it without judging others? What if I was as lavish as my husband is when he cooks with parsley or cumin?

While we desire to love both God and people more, let us remember that Jesus can't love us any more. He doesn't have to work on perfecting this love; it is THE PERFECT LOVE. There is nothing we can do to gain more of His love and nothing we can do to have it taken from us. It's sealed forever.

Hallelujah! —ALICE J. WISLER

FAITH STEP: *Ponder the word "love." How do you perfect your love for others?*

SATURDAY, OCTOBER 10

Don't worry about anything; instead, pray about everything. I tell God what you need, and don't forget to thank him for all he has done. Philippians 4:6 (TLB)

As A YOUNG BIBLE STUDY teacher, I often asked the question, "What prayers has God answered for you lately?" The absence of current, "meaty" answers bothered me. I wanted to hear more than the "Jesus-gave-me-a-parking-spot" kind of prayer from my students. In the sometimes awkward silence, one or two would regularly share their survival of a near accident or serious illness earlier in their lives.

As I matured, however—and quit judging—I soon realized a class member's answer (or silence) didn't always indicate the neglect of a vital prayer life. It could simply reflect a quiet personality, the inexperience of a new believer, or even the need for more time to reflect before responding.

Recently I asked myself that same question. No current, "meaty" answers emerged. Well, age—and fading memory—do go together, don't they? All of us experience times when answers to prayers don't slip off our tongues readily, and we fall back on "old" testimonies.

Maybe you pray fervently and specifically. But children, carpools, and overcrowded schedules take their toll. Paul's reminder—thank Him for all that He has done"—gets squished between piles of laundry. By the time Jesus answers your prayer, you've forgotten the request—or that He answered it.

Maybe that's why I've started thanking Jesus *before* He answers—for His answers. Since He knows our needs (and requests) even before we ask (Matthew 6:8), isn't He trustworthy enough to give thanks for His responses—before we receive them?

We can trust God for His answers, whatever they are. And if asked, we can offer fresh testimonies—because we've already expressed gratitude ahead of time. —REBECCA BARLOW JORDAN

FAITH STEP: *Keep your prayer requests in a small notebook. Thank Jesus for His answers as soon as you pray them. And review that notebook weekly.*

SUNDAY, OCTOBER 11

"And there is salvation in no one else, for there is no other name under heaven given among men by which we must be saved." Acts 4:12 (ESV)

As much as I've traveled in the past few years, I still feel my small town roots when the airplane lands in a large city. So when I was greeted at baggage claim by a sign-toting chauffeur on a trip last fall, I felt both elated and felt out of place.

I settled into the backseat while my driver deposited my luggage in the trunk. I'd know within minutes if he wanted to spend the trip in conversation or silence.

Conversation, definitely, enhanced by his elegant Jordanian accent.

Having served as an event driver several times that day, he asked if I was with "that Christian authors' group." I told him I was.

Watching me with glances to his rearview mirror, he said, "I have transported many Christians over the years. I have studied this *Chrrrris-ti-ani-ty*," he said, rolling the R and enunciating clearly. "And I believe I know more about Christianity than most of your people who call themselves Christians."

Sobered by the truth he'd just proposed, I agreed that he probably did.

"Your books. Are they *Chrrrris-tian*?"

"All my books share the heart of... Jesus Christ," I answered.

His eyes widened—deep brown irises surrounded by startling white. "I commend you!" he said. "You...you...*say the name* of this Jesus Christ. Some will not say the name."

Something shifted in me that day. No more hesitation for fear of whom I might offend. There's only One Whom I can't afford to offend. And His Name is Jesus. —CYNTHIA RUCHTI

FAITH STEP: *Fear will knock on your heart in myriad ways this day. Say the Name. Crises will escalate this week. Say the Name. People who have long denied Him will call you to explain who you are. Say the Name.*

MONDAY, OCTOBER 12

Let all that I am wait quietly before God, for my hope is in him.
Psalm 62:5 (NLT)

I'VE COME TO ADMIT SOMETHING about myself: I am not a naturally trusting person.

When a friend turned on me in childhood, I wondered for years what it was about me that deserved such rejection. When my teenage peers viewed my beliefs as old-school, I scrambled for a way to fit in while pretending to be secure in my faith. And when I've watched loved ones suffer at the hand of evil as an adult, I have wondered why God allows so many lies to win.

Now in my early forties I'm aware that I need to balance being both shrewd and harmless (Matthew 10:16). By this I mean that I need to approach the mistruths I encounter with grace and an unshakeable sureness that my hope is in the Lord. This is particularly difficult when it comes to trusting the deepest places of my heart to Jesus, Who allows terrible things to happen on earth.

This crippled world needs to witness Jesus-transformed lives that are characterized by *hope that trusts in Someone Who won't fail us!*

Trusting Jesus means sheltering our souls in the cleft of His protective presence. His supernatural power can break through the greatest doubt and the darkest evil and heal deep down.

Trusting Christ for lasting security invites His hope to break through and restore. It creates joyful living despite the threat of woundedness. I pray my remaining decades will reflect the joyful, welcoming sureness that my trust is in the Lord. —ERIN KEELEY MARSHALL

FAITH STEP: *Write down your biggest doubt about God. Place it in your wallet as a reminder to pray about it whenever you go to pay for something or show your ID. Ask Jesus for help to trust Him more deeply.*

TUESDAY, OCTOBER 13

Remember, the Lord is coming soon. Don't worry about anything; instead, pray about everything. Tell God what you need, and thank him for all he has done.
Philippians 4:5–6 (NLT)

I REMEMBER, AS A KID, watching a movie about Christ's second coming. For weeks afterward I feared planes plummeting and cars crashing should the rapture come and claim pilots and drivers. My imagination shifted into overdrive, and fear of being left behind when Jesus returned motivated me to behave myself. How little I understood then!

Decades have passed and, frankly, I don't profess to understand everything about Jesus's return even now. But one thing I do know—it doesn't need to scare me anymore. On the contrary, I realize now that its reality brings me cause for peace and courage.

This realization came while speaking to a missionary friend whose wife died tragically. He told me how he'd wrestled with Jesus after losing his wife, best friend, and ministry partner. How could he recover from this loss? "The light dawned one day as I read Philippians 4," my friend said. "That's when I noticed how the last stanza of verse five—'Remember, the Lord is coming soon'—prefaced 'Don't worry about anything,' and my perspective changed. When Jesus comes to take His children home, today's worries and pain won't matter anymore. Why, therefore, should I let them consume me now?"

How true! The end of our story has already been written. Someday Jesus will come in splendor and majesty to carry us home. He'll avenge injustice, heal our mortal bodies, and mend our broken hearts. Let's live today in the hope, peace, and courage that the promise of His return brings.
—GRACE FOX

FAITH STEP: *Write these words on a recipe card: "Remember, the Lord is coming soon. Don't worry about anything." Place the card on your fridge or use it as a bookmark to remind yourself of the hope that Christ's second coming brings.*

WEDNESDAY, OCTOBER 14

Heaven and earth will disappear, but my words will never disappear.
Matthew 24:35 (NLT)

I REMEMBER A TIME IN my life when thinking about Jesus or the Bible was the last thing I wanted. I was a teenager, wrapped up in music, friends, and boys. Especially boys. Yet I was unhappy, empty, and my life was full of drama. Depression set in, and I tried to remember the last time I was truly happy. It was during my elementary school years when I attended church, spent time with Christian friends, and *knew* that Jesus loved me.

One day, daring to hope that I could have that peace again, I found my Bible and flipped it open. It randomly fell to 1 Peter 1:24–25 (NLT), "As the Scriptures say, 'People are like grass; their beauty is like a flower in the field. The grass withers and the flower fades. But the word of the Lord remains forever.' And that word is the Good News that was preached to you."

The words jumped off the page at me. My mind raced. I'd turned my attention to things that weren't going to last. It was as if Jesus was speaking directly to my heart saying, "Come back to what will last forever."

I didn't change overnight. I had more struggles, more heartache to face before I finally surrendered, but that verse was a turning point. Through those words Jesus whispered to me that all of us go through life, and we must choose whether to focus on what will wither and fade or what will last forever. I'm so thankful that Jesus met me in the moment, and that the Good News led me to a forever relationship with Him. —TRICIA GOYER

FAITH STEP: *Do you know someone who used to find peace and joy in her or his life but now is wandering and trying to find happiness with things that will never satisfy? Take a moment to write out this Scripture for the person, and then share how God's Word has made a difference in your life. Then, when the opportunity comes, offer it as a gift of hope.*

THURSDAY, OCTOBER 15

He came swiftly on the wings of the wind. . . . He rescued me from my strong enemy and from those who hated me, for they were too mighty for me. They confronted me in the day of my calamity, but the Lord was my support. Psalm 18:10, 17–18 (ESV)

LAST NIGHT I WENT TO bed to the sound of wind beating against the house. Gusts blew so strong that the windows rattled. I was surprised that both kids continued sleeping through the maelstrom.

This morning I awoke to those same winds that hadn't relented through the night. I hesitated to go outside to discover all that had been upended and undone.

I had a few quiet moments to gaze out the office window before my family got up, and as I watched the treetops sway and imagined the feel of being nearly lifted up by gusts, I felt a whisper in my spirit: *I am the force who undoes all that works against you.*

Wow, for all the sermons and Bible studies I'd heard about holding on to Jesus during storms of life, I'd never envisioned *Him* as the wind, coming to wreak havoc on all that threatens me.

But that is just how the Bible describes Him in Psalm 18. He is the storm to end all storms that blow in my life. He is their undoing so they don't have to be mine.

Instead of fearing them, I can let Him draw me up to His chariot. I can exult to ride with Him and experience firsthand the force that He is against all that attempt to take down His own.

The winds are still causing a ruckus outside, and they'll likely blow all day. But I'm trusting that Jesus is commanding them, and the storm He creates means victory for me, His child. —ERIN KEELEY MARSHALL

FAITH STEP: *Pray about the winds that buffet your life. Ask Jesus to plant a vision in your mind of Him arriving in His mighty chariot to defeat the forces that blow against you.*

FRIDAY, OCTOBER 16

Therefore, there is now no condemnation for those who are in Christ Jesus, because through Christ Jesus the law of the Spirit who gives life has set you free from the law of sin and death. Romans 8:1–2 (NIV)

CURLED UP WITH A BOWL of popcorn, I watched a TV program in which chefs competed to get their own cooking show. At one point, they had to give a demonstration of a recipe in front of a focus group. The focus group held little remotes with dials. When they liked what the chef said, or how they were presenting, they would dial upward. When they didn't enjoy something, they dialed downward. The judges could monitor in real time how much the audience liked the chefs at any given moment.

Can you imagine living life with a focus group dialing in their judgment of your every word and action? I shuddered at the thought.

But then I realized that I often have that warped view of Jesus. I picture Him evaluating how much He likes me at any given moment. *Hooray!* I read an extra chapter of my Bible, God's love dial must be turned up right now. Uh-oh. I missed church this week; He probably turned the dial down. What an oppressive way to live.

Jesus makes it clear that for those who are "in Him"—who have trusted Him to be our Savior—there is now no condemnation. We don't live under the horrible pressure of a "love dial." God is not a focus group picking apart each weakness. Yes, He convicts and works in our lives to bring positive change, but always with total love and constant forgiveness.
—SHARON HINCK

FAITH STEP: *Any time today if you begin to believe Jesus's "love dial" is turned down, push back against that lie by coming back to this verse in Romans 8 and reading it out loud.*

SATURDAY, OCTOBER 17

You will know the truth, and the truth will set you free. John 8:32 (NIV)

I'VE CHALLENGED MYSELF LATELY NOT to say things I don't believe. That may sound obvious, since as Christians it's a given we should tell the truth. But a lot of times we don't. I think we mean well, and we're trying to comfort someone, but a lot of the clichés we use are just not right. And I've become determined not to say them, even if that means saying nothing at all.

What am I talking about? Things like this: something bad happens like a miscarriage and someone says to the hurting mother, *Heaven needed another angel.* Or there's a car wreck and people say to the ones who are involved, *Everything happens for a reason.* Or this one, when there's a divorce, or someone falls into sin, *There but for the grace of God go I.* There are others.

We want to offer an explanation to others—and ourselves—that somehow makes sense of something we can't understand. But the fact is, the Christian life doesn't always make sense. We won't always know what to say, and that has to be okay. The truth is Jesus's love is big enough for the things we can't understand. We need not say anything except maybe: *I'm praying for you. I love you. I'm sorry.* —GWEN FORD FAULKENBERRY

FAITH STEP: *Resist the temptation to offer clichés when people are hurting. Instead, offer them the truth that Jesus loves them—no matter what.*

SUNDAY, OCTOBER 18

But when they did not find them, they dragged Jason and some other
believers before the city officials, shouting: "These men who have caused trouble all
over the world have now come here, and Jason has welcomed them into his house.
They are all defying Caesar's decrees, saying that there is another king,
one called Jesus." Acts 17:6–7 (NIV)

MY PARENTS TAUGHT ME EARLY in life to exercise wisdom when selecting friends. The "wrong" ones could greatly influence my decisions and testimony. And for the most part, I listened.

But sometimes, associating with even the "right" friends can usher in another set of problems. Enter Jason. Scripture doesn't explain his relationship with Paul, only that as a fellow believer, he welcomed Paul and his friend Silas into his house.

Jealousy and fear riled the synagogue leaders where Paul preached about "another king." They enlisted some scoundrels to riot and then searched for the men who were turning their world upside down.

Their hunt led them to the home of Jason because of his hospitality and friendship with Paul. When they couldn't find Paul, their troublemaker, they dragged Jason and some of his Christian friends into the marketplace, accusing them of welcoming Caesar's enemies—and giving allegiance to another king, Jesus. The city officials eventually released them, but not before they extracted some kind of bond or agreement from them.

Another king, indeed. Paul, Silas, Jason, and the other believers knew Jesus was not just another king. He was the *only* King.

When we associate with well-known believers, we may suffer innocently. It's happening all over the world. But allegiance to Jesus—our only King—makes any cost worthwhile. —REBECCA BARLOW JORDAN

FAITH STEP: *Thank Jesus for your Christian friends. Remember to pray for believers all over the world today who are being persecuted for their allegiance to their only King, Jesus.*

MONDAY, OCTOBER 19

Not that I have already obtained it or have already become perfect, but I press on so that I may lay hold of that for which also I was laid hold of by Christ Jesus.
Philippians 3:12 (NAS)

RECENTLY WE PURCHASED A HOUSE, and moving in I longed for everything to be perfect. I wanted new drapes hung, and I bemoaned putting our well-loved couch in the living room. I spent an hour online trying to find the perfect new couch and accessories, but eventually the lack of money for all the new things I wanted won out over my desire. I just didn't have enough funds to create a *Better Homes and Gardens* magazine spread. And even if I did, with three preschoolers I'd never be able to keep it that way! I was reminded that my living room was supposed to be a place of connection, not a display.

I often want the same type of unrealistic perfection for myself. I want to become mature in Christ—to be made perfect—so I can display myself to others. Jesus desires to perfect me—perfect each of us—for a different reason. Jesus doesn't want to make us magazine spreads of His transforming power, but rather He wants to bring us close.

Ephesians 1:4–5 (NLT) says, "Even before he made the world, God loved us and chose us in Christ to be holy and without fault in his eyes. God decided in advance to adopt us into his own family by bringing us to himself through Jesus Christ."

It's okay to strive for perfection—for maturity—but we need to do it with Jesus's goal in mind...to draw closer to Him. This closeness is possible through Jesus Christ. Not to be a display, but to be God's child.
—TRICIA GOYER

FAITH STEP: *Write a "before" and "after" list of three things that have been transformed in your life since you became a believer. Then ask, "How have these changes brought me closer to Christ?" Finally, praise and thank Him for the changes!*

TUESDAY, OCTOBER 20

"Jesus was tired from his journey." John 4:6 (CEB)

I REMEMBER FEELING FRUSTRATED WHEN my cranky toddlers thought they didn't need a nap and fought against naptime with nuclear-energy resistance. "The day's coming," I told them—fruitlessly—"when you'll beg for a nap."

Most of my adult life, a nap remained a far-off, ethereal dream. I'd push through, no matter how much my body screamed for the chance to lie down for a few minutes. I'd close my eyes at the hair salon, claiming it was as close to a nap as I was going to get.

Others seem to have mastered the art of napping. My husband's an expert at it. Girlfriends talk about their fifteen-minute "power naps" with the same enthusiasm they have for their workouts and kale smoothies.

God invented a subtle way of reintroducing naps to my life. It's called aging. That, and wisdom.

The fourth chapter of the book of John made it a point to note that on one of Jesus's trips through Samaria, He stopped at Jacob's well because He "was tired from His journey." At midday.

Despite knowing Jesus walked the gamut of human emotions and experiences, it amazes me that He grew tired, and wasn't...afraid...to...admit...it. He stopped to rest, midday, His journey unfinished.

Because He stopped to rest, He met the woman at the well, whose life changed radically that day, and who influenced many others to come to Jesus, according to later verses in that chapter.

What scenes might I miss when I push through my tiredness rather than stop to rest? If Jesus could afford a pause in His journey, can't I?

—CYNTHIA RUCHTI

FAITH STEP: *Jesus stopped at the well because He was tired, not because He had an agenda. Tired is reason enough, and not at all unproductive. Make it a point to listen so carefully to His instructions that you'll respond when He says it's time to pause and refresh.*

WEDNESDAY, OCTOBER 21

Trust in the Lord with all your heart and lean not on your own understanding; in all your ways submit to him, and he will make your paths straight.
Proverbs 3:5–6 (NIV)

WHEN I WAS IN COLLEGE, I visited my sister and brother-in-law, Erica and Van, in southern California. Van was the music pastor at their church. They were hosting a special night for the kids in which a Christian magician would be performing, using his illusions to illustrate the truth of God's Word.

Van and I opened the service, singing a song that he had written: *Don't let your heart be troubled. Trust in the Lord. No need to fear tomorrow, trust in the Lord. For He has good things for those who wait on Him. So don't let your heart be troubled, trust in the Lord.*

It was while singing "Don't let your heart be troubled" a second time, that the magician's parrot did a fly by, near my head. At the sound of rapidly flapping wings, I ducked to the side and my eyes went wide. It was unnerving to say the least. I was more than a little troubled. I'm not going to lie; we kept on singing. Because what else do you do when a parrot is circling overhead?

And so it is with trusting, especially when the unexpected comes up: we keep trusting.

With hearts pounding, with eyes widened in surprise, and with fear edging in, we turn to Jesus, Who has seen it all. The One Who has conquered fear and death. The One Who makes paths straight and calms hurricane winds. And we say, "I'm not sure what is up ahead...I'm feeling a little nervous right now...but I am going to choose to trust You. I believe that You are in control and that You are going to take care of me."

And the best part is? He will. —SUSANNA FOTH AUGHTMON

FAITH STEP: *Write Proverbs 3:5–6 on an index card and memorize it. Whenever you begin feeling anxious, remind yourself that when you trust Jesus, He will make your path straight.*

THURSDAY, OCTOBER 22

My help and glory are in God—granite-strength and safe-harbor God—so trust him absolutely, people; lay your lives on the line for him. God is a safe place to be.
Psalm 62:7–8 (MSG)

CAN GOD BE TRUSTED? I say so, but much of the time I live as if He can't.

I recently lost the hearing in my right ear. Suddenly, seemingly, irreversibly, and totally. At first, I thought my ear was just blocked and I didn't take it seriously. I asked people to pray for me almost as an afterthought because it was annoying. After church, people came up to me with suggestions—sweet oil, peroxide—you name it. I tried them all. I prayed during my commute and even, feeling a little ridiculous, said the word, "Ephphatha," which Jesus used when healing a deaf person.

Nothing happened.

When I was referred to an ear, nose and throat specialist, I was sure the doctor could do something simple to open my ear and restore my hearing. I wasn't ready to hear that the nerve was dead and there was little he or anyone else could offer. People have been praying for me since, and I was thrilled to get some hearing back. I've had more tests and referrals. I don't know how the story will end. I do know Jesus wasn't caught by surprise even if I was.

I'd like to understand what went wrong, but I don't need to.

I'd like to hear as well as I used to. I'm asking for that. And I'm trusting Jesus.

I feel a little guilty that this looms so large in my life right now. I know other believers are dealing with far worse. Still, I ask. I trust.

I know Jesus loves me. I don't know the outcome, but I don't have to. I know Him.

And that is the victory. —SUZANNE DAVENPORT TIETJEN

FAITH STEP: *Jesus calls us to follow Him because He is faithful and can be trusted. Submit yourself to putting your trust in Him today, no matter what you're facing.*

FRIDAY, OCTOBER 23

At once I was in the Spirit, and there before me was a throne in heaven with someone sitting on it. And the one who sat there had the appearance of jasper and ruby. A rainbow that shone like an emerald encircled the throne. Surrounding the throne were twenty-four other thrones, and seated on them were twenty-four elders. Revelation 4:2–4 (NIV)

I WAS READING IN REVELATION recently, amazed at the description of heaven revealed in a vision to Jesus's disciple John. Being visual, I tried to imagine what John saw of God on His heavenly throne and of Jesus, His Son—referred to as the Lamb—along with the others surrounding Him (Revelation 5).

Picking up a pen and paper, I began sketching John's vivid images. But the more I tried to draw them, the more frustrated I became. Capturing them adequately was impossible, but not just because of my artistically challenged fingers. Even the magnificent beauty of John's recorded description, as amazing as it seems, could never do justice to what waits for those whose names are written in "the Lamb's book of life." Some feel it all sounds too extraordinary to believe.

Sometimes I feel that same frustration when attempting to explain to others what Jesus has done for me. I can try to quote verses, write passionate devotionals, and testify on glowing, visual terms. But how do you draw a picture of Jesus's amazing grace? How do you express the depth of mercy and faithfulness from One Who lavishes His love on such unworthy recipients? How do you convince someone Jesus died for them—and for the entire world—just because He loved them (John 3:16)?

Like John's description in Revelation, capturing those truths is almost impossible: awesome and beyond imagination.

But not beyond belief. —REBECCA BARLOW JORDAN

FAITH STEP: *Using pictures or words take time this week to explain what Jesus has done for you. Then thank Him for His amazing love and grace, and for preparing a place called heaven for us.*

SATURDAY, OCTOBER 24

He chose his servant David, calling him from the sheep pens. He took David from tending the ewes and lambs and made him the shepherd of Jacob's descendants—God's own people, Israel. He cared for them with a true heart and led them with skillful hands. Psalm 78:70–72 (NLT)

ONE OF MY FAVORITE THINGS is to hear rags-to-riches stories...not stories of men and women who literally went from homeless to living in a mansion, but those who did so spiritually. Christian biographies are filled with stories of ordinary people who Jesus got ahold of and through them, inspired a generation through them.

Charles Colson, D. L. Moody, and Joni Eareckson Tada were average folks—each with his and her own challenges—until Jesus got to them. What happens to turn a man or woman around? A willingness to allow Jesus to enter and fill. With Jesus inside, all those who come in contact with them get the impression that Jesus is at work. Those who allow Jesus's love in have the ability to love and care for others in remarkable ways.

Jesus raises men and women for His glory. At the end of his life David himself confessed the transformation: "These are the last words of David: 'David, the son of Jesse, speaks—David, the man who was raised up so high, David, the man anointed by the God of Jacob, David, the sweet psalmist of Israel.'" (2 Samuel 23:1 NLT).

David knew who he was. He was a mere shepherd. God was the One Who raised him—not because of David's choosing, but because of God's.

Today you may feel completely ordinary, but what does Jesus see? Jesus is an expert at raising up those who bow down low to Him. Not so those men and women will get the glory, but because His children—His sheep—will have leaders whom they can look to, to offer them hands-and-feet love and care from our true Shepherd's heart. —TRICIA GOYER

FAITH STEP: *Check out a book from the library on a saint, and take note on how Jesus took that person from rags to riches, spiritually.*

SUNDAY, OCTOBER 25

The words I have spoken to you are spirit and they are life. John 6:63 (NIV)

WHAT KIND OF WORDS DO you speak? I've been asking myself this question, especially in regard to my children. I want my words to be like Jesus's words—spirit and life. But sometimes when I hear myself nagging or complaining I know I'm not bringing life. I'm quenching any chance of the Spirit's work.

It can be difficult to know how to speak words of life if you have to give discipline. But if we follow Jesus's example, words of life are not always about butterflies and rainbows. They can be hard sayings, rebukes, corrections. All of these have their place, but the trick is how to speak them with love. I think one of the main things is to think about what we are trying to accomplish. We should be in the business of building up, not tearing down.

Another thing to think about is what kinds of words do you listen to? At times I find myself dwelling too much on words others have spoken that are neither spirit nor life. We need to let those words go, no matter who speaks them. Words of life will stir something in our spirits, spur us on to good deeds. Words of death are the opposite. They make us feel condemned. We need to recognize that those kinds of words are not from Jesus, and we can choose not to receive them.

When He lives in us, He helps us discern what words are spirit and life—both in our speaking and in our listening—because they come from Him and accomplish His purposes. —GWEN FORD FAULKENBERRY

FAITH STEP: *Practice taking a moment to think before you speak today. Ask Jesus to help you discern whether you are speaking words of life. Invite Him to speak through you. Also, when listening to others, ask Him to help you receive only words of life.*

MONDAY, OCTOBER 26

And they threw him out of the synagogue. John 9:34 (NLT)

LATELY I'VE BEEN CONSIDERING WHAT faithfulness to God involves. I've wondered whether my daily activities and my heart's focus are in line with what the Bible says about laying down my life, taking up my cross, and following Him.

Am I giving my all for His kingdom and for others as a wife, stay-at-home mom, and part-time writer? Each day am I releasing my agenda and dreams to Him, allowing Him to change my course and affect my minute-by-minute activities? In all this processing I've felt somewhat flummoxed.

And then I read John 9, a familiar story about Jesus healing a man born blind. This time He showed me something I'd never noticed.

The Pharisees, enemies of Jesus, were up in arms about how the healing happened. They even questioned the man's parents to verify whether he was truly blind since birth. His parents responded, "He is old enough to speak for himself. Ask him" (verse 21). They were afraid of answering truthfully for fear of getting kicked out of the synagogue....

And that's where my attention caught. Unfortunately, the parents' response proved their lack of faithfulness to the Lord. So programmed were they by tradition and their "acceptable" way of life, they were not willing to stand strong for truth—even when it involved their own child, not to mention Jesus.

The man, however, was forever changed by his experience with Jesus. He did get kicked out of the synagogue, but his new connection with his Lord was well worth the cost of all it seemed he was giving up.

I got the conviction I needed. My first question each morning ought to be, *Jesus, will You show me how to be fully faithful to You today?*
—ERIN KEELEY MARSHALL

FAITH STEP: *Pray and ask Jesus to show you how to be fully faithful to Him today.*

TUESDAY, OCTOBER 27

But you, dear friends, by building yourselves up in your most holy faith and praying in the Holy Spirit, keep yourselves in God's love as you wait for the mercy of our Lord Jesus Christ to bring you to eternal life. Jude 1:20–21 (NIV)

WHEN I HURT MY BACK two years ago, I stopped lifting things—because lifting things would send a shooting pain down my back, lay me out flat, and have me calling out in the name of Jesus. Even though my back has stopped hurting now, the telltale signs of two nonlifting years are all there.

My arms tell the sad, flabby tale of a back injury. I used to have the kind of arms that were ever moving, holding small people, picking up large baskets of laundry and lugging bags of potting soil to the backyard. Gone are the firm muscles that I scored lifting large children for years. In their place are some well-rounded, soft, and pliable arms. Sad arms. Addison told me yesterday as he squeezed my arm, "Mom, I love your chubby arms."

He is the only one who does. It's time for a new arm regimen.

Sometimes I feel like my spiritual life echoes my physical life. It doesn't take long for my spirit to get out of shape. Flabby. Undisciplined. Saggy. And just like my arms need some toning, so does my attitude, my character, and my focus.

When I fall out of step with Jesus, when I neglect the spiritual disciplines of prayer, reading Scripture and time with Jesus, my life shows the results of it. When I exercise my faith, taking risks, trusting Him, and listening to Him, not only does it strengthen my faith, it enables me to move forward to bigger and better things in Him. And that is something worth working toward. —SUSANNA FOTH AUGHTMON

FAITH STEP: *Go for a prayer run or walk. As you feel your heart pumping, recognize that exercising your faith in Jesus is just as vital as exercising your muscles.*

WEDNESDAY, OCTOBER 28

I am not saying this because I am in need, for I have learned to be content whatever the circumstances. I know what it is to be in need, and I know what it is to have plenty. I have learned the secret of being content in any and every situation, whether well fed or hungry, whether living in plenty or in want. I can do all this through him who gives me strength. Philippians 4:11–13 (NIV)

LAST YEAR MY FAMILY AND I went through a host of difficult circumstances. My eldest was hospitalized for the third time with mental health issues and diagnosed with borderline personality disorder. After having been on her own for three years, she came back to live with us, receive therapy, and look for a job.

As a blended family, my three children continued to struggle with their stepfather (my husband) and their own inability to follow rules. We seemed to be having one chaotic moment after another. Then, on top of it all came heavy financial burdens. Carl and I were both underemployed. Bills mounted. Our job searches were in vain.

There were times I wanted to run away.

All my life I had wondered when I read Paul's words in Philippians 4 how a person could learn to be content even in times of need. Could I learn the joy of being content even when things were crashing around me? Could I draw unto Jesus and know that He would be my hope, peace and joy? And that He is enough? —ALICE J. WISLER

FAITH STEP: *How can you be a blessing to someone going through a struggle right now? What can you offer those who are bombarded by tough circumstances?*

THURSDAY, OCTOBER 29

For this people's heart has become calloused; they hardly hear with their ears, and they have closed their eyes. Otherwise they might see with their eyes, hear with their ears, understand with their hearts and turn, and I would heal them.
Matthew 13:15 (NIV)

MY HUSBAND RECENTLY TRAVELED TO the East Coast for business, so he added a detour to see our granddaughter. She was at the exciting stage of learning to babble, stand, and crawl (although her preferred direction was backward). I longed to be there—to see and hear those special moments.

Between Face Time, Skype, and other communication tools, my husband promised to share the visit with me. I was so excited to see our granddaughter in action. But his schedule was packed with activities, and he was rarely in a place where we could get a connection. When I called, I wouldn't get an answer. When he'd call me and point the phone's camera at our granddaughter, I'd get a frustratingly brief glimpse—only to get cut off.

My longing to be able to hear and see and connect with God is even stronger than my desire to interact with my granddaughter. Just as I needed a Wi-Fi connection to see and hear her, we all need some way to bridge the distance between ourselves and our Creator. Like the Internet connection that finally allowed me to see and hear my sweet granddaughter, Jesus gives us the means to see and hear God's truth and love. He connects us, wipes away the static and noise of our sins, and allows us precious fellowship with our Father.

In today's verse, Jesus expresses His longing to help us see, hear, and understand His love for each one of us. Let's ask Him to remove any callousness from our hearts and turn toward His healing. —SHARON HINCK

FAITH STEP: *Next time you use technology to communicate with someone, stop to remember that Jesus has created a means for us to connect with God, and through Him we always have a clear, direct connection.*

FRIDAY, OCTOBER 30

For God alone my soul waits in silence; from him comes my salvation.
Psalm 62:1 (ESV)

I HAVE ALWAYS LOVED SILENCE. I miss it a lot.

Before we moved to the Upper Peninsula of Michigan, I drove to the Hiawatha Forest for one week every month. I left my flock of sheep and my work as a neonatal nurse practitioner to get away from the noise and to write.

I'd never known such quiet.

I heard the refrigerator cycling and my heartbeat in my ears while waiting for sleep. The cabin had no phone, no TV, no Internet—not even cell phone coverage. I wrote in silence and kept a list of things to research. A trip to town and five bucks in the donation jar at the Falling Rock Cafe got me online once a week. That was plenty.

I was relaxed, prayed up, and productive. When we moved north, we brought our share of human and electronic noise. Now I write in our tiny lake house, rich in quiet (except for loon calls).

Then, a few months back, I lost the hearing in my right ear. It turns out for me, deafness does not equal silence. Like phantom pain felt by an amputee, tinnitus, the brain's consolation prize for loss of aural input, clangs in my head.

I'm cranky. Disquieted. My friends and I are praying. My hearing is better, and I'm grateful. Still, the silence is gone.

But quiet may still have a chance. Jesus knew the value of pulling back from chaos. He withdrew often to talk with His Father. During a busy time, He encouraged the disciples to come away to a solitary place to rest. I can still keep silence before God as an act of worship even if it doesn't sound the way it used to. —SUZANNE DAVENPORT TIETJEN

FAITH STEP: *Silence can be holy—an act of worship. Sit in silence today. Try ten minutes or more. Imagine Jesus sitting there with you. He will be.*

SATURDAY, OCTOBER 31

For to us a child is born, to us a son is given, and the government will be on his shoulders. And he will be called Wonderful Counselor, Mighty God, Everlasting Father, Prince of Peace. Isaiah 9:6 (NIV)

RECENTLY WE HAVE WATCHED *THE Bible* on the History channel. Our boys found it to be riveting. Blood. Weaponry. Pretty girls. What more could they ask for?

I know you are thinking, "Hey, that stuff is not in the Bible!" And I am telling you, *yes, yes, it is in the Bible.* The Bible is violent and raw in places. It has real stories about real people with real problems.

It provided us with fodder for some very interesting discussions. During one dancing scene in Sodom, Jack said, "Hey, Mom! The Bible is super-inappropriate." Yep. It is.

Then Addie crawled up next to me when Samson had his eyes gouged out and said, "Mom, you know, sometimes the Bible is really gory!"

"Yes, it is!" I agreed, closing my eyes and sticking my fingers in my ears.

We found ourselves rooting for the people in the stories who were obedient, who triumphed, who lived the life they were designed for. And we realized that these true stories were all gearing up for the main story. The story of Jesus. I kept thinking, "I can't wait until He shows up!"

His is the story to end all stories. He is the great hope of the world. The Savior. He brings hope and clarity and joy when He arrives. His story shifted all of eternity. He is still showing up today in the lives of the ones who love Him and seek Him. His mercy, His forgiveness and His love permeate our stories when we follow Him. And those are the stories with the best endings. —SUSANNA FOTH AUGHTMON

FAITH STEP: *Journal how Jesus showing up in your life changed your story. Thank Him for rewriting the story of your life.*

SUNDAY, NOVEMBER 1

May your unfailing love be my comfort, according to your promise to your servant.
Psalm 119:76 (NIV)

WE HEARD THE FREEZE WARNING on the news, signaling an early winter. My beloved gardens were still producing in early November: seven-foot-tall pepper plants and tomato vines nestling multiple clusters of green tomatoes. Most of the perennials would simply fall asleep like bears in hibernation, returning the following spring.

But what about my twenty-five potted annuals, including my green and flourishing ferns? Before nightfall, my husband and I gathered the plants, covering them with sheets on the back porch. They looked like lumpy ghosts.

The next morning I checked the damage. Most of the perennials survived, but the beautiful, trailing, sweet potato vines lay shriveled, yellow, and brown, along with my colorful coleus plants. Too sad. The annuals would die.

Just when the winter doldrums were descending, I walked into the living room and found my husband had started a blazing fire, comforting and warm. Not only that, he'd collected a sack full of green tomatoes. That night we enjoyed a Deep South staple, fried green tomatoes—for the first time.

Most of us dislike winter, endless days of unchanging, frigid weather, threatening to shrivel our faith and discourage our spirits. Like those dying plants, we may feel useless and void of color.

Jesus taught me a lesson that day, one I often forget. Every season has a purpose. Jesus is like that warm, blazing fire, beckoning us to sit awhile and partake of His comfort and warmth. Even in the harshest circumstances, He will cover us with His love and may even surprise us with good things that emerge from that season, if we'll watch for them.
—REBECCA BARLOW JORDAN

FAITH STEP: *Think about a time when it felt like winter in your life. What good things came out of those experiences? Today, thank Jesus for His continuous covering of love.*

MONDAY, NOVEMBER 2

Then he said to me, "Speak a prophetic message to the winds, son of man. Speak a prophetic message and say, 'This is what the Sovereign Lord says: Come, O breath, from the four winds! Breathe into these dead bodies so they may live again.'" So I spoke the message as he commanded me, and breath came into their bodies. They all came to life and stood up on their feet—a great army. Ezekiel 37:9–10 (NLT)

WHEN MY HUSBAND, JOHN, WAS twenty years old he was in a car accident and had numerous injuries, including a broken back and internal injuries. He felt Jesus asking him if he was ready to go home...and John answered that he felt he still had more to do here. I'm so glad!

Have you ever talked to someone who has faced a near-death experience? For those who've been on the brink of eternity, each day is a gift and each breath is precious.

Many of us have not faced a near-death experience, but everything before a new life in Christ was death. Before we were a walking corpse, but Christ breathed life into our dry bones. Like the dry bones in Ezekiel's prophecy, when we turn to Jesus, He puts His Spirit in us and we come to life.

"The Spirit of God has made me; the breath of the Almighty gives me life," says Job 33:4 (NIV).

Have you taken time lately to thank Jesus for your life? Have you thanked Him lately for creating you and choosing to have you walk this earth at this time? Have you also thanked Jesus for your spiritual life? Take a moment to consider this day you have, this life you have. Realize that if you are breathing, today is a gift. Don't take it for granted.
—TRICIA GOYER

FAITH STEP: *Take in a deep breath and then blow it out. Thank Jesus for your life, your breath. Say these words, "Today is a gift. I won't take it for granted. I thank You for family and friends, for life and small moments of happiness."*

TUESDAY, NOVEMBER 3

We always thank God, the Father of our Lord Jesus Christ, when we pray for you, because we have heard of your faith in Christ Jesus and of the love you have for all God's people. Colossians 1:3–4 (NIV)

A FEW FRIENDS GATHERED AROUND my table at lunch. We were holding a writing retreat day, and after several hours of hard work in silence, we were eager to catch up and chat. Holidays were approaching, and the topic of family plans came up. Each friend shared some difficult situations, challenging relationships, and relatives who made life rough. Next the topic shifted to our local churches. Again, everyone had stories of conflicts and dysfunction.

"And for someone else, *we* are the difficult person," a friend said. We all chuckled and agreed.

"Loving Jesus isn't difficult," I said with a sigh. "But this Christian walk would be so much easier without people to deal with." It wasn't an original thought.

Charles Schulz once penned Linus saying, "I love mankind...it's people I can't stand."

Yet Jesus tied faith in Him to stepping beyond a vague love of mankind to truly loving all of God's people. In this verse, as soon as faith in Christ is mentioned, love for others follows. More than anyone else, Jesus understands how complex, needy, hurtful, and difficult people can be. Yet He still calls us to live our faith by loving those around us. In our own power, we fall far short. But just as faith leads to love in this verse from Colossians, we find out how to love the difficult by tracing the sentence backward. The power to love comes from our faith in Christ Jesus. Both parts of the equation are vital. Faith in Christ leads us to love others. We can only love others through the faith of Jesus at work in our hearts. —SHARON HINCK

FAITH STEP: *Think of one difficult person in your life. Ask Jesus to love that person through you today, and as He guides, show love to him/her in a tangible way.*

WEDNESDAY, NOVEMBER 4

"When everything is ready, I will come and get you, so that you will always be with me where I am." John 14:3 (NLT)

I STEPPED OFF THE PLANE thinking how good it would be to sleep in my own bed that night. I'd been out of town for four weeks visiting family, including my husband who was working in another state. As I waited for my luggage, I sent a text to the friend who'd offered to pick me up. Since my flight arrived around dinnertime, we'd planned to stop and eat on the way to my house. My stomach growled, reminding me that it had been eight hours since I'd fed it.

Outside in the freezing temperature, I pulled a sweater from my bag. I sent another text letting my friend know which passenger pickup I was close to. No response. I called her cell phone. No answer. Thinking she must be on another call, I left a voice mail telling her where to come. After shivering in the cutting wind for almost twenty minutes, and waiting back inside the airport for another ten, I caught a taxi ride home. My friend called me later that evening, distressed that she had completely forgotten about my flight.

One of the worst feelings ever is being stranded, realizing that somebody has forgotten about you, and then trying to figure out what to do. That's one reason I treasure the promise Jesus made to His followers. Not only is He preparing an eternal heavenly home for me, He promises to personally escort me there.

That evening at the airport wasn't the first time I've been forgotten and stranded; it probably won't be the last. But when this world seems like a cold, hard place, I can take comfort in knowing Jesus will never forget about me. I may not know when, but I can be sure He's coming to pick me up—and He will be right on time. —DIANNE NEAL MATTHEWS

FAITH STEP: *Tell Jesus how much you cherish His promise to come and take you to your eternal home.*

THURSDAY, NOVEMBER 5

You have clothed yourselves with a brand-new nature that is continually being renewed as you learn more and more about Christ, who created this new nature within you. Colossians 3:10 (NLT)

WE STARTED A GARDEN THIS past spring, and planted fruit and nut trees and began to compost. Admittedly, we aren't always in tune with moderation; it was a lot of work, but we're excited about the blessings these ventures hold for our family's health.

To create compost for the garden, we bought a worm factory. It's a multilevel bin that came with one thousand worms that have procreated into scads more. We feed them produce, bread, and other goodies.

Last week my husband checked on the worms and saw small potatoes growing in the bin. We hadn't put any into it, just some potato peels. But right before his eyes, potatoes had sprouted and found new life.

Next, he went out to the garden and dug in the dirt where he had removed our dead potato plants a few weeks earlier. He had already removed all the potatoes, but sure enough he found three more new ones. So I cooked them up, and we ate them with supper.

Who knew fresh growth could come from what had aged and gone bad?

This object lesson speaks to me most clearly on days when the fruit of my spirit doesn't exactly measure up to the quality of the Fruit of Jesus's Spirit. I love that today's verse says that, as we know our Savior better, our nature continues to be renewed. If we are His, then we have this ever-fresh source of life growing within us.

So when I'm feeling less than gracious, when mercy isn't thriving in my life, and when I'm tempted to cast off the power of gentleness, I can take a deep breath and thank Jesus that He is ready to renew me again. Only then can I be a consistent refreshment to others. —ERIN KEELEY MARSHALL

FAITH STEP: *Read Colossians 3:12–14 to find out the qualities of this new nature.*

FRIDAY, NOVEMBER 6

Love your neighbor as yourself. Mark 12:31 (NIV)

MARILYNNE ROBINSON ONCE SAID, "IF we are to consider the heavens, how much more are we to consider the magnificent energies of consciousness that make whomever we pass on the street a far grander marvel than our galaxy?" I think that's a beautiful and elevated way of saying what I hear from old country preachers from time to time: "Don't be so heavenly minded that you're of no earthly good."

The pursuit of God through Bible study is great. I enjoy diving into theology as much as the next person. I am glad there are those who are called to be Bible scholars and who teach. But sometimes I think we can get so caught up in what we are learning about Jesus that we forget the main thing is to be like Jesus. And what Jesus cared about most was love.

People don't care what religion or denomination you are from when you're visiting them in the nursing home. It doesn't matter what you believe about baptism if you're running a food bank. If you help me carry my groceries, or encourage my kid in a ballgame, I'm not concerned whether we agree on doctrine.

The truth is that the world couldn't care less about our favorite theologians, Bible translations, or even whether we tithe. People want to be loved in deep and authentic ways. They want us to be there in times of need. The only thing that matters is love.

Jesus said the whole law could be summed up into two: love God and love your neighbor. Those things are challenging enough for me, day in and day out, so that if I never master any other concept, I'll have enough to work on for the rest of my life. —GWEN FORD FAULKENBERRY

FAITH STEP: *Write down some tangible ways you can love your neighbor. Then, go and try them out!*

SATURDAY, NOVEMBER 7

*Aware of this, Jesus withdrew from that place. A large crowd followed him,
and he healed all who were ill ... This was to fulfill what was spoken
through the prophet Isaiah: ". . . A bruised reed he will not break,
and a smoldering wick he will not snuff out."*
Matthew 12:15, 17, 20 (NIV)

I'D HAD A ROUGH WEEKEND. Encounters with old friends had reminded me how many people have impressive job titles, receive generous paychecks, and feel productive on a daily basis. I was contributing little to the family budget, and there were days it felt like a great accomplishment to get one meal on the table. Instead of running to Jesus with my feelings of worthlessness, I scolded myself, "You shouldn't need outward validation. Your identity is in Christ. He loves you and you shouldn't need more than that."

All my scolding didn't bring healing to my heart. Finally I stopped pretending and prayed, "Lord, I know You value me regardless of title, paycheck, or accomplishments. But it's so hard to feel like a worthwhile, contributing part of life these days. I hurt."

To be honest, I think I expected more scolding. Instead, the very next morning an unexpected e-mail arrived with a freelance editing job that perfectly met my need to feel useful. Then the next day a friend wrote a blog about people who had been an influence in her life—and included me. Jesus didn't respond to my need with scolding. He patiently and tenderly blessed me with reminders of His love.

Do you ever hesitate to bring your longings or hurts to Jesus, because you tell yourself you shouldn't have those feelings? Perhaps some of the people in the crowd following Jesus had similar fears. Yet Jesus granted healing, and gentle understanding. —SHARON HINCK

FAITH STEP: *What is causing your heart to hurt today? Have you tried to talk yourself out of your feelings? Instead, take your needs to Jesus and trust His gentleness.*

SUNDAY, NOVEMBER 8

I will praise you, Lord, for you have rescued me. You refused to let my enemies
triumph over me. O Lord my God, I cried out to you for help, and you
restored my health. You brought me up from the grave, O Lord.
You kept me from falling into the pit of death. Sing to the Lord,
all you godly ones! Praise his holy name.
Psalm 30:1–4 (NLT)

LAST NIGHT MY HUSBAND, SCOTT, had to rush me to the hospital. It was
a race against the clock as I experienced my first-ever allergic reaction to
strawberries.

On the way out the door, I had accidentally grabbed my son's tube of
eczema lotion instead of his epi-pen, in case I needed it. The boxes look
pretty similar. I'm fairly sure that a slathering of steroid cream does not
have the same effect as a shot of life-saving epinephrine.

Clearly, my life and all of my breaths are held in the palm of the One
Who created me. And He saved me. Plain and simple. It seems that He
has more days for me to live out.

This morning a thought popped into my head, *You should read*
Psalm 30. It seems that He has given me a new directive. Not to be silent.
To tell of His faithfulness. To praise Him.

Let everything that has breath praise the Lord. That is me. I have breath.
And I am beyond grateful for it. I am thankful for the greatness of the
One Who saves. The One Who delivers. Jesus answers whispered prayers
and frightened cries for help. He lifts us up to a firm place and rescues us
from the pit of death...both figuratively and literally. He is beyond good.
Can I get an amen? —SUSANNA FOTH AUGHTMON

FAITH STEP: *Read Psalm 30 out loud. Add your own praises to the end of the Psalm,*
thanking Jesus for each breath He has given you.

MONDAY, NOVEMBER 9

... Who, although He existed in the form of God, did not regard equality with God a thing to be grasped, but emptied Himself, taking the form of a bond-servant, and being made in the likeness of men. Being found in appearance as a man, He humbled Himself by becoming obedient to the point of death, even death on a cross.... Philippians 2:6–8 (NAS)

AT A CERTAIN LITTLE BISTRO that I used to frequent, the janitor made me smile. Always talkative, asking how I was doing, she'd listen for my answer. Cleaning toilets, mopping the floor, or washing the sinks, she did a great job and had the best attitude.

I know from firsthand experience that a job of that nature is one of the most humbling. In college, for a year, it had been my job. It was the only job available—it was that or nothing.

While the girls in the dorm were grateful to me, even giving me flowers for my service of cleaning, I didn't care much for the job. Perhaps it was because I knew that society thinks there's not much prestige to this type of position. But, seriously, where would we be without those who will mop up our messes?

Although there is no mention that Jesus performed any janitorial services in the Bible, He did come to teach us how to serve one another with humility. His willingness to leave the comfort of His heavenly home to live among people in a corrupt world and then go to the Cross and die for us is the epitome of servanthood. —ALICE J. WISLER

FAITH STEP: *Which tasks of servanthood are the most difficult for you? What is the attitude of a good servant?*

TUESDAY, NOVEMBER 10

Give thanks in all circumstances; for this is God's will for you in Christ Jesus.
1 Thessalonians 5:18 (NIV)

ONE MORNING RECENTLY WE NOTICED a puddle of water on the guest bathroom floor. And no one had used the shower. *Uh-oh.*

We grabbed towels, blotting the dampness to protect the nearby carpet. We finally located a leak somewhere around the base of the toilet.

A few minutes later we heard a gurgling sound from the shower as water bubbled up like an underground spring. Not good. Then I remembered another incident a year or two earlier when the plumbing backed up through our master bathtub. Surely not! I raced to the other bathroom, and you can guess what I found. An inch of anything but spring-looking water. *Yuck!*

The leakage eventually drained, and the problem didn't require an expert this time. For that we were extremely grateful. However, the mess left behind did necessitate a thorough cleaning of both tubs, one of which I had neglected for some time. I wasn't too pleased about the interruption in an otherwise productive day, as I completed the procrastinated job of scouring weeks of scummy buildup.

Later I felt Jesus's gentle nudge, especially when I looked at the shiny surface of my clean tub. I actually heard myself uttering a prayer: "Thank you, Jesus, for that unwelcome interruption. It forced me to do an unpleasant task I had avoided far too long."

Giving thanks in everything is never easy. Some circumstances test us severely. That incident hardly mattered when compared to crises like illness, betrayal, unemployment, or a loved one's death. But the principle is the same.

Sometimes we need a heavenly prod to exercise gratitude, even to give thanks for a leaky toilet. —REBECCA BARLOW JORDAN

FAITH STEP: *If you've never done so, begin a gratitude journal. Write down a recent circumstance for which you can give thanks. And every day, add something new—even if it seems unpleasant at the time.*

WEDNESDAY, NOVEMBER 11

Then she knelt behind him at his feet, weeping. Her tears fell on his feet, and she wiped them off with her hair. Then she kept kissing his feet and putting perfume on them. Luke 7:38 (NLT)

WHILE MY DAUGHTER HAD A meeting with another mom, their two younger children played together. Even though the other mom's daughter was a couple of years older than my three-year-old grandson, they seemed to mesh well. After a session of dress-up, the girl asked Roman if she could have a kiss. "No," he answered. When the girl asked why not, Roman responded, "Because I'm saving my kisses for Lacey." (Lacey is his older sister.)

Upon hearing this story, my first thought was, *Good boy. Don't give in to our culture's promotion of loose behavior and casual relationships.* Later, I started wondering how wise I am when it comes to sharing my affection— not in a physical sense, but in a spiritual sense. Do I love worldly things more than I love Jesus? Am I careful to save first place in my heart for Him rather than other relationships, material possessions, or self-centered pleasures?

The woman in Luke 7 saved her kisses for Jesus. After living an immoral life, she met Someone who offered her forgiveness and unconditional love. The self-righteous host of the dinner party had failed to offer Jesus even the common courtesy of providing water to wash the dust off His feet. The sinful woman washed His feet with her tears and covered them with kisses. Jesus explained to Simon that the woman demonstrated great love because of her awareness that her sins had been forgiven. Whenever I'm tempted to bestow my affections on something unworthy, all I have to do is remember how much Jesus has forgiven me. Then I'll know Who I'm saving my kisses for. —DIANNE NEAL MATTHEWS

FAITH STEP: *When was the last time you lavished affection on Jesus? Take some time today to express your love for Him in a special prayer, song, or poem.*

THURSDAY, NOVEMBER 12

Seeing their faith, Jesus said to the man, "Young man, your sins are forgiven."
Luke 5:20 (NLT)

SOMETIMES I GROW WEARY OF other people's problems. That sounds horrid until I clarify that my discouragement comes not because I don't care...but because I do. It hurts to feel incompetent to fix their aches.

That admission explains why I love this verse! People often approached Jesus as He went about His ministry, and this particular story contains something subtle worth noting: our faith affects others.

One day Jesus was teaching and healing in someone's home. The crowd was thick, as were the needs. In the throng, a paralyzed man waited, desperate for Jesus's touch. God saw the man's need, and He began to meet that need through faith-filled friends whom He knew would do all they could to get the lame man to the Savior.

When they lowered the man through the roof to where Jesus was, Jesus commented on the faith that had brought them there. Instead of the Bible mentioning the lame man's faith, it says that Jesus saw "their" faith. The friends' faith played a key role in the man's healing.

When I feel powerless to help hurting souls across the globe, this story of friends' faith that led to healing inspires me to keep praying. I can trust that every prayer I offer for a needy person I don't know but love through Christ leads to that person's healing.

Jesus hears and acts on our faith for the sake of others. He uses our faith, making up for what we lack with His wisdom and power. We don't need to know what every person is going through in order to play a role in helping her/him experience the Savior. —ERIN KEELEY MARSHALL

FAITH STEP: *Pay attention to the strangers you come across while running errands or commuting to work. Give the Holy Spirit an opportunity to nudge you to pray. When we pay attention to Jesus's priorities, He can use our faith mightily for others.*

FRIDAY, NOVEMBER 13

But let the godly rejoice. Let them be glad in God's presence. Let them be filled with joy. Psalm 68:3 (NLT)

JUST THIS MORNING WHEN JACK walked into the kitchen for breakfast, I said, "Are you ready for the happy morning dance?"

"No."

"Happy morning! Happy morning! Happy morning! Dance! Dance!" I accompanied my impromptu song with an equally impromptu jig. Jack covered both eyes with his hands. "Mom...stop."

I was filled with joy. And laughter. Will walked in. "Will, do you want to see my happy morning dance?"

"No."

I started up with the song and dance.

"Cover your eyes. Don't look at her." Jack instructed his brother. They escaped to the living room.

I followed. "Don't any of you want to see my dance?" I asked.

All three boys said, "No."

"That's too bad. I was going to give you points for watching." The boys earn points for chores and good listening, redeemable at the end of the week.

"Yes! We'll watch it!"

"Too little too late!" I told them. "Maybe next time."

I danced back into the kitchen. I think Jesus would have appreciated it. Everywhere He went and everyone He touched was infused with joy. Weddings were better. Dinner parties were better. Even Scripture came to life when He spoke it. Joy is contagious. Let the joy of the Lord be your strength.

Happy morning! Happy morning! Happy morning! Dance! Dance!
—SUSANNA FOTH AUGHTMON

FAITH STEP: *Do something that brings you joy, whether it is listening to music, digging in the garden, or baking your favorite cookies. Invite Jesus to fill you with His joy.*

SATURDAY, NOVEMBER 14

When the Lord saw her, his heart went out to her and he said,
"Don't cry." Luke 7:13 (NIV)

I'VE BEEN SEEN BY A lot of doctors recently. They all have forms to fill out. Some have longer waits or more impressive surroundings. I visited the Mayo Clinic this week and even as someone who's worked many years at hospitals in several states, I was impressed to the point of being overwhelmed.

The shiny buildings and billion-dollar budgets don't make the difference for me, though.

Not every doctor I've seen has seen me.

Some were distracted. Others were engaged, asking questions and listening for answers. Others reached conclusions before considering the evidence. I respect their knowledge but can tell when I'm being viewed as a diagnosis instead of a human being. I sometimes do the same thing myself. As a neonatal nurse, when I resuscitate an infant, I concentrate on algorithms, organ systems, and actions to be taken rather than thinking of the baby as someone's precious child. Emotions can wait.

Often when Jesus helped someone, the Bible says He saw the person—Peter's mother, the woman who touched the hem of His garment, the grieving mother in today's verse. When Jesus, His disciples, and followers came upon a funeral procession, rather than just waiting for it to pass, Jesus picked out one person, the widow who'd lost her son and her hope. He saw her, felt her sorrow, and met her need.

Loving people in general isn't loving them at all. If we want to love people like Jesus does, we need to risk seeing them as individuals. To look someone in the eye and really care. We are His hands and His feet in this world. May we also learn to be His eyes. —SUZANNE DAVENPORT TIETJEN

FAITH STEP: *Today, ask Jesus to help you see what He sees, moment by moment, person by person. Take the risk of caring about each one. Before bed, examine your heart. Is it softer?*

SUNDAY, NOVEMBER 15

Let us run with endurance the race that is set before us, looking unto Jesus, the author and finisher of our faith, who for the joy that was set before Him endured the cross, despising the shame, and has sat down at the right hand of the throne of God. Hebrews 12:1–2 (NKJV)

WHEN I BATTLE DOUBT, IT is usually because of a conundrum Frederick Buechner describes this way: *God is all-powerful. God is all-good. Terrible things happen. You can reconcile any two of these propositions with each other, but you can't reconcile all three. Christianity ultimately offers no theoretical solutions at all.*

Buechner goes on to say: *It merely points to the Cross and says that, practically speaking, there is no evil so dark and so obscene—not even this—but that God can turn it to good.*

The Cross is a great silencer of doubts. Even doubting Thomas succumbed to belief when he placed his fingers where the nails had been in Jesus's hands. It's a mystery I'll never fully understand, but one that demands my awe and respect. The Cross is where I go back over and over again when doubts assail.

The promise of the Cross is, as Buechner says, and Paul writes in Romans 8:28, *all things work together for good.* Even the things that hurt. Even the things we don't understand. Even the things that are unfair. Yes— even the things that kill us. There is no theoretical solution. But faith demands that we make the leap over the gulf of our finite understanding to trust the infinite love of the Cross. —GWEN FORD FAULKENBERRY

FAITH STEP: *Do you struggle with doubt? Especially when things happen that you don't understand? Jesus knows and understands. Take your fears to the Cross and lay them at His feet. You can trust His love is big enough for all of your questions.*

MONDAY, NOVEMBER 16

"Because of our God's deep compassion . . . ." Luke 1:78 (CEB)

THE WOMAN DROPPED HER GAZE, then sighed and looked me in the eye. "It's not all bad. Finding out now is better than never knowing what was going on with him."

She was talking about her husband and the recent revelation that he suffers from an adult version of high-functioning Asperger's syndrome.

One of the manifestations of the Autism/Asperger's spectrum is an inability to empathize, to show compassion for another's physical or emotional pain. It reveals itself in a lack of responsiveness, sometimes interpreted as a lack of kindness or caring.

Not knowing had taken a toll on their marriage; knowing added a new dimension of challenge. Hard as their road would be, she no longer attributed his lack of expressed concern as a character flaw that cut her to the core.

Knowing someone cares is a vital key to our ability to endure hardship, knee-buckling crises, and the energy-draining ordinariness of life.

Years ago, I received a carved wood plaque that read, "Jesus Cares." Five moves in five years may have been the culprit in its disappearance. But the truth of that simple plaque remains. Embedded in my soul is the imprint of those words, as if the plaque had been pressed against the flesh of my heart. No matter what I face, this truth lingers: Jesus cares.

Unlike the husband who struggles to empathize, the One Who loves us perfectly is also perfectly gifted at expressing it—through comforting verses in the Bible, through a timely hug from a friend, through sweet words in a note or text or instant message, through that indescribable sense of His presence by His Holy Spirit. —CYNTHIA RUCHTI

FAITH STEP: *Make it a practice today to end every negative sentence with three fresh words: "But Jesus cares." This is hard . . . but Jesus cares. I'm heartbroken . . . but Jesus cares. My husband/friend/mother/boss didn't notice the extra effort I made . . . but Jesus cares.*

TUESDAY, NOVEMBER 17

One day Jesus was praying in a certain place. When he finished, one of his disciples said to him, "Lord, teach us to pray, just as John taught his disciples."
Luke 11:1 (NIV)

WHEN MY GRANDDAUGHTER WAS ABOUT six months old, my husband and I visited her and took advantage of the chance to take tons of photos, since we live halfway across the country.

As I was holding our little sweetie, telling her how special she was and singing to her, my husband took a series of photos of the two of us. The pictures captured how intently she studied my face, and how she concentrated on pursing her lips, moving her tongue, trying to copy what she observed, even though she was too young to form words yet. With each picture, her smile grew bigger, too, and in the last photo we are both laughing with shared glee.

Yes, I'm a doting grandma. I'm thrilled with each effort the amazing baby makes to coo or laugh or babble. I understand that she's young, and it will take time to master conversation.

While cuddling my granddaughter, it struck me how frequently I forget that Jesus dotes on us every bit as much. Sometimes as I struggle to pray about a difficult issue, I worry that I'm saying it all wrong. Yet just as I delight in helping my grandchild learn words, Jesus delights in teaching me how to pray. He doesn't frown at me for my mistakes. He joins me in joyful celebration as we communicate. And the more I study His face and copy Him, the easier it is for me to learn.

I'm just a baby at communicating with God, but I'm a baby who is loved and cherished. —SHARON HINCK

FAITH STEP: *Notice babies this week, especially those who are copying sounds and learning to speak. Ask Jesus to continue teaching you to pray.*

WEDNESDAY, NOVEMBER 18

Carry each other's burdens, and in this way you will fulfill the law of Christ.
Galatians 6:2 (NIV)

NO ONE IN MY FAMILY will sit next to me in a movie. I become emotionally involved with the story and yell things at the screen.

Years ago, during a tense scene in a movie, I yelled out, "Jesus, help him." Scott leaned over and said, "Quit bothering Jesus. He has real prayers He needs to listen to." It didn't matter that it was a fictional tale...it felt real to me.

I often find myself praying out loud as I watch the news. When we begin following Jesus, we find we care about what He cares about. People.

When someone is reeling from a tragedy, we reel with them. Their story in some way becomes our story. We weep along with the families who have lost a child, a sister, a spouse. We rejoice together at the goodness that we see in our fellow man as people help those who are hurting. We stand shoulder to shoulder with them in spirit as they move forward to heal and recover. And we pray. We cry out on their behalf, "Jesus, help them." Because He is the One Who can comfort, heal, and restore.

I try hard not to be overwhelmed by the horror of what happens in the world. I want to let my soul lift with hope at each act of kindness and courage and goodness that plays out every day.

And I want to see each news story as a sovereign opportunity to pray. To talk to Jesus about these people He loves so much. To ask for His healing, His grace, and His peace to intervene in their chaos and to ask Him to enfold them with His great love, wiping away their tears and healing their hearts. It is what He does best. —SUSANNA FOTH AUGHTMON

FAITH STEP: *While watching the news or reading headlines online, take the opportunity to bring those stories to Jesus in prayer, knowing He cares for these people with a deep love.*

THURSDAY, NOVEMBER 19

"Focus your thoughts on these things." Philippians 4:8 *(CEB)*

I ADMIT IT. AT TIMES I've dishonored a verse from God's Word with an unspoken, "Yeah, yeah, yeah." I didn't doubt the teaching's truth, but I didn't fully embrace what it was telling me or how Jesus could make it possible.

Philippians 4:8 is one of those passages. When the verse was suggested as a panacea for whatever ailed me or as a finger-shaking directive, I sometimes push it aside as not applying to my immediate need.

"From now on, brothers and sisters, if anything is excellent and if anything is admirable, focus your thoughts on these things: all that is true, all that is holy, all that is just, all that is pure, all that is lovely, and all that is worthy of praise" (CEB).

Have you ever wondered if that verse might have been born from the Apostle Paul's experience after a week at Smiley Face Spa, rather than crafted by the heart of Jesus?

After thinking about it for a couple of decades, I'm finally grasping what might lie behind that verse. Jesus—the one "well acquainted" with our griefs—understands completely that impure, unloving, dishonorable, unholy, unjust thoughts will swirl around us in the mix of everyday life. Depressing thoughts. Self-absorbed thoughts. Thoughts of revenge. He doesn't pretend they aren't there. Instead, Jesus calls us to steer our focus—with His help—to those thoughts that are for our good, not our emotional or spiritual destruction.

It's as if when our mind drifts to something unholy or defeating, Jesus holds our chin and says, "Look Me in the eyes. Focus. You are loved. You're held. You're safe with Me. And you can trust that this verse applies to you. Yes, you." —CYNTHIA RUCHTI

FAITH STEP: *If you memorized Philippians 4:8 in a traditional version, commit it to memory in another version. The exercise will refresh your understanding and pull from the verse more truth than you realized was there.*

FRIDAY, NOVEMBER 20

Send out your light and your truth; let them guide me. Let them lead me to your holy mountain, to the place where you live. Psalm 43:3 (NLT)

EVERY WEEK, WITH THE HELP of other mentors, I lead a support group for teenage mothers. It's easy to spend time with them. It's easy to love them and their children. It's harder to hold back from telling them what to do. And it's hard when we share the good news of Jesus and they stand still, not walking toward Him. Or worse, they walk the other way. It's hard not to lose heart when we see them trying to find happiness in the false pleasures that this world offers. I don't have all the answers...but I do have the most important answer to all of life's problems: Jesus.

"I have something wonderful," I tell them in numerous ways. "Someone Who will help everything. I know that something great is coming, because I've seen the first rays of His light in my heart."

Every day there are people around us seeking their own self-satisfaction. We can share what we know about Jesus, but that doesn't mean our hearers will seek what we have to offer...until they see the reality of Jesus's light lived out in our lives.

We may not think people are listening—and maybe they aren't—but they are always watching. When they see the joy and peace that Jesus's light brings into our lives, they will see Him in us. And when dark times come, we will be the ones they turn to, with hearts ready to listen.

Don't get discouraged if you are trying to share a message of hope with someone who needs it. You never know how your words will stay with and affect them. It might not be until eternity that we'll truly see the impact we had. —TRICIA GOYER

FAITH STEP: *Light a candle and watch it flicker and dance, and then pray for Jesus to show you how to be a light to those around you.*

SATURDAY, NOVEMBER 21

"I have told you these things, so that in me you may have peace. In this world you will have trouble. But take heart! I have overcome the world." John 16:33 (NIV)

NOT AGAIN! ANOTHER FRIEND HAD been diagnosed with cancer. Her daughter wrote, pouring out her anguish and fear. A teen in our city died, and the police were slow in releasing their report. People were breathing down the chief of police's neck, suspecting foul play. Over coffee, I heard that a neighbor's house had been broken into, and vehicles and valuables were stolen. Why can't things go right? Why can't people be honest? Why are disease, destruction, and death so prevalent?

From the traumatic to the annoying, our lives are constant battles of circumstances. For some reason, when I was in my early twenties, I thought that I would manage to get to this place called All My Problems Solved and that life would be smooth sailing. I had trouble when I faced trouble, unable to shake it off. I thought something was wrong with me because my life wasn't easy.

I have a different take on things now. I rejoice when things go well. I have learned to enjoy the moment.

And I know that calamities happen to everyone and therefore, are sure to happen to me. It's not about thinking anything is wrong with me or that I am somehow being punished; it's about living in a fallen world with imperfections.

I turn to the Perfect One and find comfort in knowing that Jesus has overcome. —ALICE J. WISLER

FAITH STEP: *"Don't become overwhelmed by the magnitude of your problems, become overwhelmed by the magnitude of Jesus." How will you let the magnitude of Jesus increase your faith today?*

SUNDAY, NOVEMBER 22

May the Lord of peace himself always give you his peace no matter what happens. The Lord be with you all. 2 Thessalonians 3:16 (NLT)

MY HUSBAND AND I WILL soon celebrate thirty-three years of marriage. Over time we've discovered several effective rules for fighting fair. One of them is to avoid using blanket statements. That is, we don't say things such as, "You *never* put your dirty clothes in the laundry hamper," or "You *always* seem distracted when I talk to you." Such statements are often exaggerations of the truth and serve no positive purpose.

I've tried to avoid using blanket statements after realizing their potential harm. Imagine my surprise, then, when I began seeing them sprinkled throughout Scripture. The writers often used words such as *always, never,* and *all* when describing God's attitudes and actions toward mankind. Once I started noticing their frequency, I began looking for them and enjoyed discovering new spiritual truths through them.

One of my favorites is today's key verse in which Paul expresses encouragement to Christ's followers in Thessalonica. "No matter what happens," he writes, "may the Lord of peace *always* give you his peace. The Lord be with you *all.*" Beautiful blanket statements, they are. And even though they're over two thousand years old, they're relevant today because Jesus, the Prince of Peace, still reigns.

Stress and fear may loom large, but the truths contained in Scripture's blanket statements weaken their power over us. Jesus promises His presence and peace at all times to His followers. Because of Who He is, everything's going to be okay—at *all* times and in *every* circumstance, no matter what. —GRACE FOX

FAITH STEP: *What concerns face you today? List them on a sheet of paper. Using a different color pencil or pen, write a prayer across the list, thanking the Lord for promising to fill you with peace in all circumstances. Capitalize the word all.*

MONDAY, NOVEMBER 23

All were weeping and mourning for her, but he said, "Do not weep, for she is not dead but sleeping." And they laughed at him, knowing that she was dead. But taking her by the hand he called, saying, "Child, arise." And her spirit returned, and she got up at once. Luke 8:52–55 (ESV)

IS THERE ANY SOUND ON earth more beautiful than the voices of those you love? Answering my phone and hearing the voice of my husband or one of my children fills me with pleasure. Hearing my name called by someone picking me up at an airport brings security and relief. The unexpected voice of a friend in a restaurant represents a delightful surprise.

During the time that Jesus walked on the earth, many people heard His voice. They witnessed Him preaching and teaching, confronting hypocrites, and comforting the hurting. They listened as He healed the sick and blind, commanded evil spirits to leave tormented bodies, and gave thanks before multiplying a little lunch to feed thousands. A few people heard Jesus's voice calling them from the other side of the grave.

I can't begin to imagine how Jairus's twelve-year-old daughter felt when Jesus took her hand and called her to come back from death. Did she hear a voice filled with power and the authority to command life and death? Or did a gentle voice radiating love and compassion draw her back to this earth? What was her first thought when she saw her Savior's face?

Although Jesus doesn't speak to me in an audible voice, He wants to communicate with me each day through prayer and the Word. His Spirit speaks to my spirit to guide, comfort, and heal. And I can look forward to the day when He takes my hand and calls me to arise into a new life.

—DIANNE NEAL MATTHEWS

FAITH STEP: *What can you do to hear Jesus's voice more clearly today? Spend a few minutes sitting before Him in silence as you pray, "Speak, Lord, for Your servant is listening" (1 Samuel 3:9).*

TUESDAY, NOVEMBER 24

*Humble yourselves, therefore, under God's mighty hand, that he may
lift you up in due time. Cast all your anxiety on him because
he cares for you. 1 Peter 5:6—7 (NIV)*

RECENTLY I RECEIVED AN E-MAIL with a radiology report of an X-ray, and there was an unexpected finding with scary-sounding medical jargon. I told myself that if it was anything serious my doctor would call...but I kept wondering about the abnormality and what it meant. Since it was the weekend, I couldn't make a quick call to the clinic to ask my doctor about the results.

My husband suggested I ask his brother, a doctor, about it, but I didn't want to pester him and was also afraid of sounding silly. Instead I searched for information online, which only ratcheted up my anxiety. Finally, I called my brother-in-law. He quickly reassured me that it was a harmless quirk and a common finding. Relief flooded me. A hundred terrible outcomes—invented by my wild imagination—all dissolved.

The experience made me realize how many times anxiety coils around me, subtly squeezing tighter and tighter. What if readers don't like my next book? What if a friend finds me annoying? What if my children wander from faith? What if my husband is in a car accident? What if society crumbles? Like subtle signs on an X-ray, I can see there are problems, but I don't fully know what they mean. In my ignorance I imagine the worst.

Until I remember there is someone I can call on. Jesus understands the truth and reassures me all will be well. Even better, He has the power to bring change to the situation, or change to my heart so I can bear it with more grace until His answer unfolds. —SHARON HINCK

FAITH STEP: *Choose one source of anxiety in your life right now. Discuss it with Jesus, and ask for His diagnosis.*

WEDNESDAY, NOVEMBER 25

I am with you always, even to the end of the world. Matthew 28:20 (TLB)

DAVID BROOKS, IN A WONDERFUL column in *The New York Times*, writes about something he calls "the art of presence." It's the idea that when people are suffering a trauma, the best thing we can do for them is to be there. Not to try to fix everything, or explain, or even plan; but to "sit simply through moments of pain and uncomfortable darkness."

Brooks gives some great advice. I often feel at a loss when ministering to others in pain, even though I want so much to help, to do, and say the right things. His article reminded me that the main thing is to be present. To stand up and be counted among the ones who are there when there's a need. Not necessarily there with answers. Just there. It's true that being present is what matters most. If I think back over times I've been in need, it's not really the wise sage who comes to my mind, or the great orator who spoke perfect words. It's the friend who held my hand. The sister who brought soup.

When I read the article I thought about Jesus and how He promised to always be with us. It makes sense that this would comfort others, because out of all of the things I love about Jesus, it's His presence that I need the most. There are so many things I don't understand, and even reading the Bible doesn't solve everything or give us all of the answers. But knowing that nothing can separate me from His love...He is with me always...in Him we live and breathe and have our being...this is enough. His presence is the one thing we can't do without—and thanks be to God we don't ever have to! —GWEN FORD FAULKENBERRY

FAITH STEP: *Is there someone who needs you to share the presence of Jesus today? To just be there? Step out in faith and practice the art of presence. You'll never be sorry you did.*

THURSDAY, NOVEMBER 26

Since ancient times no one has heard, no ear has perceived, no eye has seen any God besides you, who acts on behalf of those who wait for him.
Isaiah 64:4 (NIV)

ONE OF MY FAVORITE THINGS about Thanksgiving is reflecting over my last year, but sometimes the truest Thanksgiving comes when I look farther back. I love digging out my old prayer journals. This is part of a prayer from 1999:

Dear Jesus, I thank You for this new morning. I thank You that you desire to meet with me as much as I desire to meet with You—even more. I have yet to see how my life can be transformed by being solely committed to You, living a life without reservation, instead of trusting, listening and obeying in all things. Whose lives would be affected? Whom would I touch? How would eternity be forever changed?

I love looking back more than a year because so much has happened. I've celebrated twenty-three years of marriage, raised three amazing kids, led three mission trips, helped open a pregnancy center, started two teen mom support groups, started a blog, wrote numerous books, moved to Arkansas for ministry, started a radio podcast, and adopted three children!

Those are the highlights. There have been many hard moments—painful moments—too. As James 1:12 (NIV) says, "Blessed is the one who perseveres under trial because, having stood the test, that person will receive the crown of life that the Lord has promised to those who love him."

Jesus acts on those who wait for Him. He helps us persevere, and He promises a crown of life at the end of our journey. That's something to be thankful for! —TRICIA GOYER

FAITH STEP: *This Thanksgiving don't just take time to look over the past year and share things you are thankful for. Instead, look back over the last five or ten years... maybe even more. Share ways you've persevered. Share accomplishments you've achieved through and for Jesus. Finally, share how Jesus has acted as you've waited for Him.*

FRIDAY, NOVEMBER 27

Come away, my beloved, and be like a gazelle or like a young stag on the spice-laden mountains. Song of Songs 8:14 (NIV)

THIS LAST WEEKEND I WAS away speaking at a women's retreat in Washington with my friend Melissa.

We did a lot of laughing. Mostly, Melissa laughed at me because I could not maneuver climbing in and out of a top bunk bed. (Why are the rungs so far apart? Why are sleeping bags so slippery? Why do I not have any upper arm strength?)

We had chats long into the night. It was a moment to get away from life and refocus, relax, and regroup.

I like the word "retreat." In my mind, I hear it as a full battle cry. "Sweet mercy, run for your lives! RETREAT!" I picture myself, arms flailing, running all out, breathing hard to get to a place of peace. A place where the clamor of life eases up enough so I can hear myself think and give Jesus a chance to connect with me.

I am not an army tactician but I have watched enough Civil War movies to know that when the guy in charge yells, "Retreat!" it is so those who are fighting the battle can back up and get together with him. They need to disengage, get out of the fray—and they need to do it at a full-out run, so he can give them a new course of action.

I don't think a retreat has to be at a camp...though it is nice when it is. But I do think anytime you change your surroundings it helps you refocus. So this morning after I take the kids to school, I am going for a walk at the park near my kids' school. So I can get together with Jesus and find out what's next. I want Him to call the shots. Retreat. —SUSANNA FOTH AUGHTMON

FAITH STEP: *Find a place of peace where you can sit and listen to Jesus. Tell Him that you want Him to call the shots in your life today.*

SATURDAY, NOVEMBER 28

In the same way, the Spirit helps us in our weakness. We do not know what we ought to pray for, but the Spirit himself intercedes for us with groans that words cannot express. Romans 8:26 (NIV)

YESTERDAY MY HUSBAND AND I were driving home from a family gathering when our youngest daughter texted us. Since I was in the passenger seat, I picked up my husband's phone and typed in a response. However, the car was bouncing a bit, the keypad was tiny, and I didn't have my reading glasses with me. I couldn't see what I was typing, and AutoCorrect is prone to insert its own interpretation. She finally sent the message, "I can't figure out what you're trying to say."

Another time when I was texting with our older daughter, I finally acknowledged, "I'm a bad texter." And the phone changed my message to "I'm a bad texture." Our kids have saved some of the strange texts they've gotten from me for when they need a laugh.

There are days when my prayer life feels as clumsy as my efforts to text. Recently our church has been dealing with conflicts and difficulties. My heart breaks to see friends hurt. I begin to pray and try to frame a solution, but have no idea what to ask for or what will bring healing.

What a comfort that Jesus gave us the Holy Spirit to guide and direct our prayers. We don't need to tell Jesus the answers and solutions. We don't even have to know all the right questions to ask. Our prayers may look like a garbled text with misspellings, but we don't have to fear our petitions aren't good enough or our language isn't fancy enough. We can trust that Jesus not only understands our garbled efforts to communicate, but that He hears and responds in love. —SHARON HINCK

FAITH STEP: *Today, each time you text someone (or e-mail, phone, or write), take a moment to thank Jesus for sending His Spirit to guide our prayers.*

SUNDAY, NOVEMBER 29

And his name will be the hope of all the world. Matthew 12:21 (NLT)

HAVE YOU NOTICED ABOUT THIS time of year how often we hear the word "hope"? Perhaps that's not by accident.

We will always hear of hurts and disappointments, and even experience them ourselves. But at Christmastime needs rise to the surface like the fat of rich cream. I see it in newspaper headlines, Internet news features, and in the heart-tugging requests of people who comment on my blog about discouragement in their lives. Everyone wants—and needs—hope.

Perhaps the cheerful celebrations at Christmas stir up an intense longing for encouragement. Those "without" look into the windows of those "with" and feel the weight of despair and loneliness exaggerated.

Cries for help do reach willing servants, moved by love and compassion to meet the most desperate needs. Churches and other helpful organizations search for impoverished families to "adopt," while nonprofit groups beg for more to supply the greatest demands. But we cannot meet them all. And at best, even the most generous philanthropists can't restore the losses and fill the stockings of every person in crisis.

There is, however, One Who can. He may choose not to fix every physical need until heaven. But the soul's most pressing need, "the hopes and fears of all the years," has already been met. Jesus, God's most precious gift, is the hope of all the world.

Our pocketbooks will empty, but our hearts can remain full year round. This year, be generous to meet physical needs. When others long for hope and encouragement, don't forget to also share with them the gift that lasts forever: the good news of Jesus. —REBECCA BARLOW JORDAN

FAITH STEP: *This Christmas, do without something you enjoy, and give the "savings" to someone in need. As you do, share the hope Jesus can bring all year long.*

MONDAY, NOVEMBER 30

And now, just as you accepted Christ Jesus as your Lord, you must continue to live in obedience to him. Colossians 2:6 (NLT)

BABYSITTING FOUR GRANDCHILDREN LESS THAN six years of age means toys lay strewn across our living room. It also means someone has to clean up before bedtime. And so my husband and I issue the command: "C'mon, kids. Let's put the toys away now."

Invariably, the call to action receives mixed reviews. One child responds immediately with a cheerful, "Okay!" Another stalls for a minute, hoping grandparents and siblings will get the job done without his help. A third—absorbed in playtime or a good book—ignores the command altogether, while the fourth escapes the room.

I'm not a behavioral expert, but I know what obedience looks like. I also know that kids aren't the only ones who struggle with it. Grown-ups do too. We don't always feel like responding with a cheerful okay when the Holy Spirit prompts us to say or do something specific. Sometimes we stall, hoping someone else will assume the task. Sometimes we ignore the prompting because a different, more appealing, activity absorbs our attention. And at other times, well, we try to escape. Can you relate?

Scripture tells us how we, as Christ's followers, ought to behave when He gives us a task. It's simple, really—we ought to say yes, immediately and cheerfully. No eye rolling marked with a sarcastic, "All right. Whatever." No foot stamping accompanied by a protest, "But I don't want to!" And no running away.

If we declare Jesus as our Lord, then He's the boss and deserves our implicit obedience. Let's respond to His commands in a way that honors Him as He deserves. —GRACE FOX

FAITH STEP: *Perhaps the Holy Spirit has nudged you to do a particular task but you're struggling with obedience. Ask Him to give you the victory over hindrances and excuses and to grant you a heart that's eager to obey Him.*

TUESDAY, DECEMBER 1

*As he went along, he saw a man blind from birth. His disciples asked him, "Rabbi,
who sinned, this man or his parents, that he was born blind?" "Neither this man
nor his parents sinned," said Jesus, "but this happened so that the works
of God might be displayed in him." John 9:1–3 (NIV)*

WHEN MY SON CORY WAS just a baby he had a horribly high fever. My
husband, John, and I were questioning whether or not to take him to the
emergency room, when John said, "We should pray."

John put his large hand on Cory's forehead and prayed for healing.
Then his eyes grew wide. I reached up and touched Cory's forehead and
it was cool. The fever was gone! John and I have prayed for many things
over the years. Not every prayer was answered in such a miraculous way,
but the fact that one was urged us to continue to bring our requests before
Jesus.

In the Bible, Jesus performed many miracles, and through them many
got a glimpse of Who Jesus was. It took a storm for the disciples to see
that Jesus had power to calm even the winds and the waves. It took a
famished crowd for the disciples to realize that little is much in the hands
of their Lord. It took broken bodies for Jesus to be called "Healer." Dis-
eased minds allowed Jesus to be labeled "Deliverer." And renewed hope in
empty, hurting souls let those around Jesus see Him as "Lord."

It's only because of the darkness that we can see the light. It's only
through pain and suffering that we can receive Jesus's comfort. Sometimes
we may question why we have to go through what we do. First, because
we live in a sinful world marked by struggle, but also because Jesus has
more of Himself to reveal to us. His power, His love, His provision that
we can't discover any other way. —TRICIA GOYER

FAITH STEP: *Do you have a sick friend? Visit that person and pray, expecting Jesus
will meet you as you join together with heads bowed.*

WEDNESDAY, DECEMBER 2

Then we'll be a choir—not our voices only, but our very lives singing in harmony in a stunning anthem to the God and Father of our Master Jesus!
Romans 15:6 (MSG)

I LOVE TO SING, ESPECIALLY in parts. Years ago I sang in a gospel quartet, and I sing tenor in the church choir. My voice isn't beautiful but I can hit the right notes. Once I know them.

You see, I'm not very good at reading music. My musical friends sight-read. They look at the written music and hear the song in their heads. I don't. I need to hear the starting note or I'm halfway through the verse before I find the harmony. I do even better if the accompanist plunks out my part. Sometimes I ask her to play a particularly difficult interval over and over while I match pitches. I drum it into my head all week long and by Sunday I can sing it easily, able to pay attention to the director and the dynamics.

In one sense, written music is the song. If you purchase the sheet music to Handel's *Messiah*, you hold it in your hands. But that isn't all it was designed to be. The *Messiah* is meant to be experienced in a candlelit cathedral where beautiful voices lift the listeners to a place the score could never take them. So, too, God's written Word is complete, strong, and sufficient to achieve His purposes. But it is intended to be more—something seen and heard, more than words on paper or concepts in our minds. His Word is meant to work in us, capture our hearts, and transform us so that our changed lives, impossible to hide, are experienced by an audience who'll see Jesus in our attitudes and actions even if they've never read the Word at all. —SUZANNE DAVENPORT TIETJEN

FAITH STEP: *You need to know a song to sing it, and you need to know the Bible to live it. Read the Word, hear it, and study it. Consider how it applies to you and respond. It'll show.*

THURSDAY, DECEMBER 3

"I am the world's Light. No one who follows me stumbles around in the darkness. I provide plenty of light to live in." John 8:12 (MSG)

DURING A HIGH-SCHOOL MISSIONS TRIP many years ago, our group took an afternoon off to go spelunking.

The cave we explored wound for miles, and we journeyed through probably a quarter of it. We crawled through narrow passageways, hefted each other up over ledges, and even crossed a narrow gorge on a plank bridge.

At one point we reached a chamber large enough for all fifteen of us to crawl inside. Our guide told us to sit and take a break, and to shut off our flashlights. *Click, click, click.* Each click dimmed the space a bit more until the final light was extinguished.

Being engulfed in pitch darkness could have been terrifying, especially with no knowledge of how to free ourselves without our guide's assistance. But something about having no other choice than to trust the guide simplified my faith that all would be okay. Fortunately, that faith proved true, and we were led out of bondage from that cave.

Christmas is quickly approaching, and it seems everywhere I go and every song I listen to, I'm reminded that Jesus's birth brought light into a sin-darkened world. The world finally had the Guide who could and would carry us into His light.

This world serves up many forms of bondage, and during the holidays especially, those trappings can feel especially painful. We yearn for release from whatever holds us back and keeps us from living free.

This season be reminded of your faithful Guide, Jesus, Who will be true to you. Follow Him, and He will provide His light to show the way through your specific circumstances. —ERIN KEELEY MARSHALL

FAITH STEP: *Memorize John 1:5 (NLT), "The light shines in the darkness, and the darkness can never extinguish it."*

FRIDAY, DECEMBER 4

So we fix our eyes not on what is seen, but on what is unseen, since what is seen is temporary, but what is unseen is eternal. 2 Corinthians 4:18 (NIV)

WHEN OUR CHILDREN WERE YOUNG, we wanted them to be engaged in our family Advent devotions. Besides the symbolic candles in the Advent wreath, we created a basket full of small boxes. After our Bible reading time, one of the children would choose a box and open it, and create a "devotional thought" based on the object inside. A marble, a thimble, a wooden butterfly, a button, a pompom, a piece of sponge, or a seashell. Whatever they found, they would explain some truth about Jesus: we can hold a marble in our hand, the way our Creator holds the world. A thimble protects our thumb, as Jesus protects our souls. A butterfly dies and is reborn, as we will be one day because of the death and Resurrection of Jesus.

Each tangible object—a thing that is seen—could remind us of a larger truth—the thing that is not seen.

Some days it's a challenge to see Jesus at work in our lives. The temporary "what is seen" fills our entire field of vision, distracting us and even causing us to obsess over it. Our days fill with goals we want to reach, people we wish would change, troubles that grab our focus. Yet in the midst of our day, those tangible objects and visible events can springboard our thoughts toward the eternal.

The goals that feel overwhelming can remind us of our reliance on Christ and His provision. The irritating family member can provide a place to practice Jesus's call to forgiveness. Our struggle with pain can call to mind the beautiful mercy of Jesus and the promise of new, whole bodies one day.

Each day becomes an adventure when we find ways to look beyond what is seen, to what is eternal. —SHARON HINCK

FAITH STEP: *Look around the place where you're sitting. Choose one tangible object and think of a way it can remind you of a truth about Jesus.*

SATURDAY, DECEMBER 5

I lie down and sleep; I wake again, because the Lord sustains me.
Psalm 3:5 (NIV)

TWO O'CLOCK IN THE MORNING was not the time to focus on troubles. But I lay wide awake, my problems looming larger than life. Fear crept in like a burglar. I was worried about how my daughter, who had moved out on her own, was doing and kept replaying in my mind some disturbing text messages she had sent the day before. *Is she safe? Is she taking her medication?* "You've given her over to Jesus," I reminded myself. "Don't take it back. Don't entrust your burden to Jesus and then take back that burden."

Parents think we are supposed to worry about our children. And we do it so well! Yet, Jesus tells us not to be anxious and worry for many reasons—one being, worry is a waste of time and energy, and it produces no fruit; it does not accomplish a thing!

I prayed for peace and for sleep and, eventually, they came. The next morning, I was somewhat refreshed and grateful for the mercies that God brings us that are new every morning. He is faithful to sustain us with all we have to deal with. Nothing gets past His vision. —ALICE J. WISLER

FAITH STEP: *Look up the word* sustain *in a dictionary and then journal about it. What does it mean? What does the Lord's ability to sustain you through your hardships mean to you?*

SUNDAY, DECEMBER 6

This Son perfectly mirrors God, and is stamped with God's nature.
Hebrews 1:3 (MSG)

WE'VE PROBABLY ALL TRIED TO make Christmas a perfect celebration at least once: buying gifts the day after Christmas for the next year, devising lists to complement other lists. Decorated trees with color-coordinated ornaments appearing in every room by October. And the entire house filled with candles, music, and lights.

I remember years ago when our children wanted a perfect Christmas tree, sort of like Goldilocks at Christmas: "Too short, too tall; oh, this one is just right." It would have been so simple if we'd had only three trees to choose from. But we had to examine all two hundred fifty trees in the lot before we found that "perfect" one. And it had to be a fresh—one that we'd cut ourselves.

That tradition ended the day I found ticks spilling out of every tree limb onto my windowsill and carpet. The next year, we bought an artificial tree, still in use.

The circumstances surrounding that first Christmas over two thousand years ago were anything but perfect. An overcrowded city. A messy barn. Noisy animals. A teenager in labor. Yet the night was accompanied by a powerful, twinkling star, a host of heavenly angels, and the fragrance of a Holy God (Luke 2:1–20). The one thing that mattered about that heavenly event still matters today. The One born that night was God's perfect gift to us—the Light of the World, Jesus. It had been God's perfect plan all along.

Traditions are okay, as long as our focus is right. It's not the outward traditions of Christmas that spell perfection, but the inward celebration of the birth of our Savior, Jesus, the perfect Son of God. —REBECCA BARLOW JORDAN

FAITH STEP: *Ask Jesus to help you simplify Christmas this year. Thank Him that He is the one perfect celebration about Christmas you never want to ignore.*

MONDAY, DECEMBER 7

"Ask and it will be given to you; seek and you will find; knock and the door will be opened to you. For everyone who asks receives; the one who seeks finds; and to the one who knocks, the door will be opened. Matthew 7:7–8 (NIV)

I HAVE STARTED THINKING THAT I am most likely a visual and kinetic pray-er. If I try to pray with my eyes closed, I can count on falling asleep in two or three seconds. But if I put pen to paper or fingers to keyboard, my mind can stay focused, my prayers can flow like a small river of petitions sent heavenward. If I am walking and listening to music, prayers of thanks gather at my lips and fall out with each step.

Weird, I know. But really, Jesus is creative. Why wouldn't He want our prayers to be creative? Maybe He tires of hearing only bedside prayers so He made only a few of us able to pray when we are doing sprints on the track...or possibly there are some of us who can only focus on praying for others when we are holding their pictures in our hands—the touch and feel of the frame draws our thoughts toward Jesus. Maybe there are some of us who have to dance our prayers with leaps and deep pliés. (That one I will leave to my dancing friends.)

But I have started illustrating my prayers in my journal. Drawing pictures after different thoughts. Writing out Scriptures in bubble letters. It makes them come alive and, more than that, it seems to etch Jesus's Word on my soul.

And that, I think, is the point of prayer after all. His words, His thoughts, His dreams written on our hearts and lived out in our lives.
—SUSANNA FOTH AUGHTMON

FAITH STEP: *Draw a picture of your favorite Scripture verse and pin it on your fridge so you can meditate on it throughout the day.*

TUESDAY, DECEMBER 8

Now after they had left, an angel of the Lord appeared to Joseph in a dream and said, "Get up, take the child and his mother, and flee to Egypt, and remain there until I tell you; for Herod is about to search for the child, to destroy him." Matthew 2:13 (NRSV)

THE "FLIGHT TO EGYPT" IS something I've not given much thought. I once saw a painting in a museum called *The Slaying of the Innocents*, depicting what happened in Bethlehem after Mary and Joseph fled to Egypt. Herod was angry that the wise men did not return to tell him where the Baby Jesus was, and so he ordered all children under the age of two slaughtered. The painting made an impression on me; it was horrible. Full of blood and violence and harrowing loss.

I was reading these verses again this year, however, and it seemed to jump out at me that Mary and Joseph and the Baby Jesus fled in the night. What must that have been like? And how far ahead were they from the soldiers who came to kill the innocent children of Bethlehem? Could they hear the cries of the mothers and fathers from where they were on the road? Did they narrowly escape?

Whatever the exact timetable, they fled in darkness, and from darkness. It must have been terrifying for them, for Joseph, most of all. I imagine the baby nestled against Mary, trusting in her, and Mary trusting in Joseph. Who did Joseph have to trust in but God and God alone? The One Who sent the angel in the dream.

Sometimes we are in darkness, called, like Joseph, to walk through the night. Even though He could, God doesn't always dispel the darkness. Instead, He has provided Jesus to walk through it with us as our companion, our guide, our light. —GWEN FORD FAULKENBERRY

FAITH STEP: *If you are walking through a dark place, take the hand of Jesus. Trust Him to be your hope and your strength every step, and to bring you safely through to morning.*

WEDNESDAY, DECEMBER 9

So the Lord himself will give you this sign: A virgin will become pregnant and give birth to a son, and she will name him Immanuel [God Is With Us].
Isaiah 7:14 (GW)

LAST YEAR I HAD A different kind of Christmas. I didn't put up a tree; the only decorating I did was to hang a wreath on the front door. I didn't attend any Christmas plays, musicals, or special events. Didn't wrap a single present or bake a single cookie or mail a single card. Selling your house right after Thanksgiving and then moving across country the week before Christmas puts a big dent in normal celebrating.

Even before the house sold, I had been flying back and forth between two states to visit my husband. Occasionally, I had brief panic-filled moments when I thought, *Oh no! I'm missing Christmas!* Sometimes I felt cheated out of enjoying the things I love about the season. My perspective changed during the long drive to visit loved ones before heading to our new location. Finally, I was forced to slow down as Christmas music on the radio prepared me to celebrate the essence of Christmas instead of its trappings.

Having a Christmas stripped of all the usual activities and traditions drew my focus to the real blessings. Instead of having my children and grandchildren over for a home-cooked feast, we gathered at a cook-your-own steakhouse. Not my first choice for a celebration, but we were together. I couldn't present all my family members with carefully chosen gifts, but I could shower them with love.

More important, my pared-down version of Christmas left more room for the miracle we celebrate: God coming down to earth in the form of a baby. A love that compelled Jesus to die in our place so we can live forever. Gifts of mercy, forgiveness, and grace freely offered to those who believe. Immanuel, God with us. —DIANNE NEAL MATTHEWS

FAITH STEP: *Ask Jesus if you need to strip away anything from your holiday busyness so you can focus more on Him this Christmas season.*

THURSDAY, DECEMBER 10

The Lord is my shepherd; I shall not want. He maketh me to lie down in green pastures: he leadeth me beside the still waters. Psalm 23:1–2 (KJV)

I'D BEEN FUSSING TO JESUS for several weeks. Most of my friends had "real" jobs, places to go each day, people to interact with, regular paychecks to depend on. My freelance writing and editing were fulfilling and a blessing to me, but I had no control over when projects would arrive. I was nearing completion of my current writing contract and after that my work calendar was a big empty space. It was a terrifying feeling. I reminded myself that my identity was settled in Jesus's love for me, not my five-year career plan (or lack of one). Yet I admitted to my Shepherd that having no clear new direction from Him was not my preference. I grappled with the challenge of trusting Him during a time of stillness in a green pasture.

The next day a large editing job arrived with a tight deadline, then a few smaller requests came in as well. In fact, with my writing work, the editing, and the holiday season all overlapping, I was suddenly drowning in work.

I had to laugh at myself. I'd been so worried about a lull, and now I was dog-paddling, longing to reach a place where I could catch my breath. Jesus reminded me that I could trust Him to lead me to the next new place, the next project. As I began to panic at the stress of the new projects, He also invited me to trust Him to provide the strength and wisdom I needed.

When Jesus identifies Himself as our Good Shepherd, He is reminding us that He can protect and guide us over all sorts of terrain. Since the terrain of our lives is ever-changing, I'm grateful for that reassurance.
—SHARON HINCK

FAITH STEP: *Look back at the past year. Have there been times of quiet, even emptiness? Times of feeling too busy and overwhelmed? How did Jesus guide you? Reflect and then thank Him for leading you through this year.*

FRIDAY, DECEMBER 11

"Think of the various tests you encounter as occasions for joy."
James 1:2 (CEB)

"WON'T *THIS* BE AN ADVENTURE!" my friend said, noting that the lights had gone out not only in the vacation condo we'd rented, but all over the city, judging from the darkened landscape we could see through the window. Midmorning in an unfamiliar setting is one thing. Nightfall is another.

Some complain when the lights go out, but my friend's first reaction was curiosity about the kind of adventure we'd experience because of it. That was her response to most things other people might find irritating or disruptive.

She wasn't out of touch with reality. On the contrary, she was deeply in touch with the reality Jesus came to bring. He told us His joy could be ours (John 15:11). His Word says that His joy is our strength—and why would that matter if we weren't constantly desperate for strength?—and that we can "count it all joy" when trouble comes (James 1:2). Consider those challenges "occasions for joy," as the Common English Bible puts it. *Adventures.*

James 1:2 is a verse that can evoke confusion, disbelief, or anger for some. Joy? Out of a disheartening situation? That doesn't even make sense . . . unless you understand that because of the intense love of Jesus, we can trust His assurance that even the things we suffer make us more complete individuals (James 1:3–4). The process doesn't have to empty us. It can make us full because of the presence of Jesus made more tangible than ever in our time of need.

In that light, at times life feels like an amusement park with too many rides and a world-class roller coaster. But our hearts not only beat faster, they're stronger when we reach the adventure's end. —CYNTHIA RUCHTI

FAITH STEP: *Have you logged your current situation into the "Occasions for Joy" column yet? Because Jesus supported the idea, you can reframe an aspect of today's trial as "Adventure with Him." See what happens.*

SATURDAY, DECEMBER 12

Anyone who holds onto life just as it is destroys that life. But if you let it go, reckless in your love, you'll have it forever, real and eternal. John 12:25 (MSG)

GOD HAS BEEN TEACHING ME about vulnerability, a gift I never wanted.

Growing up, we learn to protect ourselves. To never admit certain things. To hold back our tears. If we didn't learn this before high school, we were in big trouble. We—sadly, not all of us—survived. Along the way we wore so many masks we don't remember how to be real.

It's strange, because I'm touched when others are authentic. They bravely share their unguarded hearts, and I tell myself they can do it because *they* have their acts together.

Unlike me. I am a mess! And I can't afford for anyone to know.

Until recently, anyway. I'm in an online group of Christians who support each other's creative efforts along with each other's efforts to be human. And honest. We gather face to face every year. To keep it real. Last year's opening prayer issued this challenge: "Help us to pay attention. Remember, everyone has something to offer."

That resonated with me. I fought my introversion and sat with different people at every meal. I looked at and listened to each person without writing off anyone. I forgot about myself.

I imagine Jesus looked at people like that. The experience of being really seen yet still loved may explain why so many dropped everything and followed Him, why so many still do today.

For me, the experiment is ongoing. People look very precious to me. It's scary, giving it your all. Being all in. But what are we really here for anyway? Could it be to see and take care of each other? Maybe I'm learning how. —SUZANNE DAVENPORT TIETJEN

FAITH STEP: *Try it yourself with the people God brings into your life. Hear what they're saying. Ask questions. Give up the need to make your own point. How does this feel? What do you see?*

SUNDAY, DECEMBER 13

---

*But the angel said to them, "Do not be afraid. I bring you good news that will cause
great joy for all the people. Today in the town of David a Savior has been born to
you; he is the Messiah, the Lord... When they had seen him, they spread the word
concerning what had been told them about this child, and all who heard it were
amazed at what the shepherds said to them. Luke 2:10–11; 17–18 (NIV)*

OUR FIRST GRANDCHILD WAS BORN on Christmas Eve. As soon as we
received the call from our son-in-law, we headed out and drove several
hours, eager to arrive in time for the birth.

The hospital looked deserted as the small crew of excited relatives waited
in the halls outside our daughter's room. Not long after, we heard the loud
cries of an infant. Our granddaughter was here! One glimpse of that baby
girl filled everyone's hearts in that hospital room, from parents to each
doting grandparent.

Smiles as big as Christmas, accompanied by tears of joy and baby brag
books emerged from their hiding places. Those happy feelings didn't van-
ish the moment we left the hospital. No, we repeated those "sounding
joys," as the familiar Christmas carol goes, to everyone who'd listen—each
time a new grandchild was born. A new baby! Light of our lives! We
would never be the same.

Over two thousand years ago a baby was born: the Son of God—
Jesus, the long-awaited Savior. Just like us, the shepherds, on that
starry night Jesus was born, couldn't keep the joy to themselves. Like
us, they had to spread the good news of great joy to all who would listen. And because of Jesus, our lives—and theirs—changed forever.
—REBECCA BARLOW JORDAN

FAITH STEP: *Read through or sing the words to the Christmas carol, "Joy to the
World." Then ask Jesus to help you "repeat the sounding joy" to someone who needs to
hear that good news this Christmas.*

MONDAY, DECEMBER 14

Hear my prayer, O Lord, and give ear to my cry; hold not your peace at my tears! For I am a sojourner with you, a guest, like all my fathers. Psalm 39:12 (ESV)

I GREW UP AS A missionary kid in Japan and, from the time I was fifteen, I was required by law to carry an AR with me at all times. An AR is an Alien Registration and if that won't make you feel like something foreign, nothing will. All foreigners fifteen years of age and older had to carry this small pocket-size booklet. At any time we could be asked by authorities to show it. Even though I was born in Japan and considered it my home, I could never legally be a citizen of the country since my father was an American citizen.

Jesus was an alien too. He came to earth from another place—heaven. He lived among the people, although earth was not his home.

Likewise, as Jesus's adopted brothers and sisters, we are foreigners here, too, sojourners, traveling this path called life. The path does get rocky at times and our tears fall. We sometimes feel like we don't belong and wonder how much longer it will be before Jesus returns. We are constantly reminded that we weren't created just for this earth. Our real home is in heaven with Jesus. We can be hopeful; the glory will soon come!
—ALICE J. WISLER

FAITH STEP: *As Christians, we fluctuate between wanting to feel comfortable and make this world our home, and knowing that we are not to get too attached. What are some reminders you encounter that make you aware that you are only a sojourner for a short time on earth?*

TUESDAY, DECEMBER 15

In his hand is the life of every creature and the breath of all mankind.
Job 12:10 (NIV)

I HAVE THREE PRESCHOOL-AGE CHILDREN, and one of their favorite songs is, "He's got the whole world in His hands." I love how their voices raise in squeaky melodies. I love singing along with them, but I often wonder, *Do I really, really believe it?* Do you?

What concerns you today? Are you worried about your family, your marriage, or your children? Jesus says, "I have the whole world in My hands."

Are you concerned about your job or daily duties? Hear Jesus saying, "I have the whole world in My hands."

Are your anxious thoughts carrying you away? Hear Jesus saying, "I have the whole world in My hands."

Do you have health problems that are wearing you down? Hear Jesus saying, "I have the whole world in My hands."

Are you concerned about your family members and friends who don't want anything to do with Jesus? Jesus has them in His hands too.

Jesus not only holds the world, He created it. "God, the Lord, created the heavens and stretched them out. He created the earth and everything in it. He gives breath to everyone, life to everyone who walks the earth. And it is he who says, 'I, the Lord, have called you to demonstrate my righteousness. I will take you by the hand and guard you, and I will give you to my people, Israel, as a symbol of my covenant with them. And you will be a light to guide the nations'" (Isaiah 42:5–6, NLT).

Jesus's hands are large enough to carry all the burdens of our world, but intimate enough to reach out to hold the hand of a single person in need and wipe a stray tear. Thank Him for that...or better yet, sing it. "He's got the whole world in His hands." —TRICIA GOYER

FAITH STEP: *Sing some of your favorite childhood Bible songs and consider what the words mean to you now.*

WEDNESDAY, DECEMBER 16

While they were stoning him, Stephen prayed, "Lord Jesus, receive my spirit."
Then he fell on his knees and cried out, "Lord, do not hold this sin against them."
When he had said this, he fell asleep. Acts 7:59–60 (NIV)

"CAN A PERSON CHANGE?" I asked Jesus in prayer one night. "More to the point, can I change? Will I ever become more like You?"

I was frustrated with myself. I'd begun the day with great intentions to be a faithful servant of Christ, but slipped into old patterns of worry, selfishness, and discouragement. Some days it feels like the older I get, the less I'm being conformed to the likeness of Christ, when I long for the opposite.

I wonder if Stephen ever asked similar questions. If so, I found a surprising answer in Acts 7. As Stephen was dying—unjustly attacked, in horrible pain—he prayed for those stoning him. My human nature would be tempted to pray, "Smite them!" But Stephen used similar words to the ones Jesus used on the Cross in Luke 23:34: "Father, forgive them, for they do not know what they are doing." In his moments of greatest distress, Stephen emulated Jesus and trusted Jesus to receive his spirit.

His story gives me great hope. Jesus can indeed live through us. Not through our own feeble efforts, but through His grace. Like Stephen, we may find words coming from us that are straight from the heart of Christ. We may respond in a way that supersedes our human nature. We can give our spirit to Jesus one day when we face death, and we can also give ourselves to Him each day of our lives. —SHARON HINCK

FAITH STEP: *Invite Jesus to shape you and change you today. Ask Him to live through you, so that the words you speak come from a heart full of His love.*

THURSDAY, DECEMBER 17

"For the joy that was set before him endured. . . ." Hebrews 12:2 *(ESV)*

UNDER THAT UGLY, LINT-MAGNET MAROON carpeting in our dining room lay maple flooring original to this one-hundred-year-old house. When the backing threads began to show through in high-traffic areas years ago, I knew it was time to commit: restore the hardwood or install different carpeting.

I removed the Daily Annoyance Carpet, exposing a layer of linoleum tiles that must have been installed in the forties. The tiles released their hold reluctantly. Underneath, a black, tarry glue resisted all normal removal techniques other than me on my knees with a putty knife.

Then sanding. Then removal of all evidence of sanding. Then staining. Then a polyurethane coat followed by drying time, light sanding, wiping off the residue, another polyurethane coat, and repeat three times.

Now the floor glows with a warm sheen. Worth it? Definitely!

I pressed on through that task because of the promise of a joy-filled end-result. In the Bible, we read about what Jesus endured for the joy set before Him. "He endured the cross, ignoring the shame, for the sake of the joy that was laid out in front of him" (Hebrews 12:2, CEB).

What joy? He endured the Cross for the joy of pain relief when He returned to life again? The joy of being freed from the world that misunderstood Him so badly, treated Him so cruelly?

According to the rest of what we read in God's Word, those were secondary to the goal of seeing us restored, affording us the opportunity to shine, our sins forgiven, with unlimited access to the Father God through the Son! *That* joy. He endured the Cross out of love for us. Never-ending relationship with us was the joy-set-before-Him. —CYNTHIA RUCHTI

FAITH STEP: *"I am the joy for which He endured." Have you said it out loud? Does this reality flood your heart with gratitude? Consider three ways today that your life can shine because of what Jesus endured for you. Tomorrow, consider three more.*

FRIDAY, DECEMBER 18

As I learn your righteous regulations, I will thank you by living as I should!
Psalm 119:7 (NLT)

CHRISTMAS IS NEARLY HERE AS I write this. Two days ago, a neighbor dropped off a package of soup ingredients. Yummy. Yesterday a different neighbor surprised me with a bag of homemade molasses cookies. Double yummy. Today an aunt delivered a big box of Belgian chocolates. Need I say more?

I appreciate the gifts, but even more I appreciate these women's friendship. To express my gratitude, I plan to treat them to a sweet surprise from my kitchen—cinnamon rolls, perhaps.

This season we celebrate the most precious gift ever given to humankind—God's Son, Jesus Christ. He became one of us, lived among us, and then suffered and died so we might be reconciled to God and spend eternity with Him. He also came to show us, and give us specific instructions about, how to live well until that time comes.

Jesus taught us how to treat our enemies, respect authority, and honor our spouses. He instructed us about how to handle money, regard time, and care for the poor. He showed us how to deal with suffering and how to walk in integrity. He did this because He loves us and cares for our well-being.

How should we respond to Jesus's love and kindness? For sure, we ought to say thank you, but, frankly, talk is cheap. Anyone can say thanks but not mean it. We best express our gratitude by placing our trust in Him and doing what He says.

This season and all year long, let's say thank you to Jesus in a meaningful way. Let's show our gratitude by living in a way that honors Him.
—GRACE FOX

FAITH STEP: *Have you decorated your tree yet? If not, express thanks to Jesus for something specific with each bulb you hang. If you have, then enjoy looking at the bulbs already on the tree. With each one you see, recall one God-given gift for which you are thankful.*

SATURDAY, DECEMBER 19

Answer this question: Does the God who lavishly provides you with his own presence, his Holy Spirit, working things in your lives you could never do for yourselves, does he do these things because of your strenuous moral striving or because you trust him to do them in you? Galatians 3:5 (MSG)

I SPEND HOUR UPON HOUR each week picking up toys, cleaning toilets, and scrubbing mystery stains from the carpet. But you can't tell I have done anything thanks to the three small people who are constantly working against me.

The truth is, not only is my house messy, my entire life is messy. It is a hodge-podge of kids, family, friends, ministry, bad news, great news, joy, sadness, homework, housework, coffee dates, and rotten apple cores tucked into the corners of the minivan.

Try as I might, I have found I am incapable of untangling the threads of my life. Just like I can't keep my house clean, I can't make sense of the hardships, the sweet goodness, the questions, the overwhelming blessings—and how they should all fit together. I want my life to be quiet and neat and clean, but I don't see that happening anytime in the near future.

Uncluttering my life is not something that I can actually do...only Jesus can. Do I knock myself out trying to order my own life or do I trust the One Who created me to shape my life in a way that I could never do on my own? My heart's cry needs to shift from "I want my life to be uncluttered" to "I am trusting You with my mess." I have a feeling that the One Who ordered the universe is the One Who can bring beauty from chaos. With or without a clean house. —SUSANNA FOTH AUGHTMON

FAITH STEP: *Leave your house messy and use those extra minutes you would spend on cleaning to find a quiet place and pray, "Jesus, I am trusting You with my mess."*

SUNDAY, DECEMBER 20

*Even the sparrow has found a home, and the swallow a nest for herself,
a place near your altar, Lord Almighty, my King and my God.*
Psalm 84:3 (NIV)

WE TAILORED OUR DECORATIONS THIS year: lighted tree, mantel and hearth, a wreath on the door, and a nativity scene in the front yard. I fashioned the wreath on the door years ago, so it has endured multiple Christmas seasons in all kinds of Texas weather. Though aged, it still cradles a host of Christmas cheer with its smiling gold angel, burgundy ribbon, and a variety of Christmas symbols.

This season we've already experienced unusual days with record low temperatures. An icy storm left huge tree limbs downed and dangling across property, streets, and power lines. Our huge oak trees, still dressed in the orange and gold leaves of fall, sat with their heavy, icy arms drooping almost to the ground, some laying across the roof.

I wondered how this storm had upset the homes of our neighborhood birds. One morning we opened the front door and noticed something fly out of the wreath. This happened several days in a row. Finally we realized a bird had found a warm, comfy spot and taken up residence in the simple circular "branches" of our Christmas door wreath.

That incident reminded me of Jesus's tender care for all His creation, including us, through all kinds of inclement weather. But more than that, I saw Jesus, the Son of God, a Babe, resting in the simple but warm "nest" of an animal trough that cold, wintry Christmas night. God's eternal love, wrapped in a blanket, the King of kings would soon become the peaceful resting place for our seeking souls: a home near His heart forever.

We, too, can nestle in His wreath of love—an eternal provision for His children. —REBECCA BARLOW JORDAN

FAITH STEP: *If any birds visit your yard, take time to feed them. Then thank Jesus for His eternal love and provision for you.*

MONDAY, DECEMBER 21

All spoke well of him and were amazed at the gracious words that came from his lips. "Isn't this Joseph's son?" they asked. Luke 4:22 (NIV)

WHEN I COMPILED MY THIRD cookbook of memories that I published myself, I looked it over and felt pleased with my accomplishment. Those who had contributed recipes and memories of loved ones for it were excited to purchase a copy. The orders came in as did praise for the book. People liked having a tangible book with food-related memories and favorite recipes in memory of their loved ones.

My friend Jane ordered a large number of copies for her family in memory of her daughter who had died. When we met months later for lunch, Jane told me that the birth date on her daughter's page was incorrect. The perfectionist side of me cringed. How could I have let that error slip by? I also felt bad for a more significant reason. This was Jane's daughter, and I know how we bereaved mothers can be about misprints when it comes to our deceased child. All we have left are the memories, and birth and death dates need to be recorded correctly. Yet instead of complaining, Jane said it didn't matter, and bought another four cookbooks.

How gracious can you be? Jane's understanding toward me taught me volumes about graciousness. She didn't let my mistake mar our friendship. Realizing that I had made an innocent error, she urged me not to feel bad about it. I admired her ability to find beauty in the cookbook even if I had typed in the wrong birth date for her daughter. For Jane, our friendship meant more to her than any oversight. —ALICE J. WISLER

FAITH STEP: *How does Jesus's attitude toward His disciples show graciousness? How can you cultivate a similar way of dealing with others—even when they are not gracious?*

TUESDAY, DECEMBER 22

Glory to God in the highest, and on earth peace, good will toward men.
Luke 2:14 (KJV)

MY SIX-YEAR-OLD DAUGHTER, ADELAIDE, INHERITED the decorating gene from me when it comes to holidays. She and I were ready to put up the Christmas tree as soon as we took down our fall pumpkins at the end of October. It took us until close to Thanksgiving to get our elf-helpers into the mood. Finally, the tree was brought down from the attic and assembled by a brawnier elf than ourselves, and the village was lit by one a bit more technically inclined. And although Harper no longer cared to put up his tree with the cowboy ornaments, and Grace declined the *Tale of Three Trees* display I offered for her desk, Adelaide happily decked out every square inch of her room with Christmas cheer.

Unfortunately, Adelaide also inherited my gene for clutter. When she showed me her room, I complimented her tree and the reindeer antlers that adorned her stuffed animals. But her dresser, which resembles my desk at work, was a hodgepodge of snow globes, Santas, snowmen, and ornaments.

"You know what is my favorite, Mommy?"

I couldn't imagine, since I was unable to focus on any one thing.

"It's this one with the sweet little Baby Jesus."

She pointed to a tiny painted pewter nativity I'd had since I was a child. It's so small that I hadn't even spotted it in the midst of everything else. Adelaide had placed the manger in the center, and Mary and Joseph, the shepherds, and all of the little animals were squeezed around it, as close as they could get.

"See, they are all looking at Him."

And so they were. In the midst of a crazy, cluttered, Christmas extravaganza, Adelaide had created a space for stillness. A place for peace.

—GWEN FORD FAULKENBERRY

FAITH STEP: *As the Christmas season cranks up around you, create a peaceful place where you can sit and contemplate Baby Jesus.*

WEDNESDAY, DECEMBER 23

*And she brought forth her firstborn son, and wrapped him in swaddling clothes,
and laid him in a manger; because there was no room for them in the inn.*
Luke 2:7 (KJV)

AFTER AN MRI, WE THOUGHT my dear friend Cheryl had Stage 2 breast cancer, which was bad enough. A few days later the PET scan turned something already bad into something dire. The disease had metastasized from breast to lymph nodes to the spine. Now it was Stage 4.

Her first chemotherapy treatment was in early December. I was teaching classes that day but kept in touch by texting with her daughter who sent me updates through the whole grueling experience. I saw them later that night. Cheryl gave my kids an "Elf on the Shelf," and I just sat in a kind of stupor holding her hand and patting it, not wanting to let her warmth and softness go.

After I got home that night and tucked my kids into bed, I lay in my own bed looking up at the ceiling. It was dark so I couldn't see anything. My eyes stared into a black void.

Where are You, Jesus? It seemed particularly cruel that all of this was happening at Christmas, Cheryl's favorite holiday. I started to think about our special traditions, how we exchange ornaments and eat dinner together every year. This year even in the midst of her ordeal she'd managed to start a new tradition with my kids.

Finally, my thoughts turned to the baby in the manger. It occurred to me that *here* is Jesus. He came to us not in the glistening splendor of a throne room but in the mess and straw of a stable. And He comes to us now...in our chemo, our divorces, our brokenness, and losses, and messes of every kind. —GWEN FORD FAULKENBERRY

FAITH STEP: *Look around you. Is there a messy place Jesus wants you to go with Him to bring help and healing?*

THURSDAY, DECEMBER 24

When He had given thanks, He broke it and said, "Take, eat; this is My body which is broken for you." 1 Corinthians 11:24 (NKJV)

AT OUR CHURCH ON CHRISTMAS EVE, we always have a candlelight service. My whole family goes, and we sing Christmas songs and take the Lord's Supper. There is no nursery provided—we are all in the sanctuary—and so this Christmas Eve I was holding Stella, my almost-two-year-old, when the plate with unleavened wafers came by.

I took one and considered it prayerfully. During this reverent moment, Stella lurched forward to try to reach the plate that was thankfully held secure by one of the deacons. "I do, I do!" She said. This is what she says when she wants to do something herself.

Since it was dinnertime and we hadn't eaten, I surmised that she might be hungry. I think this is why the tray of crackers was so important to her. When it was safely past us and out of her reach, she began to kick her legs. "I want one!"

In order to keep the peace, or at least have it restored, I did what any God-fearing mother would have done. I gave her my wafer. She took it in her little hand and plopped it into her mouth, biting into the symbolic body of Christ with gusto.

After the service, I went up to the table and got a new wafer for myself. As I chewed it I thought about Jesus's sacrifice. I also thought about Stella and how funny the whole situation had been. But really, her antics provide a pretty good picture of the gospel of Jesus. The whole world is hungry, and what they need seems out of reach. But we hold Him in our hands. There's plenty to go around. We can offer them Jesus.
—GWEN FORD FAULKENBERRY

FAITH STEP: *Make a list of people you know who need Jesus. Beside each name, write down a way you can invite them to taste and see that He is good (Psalm 34).*

FRIDAY, DECEMBER 25

For if the willingness is there, the gift is acceptable according to what one has, not according to what one does not have. 2 Corinthians 8:12 (NIV)

WHEN OUR CHILDREN WERE YOUNG, on Christmas Day we wanted to emphasize the gift Jesus gave us by coming to earth and saving us, so we encouraged each child to give birthday gifts to Jesus in a creative way.

After church, when we gathered to open presents, each of us would offer a gift of our talents to Jesus before opening one of the boxes under the tree. The children might do a skit, or recite a Bible verse. My husband might read a classic story, and I would play a carol on the piano. Sometimes we'd all join together lifting up a song with our voices and various instruments. Our hope was that even in our exchange of presents, our focus would be on Jesus.

One of my favorite carols has always been "The Little Drummer Boy." Even the youngest children could play along on rhythm instruments when we'd sing. I identified with the lyrics, "I have no gift to bring... That's fit to give our King...I played my drum for him."

Wonder floods me when I'm reminded that my unique, humble skills and interests are the very gifts Jesus treasures from me. I don't need to possess huge financial resources, fame, or spectacular talent. I can offer the simple love that swells in my heart as I worship. Each of us has ways to worship Jesus that fit our personalities, our communication style, and our callings, and that gift is acceptable, according to what one has.

—SHARON HINCK

FAITH STEP: *Give Jesus a birthday gift this Christmas Day. Write Him a poem, draw a picture, sing a song, or use whatever means most helps you share from the heart.*

SATURDAY, DECEMBER 26

And he brought him to Jesus. Jesus looked at him and said, "You are Simon son of John. You will be called Cephas" (which, when translated, is Peter). John 1:42 (NIV)

GROWING UP I DIDN'T THINK much of my name, but the older I've gotten the more I've appreciated it. When people use my name, a lot is summed up in it. For my husband my name reflects companion, friend, bride. It resonates with intimacy and unity. For my children my name brings comfort and "home." My friends might consider my laughter and my quirks when they hear my name. My readers relate it to a type of book. My name came first, and it now reflects who I've become.

Yet only Jesus can offer a new name, as He did with Peter. Jesus saw not only what Peter was, but what he would be. "And I tell you that you are Peter, and on this rock I will build my church, and the gates of Hades will not overcome it" (Matthew 16:18, NIV).

Jesus saw in Simon what Simon couldn't see in himself. Jesus saw "Peter," a rock. Jesus knew that Peter's confession of Christ was the foundation for the church to come.

We will get a new name too. Revelation 2:17 says, "To the one who is victorious, I will give some of the hidden manna. I will also give that person a white stone with a new name written on it, known only to the one who receives it" (NIV).

Some day we will get a new name, just like Peter. It will represent not how our family, friends, or the world sees us—but how Jesus does. And I can't imagine a more intimate gift than to have all that I am summed up in a name given by the One Who knows me and created me. —TRICIA GOYER

FAITH STEP: *Take time to ponder your new name in heaven. What do you hope your new name will sum up about you?*

SUNDAY, DECEMBER 27

"Bring the whole tithe into the storehouse, that there may be food in my house. Test me in this," says the Lord Almighty, "and see if I will not throw open the floodgates of heaven and pour out so much blessing that there will not be room enough to store it." Malachi 3:10 (NIV)

HAVE YOU SEEN THE TV show *Storage Wars?* There's something exciting and hopeful about throwing open a storage-unit door to discover potential treasure inside.

The search for treasure is an age-old one. Jesus spoke of it in Matthew 6:19–21 and 13:44–46. He understands our yearning for more, and He is passionate about overflowing this world of souls He loves so much.

But when it comes to wanting more, I don't recall many places where the Lord tells us to test Him about it. Testing Him seems taboo to me, which makes this Malachi challenge stand out. The first time I heard it I was stunned by its potential.

Maybe the key to this challenge lies in its focus on giving to build Jesus's Kingdom instead of hoarding everything for ourselves.

Next to his invitation to salvation, this invitation is my favorite because there's no limit. Throwing open floodgates... imagine it! Imagine the deluge of blessing He longs to pour on a needy world if we'll only adopt His habits of giving.

When we give and give some more to His causes, He promises to overwhelm with His abundance. Giving of this type does not need to be large if the resources are small. A small but sacrificial gift is all it takes to release the outpouring of the Savior's heart. When we give, He provides more so we can give more.

Who needs the flood your giving can prompt? Don't miss this opportunity to experience more of Jesus. —ERIN KEELEY MARSHALL

FAITH STEP: *In faith, ask Jesus to multiply and bless your sacrificial gift. Ask Him to open the floodgates, and then give some more.*

MONDAY, DECEMBER 28

Peter came to Him and said, "Lord, how often shall my brother sin against me, and I forgive him? Up to seven times?" Jesus said to him, "I do not say to you, up to seven times, but up to seventy times seven." Matthew 18:21–22 (NKJV)

In THE PAST WHEN I'VE encountered this verse, the focus seemed to be on lavish forgiveness for the good of others. There's the impression this is our duty—even though someone wrongs us repeatedly, we extend forgiveness because that's what Jesus would do. And I'm sure it is. But the more I get to know Jesus, the more I believe Jesus is giving us a prescription for personal spiritual health as much or more than He is giving us an evangelistic directive.

Consider the testimony of Nelson Mandela. Bill Clinton tells about a time he asked Mandela how he felt about the people who imprisoned him. Mandela answered, "I hated them for a long time. I broke rocks every day in prison, and I stayed alive on hate. They took a lot away from me. They took me away from my wife, and it subsequently destroyed my marriage. They took me away from seeing my children grow up. They abused me mentally and physically. And one day, I realized they could take it all except my mind and my heart. Those things I would have to give to them, and I simply decided not to give them away."

Clinton asked about when he was released from prison. Mandela explained, "As I felt the anger rising up, I thought to myself, 'They have already had you for twenty-seven years. And if you keep hating them, they'll have you again.' And I said, 'I want to be free.' And so I let it go. I let it go." He went on to lead a nation in the path of forgiveness.

When Jesus advised Peter to keep on forgiving, He knew it would help others. But He also knew it would help Peter to live in freedom and peace.
—GWEN FORD FAULKENBERRY

FAITH STEP: *If you are holding unforgiveness in your heart, let it go. Don't let whoever hurt you keep the keys to your personal prison. Forgiveness sets us free.*

TUESDAY, DECEMBER 29

[Jesus] went on from there to teach and preach in the towns of Galilee. When John, who was in prison, heard about the deeds of the Messiah, he sent his disciples to ask him, "Are you the one who is to come, or should we expect someone else?"
Matthew 11:1–2 (NIV)

I GREW UP SINGING "JESUS Loves Me," praying every night before going to sleep, and playing church with my stuffed animals in our missionary home in Osaka, Japan. After a stint of teenage rebellion, I said I would follow Jesus as my Lord at the age of sixteen. I believed. I trusted.

But when my son Daniel died at the age of four, for the first time in my life, I doubted. It wasn't just a little doubt; it was scary doubting, with a capital D. Perhaps Jesus was not Who He said He was. Maybe He wasn't for me. After all, how could He allow a child to die? Countless people had been praying for my son's healing all over the world. Why hadn't those prayers been answered? *Are you the One?*

Like the disciples, we think that Jesus should come in and make it all right—now. We might think that when He doesn't operate as we think He should, then He isn't who we once thought He was.

Are you the One? In times like these, we have to cling to Who He says He is. We have to pray against all doubt that we will know that He is God's son Who died for us and was resurrected from that tomb of death. We don't understand much of what happens to us, but we draw to the One Who understands our doubt, and like a shepherd, soothes our troubled minds, and holds us close.

There is no other. —ALICE J. WISLER

FAITH STEP: *Sometimes when doubts loom, we forget all that Jesus is. Take a sheet of paper and write, Are You the One? Then list attributes of Jesus that testify to His power and authority.*

WEDNESDAY, DECEMBER 30

They will tell people yet to be born about his righteousness— that he has finished it.
Psalm 22:31 (GW)

MY HUSBAND AND I ARE in the process of having a new house built. I've been pleasantly surprised to find out what is included in the price of our home. I can't help contrasting it to our last experience in another area. Our previous builder's basic model included the cheapest surfaces, paint, carpet, trim, and appliances. We paid extra to upgrade most features and later added a few items like ceiling fans, plus bought new appliances. Outside, the builder installed a sprinkler system (a must in that area) and laid sod in the front yard only. When we sold the house three years later, our planned upgrades had not been completed, the side yard and back-yards hadn't been done, and the basement was completely unfinished.

Our current builder uses beautiful carpet, wood, and tile flooring. Ceiling fans are included. The kitchen and bathrooms include granite countertops, high-quality fixtures and lighting, gorgeous cabinets, and special decorative touches. Both front and backyards will have sprinkler systems and sod. The front will be completely landscaped and the backyard will have a wood fence. Once this home is finished, it will be *really* finished. We won't have to do much more than move in and start enjoying it.

The final words that Jesus uttered from the Cross pinpoint what makes Christianity different from most other belief systems: "It is finished!" (John 19:30). Jesus had completed the work He came to do; the penalty for our sins had been paid in full. We have no need to offer sacrifices, observe rituals or strict rules, or work to try to earn His favor. All we have to do is accept His gift of forgiveness and start enjoying a personal relationship with Him. Finished is definitely better. —DIANNE NEAL MATTHEWS

FAITH STEP: *Are you living like your salvation is finished or unfinished? Meditate on the full meaning of Jesus's words, "It is finished!" Think about how that affects your relationship with Him.*

THURSDAY, DECEMBER 31

Do everything without complaining or arguing, so that you may become blameless
and pure, children of God without fault in a crooked and depraved generation,
in which you shine like stars in the universe as you hold out the word of life.
Philippians 2:14–16 (NIV)

IT'S NEW YEAR'S EVE AND I'm considering resolutions. In the last few years, one in particular has soundly and repeatedly defeated me.

Doomed or not, I'm dusting it off again. I'm resolving not to complain—defined as expressing dissatisfaction or annoyance about a state of affairs or an event (praying about a situation doesn't count). The first year I tried not to complain; I made it into February, but I hadn't been counting exasperated sighs, facial expressions, or eye-rolling. Now that I do, I haven't lasted a week. When I trip up, God forgives me and I start over.

It's a huge mistake to consider complaining a small offense. Murmuring lays bare an attitude of ungratefulness, greed, and disrespect for God. When I complain, I'm acting no better than the Israelites, who tired of eating a miracle and complained about manna—tempting God and sorely trying His patience. Some of them died as a result. Their story is an example for us. God hates this sin.

Jesus never complained. He always pleased the Father. I want to be like Jesus, cooperating with the Holy Spirit as He transforms me into His likeness. Still, sometimes I speak before thinking and find myself complaining. When I do, I'm saying God doesn't know what to bring into my life.

Is that really what I think? Maybe, sometimes, it is. For me, having the resolution spotlights the behavior. It shows me my complaining heart. So I can go to Jesus contrite, repenting. And, forgiven, begin again.
—SUZANNE DAVENPORT TIETJEN

FAITH STEP: *Hate resolutions? Do you start well and quit when you stumble? Pray for guidance. Offer Jesus the habit, then picture Him helping you one moment at a time.*

ABOUT THE AUTHORS

 SUSANNA FOTH AUGHTMON is the mother of Jack, 12, Will, 10, Addison, 7, and the wife of Scott, the lead pastor of Pathway Church in Palo Alto, California. Their family has been church-planting for eight years. Susanna has led worship, worked in children's ministry, and done the odd janitorial job during their ministry. Susanna's books include *All I Need Is Jesus and a Good Pair of Jeans*, *My Bangs Look Good and Other Lies I Tell Myself*, and *I Blame Eve*. She blogs regularly at tiredsupergirl.blogspot.com.

 GWEN FORD FAULKENBERRY lives and writes in the Ozark Mountains of Arkansas. Her passion is Jesus—and the family He has given her. She loves to talk literature with Grace, 13, go fishing with Harper, 11, bake goodies with Adelaide, 7, and feed goats with Stella, 2. Gwen is the author of *God's Heart Through You*, *Love Finds You in Romeo, Colorado*, *Love Finds You in Branson, Missouri*, *Love Finds You Home for Christmas*, *A Beautiful Life*, *A Beautiful Day*, *Jesus, Be Near Me*, and *Sixty Promises to Pray for Your Marriage*. A new novel, *Seeing Stars*, comes out this year.

 GRACE FOX is an international speaker whose passion is to connect the dots between faith and real life for her readers and audiences. Her writing has appeared in *Focus on the Family*, *Power for Living*, and *Insights Canada*. She's written eight books, including *Morning Moments with God*, *Tuck-Me-In Talks with Your Little Ones*, and *One-Minute Romance for Couples*. She

also produced the award-winning DVD-based Bible study *Moving from Fear to Freedom: A Woman-to-Woman Conversation*. Connect with Grace by visiting gracefox.com, read her devotional blogs at gracefox.com/blog, and meet her at fb.com/gracefox.author and twitter.com/gracelfox.

USA Today best-selling author TRICIA GOYER has written more than forty books, including the novelization of the movie *Moms' Night Out*, and over five hundred articles for national publications and blogs for TheBetterMom .com and MomLifeToday.com. Tricia and her husband, John, live in Little Rock, Arkansas, where she coordinates a teen MOPS (Mothers of Preschoolers) group. They have six children. You can find her at TriciaGoyer.com.

SHARON HINCK writes "stories for the hero in all of us," about ordinary people experiencing God's grace in unexpected ways. Her award-winning novels include *Stepping into Sunlight* and her ground-breaking Sword of Lyric series with the recently released *Restorer's Journey, Expanded Edition*. This is Sharon's fourth year writing for *Mornings with Jesus*, and she loves spending mornings—and all day—with Jesus. She welcomes visitors to her Web site sharonhinck.com.

REBECCA BARLOW JORDAN is a best-selling inspirational author who has penned eleven books and over two thousand greeting cards, articles, and devotions. She is passionate about motivating others heart-to-heart and helping them find intimacy with God. Rebecca's books include *Day-votions* three-book series for women, mothers, and grandmothers. She and her minister-husband have two children and four grandchildren and live in East Texas, where she loves gardening and reading great fiction. Learn more about her at rebeccabarlowjordan.com.

ERIN KEELEY MARSHALL is the author of *Navigating Route 20-Something* and *The Daily God Book*, and is a contributing writer to *Mornings with Jesus 2012, 2013, 2014* and *365 Pocket Prayers for Mothers*. She writes and edits from home while being a wife to Steve and a mom to Paxton and Calianne. You can find Erin on the Web at erinkeeleymarshall.com and on Facebook, LinkedIn, and Twitter @EKMarshall.

DIANNE NEAL MATTHEWS is the author of four daily devotional books, including *The One Year Women of the Bible* and *Designed for Devotion: A 365-Day Journey from Genesis to Revelation*. She and her husband, Richard, have been married forty years and currently live in southeast Texas, too far away from their three children and two adorable grandchildren. To learn more, visit DianneNealMatthews.com or connect with her through Facebook or Twitter @DianneNMatthews.

CYNTHIA RUCHTI is an award-winning author and speaker who tells stories of "hope that glows in the dark" through her novels, novellas, devotions, nonfiction, and speaking events for women and writers. Recent releases include *When the Morning Glory Blooms*, *All My Belongings*, and *Ragged Hope: Surviving the Fallout of Other People's Choices*. In 2015, *As Water Gone By* and *Tattered & Mended: The Art of Heal the Soul* will join them. Connecting with readers is among her greatest joys. You'll find Cynthia at cynthiaruchti.com or facebook.com/CynthiaRuchti ReaderPage.

SUZANNE DAVENPORT TIETJEN is the author of *The Sheep of His Hand: Reflections on the Psalms from a 21st-Century Shepherd* and *40 Days to Your Best Life for Nurses*. A few years back, she and her husband, Mike, moved to a cabin deep in the forest, where they enjoy breathtaking beauty and an outdoor lifestyle. A former shepherd, she works as a transport nurse at the only level III neonatal ICU in Michigan's Upper Peninsula. You can find out more at suzannetietjen.com or follow Suzanne on Twitter @suzishepherd.

 ALICE J. WISLER was born in Osaka, Japan, to Presbyterian missionaries. She is the author of *Rain Song, How Sweet It Is, Hatteras Girl, A Wedding Invitation, Still Life in Shadows,* and *Getting Out of Bed in the Morning: Reflections of Comfort in Heartache.* Her sixth novel, *Under the Silk Hibiscus,* comes out in November. In memory of her son Daniel, Alice speaks on grief and loss at conferences across the country and teaches grief-writing workshops. Join Alice at her Web site alicewisler.com.

SCRIPTURE REFERENCE INDEX

TOPICAL INDEX

A NOTE FROM THE EDITORS

We hope you enjoy *Mornings with Jesus 2015*, created by the Books and Inspirational Media Division of Guideposts, a nonprofit organization that touches millions of lives every day through products and services that inspire, encourage, help you grow in your faith, and celebrate God's love in every aspect of your daily life.

Thank you for making a difference with your purchase of this book, which helps fund our many outreach programs to military personnel, prisons, hospitals, nursing homes, and educational institutions. To learn more, visit GuidepostsFoundation.org.

We also maintain many useful and uplifting online resources. Visit Guideposts.org to read true stories of hope and inspiration, access OurPrayer network, sign up for free newsletters, download free e-books, join our Facebook community, and follow our stimulating blogs. To delve more deeply into *Mornings with Jesus*, visit Guideposts.org/MorningswithJesus.

You may purchase the 2016 edition of *Mornings with Jesus* anytime after July 2015. To order, visit ShopGuideposts.org, call (800) 932-2145, or write to Guideposts, PO Box 5815, Harlan, Iowa 51593.